VOLUME 4

LATIN

AMERICAN

URBAN

RESEARCH

LATIN AMERICAN URBAN RESEARCH

This series is published in cooperation with

The Center for Latin American Studies, University of Florida

Other volumes:

1. Latin American Urban Research (1971)
   Francine F. Rabinovitz and Felicity M. Trueblood, Editors

2. Regional and Urban Development Policies: A Latin American Perspective (1972)
   Guillermo Geisse and Jorge E. Hardoy, Editors

3. National-Local Linkages: The Interrelationship of Urban and National Polities in Latin America (1973)
   Francine F. Rabinovitz and Felicity M. Trueblood, Editors

Latin
American
Urban
Research

VOLUME 4

ANTHROPOLOGICAL PERSPECTIVES
ON LATIN AMERICAN URBANIZATION

WAYNE A. CORNELIUS
and
FELICITY M. TRUEBLOOD
Editors

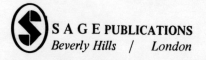
S A G E PUBLICATIONS
Beverly Hills / *London*

For information address:

SAGE PUBLICATIONS, INC.
275 South Beverly Drive
Beverly Hills, California 90212

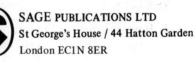

SAGE PUBLICATIONS LTD
St George's House / 44 Hatton Garden
London EC1N 8ER

Printed in the United States of America

International Standard Book Number 0-8039-0313-8 (cloth)
0-8039-0852-0 (paper)

Library of Congress Catalog Card No. 73-86706

SECOND PRINTING

CONTENTS

Introduction
                WAYNE A. CORNELIUS   9

Part I. CITYWARD MIGRATION

   1. Family and Household Organization among
      Tzintzuntzan Migrants in Mexico City
         ROBERT V. KEMPER   23

   2. Mediation and Rural-Urban Migration in Mexico:
      A Proposal and a Case Study
         JACK R. ROLLWAGEN   47

**Part II. THE SOCIAL AND ECONOMIC ORGANIZATION OF
THE CITY**

   3. Housing-Settlement Types, Arrangements for Living,
      Proletarianization, and the Social Structure of the City
         ANTHONY LEEDS   67

   4. The Concept of "Marginality" as Applied to
      Squatter Settlements
         LISA R. PEATTIE   101

**Part III. THE DEVELOPMENT AND ORGANIZATION OF
URBAN NEIGHBORHOODS**

   5. The Interaction of Population and Locality in the
      Development of Squatter Settlements in Lima
         DOUGLAS UZZELL   113

   6. The Social and Economic Organization of a
      Mexican Shantytown
         LARISSA LOMNITZ   135

7. Neighbors at a Distance: Life in a Low-Income
   Colombian Barrio
   MICHAEL B. WHITEFORD   157

8. Grass-Roots Political Organization in Cuba: A Case of the
   Committees for the Defense of the Revolution
   DOUGLAS BUTTERWORTH   183

Part IV. THE RURAL-URBAN INTERFACE

9. The Interrelationships of City and Provinces in
   Peru and Guatemala
   BRYAN R. ROBERTS   207

10. The Influence of Migrants upon Traditional Social and
    Political Concepts: A Peruvian Case Study
    BILLIE JEAN ISBELL   237

SELECT BIBLIOGRAPHY, 1972-1974

Capital or Major Cities   263
Other Cities by Country   272
Countries in General   276
General Urban Studies on Latin America   288
Urban and Regional Planning   293
General Urban Studies Dealing in Part with Latin America   294
Bibliographies   295

VOLUME 4

LATIN

AMERICAN

URBAN

RESEARCH

ABOUT THE EDITORS

WAYNE A. CORNELIUS is Assistant Professor of Political Science and Research Associate, Center for International Studies, at the Massachusetts Institute of Technology. He received his Ph.D. at Stanford University, and has been a visiting researcher at El Colegio de México (Mexico City) and the Center for International Affairs at Harvard University. His teaching fields include comparative urban politics and Latin American politics. He has done field work in Mexico, and is currently engaged in research on the impact of government policies and programs on out-migration from rural communities in that country. His recent publications include *Politics and Poverty in Urban Mexico* (forthcoming); "Urbanization and Political Demand Making: Political Participation Among the Migrant Poor in Latin American Cities" (*American Political Science Review,* September 1974); *Political Learning Among the Migrant Poor* (Sage Publications, 1973); and *Crisis, Choice, and Change: Historical Studies of Political Development* (co-author; Little, Brown, 1973).

FELICITY M. TRUEBLOOD is Assistant Professor of Latin American Studies and History at the University of Florida, Gainesville. She also serves as executive secretary of the Latin American Studies Association (LASA). She is editor of the *LASA Newsletter* and a former editor of the *Southeastern Latin Americanist* and the *Journal of Inter-American Studies.* She is a consultant to various presses specializing in Latin American-related publications, and has published translations of Spanish language fiction and nonfiction.

Introduction

WAYNE A. CORNELIUS

The past decade has witnessed a resurgence of interest in the field which has come to be known as "urban anthropology." Long preoccupied with the study of traditional, primitive or peasant societies dwelling in rural areas, social and cultural anthropologists have turned their attention increasingly to modern, complex, urban-dwelling societies. As urban-industrial development began to impinge upon formerly "closed" rural communities and millions of peasants migrated to cities in Third World countries, anthropologists moved along with their subjects to study their adaptation to urban life. The resulting increase in anthropological research in urban settings is reflected in the founding in 1972 of three journals devoted entirely to such research *(Urban Anthropology, Urban Anthropology Newsletter,* and *Urban Life and Culture)* and the appearance of several anthologies and textbooks consisting of field research reports and methodological essays by anthropologists concerned with cities and the urbanization process (Eddy, 1968; Mangin, 1970; Spencer, 1971; Weaver and White, 1972; Southall, 1973; Foster and Kemper, 1974; Uzzell, 1974).

Perhaps because Latin America was faster than other contemporary developing regions to achieve a relatively high level of urban development, Latin Americanists have been very prominent among the group of anthropologists who have contributed to this literature. Anthropologists have also been responsible for some of the highest-quality work in the interdisciplinary field of Latin American urban studies in recent years (for bibliography, see Kemper, 1971a; Gutkind, 1973). This volume of *Latin American Urban Research* is intended to introduce urbanists in other disciplines to the work of "urban anthropologists," and to illustrate the utility of an anthropological perspective in understanding the dynamics of urban life and the urbanization process in Latin America.

The anthropologists' migration from rural to urban areas has not been without problems and frustrations. The social units which they encountered in the urban setting tended to be larger, more heterogeneous, and less easily "bounded" than those traditionally studied by anthropologists in rural areas.

The great scope and complexity of urban phenomena seemed to be incompatible with the field methods and analytic approaches developed for microethnography in the countryside. The urgent need to confront and resolve these dilemmas has given rise to lively debates among anthropologists seeking to define the boundaries of the "urban field" of their discipline and to specify the most appropriate units of study, research methods, and conceptual frameworks to be employed within it (see Gulick, 1968, 1973; Leeds, 1968; Whiteford et al., 1972; Michaelson, 1972; Epstein, 1973: 17-19; Swartz, 1973; Plotnicov, 1973; Snyder, 1973; Weaver, 1973; Foster and Kemper, 1974: 1-17). While it would be presumptuous of us, as non-anthropologists, to attempt to make a case for or against the intellectual integrity of "urban anthropology" as a separate field of inquiry, or to take sides on any of the other conceptual and methodological issues currently dividing "urban anthropologists," we would not hesitate to argue that the *anthropological approach* to urban studies is particularly well suited to answering a variety of key questions about cities and the urbanization process in Latin America and other developing regions.

One of the major strengths of the anthropological approach grows out of its deep concern for what happens at the grass-roots level of society. While many economists, political scientists, historians, and urban planners share this concern, their analyses are more often than not pursued at the level of whole cities, systems of cities, or even nation-states, using the kinds of data which make it difficult or impossible for them to make valid statements or inferences about the attitudes and behavior of individual city dwellers. The anthropologist may also engage in macro-level analysis and theorizing, but his work is based in the first instance upon micro-level data referring to individuals. These data are usually gathered through a variety of field research techniques, including participant-observation, intensive, unstructured interviewing, projective tests, censuses or sample surveys, household budgets, inventories of possessions, and the gathering of life histories. This methodological eclecticism is another important strength of the anthropologist's approach to urban research, insofar as it supplies both qualitative and quantitative data bearing upon the research question and provides a basis for convergent validation of research findings.

Certain data-gathering techniques traditionally favored by the anthropologist, especially participant-observation and collection of life histories, are especially appropriate to the study of *change processes* at the individual, neighborhood, or city level: How do rural migrants adjust to urban life? How do they become incorporated into the urban labor market? How do they become involved in political activity? How do the urban poor develop strategies for economic survival? How do urban neighborhoods develop into social and political communities? What mechanisms hold such communities together over time? How do rural communities change under the impact of out-migration and return-migration from the cities? These and other pressing questions about urbanization in Latin America require the kind of intensive, process-oriented, firsthand treatment which is the hallmark of the anthropological approach; an approach which emphasizes living with people in order to learn their ways of thinking and doing things.

We believe that the papers assembled in this volume are broadly representative, in terms of methodology, analytical frameworks, and substantive concerns, of recent anthropological research on Latin American cities and city growth. Part I of the volume is devoted to studies of cityward migration, which represents perhaps the most highly developed area of the "urban anthropology" literature (see Kemper, 1970; Spencer, 1971; Cornelius, 1971: 118-119). The pioneer in this area was Oscar Lewis (1952, 1965), whose study of migrants from the village of Tepoztlán, Mexico, to the Mexican capital served as a model for subsequent studies in which anthropologists traced out-migrants from particular rural communities of origin and studied their adjustment to urban life at one or more points of destination (Butterworth, 1962; Bradfield, 1963; Rollwagen, 1968; Kemper, 1971b; Orellana, 1973; Alderson-Smith, forthcoming).

Robert V. Kemper's article in this volume sheds new light on a question of long-standing interest to "urban anthropologists" and urbanists in general: How does cityward migration and urban residence affect the institution of the family? Among migrants from the peasant village of Tzintzuntzan, Mexico, to Mexico City, he finds that the nuclear family has remained cohesive and continues to play an important and positive role in economic assimilation and psychological adaptation to urban life. Tzintzuntzan migrants "have established a spatial-temporal network through which a constantly changing set of actors aids one another to find housing and jobs." But if kinship networks are important to economic success in the city, they do not represent a simple transfer of rural patterns of family organization to the urban setting. Some of Kemper's most significant findings relate to the "subtle and profound changes in the family life of Tzintzuntzeños in Mexico City." For example, Kemper notes an improvement in the quality of interpersonal relations among family members in the city, by comparison with norms prevailing in the migrants' community of origin. Husband-wife relations become more egalitarian and mutually supportive in the urban setting, while fathers adopt a more affectionate, less authoritarian posture toward their children. Such changes are interpreted by Kemper as a rejection of the behavior associated with rural *machismo*. Concluding that the changes which have occurred thus far in the migrants' family life have been "overwhelmingly integrative rather than disorganizing," Kemper goes on to analyze the economic basis for these changes. He attributes much importance to urban opportunities for steady and higher-paid employment for male heads of family, which provides them with statuses and roles which help to stabilize family relationships. Kemper's research also illustrates the utility of a follow-up study of migrants from a rural community of origin which is already well documented in ethnographic studies (see Foster, 1967; Kemper, 1974).

Jack Rollwagen's contribution to the volume presents an elaboration of a theoretical construct which may be used to guide attempts at generalization about the migration process at the national level. Observing that rural-urban migration is often conceived in terms of "national forces" operating directly upon undifferentiated "rural populations," he argues that the concept of "mediation" may clarify how particular rural communities or groups within such communities are drawn into the national economy and society. Building upon the efforts of Eric Wolf and Sydel Silverman to conceptualize processes of cultural and economic mediation or brokerage between the local community and the nation, Rollwagen shows how a group of successful migrant entrepreneurs originating in the village of Mexticacán, Mexico, became assimilated into the national economy and came to exert a decisive social and economic influence upon their community of origin. The mechanism of influence which Rollwagen focuses upon is the entrepreneurs' control over urban employment opportunities for prospective migrants from the village. He also identifies the circumstances which led the entrepreneurs to gradually divest themselves of their mediator role vis-à-vis the Mexticacán villagers. Rollwagen's article makes a contribution to our all-too-limited knowledge of the roles that permanently urban-based migrants may play in the economic and social life of their communities of origin. His work also illustrates some of the ways in which urbanization creates mechanisms that accelerate social and economic mobility among a significant segment of the migratory stream to Latin American cities.

The papers included in Part II of this volume are representative of a small but rapidly expanding group of anthropological studies which attempt to provide either a holistic view of a particular city or an analysis of citywide patterns of social and economic organization (see Harris, 1956; Whiteford, 1964; Epstein, 1973; Gonzalez, 1974; Price, 1973; Reina, 1973).

Anthony Leeds presents a broadly conceived portrayal of the basic social structure of the city of Rio de Janeiro (with frequent comparative reference to Lima, Peru), as a tentative model for discussing the social orders of cities as units of analysis. Starting from the lower-income household as a locus of organization, especially with respect to location of residence within the city, Leeds traces the extension of social links among members of the lower class through various networks and organizations as low-income people "circulate" among specialized types of housing-settlement zones. He observes that intracity residential mobility and the interpersonal networks of communication and discussion resulting from such movement provide the *potential* basis for classwide solidarity and political action. But the potential remains largely unrealized, due to the fragmentation of the proletarian class stemming from the structure of the national economy, the urban labor market, and residential segregation, as well as deliberate action on the part of the upper class (e.g., pejorative treatment in the mass media) to foster divisiveness among the proletariat. The upper class itself tends toward fragmentation, however, due to the nature of capitalist economic competition and because of immigration. The resulting fragments seek support in their struggle for power, wealth, and prestige, among certain fragments of the lower class.

Leeds describes how the competition and division inside both upper and lower classes leads to cross-class political coalitions which criss-cross the entire physical city. His analysis thus identifies some of the key obstacles to demand-making by low-income city dwellers based on perceived class interests or class solidarity (see also the studies summarized in Cornelius, 1974). Leeds also draws some important implications of this view of the organization of the city for urban planning—viz, that planners, being representative of the upper class, conceive their planning in terms of upper-class interests. But at any given point in time, the physical structure of the city—housing, buildings, open spaces, sewage systems, and so on—is a crystallization of the *total* social and ideological order of the city and the nation of which it is a part. Leeds argues that the failure of urban planners to take account of the entire social order of the city makes failures of planning inevitable.

Lisa Peattie's contribution to this section of the volume also demonstrates the importance of exploring the *interrelationships* between whatever segment of the urban population one studies and the larger social, economic, and political systems in which it is enmeshed. Continuing and deepening the attack upon the concept of urban "marginality," an assault in which anthropologists have played a prominent role (see, for example, Leeds and Leeds, 1970; Epstein, 1972: 52-53), she questions the applicability of the concept to the populations of squatter settlements and more generally to unskilled poor people in Latin American cities. Her critique is based on empirical evidence reported in the literature as well as her own field work in Ciudad Guayana, Venezuela. She concludes that, regardless of whether we refer to economic, social, political, or cultural phenomena, *structured inequality* rather than "marginality" seems to characterize more accurately the situation of squatter settlement residents. Why, she asks, do we describe as "economically marginal" a segment of the urban population which makes a substantial contribution to the urban labor force, which buys goods and services in the urban consumer market, and which contributes in a number of other ways to the formation of capital? As in the economic sphere, many other elements of the squatter's way of life appear to be shared by the larger urban society. Peattie's discussion should not be dismissed as just another scholastic exercise in conceptual clarification, since, as she correctly points out, the manner in which we view the interrelations between squatter settlements and the larger society has highly important implications for the elaboration of public policies. Thinking in terms of "marginality" as usually conceived leads to a view of the problems of squatter settlements as resulting primarily from the residents' lack of ties or integration into the larger society. The evidence discussed by Peattie is consistent with a very different view, which holds that "it is not any *lack* of ties with the dominant sectors of the society that is the problem, but the *kinds* of ties which exist" (Epstein, 1972: 53, emphasis added).

It is worth noting that Peattie began her exploration of the topics discussed in her contribution to this volume with a careful ethnographic study of a single urban neighborhood (see Peattie, 1968). The work of Peattie and other contributors to this volume is at sharp variance with the stereotype of anthropology as a discipline capable of producing only charming case studies whose findings are nongeneralizable and do not contribute to general theory building. It demonstrates that intensive microethnography in an urban setting can ultimately provide a basis for macro-level explanation and conceptualization which leads to important insights into the dynamics of urban life. Leeds (in this volume, and Leeds, 1973) and Peattie also illustrate the utility of the anthropological approach for scrutinizing the "facts" and assumptions on which urban policies are based.

The papers presented in Part III deal with the organization and development of specific low-income neighborhoods in four different Latin American cities. Douglas Uzzell's paper is an effort to explain the way in which squatter settlements in Lima, Peru, develop, by reference to the interaction between characteristics of the locality and characteristics of its population over time. Proceeding from the assumptions that different localities attract different kinds of residents, and that the behavior of people changes the character of the places where they live, Uzzell attacks the impression given by some previous studies of squatter settlements that "a given population comes to a locality in the beginning and, except for the effects of the life cycle, remains stable." He emphasizes the effects of movements of people into and out of the squatter settlement upon the rate and pattern of its development, in terms of the extent of capital and labor investment, the extent of physical planning, and other aspects of community development. Uzzell's findings lead him to question the validity of establishing fixed typologies of squatter settlements based on their physical appearance at a given point in time and then associating each type of locality with one or two types of residents—e.g., "down-and-out" versus "poor-but-ambitious."

Larissa Lomnitz's study of a low-income neighborhood in Mexico City is addressed to a fundamental question of interest to all urbanists: How do poor people—many of them of rural origin—manage to survive economically in a competitive urban environment, without savings or salable skills, and unassisted by organized systems of social welfare? Characterizing residents of the neighborhood which she studied as "urban hunters and gatherers," economically "marginal" people (in the sense that they suffer from unemployment or underemployment, lack a stable family income, and have the lowest level of income within the urban population), Lomnitz describes the sociocultural defense mechanisms and strategies for survival which they have developed. While "social network analysis" has been a frequent concern of anthropologists working in African cities (see, for example, Mitchell, 1969), systematic, empirical studies of informal interpersonal networks among city dwellers in Latin America have been rare. Lomnitz's analysis of social networks consisting of clusters of neighboring nuclear families who practice continuous, reciprocal exchange of information, job training and aid in job procurement, loans, and other forms of material and emotional support thus constitutes an important contribution to our knowledge in this area. She specifies the basic units of exchange as well as the mechanisms (e.g., fictive kinship, and *"cuatismo,"* a Mexican form of male friendship) which reinforce the mutual aid networks. Lomnitz concludes that these networks function as an economic structure parallel to the market structure which dominates urban economic organization. In her view, the economic survival of residents of the settlement she studied depends upon the creation and maintenance of a system of exchange which is entirely distinct from the functioning of the market place; a system based on locally available resources in kinship and friendship. Persisting in time, rather than characterized by the causal, momentary relation of the market, the reciprocal exchange institutionalized by mutual aid networks serves to maximize economic security among low-income people. It is also these networks, she points out, which represent the "effective community" for individual residents of the neighborhood, which lacks any other form of social or political organization.

Some of the same themes developed in Lomnitz's paper are taken up by Michael Whiteford in his study of a low-income neighborhood on the periphery of Popayán, Colombia. Whiteford also found a *barrio* characterized by very little community cohesiveness, whose inhabitants preferred to remain aloof from social entanglements but had nevertheless found it necessary to develop loosely knit networks for reciprocal exchange of goods and services. Whiteford's study is particularly valuable for the insights which it provides into the way in which residents of the neighborhood view the dominant society and polity and their position within this sociopolitical order. He finds that they view life in terms of a continuous struggle for survival, in which they must defend themselves against the abuses of government, employers, labor unions, and other elements of "an unscrupulous oligarchy that takes advantage of them at every turn." Their struggle is rendered even more difficult by the labor surplus and the lack of industrial employment opportunities in a small but rapidly growing city such as Popayán.

It is noteworthy that neither of the settlements studied by Lomnitz and Whiteford originated in a squatter invasion. They are both low-income neighborhoods created by the subdivision of land by a private landowner, from whom the original residents purchased plots of land for self-built housing. Thus their inhabitants have not been exposed to the kinds of stressful experiences which accompany the invasion and defense of land in a squatter settlement, and which appear to be quite important to the development of a sense of community solidarity and a high level of community-wide organization (see Portes, 1971: 243; Cornelius, 1973: 41-42).

The last of our papers focusing on specific urban neighborhoods, by Douglas Butterworth, represents the first published report of data gathered as part of a field study in Havana, Cuba, directed by the late Oscar Lewis. Butterworth supervised that portion of the study concerned with the residents of a new housing project, many of whom had been relocated from Las Yaguas, which he describes as "the most infamous slum in pre-revolutionary Cuba." Butterworth's paper provides a rare glimpse of the functioning of the Committees for the Defense of the Revolution (CDRs), a key form of mass-based political organization in Cuba under Castro, in an urban setting. Originally created for internal security ("vigilance") and political indoctrination purposes, the CDRs have gradually acquired a variety of developmental and administrative functions, such as the taking of a national census, health education, collection of raw materials for reuse, and construction of public works. The CDRs in the housing project which Butterworth studied experienced a limited amount of success in accomplishing their goals for about two years after their founding; but by 1970, when Butterworth's field work was undertaken, they had ceased to function at all. The reasons for this failure of grass-roots political organization are Butterworth's principal concern. Drawing extensively upon depth interviews conducted with project residents, he depicts a situation of intense personal rivalries and animosities, coupled with a breakdown in communication and cooperation between the CDRs operating in the housing project and the Sectional (or zonal) CDR having jurisdiction over them.

Butterworth argues that, underlying these problems, was a huge cultural gap between the former residents of the Las Yaguas slum and the people with whom they had to interact—neighbors, officials of the Sectional CDR, and higher-level bureaucrats. The people removed from Las Yaguas had little previous organizational experience; Butterworth describes them as prime examples of persons living in the "culture of poverty," whose most distinguishing characteristics are "a lack of effective participation and integration of the people in the larger society, and a minimum of organization beyond the family." Butterworth contrasts the conditions prevailing in the housing project and six other areas where former residents of Las Yaguas had been resettled, and where the local CDRs had also fallen into decay, with those obtaining in a neighborhood inhabited by sugar workers, whose long experience with union organization provided the basis for the impressive accomplishments of the local CDR. Butterworth is not inclined, however, to rely entirely upon a "culture of poverty" explanation of his findings in the housing project. He shows that the failure of grass-roots political organization in the project is also a consequence of attention to the local CDR by officials at higher levels of authority. The brief period of success experienced by the project's CDR suggests that external assistance may in large measure overcome the obstacles to political organization rooted in poverty and local subcultures.

The papers comprising Part IV of this volume are addressed to the nexus between urban and rural populations. As defined in a recent survey of the "urban anthropology" literature (Snyder, 1973: 105-106), the interests of anthropologists in the rural-urban interface lie in two areas: (1) How rural cultural constraints and patterns of social and economic organization affect the urban adaptation of migrants; and (2) the impact of urbanites and returned migrants from urban areas upon rural populations, in terms of modernizing influences.

Bryan Roberts' comparative analysis of the cases of Peru and Guatemala is addressed primarily to the first of these questions. He seeks to explain differences between the urban behavior of migrants in these two countries in terms of the persistence and strength of rural ties and cultural practices in the urban setting. He stresses that urban behavior must be understood not simply as a response to certain aspects of the economic and political organization of the migrant's city of destination:

> Interrelationships between city and provinces are additional, significant variables in the comparative analysis of urban behavior. An important factor in whether migrants maintain a distinctive identity in the city is the extent to which urban life involves continuing social and economic relationships with the provinces.

Roberts found these relationships to be much stronger in Peru than in Guatemala, and he attributes this difference to the greater availability of economic opportunities in rural communities of Peru as well as a much more complex and "aggressive" pattern of social and political organization in rural Peru. These differences are, in turn, reflected in the greater organizational capacity and the greater material rewards obtained by poor people in Peruvian cities, as compared with those in Guatemala City. Roberts' analysis, combining both historical data and data gathered through field work among contemporary populations in rural and urban areas, specifies the kinds of exchanges which occur between villagers and city dwellers. This reciprocity of influence is found to be highly important to an explanation of urban behavior and patterns of social and political organization in Peru. As Roberts puts it, this is not just a case of "the city dominating the countryside."

Billie Jean Isbell's study of an Indian village in Highland Peru is one of the first detailed inquiries into the impact of "return migration" from the city upon a rural community. She provides an innovative description and analysis of the returned migrants' conceptions of social space, ritual, and religious cults, and how these differ from the traditional concepts shared by nonmigrant villagers. She describes how the migrants' experiences of movement to the city, invasion of urban land to form squatter settlements, and return to their place of origin have led them to modify or reinterpret certain traditional concepts. Thus, for example, the closed, dualistic conception of social space traditionally held by residents of the village has been rearranged in a way that indicates a potential for integration into the national culture. Isbell also documents the ways in which returned migrants have acted as legal-political representatives and "cultural brokers" for the village, occupied key positions in local governing bodies, and launched important developmental initiatives, including a campaign to confiscate the Church's local holdings in land and livestock and convert them into a cooperative to be run in the interests of the village. Isbell predicts that the rate of change in the village will increase due to the presence of returned migrants, who perceive themselves as members of both the village and national communities.

The papers with which we conclude this volume of *Latin American Urban Research* represent an appropriate point of transition to the fifth volume in the series, scheduled for publication in 1975. Tentatively entitled "The Political Economy of Urban Development in Latin America," most of its contributors will analyze the economic and political relationships existing between rural and urban areas in Latin American countries. The rationale for the volume depends heavily upon the argument implicit in the papers by Roberts and Isbell–i.e., that an adequate understanding of the determinants and consequences of urbanization in Latin America must encompass rural as well as urban areas–the points of origin for cityward migrants as well as their places of destination. In recent years, anthropologists and other social scientists have begun to question the practice of comparing "the urban" and "the rural" as distinct entities in urbanization studies. Perhaps a more realistic approach would focus upon the nature and quality of the interfaces between the two (cf. Snyder, 1973: 106; Orellana, 1973; Leeds, 1974). Hopefully, Volume 5 of this series will provide additional impetus for the reintegration of the countryside into research on Latin American urbanization.

REFERENCES

ALDERSON-SMITH, G. (forthcoming) "Individual orientations toward action: a micro-study among 'marginal' city dwellers in Lima, Peru." Ph.D. dissertation. University of Sussex, England.

BRADFIELD, S. (1963) "Migration from Huaylas: a study of brothers." Ph.D. dissertation. Cornell University.

BUTTERWORTH, D. S. (1962) "A study of the urbanization process among Mixtec migrants from Tilantongo in Mexico City." América Indígena 22: 257-274.

CORNELIUS, W. A. (1974) "Urbanization and political demand making: political participation among the migrant poor in Latin American cities." American Political Science Review 68 (September).

––– (1973) Political Learning Among the Migrant Poor: The Impact of Residential Context. Beverly Hills, Calif.: Sage (Sage Professional Papers in Comparative Politics, No. 01-037).

––– (1971) "The political sociology of cityward migration in Latin America: toward empirical theory," pp. 95-147 in F. F. Rabinovitz and F. M. Trueblood (eds.) Latin American Urban Research, Volume 1. Beverly Hills, Calif.: Sage.

EDDY, E. M. (ed.) (1968) Urban Anthropology: Research Perspectives and Strategies. Southern Anthropological Society Proceedings, No. 2. Athens, Ga.: University of Georgia Press.

EPSTEIN, D. G. (1973) Brasília, Plan and Reality: A Study of Planned and Spontaneous Urban Development. Berkeley, Calif.: University of California Press.

——— (1972) "The genesis and function of squatter settlements in Brasília," pp. 51-58 in T. Weaver and D. White (eds.) The Anthropology of Urban Environments. Boulder, Col.: Society for Applied Anthropology (SAA Monographs No. 11).

FOSTER, G. M. (1967) Tzintzuntzan: Mexican Peasants in a Changing World. Boston: Little, Brown.

——— and R. V. KEMPER (eds.) (1974) Anthropologists in Cities. Boston: Little, Brown.

GONZALEZ, N. L. (1974) "The city of gentlemen: Santiago de los Caballeros," pp. 19-40 in G. M. Foster and R. V. Kemper (eds.) Anthropologists in Cities. Boston: Little, Brown.

GULICK, J. (1973) "The city as context: the city as microcosm of society." Presented at the Annual Meeting of the American Anthropological Association, New Orleans, La., November-December.

——— (1968) "The outlook, research strategies, and relevance of urban anthropology: a commentary," pp. 93-98 in E. M. Eddy (ed.) Urban Anthropology: Research Perspectives and Strategies. Southern Anthropological Society Proceedings, No. 2. Athens, Ga.: University of Georgia Press.

GUTKIND, P.C.W. (1973) "Bibliography on urban anthropology," pp. 425-489 in A. Southall (ed.) Urban Anthropology: Cross-Cultural Studies of Urbanization. New York and London: Oxford University Press.

HARRIS, M. (1956) Town and Class in Brazil. New York: Columbia University Press.

KEMPER, R. V. (1974) "Tzintzuntzeños in Mexico City: the anthropologist among peasant migrants," pp. 63-92 in G. M. Foster and R. V. Kemper (eds.) Anthropologists in Cities. Boston: Little, Brown.

——— (1971a) "Bibliografía comentada sobre la antropología urbana en América Latina." Boletín Bibliográfico de Antropología Americana (Instituto Panamericana de Geografía e Historia, México, D.F.) 33-34: 85-140. (Reprinted in Latin American Reprint Series, Center for Latin American Studies and Institute of International Studies, University of California, Berkeley, No. 393.)

——— (1971b) "Migration and adaptation of Tzintzuntzan migrants in Mexico City." Ph.D. dissertation. University of California, Berkeley.

——— (1970) "The anthropological study of migrants to Latin American cities." Kroeber Anthropological Society Papers 42: 1-25.

LEEDS, A. (1974) "Urban society subsumes rural: specialties, nucleations, countryside, and networks: metatheory, theory, and method." In Acts of the Fiftieth International Congress of Americanists. Rome, Italy: International Congress of Americanists.

——— (1973) "Political, economic and social effects of producer and consumer orientations toward housing in Brazil and Peru: a systems analysis." In F. F. Rabinovitz and F. M. Trueblood (eds.) Latin American Urban Research, Volume 3. Beverly Hills, Calif.: Sage.

——— (1968) "The anthropology of cities: some methodological issues," pp. 31-47 in E. M. Eddy (ed.) Urban Anthropology: Research Perspectives and Strategies. Southern Anthropological Society Proceedings, No. 2. Athens, Ga.: University of Georgia Press.

——— and E. LEEDS (1970) "Brazil and the myth of urban rurality: urban experience, work, and values in 'squatments' of Rio de Janeiro and Lima," pp. 229-285 in A. J. Field (ed.) City and Country in the Third World: Issues in the Modernization of Latin America. Cambridge, Mass.: Schenkman.

LEWIS, O. (1965) "Further observations on the folk-urban continuum and urbanization with special reference to Mexico City," pp. 491-503 in P. M. Hauser and L. F. Schnore (eds.) The Study of Urbanization. New York: John Wiley.

––– (1952) "Urbanization without breakdown: a case study." Scientific Monthly 75 (July): 31-41.

MANGIN, W. (ed.) (1970) Peasants in Cities: Readings in the Anthropology of Urbanization. Boston: Houghton Mifflin.

MICHAELSON, K. L. (1972) "Field and 'boundary' and the methodology of urban anthropology." Presented at the Annual Meeting of the American Anthropological Association, Toronto, November.

MITCHELL, J. C. (ed.) (1969) Social Networks in Urban Situations. Manchester, England: University of Manchester Press.

ORELLANA S., C. L. (1973) "Mixtec migrants in Mexico City: a case study of urbanization." Human Organization 32 (Fall): 273-283.

PEATTIE, L. R. (1968) The View from the Barrio. Ann Arbor, Mich.: University of Michigan Press.

PLOTNICOV, L. (1973) "Anthropological field work in modern and local urban contexts." Urban Anthropology 2 (Fall): 248-264.

PORTES, A. (1971) "The urban slum in Chile: types and correlates." Land Economics 47 (August): 235-248.

PRICE, J. A. (1973) Tijuana: Urbanization in a Border Culture. Notre Dame, Ind.: Notre Dame University Press.

REINA, R. E. (1973) Paraná: Social Boundaries in an Argentine City. Austin, Texas: University of Texas Press (Institute of Latin American Studies, Monograph No. 31).

ROLLWAGEN, J. R. (1968) "The paleteros of Mexticacán, Jalisco: a study of entrepreneurship in Mexico." Ph.D. dissertation. University of Oregon, Eugene.

SNYDER, P. Z. (1973) "Comparative urbanization: an anthropological perspective," pp. 101-113 in E. W. Soja et al., Research Traditions in the Comparative Study of Urbanization: Towards an Interdisciplinary Approach. Los Angeles, Calif.: School of Architecture and Urban Planning, University of California, Los Angeles.

SOUTHALL, A. (ed.) (1973) Urban Anthropology: Cross-Cultural Studies of Urbanization. New York and London: Oxford University Press.

SPENCER, R. F. (ed.) (1971) Migration and Anthropology: Proceedings of the 1970 Annual Spring Meeting of the American Ethnological Society. Seattle, Wash.: University of Washington Press.

SWARTZ, M. J. (1973) "The 'close' study of politics: a kind of commentary." Journal of Comparative Administration 4 (February): 481-498.

UZZELL, D. (1974) Urban Anthropology. Dubuque, Iowa: William C. Brown.

WEAVER, T. (1973) "The anthropology of urban and complex societies." Presented at the Annual Meeting of the American Anthropological Association, New Orleans, La., November-December.

––– and D. WHITE (eds.) (1972) The Anthropology of Urban Environments. Boulder, Col.: Society for Applied Anthropology (SAA Monograph Series, No. 11).

WHITEFORD, A. H. (1964) Two Cities of Latin America: A Comparative Description of Social Classes. Garden City, N.Y.: Doubleday-Anchor Books.

––– J. GULICK, A. LEEDS, and W. A. SHACK (1972) "Letters and commentary." Urban Anthropology Newsletter 1 (Spring): 2-6.

PART I

CITYWARD

MIGRATION

ROBERT V. KEMPER is Assistant Professor of Anthropology at Southern Methodist University. He received his Ph.D. from the University of California, Berkeley, in 1971 and held a Post-Doctoral Fellowship in Mexican-American Studies from the National Endowment for the Humanities during the academic year 1971-1972. His interests in urban studies, migration, culture change, and applied anthropology have been pursued through field research in Mexico, California, and Texas. He is the founding editor of *Urban Anthropology Newsletter* and (with George M. Foster) has co-edited *Anthropologists in Cities* (Little, Brown, 1974). His other published papers include: "The Anthropological Study of Migration to Latin American Cities" (*Kroeber Anthropological Society Papers*, Vol. 42, 1970); "Bibliografía comentada sobre la antropología urbana en América Latina" (*Boletín Bibliográfico de Antropología Americana*, Mexico, D. F., Vol. 33/34, 1970/71); and "Rural-Urban Migration in Latin America: A Framework for the Comparative Analysis of Geographical and Temporal Patterns" (*International Migration Review*, Spring 1971).

Chapter 1

FAMILY AND HOUSEHOLD ORGANIZATION AMONG TZINTZUNTZAN MIGRANTS IN MEXICO CITY

ROBERT V. KEMPER

What happens to migrant families in Latin American cities? With a well-established professional predilection for studying kinship and social organization, anthropologists have been intrigued by this question for several decades. Thus, in his pioneering multi-community project in Yucatan, Redfield (1941) suggested that movement from village to town to city would be accompanied by disorganization, secularization, and individualization. This paradigm of the urbanization process, borrowed from earlier works by European and American sociologists, was put to a crucial ethnographic test by Lewis's investigations in Tepoztlán and among Tepoztecan migrants in Mexico City. In contrast to what had been predicted, he discovered that "families remain strong; in fact, there is some evidence that family cohesiveness increases in the city in the face of the difficulties of city life" (1952: 36). Subsequent research in Mexico City slums led Lewis to refine his views on how migrants adjust to urban life. He postulated that landless rural workers are more likely to encounter family problems (and fall into the "culture of poverty") than are migrants from stable peasant villages (1966: 24).

Although the concept of the "culture of poverty" has been criticized by many anthropologists (e.g., Leeds, 1971; Peattie, 1971), the notion that the family plays a major *positive* role in migrant adjustment to city life is now generally accepted. However, in Latin America the field of family and kinship remains very understudied (Carlos and Sellers, 1972: 99), and insufficient attention has been given to research designs which will specify more precisely how and why migrant families prosper in urban settings. This is particularly unfortunate since Lewis himself suggested long ago (1952: 41) that the best procedure would be to conduct follow-up studies of migrants from rural communities already well documented ethnographically.

Perhaps because of anthropology's lingering rural tradition, only a handful of such comparative rural-urban studies have been carried out. The well-known studies by Butterworth (1962), Doughty (1970), and Mangin (1965), although not focused primarily on family life, illustrate the many advantages of this approach to the study of rural-urban migration. Thus, when the opportunity arose for me to carry out similar research among migrants from the peasant village of Tzintzuntzan, Mexico, I eagerly accepted. For several reasons this seemed like an ideal study for assessing migrant adaptation to urban life in general and examining migrant family life in particular. Most important, Tzintzuntzan is very well documented ethnographically through the long-term, ongoing research carried out by George M. Foster and his students (Foster and Ospina, 1948; Foster, 1967). Complete village household censuses for 1945, 1960, and 1970 provide superb demographic data on family organization, while detailed genealogies and voluminous fieldnotes exist on many migrants and their families. Thus, I could concentrate on a single phase of what for other ethnographers had been a time-consuming two-stage project. In addition, Tzintzuntzan emigrants share with many Mexican peasants—including those of Tepoztlán and Tilantongo—a preference for settling in Mexico City. This meant that I could compare my findings more directly with those of Lewis and Butterworth while avoiding the arduous task of locating Tzintzuntzeños in a number of Mexican cities. Under these conditions, I conducted fieldwork in Mexico City for seventeen months from April 1969 to August 1970.[1]

RURAL BACKGROUND AND URBAN DESTINATION: FROM TZINTZUNTZAN TO MEXICO CITY

Since 1940 the population of Mexico has increased from twenty to more than fifty million persons. During the same period, Tzintzuntzan has undergone a minor population explosion of its own. The 1,077 persons of 1940 became 2,169 by 1970, despite a rapid increase in emigration during the 1960s. Thus, far from facing the depopulation reported for some Mexican villages, Tzintzuntzan appears to be bulging at its demographic seams.

Rapid population growth has not been matched by an equivalent expansion of local economic opportunities. The most important traditional occupation —pottery making—has declined from 57 percent of the labor force in 1945 to 46 percent in 1970, as potters' sons abandon the craft for day labor or leave the village altogether. And only a few villagers have benefited significantly from greater demand for local crafts. Furthermore, a vital economic resource disappeared when the *bracero* program was terminated in 1964. Its effect on Tzintzuntzan—as on many communities in central Mexico—was impressive: 53 percent of all village households heads worked across the border at least once and many made several trips (Foster, 1967: 275-277). The impact of their remittances and the "demonstration effect" of their success has reverberated throughout Tzintzuntzan. Thus, peasants accustomed to inferiority and repression realized that opportunities beyond traditional channels were within their grasp.

As a result, the past three decades have witnessed many changes in Tzintzuntzan life. Homes have been improved, villagers enjoy better health, children have more educational opportunities, and a few families even possess amenities once limited to affluent urbanites. This progress has not come without consequences for traditional patterns of social stratification and cultural values. As the disparity between poverty-stricken and relatively wealthy peasants grows, the local saying *aquí somos todos iguales* is rendered obsolete. Still, few Tzintzuntzeños are secure enough to weather a severe recession, particularly since external forces determine the demand for what they produce and set the prices on what they buy.

This transformation, a crucial step in the modernization process, also reflects Tzintzuntzan's greater involvement in Mexican national life (for details, see Kemper, 1973a). Through radio, television, and newspapers, villagers have discovered the world beyond the local orbit. And since the highway cut through Tzintzuntzan in 1939, traditional craft markets have expanded, and thousands of Mexican and American tourists have stopped to visit the Tarascan *yácatas* ("pyramids") or to buy crafts at roadside stands. Thus exposed to the outside world on a daily basis, increasing numbers of Tzintzuntzan peasants elect to board the bus at the village plaza to pursue what they see on television and witness along the highway. They do not flee ignorantly from grinding poverty; they leave to find their fortune and their future—as they say, to search for life, *buscar la vida.*

Where does the highway take Tzintzuntzan emigrants? According to my analysis of Foster's unpublished census materials, a total of 738 villagers have emigrated since the late 1930s, of whom only 43 (6 percent) returned permanently to Tzintzuntzan. Of the remaining 695 "full-time" emigrants, 310 (45 percent) stayed in Michoacán, 246 (35 percent) went to the Mexico City metropolitan area, 96 (14 percent) settled elsewhere in Mexico, and another 43 (6 percent), crossed into the United States. Tzintzuntzeños clearly favor "urban" (Unikel, 1968: 15) destinations, since 498 (72 percent) have settled in localities with more than 15,000 inhabitants. After Mexico City, the most popular cities were Morelia, the state capital, with 76 emigrants; Pátzcuaro, a nearby market town, with 69; and Uruapan, a rapidly growing city in western Michoacán, with only 28. No other destination received more than 20 Tzintzuntzeños. Furthermore, as emigration has increased—71 percent has occurred since 1960—Mexico City has become a more important destination while migration within Michoacán has diminished.

Tzintzuntzan migrants in Mexico City represent a positively selected segment of the Tzintzuntzan population.[2] A fundamental aspect of their selectivity is demographic: the great majority were below thirty years of age at time of departure; slightly more males than females have emigrated; and few adult migrants were widowed or separated from spouses at time of departure. Tzintzuntzeños in Mexico City also show positive selectivity on other indicators such as education, occupation, living standards, and innovativeness (for details, see Kemper, 1971: 67-79). However, as the number of migrants increased during the 1960s and life in Tzintzuntzan improved for most village families, selectivity suffered the predictable "regression toward the mean" (Browning and Feindt, 1969: 356). This confirms the view that under desperate conditions few persons risk emigration, whereas when wealth increases and living conditions improve, the number of emigrants increases and the degree of positive selectivity declines.

A theoretical consequence of this trend is for recent migrants to suffer greater difficulties than did earlier migrants in coping with urban life. However, potential migrants to Mexico City have largely overcome this problem by receiving assistance from Tzintzuntzeños already established there. And as more villagers settle in the capital their presence encourages still others to follow. Thus, what was once a series of unrelated, individual moves to Mexico City has become a spatial-temporal network through which a constantly changing set of actors aids one another to find housing and jobs. In this way, more than 90 percent of the migrants have become successfully established in the capital.[3]

Tzintzuntzeños in Mexico City are especially dependent on family and kinsmen because they have no migrant club or regional association to turn to and because they live in more than forty neighborhoods distributed through the metropolitan zone. Here the nexus of urban adaptation lies with the individual and his family connections. Examining the family life of Tzintzuntzan migrants in Mexico City thus becomes a crucial first step in understanding their urban experiences. Therefore, I now turn to a detailed analysis of their family and household structure, the interpersonal relations within families, and the economic situation of migrant households in the urban setting.

FAMILY AND HOUSEHOLD STRUCTURE

Before describing the migrant situation in Mexico City, it is appropriate to summarize the main features of family and household structure in Tzintzuntzan (see Foster, 1967: 55-59). In 1970, the village population was divided among 360 households, of which 252 (70 percent) were nuclear, 59 (16.4 percent) were joint, and the remaining 49 (13.6 percent) were "truncated."[4] These three household categories contained 371 married couples plus the aforementioned 49 truncated families, for a total of 420 families. Despite recent demographic pressures on a limited land and housing supply, 88 percent of the villagers reside in their own homes. Renting and caretaking are gradually becoming more important, however, as emigrants leave behind empty houses and the urban elite from the state capital build summer houses on the shores of Lake Pátzcuaro near Tzintzuntzan.

Although the nuclear bilateral family is the most significant socioeconomic unit in the village, and most households are composed of a single conjugal family unit, it is a rare Tzintzuntzeño who never resides in a household containing two or more families during his lifetime. This is due to local partible inheritance practices and to a preference for post-marital patrilocal residence. In such a setting, the joint household often serves as a transitional phase in which some combination of cooking and budget arrangements bring together two siblings' families or the families of parents and sons (Nutini, 1967: 390). The truncated household, by contrast, results not from choice or expediency but from circumstances of death or separation, and thus creates an imbalance between family needs and their ability to meet them. Under all conditions, extended family ties are usually weak and sometimes are lacking completely. In sum, as Tzintzuntzan peasants grow up, marry, have children, and eventually watch them depart, they usually belong to a series of nuclear, joint, and truncated households. These correspond to the requirements of different segments of the typical peasant family developmental cycle, and as such constitute complementary rather than antithetical aspects of village social life.

With this brief description of village patterns in mind, I now consider the family and household structure of Tzintzuntzan migrants in Mexico City.

According to my project census, at least 483 persons resided in Tzintzuntzan-affiliated households in Mexico City during 1969-1970. A detailed breakdown yields 246 "full-time" Tzintzuntzan migrants, 38 "part-time" Tzintzuntzan migrants, 39 spouses born outside Tzintzuntzan, 116 children born in the capital, 24 children born elsewhere, 10 non-Tzintzuntzan in-laws, and 10 non-Tzintzuntzan non-kinsmen. This population was divided among 74 households, of which 46 (62.2 percent) were nuclear, 7 (9.4 percent) were joint, 16 (21.6 percent) were "truncated," and 5 (6.7 percent) were of unknown status. A total of 80 families and an additional 16 young adults boarding at the city's secondary schools, seminaries, convents, and universities composed the migrant group. In contrast to village norms, less than one-fifth of Tzintzuntzeños in the capital own their homes; nearly two-thirds rent rooms, apartments, or houses; and only a few (domestic servants) fall into the caretaker category. Furthermore, a substantial minority of the migrant households contain persons outside the conjugal unit of parents and children. The large number of temporary guests living *arrimado* ("up close to"; i.e., rent-free) in migrant homes combines with a high birth rate to generate a mean household size of 6.7 persons. This is slightly higher than that in Tzintzuntzan (6.2) and significantly higher than the Mesoamerican average of between 4.0 and 5.5 persons (Nutini and Murphy, 1970: 96).

Nuclear Households and Extended Families

Despite some differences in household composition and ownership patterns, one might conclude that the family and household structure among Tzintzuntzan migrants is substantially similar to that in the village; in other words, that migrants simply transfer their family and household patterns to the urban setting. However, attention to the role of the *extended family* among the migrants shows the insufficiency of this view. The following example illustrates how the socioeconomic functions of the migrant nuclear household are influenced by urban residence conditions:

Abel and his brother Gabriel—each married with young children—live in the same *vecindad* in Colonia Buena Ventura. They usually spend their leisure time together, just as their wives devote much of each day to joint activities, including washing clothes, doing dishes, making meals, and watching over the children. Nevertheless, each family pays its own rent and considers itself a separate household.

Thus, the nuclear household is a relatively autonomous economic unit among Tzintzuntzeños in the capital, with the key being separate rent payments and budgets. But when kin-related families live in the close proximity of a *vecindad* or even in the same neighborhood, they often share many important social and domestic activities (see also Lomnitz, 1973). By reanalyzing my data on family and household categories among the Tzintzuntzan migrants, I discovered that the incidence of such "extended family enclaves" (Leeds and Leeds, 1970) was relatively high. The number of nuclear households with no significant extended family ties falls to only 24 (32.5 percent) of the 74 migrant households, whereas extended families jump to 31 (41.9 percent) when the co-residence criterion is eliminated. In fact, more nuclear households exist in an extended family relationship to other Tzintzuntzeños in Mexico City than live in isolation (25 versus 24). For many Tzintzuntzan migrants in the capital, therefore, extended families serve as significant adjuncts to the nuclear household in easing urban adaptation. New arrivals are not limited to a single family unit in the search for housing and a job. They turn to any number of kinsmen living in the vicinity of the family with whom they are staying *arrimado* (for details on the *arrimado* pattern, see Kemper, 1973b).

Joint Households

Although there are only seven joint households among Tzintzuntzeños in Mexico City, their differences from the rural patterns further show how the urban setting influences the organization of outwardly similar social forms. These joint households develop in two main ways. Among poor families, sharing cramped quarters to stretch otherwise insufficient incomes, they grow by accretion in response to urban housing availability. Thus, a truncated household may become a nuclear household, then a joint household, and may split again into two nuclear households, forming an extended family enclave. The following example illustrates this general pattern:

> Saúl came to Mexico City in 1963 and lived *arrimado* with an uncle (since deceased) in a *vecindad* zone where he still resides. Later, a younger brother joined him. First Saúl and then his brother married, with the result that the tiny wooden shack in which they lived became very cramped. To add to the space problem, their father migrated to the city in 1968 when his wife died, leaving no one at home to help him with the family pottery-making. In March 1970, the household contained three generations: father, married sons, and two grandchildren. However, when an apartment became available across the street during the summer, Saúl took his wife and child to live there, although still keeping up many of the previous social and domestic activities with his brother's family.

Joint households also occur among more affluent Tzintzunteños in the city. With these families, co-residence and sharing of domestic functions arise not from their need to dilute the effect of poverty but from parental desire to inculcate proper behavior in their newlywed sons and daughters-in-law. Note that this rationale for the joint household resembles the traditional village pattern more than does the other migrant type described above. This paradox—that affluent migrants seem to behave more like villagers than do poor migrants—reminds us that the urban joint household does not respond to the same circumstances as in the village. In fact, only affluent migrants own homes or rent apartments large enough to comfortably contain two or more families.

Nevertheless, all migrant joint households do adhere to a universal village rule—i.e., they are formed only among kinsmen. Of the seven migrant joint households, four exist between fathers and sons, two between brothers, and one between cousins. However, even in the father-son alliances, only a single instance developed in response to a son's marriage. Thus, the joint household among Tzintzunteños in Mexico City does not result from attempts to re-create traditional rural residence patterns. In fact, the rarity of the joint household and the large number of renters attests to the tightness of Mexico City's housing market.

Truncated Households

Among Tzintzuntzan migrants in Mexico City, truncated households occur in several situations. First, desertion or separation often causes a spouse (with or without children) to migrate to Mexico City. Domestic servants also form an important segment of truncated households. Third, widowed parents sometimes follow their children to the capital. Finally, young bachelors sometimes establish independent residences after a period of living with kinsmen. In addition, a number of students have been sent by their parents to attend boarding schools in the capital. (By virtue of the tightly controlled world in which they reside, these students seldom see many other Tzintzuntzeños in Mexico City. Their social ties are primarily to the village, to which they return during vacations and from whence they receive visits and gifts from parents and relatives.)

Thus, truncated households are an important modification of traditional Tzintzuntzan family and residence patterns in the urban setting: occupational and educational requirements usually determine the urban type, whereas death, separation, or emigration produce the rural counterpart. Of course, truncated households are generally transitional, since marriage and subsequent intra-urban movements shift individuals into nuclear or joint household categories (Hammel, 1961, 1964).

Matrifocal Families Among Tzintzuntzan Migrants

The literature on working-class families in Latin American cities suggests the prevalence of the "matrifocal family" or "female-based household," in which kin relations emphasize the female line, the husband (if present) assumes a marginal position in the economic survival of the household and in the children's daily discipline, and the transient relations between husbands and wives can be described as serial monogamy or even serial polyandry (e.g., Gonzalez, 1965, 1969; Legerman, 1969; Lewis, 1965; Peattie, 1968; Safa, 1964). The principal causes for the male's limited role are job insecurity (due to lack of adequate education, job skills, and opportunities for upward mobility) and the woman's ability to support the family through self-employment in domestic services, which further weakens and threatens the male's position as chief economic provider and *jefe de familia* (Patch, 1961: 20).

In contrast, the matrifocal family is rare among Tzintzuntzeños in Mexico City. Several women (widows with children or abandoned mothers with children) do head households, but only twice have women formed *uniones libres* with more than one husband. Examination of one of these cases reveals how the matrifocal family among Tzintzuntzan migrants differs from the typical urban Latin American pattern:

Señora Corona, age 43, works as a school teacher in the day and as a secondary school vice-principal at night to support the seven people in her household (herself, four school-age children by two previous husbands, a nephew attending college, and a 21-year-old man whom she recently "married" and is putting through college). Her high income (more than $5,000 pesos per month) permits many luxuries, such as a two-week vacation in Acapulco, unknown to most migrants. Also, she has contracted for the building of a second story on her house, which is being paid off through a government-subsidized, long-term loan. Señora Corona is "notorious" for having left Tzintzuntzan as a teenager to attend secondary school and then Normal School, living a "bad" life in the city, and "wed" only in free union rather than through the Church. Certainly, much of her notoriety results from other villagers' envy of her exceptional success: her native intelligence, hard work, and driving ambition evoke pious outrage among those who have been less successful in Mexico City.

This woman little resembles the usual picture of the poverty-stricken female struggling to keep her family together in the absence of a male economic provider. Female-headed households lacking steady male employment or suffering underemployment do appear among the Tzintzuntzeños in Mexico City; however, only domestic servants fall into that category, and no women are reputed to survive through prostitution or similar activities.

Since the matrifocal family is rare among Tzintzuntzan migrants in Mexico City, what accounts for the predominance of its opposite—the bilateral conjugal household? I believe that the prevalence of steady male employment provides men with statuses and roles which stabilize the marital relationship (Schulz, 1968: 658-659). In Tzintzuntzan, where the peasant household represents the basic production unit, male employment is high and male-dominated nuclear households are the rule. Although work is performed outside the migrant household, employment rates among husbands are surprisingly high, with the result that the matrifocal family does not flourish.

FHH does not appear w/ strong urban employment opp for men

INTERPERSONAL RELATIONS IN THE MIGRANT FAMILY

Husbands and Wives

As we have seen, the conjugal family, whether manifest in the nuclear household or the extended family enclave, predominates among Tzintzuntzeños in Mexico City. However, analysis of family and household structure reveals little about the quality of interpersonal relations among family members. In Tzintzuntzan, "villagers are in general agreement about ideal role behavior within the family: the husband is dominant, owed obedience and respect by his wife and children even after the latter reach adulthood. The wife should be faithful and submissive, frugal and careful in managing family resources, and kind and loving with her children" (Foster, 1967: 59).

Such attitudes are reflected in the traditional division of labor in peasant families; as the saying goes, *el hombre en la plaza, y la mujer en la casa* ("the man's place is at work, the woman's at home"). Migrant attitudes toward ideal role behavior and proper division of labor between spouses vary considerably from the traditional Tzintzuntzan view. To be sure, husbands are the principal participants in the urban wage labor market, while their wives remain responsible for the smooth functioning of the household.[5] But husbands (as well as male children) often also perform such tasks as sweeping patios, washing dishes, and tending younger children. Such active and willing participation in household tasks, rare in Tzintzuntzan, shows that migrant men are neither helplessly dependent on their wives nor concerned about loss of "masculinity" (Leñero Otero, 1968: 132-133).

For instance, among the young bachelors who have spent time in Mexico City to complete their education, the ethic of male dominance is largely replaced by a belief in marital democracy which allows women equal authority and responsibility in the family affairs (Leñero Otero, 1968: 134). Furthermore, according to this "modern" attitude, wives may even continue in their careers after marriage. Thus, a preoccupation with economic success may override the traditional attitude that a woman's place is in the home.

Relations between spouses in migrant families are also significantly influenced by the absence of the groom's mother, who in the Tzintzuntzan peasant family exercises dominion over a son's wife when the newlyweds live in her home. The mother-in-law traditionally is considered a hard taskmaster who exploits her son's wife and thereby creates serious strains among herself, her son, and his wife. But when the mother-in-law is absent, as she usually is among migrant families, relations between husband and wife tend to be more egalitarian from the outset. Thus, separation from village and husband's mother liberates the migrant wife from much of her traditional suffering and exploitation (Esteva Fabregat, 1969: 205).

Responses to the Thematic Apperception Test (TAT) and data from life histories provide additional insights into sensitive areas of migrant husband-wife relationships.[6] The following example reveals a basically egalitarian relation between spouses.

CARD 4: a young woman is clutching the shoulders of a man whose face and body are averted as if he were trying to pull away from her.

NARRATOR: José Zavala, a 48-year-old married man.

I have always felt that in addition to dedicating oneself to a career, one should share happiness with his wife. . . . To me, my wife has been like my second half, with myself as the first half. We have struggled through life together, in happy times and in suffering, and we hope to have a happy future. . . . One improves himself, but not alone, rather always with the support of his wife. What is a wife if not a help-mate? For me, the wife is no slave, but has her own principles—just like the husband—and her own obligations and makes her own mistakes, all of which should be recognized and shared together. . . . This is my intention: to have a stable future so that I can share my happiness and success with my wife, who is the only person who has suffered with me through all my disappointments and through my happiness.

His wife's life history is replete with references to her reasons for marrying José, to their attitudes toward each other and toward their children, and to their aspirations and ambitions for the future:

After I married José, everyone in Tzintzuntzan criticized me and wanted to know why I, a widow with two young children, would be interested in him. I replied that I wanted to marry someone who would bring up the children correctly, would take me out of Quiroga where I was living in the house of my deceased husband, would take good care of me, and would see to the children's education. And besides, we had been *novios* at an early age and had always liked each other, despite my marriage at age 13 to an elderly man from Quiroga and despite José's departure to Morelia to finish his education. José could have married someone else, just as I might have done, but I rejected several other suitors because my interest was in the betterment of myself and my children, and José's career and his personal concern appeared to offer a sound base for our future. José has always respected me, without regard to the property left to me by my first husband; he wanted our relationship to be based on love and understanding, not on material goods. José and I always come to an agreement on our problems, whether it is over money or our plans, or vacations, or clothes purchases, or our food and meals. We share things between us so that we can achieve our goals in life without falling into debt or suffering unduly. In fact, we have lived well, have had no difficulties to speak of, and have gotten as far in life as our money would take us.

In sum, husband-wife relations in migrant families tend to be egalitarian and mutually supportive: most men assist and cooperate in domestic chores and progressive, younger women are career- as well as family-oriented. Regardless of their specific arrangements for income production and domestic duties, nearly all families demonstrate a low level of male authoritarianism and a high degree of "democratic" conflict resolution between spouses.

Parents and Children

If the great triangle of adulthood in Tzintzuntzan peasant families is husband, wife, and mother-in-law, then the major triad of childhood is mother, father, and child. In the traditional Mexican peasant family, males assert their masculinity by adopting the role of *El Macho* ("the He-Man"), while females fall in the opposing role of *la madre abnegada* ("the long-suffering mother").[7]

Among Tzintzuntzan migrants in Mexico City, however, fathers are more apt to be affectionate toward their children, open and understanding in their counsel, eager to labor for their children's betterment, and concerned with being a friend rather than a symbol of ultimate authority—that is, they tend to reject behavior associated with rural *machismo*. Again, TAT responses illustrate several important elements of these migrant attitudes: the first story demonstrates a perceptive understanding—and a rejection—of the traditional relationship between father and children; the second provides guidelines for more effective father-child relations; and the third shows how fathers and their children should jointly resolve their difficulties in order to turn suffering into success, poverty into progress.

CARD 7BM: a gray-haired man is looking at a younger man who is sullenly staring into space.

NARRATOR: a 26-year-old bachelor.

The mother is always idolized, and is considered very different from her husband. Children feel that the parents do not have the same affection for their own children, but upon a bit of reflection we realize that the father, in spite of not showing affection in the open manner of the mother, may love us, even more than she does. This can be better explained by example: There was a family formed, like all families, by the parents and the children. In this family the father always felt restrained. Whenever the children assembled, he found some way to separate himself from the group. Despite this, he felt that he loved his children even more than their own mother did, but the children did not respond. Once, a son noticed his attitude, approached him, and inquired as to why the father always retired from these family gatherings. The father replied that he felt inferior since all the children's affection was directed at his wife. The son, who loved his father, confessed this feeling of affection to his father, and made him understand that the children loved the father just as much as the mother, but that they couldn't demonstrate it as directly since the mother—being of the opposite sex—could receive their affection in a more direct form than the father. From then on, the father understood the children's attitudes and ever since has always participated in all the family gatherings.

NARRATOR: a 48-year-old married man.

When one has children, there is no better way to guide them than through the example of one's own behavior. The children take up many good habits from the father: if one is exacting at home, then they learn a habit valuable in their education and for their role in society.

How many times does a child ask advice of his father? But there are times when he is not brave enough to ask the father for counsel. In that case, the father must be a friend to his child. There can be no better friend than a father. The father should be a friend, not just an authority figure.

The father gives his all to his children and wants them to enjoy life to the fullest. What is very important is for the father to be a man of strong principles, to understand life, and to take part in the resolution of the world's problems, so that through such principles he may benefit the progress of his children.

NARRATOR: an 18-year-old bachelor.

For the past 15 years the father had been without a wife and the son without a mother. During this time, they had been very poor, but the father was a hard worker who hated vice as much as he strived to bring about a good future for his son. The son was put in school and the father labored to pay for it until the son finished. The son also worked to help pay for his studies. They had many adventures together, but since they were so poor they sometimes went hungry and went without sleep because they always worked so hard and so much. So, the son studied hard, thought about the future, a future when he would accomplish something because of his studies. And his father thought the same thing, and kept helping his son. So, the son studied until he was named President of the Republic. And he felt satisfied at having achieved what he thought about. And they were happy, and the son married and so did the father—and they all lived together and were very happy.

What accounts for such different views of father-child ties among traditional peasant families and Tzintzuntzan migrants? First, the absence of the man's mother relieves him from playing the conflicting roles of son and husband at the same time. Consequently, the authoritarianism of village fathers, expressed through *machismo* can be replaced by closer emotional ties between father and children. For example, child-beating is common in Tzintzuntzan but rare among the migrants in Mexico City. Discipline in the city seems rather lax, in fact, with rebukes most often limited to mild verbal urgings for proper behavior. One man perceptively remarked that his wife should discipline their children when they misbehaved during the day; he did not relish returning home each night to enforce discipline long after an incident had been forgotten. Besides, he pointed out, this would make him an authoritarian disliked by his children, whereas by not scolding them the wife would remain their friend and advocate!

Traditional *machismo* also has an economic referent (see Swartzbaugh, 1970: 5). Peasant fathers retreat to public declarations of their masculinity, often expressed through authoritarianism, self-isolation and defensiveness, and drinking,[8] when their actual accomplishements are severely constrained by ecological and economic forces (Esteva Fabregat, 1969: 222 ff.). That is, adoption of the symbols of *El Macho* allows males to establish a "social front" (Nelson, 1971: 74) by which they can avoid ultimate responsibility for their failure to properly provide for their families.

Among Tzintzuntzeños in Mexico City, a father provides daily evidence of his manhood through his stable and continuing economic contributions to his family's prosperity, and so exchanges—at least symbolically—traditional *machismo* behavior for a preferred status within the family group. Nearly all migrant men reject the ethic of *machismo* as unreasonable, disreputable, *sin urbanidad* ("uneducated"), and associate it with the rural traditions they abandoned.

Although migrant males tend to slough off the symbols and reject the model of *El Macho*, females retain much of their traditional status as the long-suffering and self-sacrificing mother, *la madre abnegada*.[9] In Mexican families dominated by a *machismo*-oriented father, the mother struggles to overcome his lack of support in raising the children and in instilling in them her Christian values and attitudes. In contrast, among nearly all Tzintzuntzan families in Mexico City, there exists a strong bond between spouses that is at once egalitarian and mutually supportive. The steady economic contributions of most husbands permits the wife to devote her attention to bringing up the children in the urban setting. The mother, therefore, retains a strong link to her children, and her suffering and sacrifice are not expressive and manipulative, but instrumental and achievement-oriented. She struggles, in cooperation with her husband, to assure her children a better place in the future by easing their progress over the hurdles which impede their economic and social mobility in the city.

The proper resolution of the conflict between traditional family role models and those in most migrant families is aptly expressed by the following TAT response:

CARD 6BM: elderly woman with tall young man.

NARRATOR: a 48-year-old married man.

The mother is a second element in the home. In general, Mexicans do not pay enough attention to the mother: they relegate her to secondary status, and give primary importance to the father. She is not consulted; at times even has no rights in her own home. This is bad and should be corrected–the mother should have her rights as well as her obligations. . . . The mother obviously should have much *confianza* with her children and should also be their friend. A friendly mother can resolve many problems, she should set a good example for her children to follow. The mother should not be a dictator, but should ask herself what is best for the children. The mother is so important that we must not mistreat her; she is always an object of our love and affection. Even when we die, the word "mother" is on our lips, and is our own special benediction.

THE ECONOMIC SITUATION OF MIGRANT HOUSEHOLDS

In the preceding sections, I have described the structure and organization of Tzintzuntzan migrant families and households in Mexico City. Since their lives also reflect the economic tensions of urbanization, analysis of their economic situation is appropriate.

Many Tzintzuntzan migrant households have more than one wage earner. In fact, for the 66 on which I obtained reliable data, only 32 (48.3 percent) have a single worker, while 29 (43.8 percent) have two, and another five (7.9 percent) have three or more, with a maximum of six reached in one large household. Thus, during the period of my census (March to July 1970), a total of 110 persons was employed full-time, an average of 1.66 per household. If students and retirees are omitted, only four of 91 adult males were without work. This high participation rate in the urban economy is not so surprising since these migrants represent some of the best educated, ablest, and most motivated members of their home community.

Despite the high number of households with more than a single worker, only five contained individuals with two jobs: two school teachers are principals at night; two church organists give music lessons between Masses; and a motorcycle telegraph messenger worked as a bill collector in the morning. In each case, the jobs require similar skills combined with relatively short hours for a single shift. For the great majority of Tzintzuntzeños in Mexico City, holding two jobs would be a physical hardship, if not an impossibility, since a normal work-week lasts 48 hours.

How can we account for the high participation rate of these migrants? In addition to providing temporary lodging, the more experienced migrants intercede as *palancas* ("levers") to obtain employment for new arrivals. Usually, the members of the household in which the new arrival lived upon reaching the city proved to be key resources. However, utilizing these personal ties constrains the job search, since one's opportunities are usually limited to positions inferior to those occupied by members of one's household and their ancillary social networks.

Recent migrants are usually content with wages sufficient for the basic needs of their families, since these far exceed what they earned in Tzintzuntzan. Thus, their sense of self-esteem is measured by rural as well as urban standards. "Relative deprivation" has its obverse in "relative satisfaction": many recent Tzintzuntzan migrants in Mexico City compare their present situation with that of their fathers and their siblings still in the village and most conclude that the urban condition is far superior.

A shift from rural to urban concepts of economic status forms an integral part of the assimilation process undergone by Tzintzuntzan migrants in Mexico City. One indication that even working-class migrants eventually become more sophisticated and better understand the demands of the urban economy is that, whereas nearly all found their first urban jobs through family ties, more experienced workers prefer to consult non-Tzintzuntzeño allies, especially job superiors, union friends, or government bureaucrats. Thus, Tzintzuntzeños in Mexico City eventually realize that while kinsmen can help with initial urban employment, subsequent upward mobility depends on individual initiative, hard work, and good contacts with non-migrants. Upward occupational mobility not only means shifting one's allegiance to a new set of achievement models, but also destroys the feeling of "community" with those who fail to attain similar socioeconomic success. The rift between *"los inferiores"* and *"los superiores,"* as one middle-class informant expressed it, mirrors Tzintzuntzan's incipient class distinctions, but with a further consequence: the urban setting provides much greater opportunity for widening the gap, and thereby increasing feelings of envy and suspicion between poor and affluent migrants.

Income and Consumer Behavior

A principal difference between village and migrant households is their relative dependence on cash income: unlike their counterparts in Tzintzuntzan, who usually keep gardens, fruit trees, and domestic animals to supplement the meager cash income from pottery-making, farming, and other traditional occupations, Tzintzuntzeño families in Mexico City are completely subject to the vagaries of the cash nexus. In the 51 migrant households for which I have detailed economic data, productive gardens and fruit trees are completely absent and domestic animals are present in only seven, with none having more than four chickens or a single pig. The absence of such supplements to cash income is due mainly to lack of space in most migrant households.

Most Tzintzuntzan migrants working in Mexico City earn slightly more than the minimum wage for a six-day week, although a few earn as much as $6,000 pesos per month.[10] Thus, the great majority of Tzintzuntzan migrants in Mexico City fall into stable working-class or professional sectors.

Migrants are well aware that "the job" provides the basis for urban livelihood and so quickly learn to adjust residence patterns, social relations, and child-raising practices to its exigencies. Persons without full-time jobs do not usually contribute to income production. Children, especially, are told to devote their time and attention to school work rather than to sell gum or newspapers on street corners. In fact, in only one household does a person below age sixteen work at all.

Thus, urban job requirements and parental attitudes reverse the traditional view of the economic struggle found in most Tzintzuntzan families, where

> a living . . . is earned by nearly everyone in bits and pieces. Every family member is alert to the possibility of picking up a few extra pesos here or there, and rare is a person who, in addition to his primary occupation, does not try his hand at other tasks [Foster, 1969: 47].

Despite much higher income levels than they would enjoy in Tzintzuntzan, most migrant families must struggle with elevated prices for consumer goods and services. Whereas few persons earn more than $100 pesos a week in Tzintzuntzan, and $50 pesos is closer to the average, families in the capital require approximately $300 pesos a week to eke out a minimal urban living standard. In an effort to assess the actual relation between income and expenses for Tzintzuntzan migrants in Mexico City, I asked three families to keep careful budgets for a fifteen-day period in June 1970 (for details, see Kemper, 1971: 131). The families were chosen to represent three distinct, but typical levels of income and living standards. The first, containing a young married couple and their baby daughter, lives in a single-room, dirt-floored shack with exterior toilet and washing facilities located in a rubble-strewn yard. The second, containing seven persons (husband, wife, their three adolescent children, and two nephews), owns their home, which has five rooms, a newly built bathroom, cement-covered patio area, and outdoor washing basin. The third, containing six persons (husband, wife, their two young children, their older, married son, and his bride), lives in a government-subsidized, two-bedroom apartment, with bath, kitchen, and living room, which is located in a large housing project.

Based on detailed budgetary data from these households and on general census information for the rest of the migrant households, I believe that nearly all Tzintzuntzeños in Mexico City spend virtually their entire incomes on basic food, clothing, and housing costs, with the percentages varying somewhat between poorer and more affluent families. The poorest migrants spend about 50 percent on food, 20 percent on housing, and 20 percent on clothing, so that little remains for the purchase of major consumer goods. In contrast, middle-class households, spend only 20-30 percent on food, 15 percent on housing, 20-30 percent on clothing, which leaves a substantial surplus for buying television sets, refrigerators, stoves, cars, and other expensive consumer goods. Thus, the essential difference between the poorest and most affluent Tzintzuntzeños in the city is the frequency with which such "luxuries" can be purchased: steady income permits survival in the city, but only higher income allows migrants to enjoy the amenities of urban living.

The relation between income and consumer behavior can also be examined through analysis of the distribution of major material possessions. In comparison with village households, migrant homes contain far more consumer goods (see Kemper, 1971: 133). For instance, the traditional *petate* is replaced in migrant households by store-bought mattresses, frames, and bedding, ideally with separate beds for each child and a large double bed for the parents. In addition to bedroom furniture, all migrant households contain at least a table, chairs, wardrobe closets, and dish shelves. Stoves (usually propane, less often kerosene—thus reversing their order of importance in Tzintzuntzan), radios, electric irons, and television sets are also found in most homes. Ownership of electric blenders, sewing machines, refrigerators, automobiles, automatic washing machines, and telephones is generally restricted to the more affluent.

Housing Quality and Living Standards

Tzintzuntzan migrants in the capital usually inhabit dwellings with more conveniences than their village counterparts enjoy (for details, see Kemper, 1971: 137). For example, they more frequently have improved bathroom facilities, hard floors, and glass windows than those in the village. However, Tzintzuntzeños dislike the lack of privacy and independence in cramped urban apartments. On the one hand, they recall the relative spaciousness of village compounds; on the other, they admire the luxuriousness of upper-class urban homes, whose grounds are surrounded by high walls topped by broken glass and barbed wire. In Mexico, a preoccupation with privacy pervades city and countryside; unfortunately, to obtain "rural" open space in the city requires much greater wealth than Tzintzuntzan migrants possess, so the only alternative lies in moving to the metropolitan periphery. For poor migrant families, this means a small plot of marginal land; for the affluent, a suburban subdivision where uniform building codes and long-term mortgages maintain appropriate standards.

Despite these qualms over urban living, Tzintzuntzeños in Mexico City possess better-quality housing and more consumer goods than do their rural counterparts. On a 30-point Standard of Living Index, the mean score (17.7) for migrant households was measurably higher than the village average (10.8). Whereas no migrant household has a score below seven, 29.9 percent of the village households are in this range; the 7-12 category includes 15.7 percent of migrant households versus 30.8 percent of the village households; the 13-18 group reverses the ratio (49.1 percent versus 28.3 percent) as does the 19-24 group (13.8 percent versus 8.7 percent). The most striking contrast appears at the top of the scale, however, with 21.6 percent of migrant household between 25-30 versus a mere 2.2 percent for village households. Their economic prosperity vis-à-vis Tzintzuntzan constantly revalidates the migrants' original decision to *buscar la vida* in Mexico City.

Although no Tzintzuntzeños in the capital belong to the urban elite, all but a few very poor households fall well outside the "culture of poverty." In compiling a list of "the possessions of the poor," Lewis examined households in a poor tenement building in the central-city slums. He found that "substantial proportions of the people's possessions had been bought secondhand," that "the tenants' principal possession was furniture, accounting for about a third of all their expenditures on material goods," that "in most households some members (usually the older sons) had to sleep on straw mats or rags on the floor," and concluded that "brevity of possession, and the singular absence of heirlooms passed down from generation to generation, suggest that the life of the very poor is weak in tradition and is oriented almost exclusively to day-to-day concerns" (1969: 115, 116-117, 124).

In contrast, only the poorest Tzintzuntzan migrants purchase any goods secondhand, furniture ceases to be their most important possession as affluence outstrips the available space in apartments and homes, and no one sleeps on *petates*. That the life of the Tzintzuntzan migrant families is weak in tradition is debatable, since few have been in Mexico City more than a generation, and they think of "tradition" as rural ways devalued by the act of emigration.

Thus, to Tzintzuntzan migrants in Mexico City, poverty is a condition to be overcome. They made the first step toward conquering it when they left the village and achieved the second with steady urban employment. The third, perhaps penultimate, step occurs as their children inculcate urban economic behavior, educational standards, and consumer attitudes, and adopt a positive, future-oriented world view. Few Tzintzuntzan migrants are pessimistic; most would agree with the informant who remarked, "What are my dreams? Well, with hard work a person begins to think about his future, in having his own home, in helping his children, and in seeing them achieve a social and economic level that he himself does not now enjoy."

SUMMARY AND CONCLUSIONS

In this paper, I have examined family and household structure, interpersonal relations, and the economic situation among Tzintzuntzan migrants in Mexico City. My analysis is based on the assumption that the effects of urbanization on family life and the acculturation of migrants to the city involve three interrelated factors: the rural background, the urban destination, and the personal attributes of the migrants themselves. To focus first on rural background, Tzintzuntzan is a traditional peasant village undergoing rapid population growth without sufficient economic expansion to satisfy those aware of opportunities in the outside world. As an urban destination, Mexico City offers an expanding economy with a relatively open labor market, but suffers from a tight housing supply and a high cost of living. To turn to the migrants themselves, the Tzintzuntzeños in the capital represent a "positively selected" population interested in raising their living standards, concerned for the education of their children, and intensely motivated to achieve success.

In this context, what happens to Tzintzuntzan migrant families in Mexico City? The nuclear household remains the center of family and household structure, although recent migrants also depend on extended family ties to find housing and jobs. Joint households, particularly those due to post-marital patrilocal residence, have diminished in importance while new forms of "truncated" households have arisen in the urban setting. The pattern of matrifocality widely reported among poor urban migrants in Latin American cities is rare among Tzintzuntzeños.

The quality of interpersonal relationships within migrant families is also affected by urbanization. Husband-wife and parent-child rapport improves as males slough off the "social front" of *machismo,* women reinterpret the role of *la madre abnegada,* and children grow up in an environment stressing independence and achievement. Furthermore, the absence of the husband's mother and his steady economic contributions in nearly all migrant households result in a more equalitarian family life.

Finally, economic success engenders a sense of family cohesiveness. The great majority of migrants have attained living standards superior to those of their village counterparts, while in competition with other urbanites they have achieved stable working-class and professional occupations. None suffers the depths of poverty visible in the slums, nor have any joined the ranks of the wealthy elite. Parents and children alike expect the next generation to make further strides.

Thus, urbanization has wrought changes subtle and profound in the family life of Tzintzuntzeños in Mexico City. So far these changes have been overwhelmingly integrative rather than disorganizing. In fact, a recent study in São Paulo reaches strikingly similar conclusions:

> In giving the migrant a chance to improve his position in life, the industrial city has made it possible for him to experience success. The results of this experience are an increased sense of efficacy, new values, and different perceptions of how the world is organized. When these changes in personal orientation and perspective occur, the family—at first the target of change—becomes its active agent. New patterns of family interaction develop, characterized by more equality, increased openness and responsiveness, and a greater concern for achievement [Rosen, 1973: 211].

I believe that research among similar populations will yield further support for this interpretation of the effects of urbanization on migrant family and household organization. At a time when Latin American urbanization proceeds at a dizzying pace, the positive role played by the migrant family certainly demands our attention. Indeed, in its role as "an institution prevailing over rapid change" (Carlos and Seller, 1972: 114), the migrant family serves as a flexible vehicle for social and economic progress.

NOTES

1. Fieldwork in Mexico City and subsequent analysis of census and ethnographic materials was supported by NIGMS Grant GM-1224. I have received constant encouragement and many perceptive suggestions from George M. Foster, whose diligent research and good name among the people of Tzintzuntzan made my own work possible. Since the methodology and techniques employed in the fieldwork have been described in detail elsewhere (Kemper, 1974), I will only mention here that I used the standard array of anthropological data gathering procedures: participant observation, censuses, household budgets, interviews, questionnaires, projective tests (Thematic Apperception Test), and life histories.

2. There are several ways of looking at migrant selectivity: one is to analyze the differences between migrant and native-born populations within a specific urban community; a second is to compare and contrast the characteristics of migrants from the same community of origin who have traveled to different urban destinations; a third is to evaluate differences between migrants from different places of origin within a specific urban community; and the fourth is to compare migrants and nonmigrants in the community of origin. Here I concentrate on migrant versus nonmigrant differences in Tzintzuntzan with analysis carried out at the household level. Thus, I inquire into the backgrounds of the migrants rather than into the particular characteristics of individual migrants. For a similar approach see Conning (1966/67).

A brief explanation of the procedure used in establishing the migrant and nonmigrant household samples is necessary. The 246 Tzintzuntzan migrants to Mexico City came from a total of 114 households. I have used the 91 for which comparative data were available as the migrant sample. Nineteen of these are from the pre-1960 period. The corresponding nonmigrant sample consists of 300 households, also divided into pre- and post-1960 periods.

3. This dependence on friends and relatives in rural-urban migration has been widely reported throughout Latin America (e.g., Browning and Feindt, 1971; Butterworth, 1962; Germani, 1961; Peattie, 1968; Roberts, 1970; Whitten, 1965).

4. In distinguishing between family and household, I follow Bender (1967: 495), who notes that family and household are logically distinct because the referent of the former is kinship, that of the latter, residence. Furthermore, he points out that the concept of household embodies two complementary, but separate, variables: co-residence and domestic functions. On the basis of these distinctions, four theoretical types are possible: Independent Nuclear Households; Joint Domestic Groups; Joint Residence Groups; and Joint Households. Thus, a nuclear household refers to a married couple (with or without children), while a joint household contains two or more married couples (with or without children) sharing co-residence and domestic functions. A "truncated" household is defined here as a residence group in which no married couple is present.

5. Only 23 females (in 21 households) were working during 1969-1970. Of these, 12 were young single women, 8 were married, and the rest were widowed or separated. Ten were maids, 4 ran small stands, 2 did washing and ironing, and the others included a seamstress, a clerk, a secretary, a public baths inspector, a doughnut maker, and a school

teacher. Significantly, only the maids and the teacher provided their household's major source of income; the rest simply supplemented wages earned by spouses, fathers, or other males.

6. Murray's Thematic Apperception Test (TAT) was administered to 15 adult migrants (10 males and 5 females). Each subject was shown a set of standardized pictures (14 for females and 15 for males) and was asked to tell a story about each. Behind this test lies the assumption that the subject projects himself into the action and that his stories reveal his world view. In giving the TAT to Tzintzuntzan migrants, I was primarily interested in the manifest cultural content of their stories rather than in analyzing their individual personalities. The TAT has seldom been used to study rural-urban migrants, but it can be a very useful tool to supplement other ethnographic procedures (see DeRidder, 1960; García Pacheco, 1963; Mangin, 1970).

7. Nelson (1971: 71) describes the differences between *El Macho* and *la madre abnegada* in these words: "The mother is open, receptive, passive, submissive; El Macho is impenetrable, closed within himself, capable of guarding himself and what is his, defensive, dominating, unpredictable, and arbitrary."

8. Sexual profligacy, often considered a fundamental characteristic of *macho* behavior (Lewis, 1951: 328, 1959: 17) is not common in Tzintzuntzan nor among the Tzintzuntzeños in Mexico City. In particular, the *Casa Chica* syndrome—i.e., keeping a separate house for women with whom one has an extra-marital affair, is considered repugnant among villagers and migrants.

9. Corwin (1963: 37), among others, has remarked on a "cult of motherhood" in contemporary Mexico: "Nothing better illustrates the Motherhood Cult than Mother's Day itself, which like Christmas, has become a great commercial institution both in the United States and Mexico. But in Mexico the commercial facts are not so impressive as the overwhelming emotional fervor released on *el día de la madre*. The entire society seems to lift its eyes beyond the sad, proletarian image of helpless maternity to the idealized and undefiled, unselfish and disinterested."

10. At the time of fieldwork, the conversion rate was $1.00 U.S. to $12.50 Mexican pesos.

11. The 30-point Standard of Living Index combines household improvements and possession of major consumer goods. It consists of the following items (each of which is given with its weight in the index):

Household Improvements—raised hearth (2); patio water tap (2); latrine (2); electricity (2); whitewashed exterior (1); glass window (1); shower bath (2); flush toilet (1).

Major Consumer Goods—raised bed (2); radio (1); electric iron (1); sewing machine (1); store-bought mattress (1); stove [propane (2), kerosene (1)]; television set (2); electric blender (1); automobile/truck (2); automatic washing machine (1).

The index was the same for both village and migrant populations, except that "raised hearth (2)" (an item absent in the city) was replaced by "refrigerator (1)" and "telephone (1)."

REFERENCES

BENDER, D. R. (1967) "A refinement of the concept of household: families, co-residence, and domestic functions." American Anthropologist 69, 5: 493-504.

BROWNING, H. L. and W. FEINDT (1969) "Selectivity of migrants to a metropolis in a developing country: a Mexican case study." Demography 6, 4: 347-357.

——— (1971) "The social and economic context of migration to Monterrey, Mexico," pp. 45-70 in F. F. Rabinovitz and F. M. Trueblood (eds.) Latin American Urban Research, Volume I. Beverly Hills: Sage.

BUTTERWORTH, D. S. (1962) "A study of the urbanization process among Mixtec migrants from Tilantongo in Mexico City." América Indigena 22, 3: 257-274 (México, D.F.)

CARLOS, M. L. and L. SELLERS (1972) "Family, kinship structure, and modernization in Latin America." Latin American Research Review 7, 2: 95-124.

CONNING, A. M. (1966/67) "Variables comunitarias y familiares en el estudio de la migración rural-urbana desde la zona central rural de Chile. Notas sobre un estudio en marcha." Antropología, Revista del Centro de Estudios Antropológicos 4: 21-34. (Santiago de Chile)

CORWIN, A. F. (1963) Contemporary Mexican Attitudes toward Population, Poverty, and Public Opinion. Gainesville: University of Florida Press.

DeRIDDER, J. C. (1960) The Personality of the Urban African in South Africa. London: Routledge & Kegan Paul.

DOUGHTY, P. L. (1970) "Behind the back of the city: 'provincial' life in Lima, Peru," pp. 30-46 in W. Mangin (ed.) Peasants in Cities: Readings in the Anthropology of Urbanization. Boston: Houghton Mifflin.

ESTEVA FABREGAT, C. (1969) "Familia y matrimonio en México: el patrón cultural." Revista de Indias 115-118 (enero-diciembre): 173-278. (Madrid)

FOSTER, G. M. (1967) Tzintzuntzan: Mexican Peasants in a Changing World. Boston: Little, Brown.

——— assisted by G. OSPINA (1948) Empire's Children: The People of Tzintzuntzan. México, D.F.: Smithsonian Institution, Institute of Social Anthropology, Publication 6.

GARCIA PACHECO, C. (1963) "Rasgos culturales de un grupo de mestizos serranos a traves del TAT," pp. 283-289 in B. Caravedo, H. Rotondo, y J. Mariátegui (eds.) Estudios de Psiquiatría Social en el Perú. Lima: Ediciones del Sol.

GERMANI, G. (1961) "Inquiry into the social effects of urbanization in a working-class sector of Greater Buenos Aires," pp. 159-178 in P. Hauser (ed.) Urbanization in Latin America. New York: International Documents Service.

GONZALEZ, N. (1965) "The consanguineal household and matrifocality." American Anthropologist 67, 6: 1541-1549.

——— (1969) Black Carib Household Structure: A Study of Migration and Modernization. Seattle and London: University of Washington Press.

HAMMEL, E. A. (1961) "The family cycle in a coastal Peruvian slum and village." American Anthropologist 63, 5: 989-1005.

——— (1964) "Some characteristics of rural village and urban slum populations on the coast of Peru." Southwestern Journal of Anthropology 20, 4: 346-358.

KEMPER, R. V. (1971) "Migration and adaptation of Tzintzuntzan migrants in Mexico City." Ph.D. dissertation. University of California.

——— (1973a) "Contemporary Mexican urbanization: a view from Tzintzuntzan." Proceedings of the Fortieth Congresso Internazionale degli Americanisti. (Rome)

——— (1973b) "Factores sociales en la migración: el caso de los Tzintzuntzeños en la Ciudad de México." América Indígena 33 (October-December): 1095-1118.

——— (1974) "Tzintzuntzeños in Mexico City: the anthropologist among peasant migrants," pp. 63-91 in G. M. Foster and R. V. Kemper (eds.) Anthropologists in Cities. Boston: Little, Brown.

LEEDS, A. (1971) "The concept of the 'culture of poverty': conceptual, logical, and empirical problems with perspectives from Brazil and Peru," pp. 226-284 in E. B. Leacock (ed.) The Culture of Poverty: A Critique. New York: Simon & Schuster.

——— and E. LEEDS (1970) "Brazil and the myth of urban rurality: urban experience, work, and values in 'squatments' of Rio de Janeiro and Lima," pp. 229-285 in A. J. Field (ed.) City and Country in the Third World: Issues in the Modernization of Latin America. Cambridge: Schenkman.

LEGERMAN, C. (1969) "Haitian peasant, plantation and urban lower class family and kinship organization: observations and comments," pp. 71-84 in R. P. Schaedel (ed.) Research and Resources of Haiti. New York: Research Institute for the Study of Man.

LEÑERO OTERO, L. (1968) Investigación de la familia en México. México, D.F.: Instituto Mexicano de Estudios Sociales, A. C.

LEWIS, O. (1951) Life in a Mexican Village: Tepoztlán Restudied. Urbana: University of Illinois Press.

——— (1952) "Urbanization without breakdown: a case study." Scientific Monthly 75: 31-41.

——— (1959) Five Families. New York: Basic Books.

——— (1965) "Further observations on the folk-urban continuum and urbanization with special reference to Mexico City," pp. 491-503 in P. M. Hauser and L. Schnore (eds.) The Study of Urbanization. New York: John Wiley.

——— (1966) "The culture of poverty." Scientific American 215, 4: 19-25.

——— (1969) "Possessions of the poor." Scientific American 221, 4: 114-124.

LOMNITZ, L. (1973) "Supervivencia en una barriada en la Ciudad de México." Demografía y Economía 7, 1: 58-85. (México, D.F.)

MANGIN, W. (1965) "Similarities and differences between two types of Peruvian communities." Sociologus 16, 1: 53-65. (Berlin)

——— (1970) "Tales from the barriadas," pp. 55-61 in W. Mangin (ed.) Peasants in Cities: Readings in the Anthropology of Urbanization. Boston: Houghton Mifflin.

NELSON, C. (1971) The Waiting Village: Social Change in Rural Mexico. Boston: Little, Brown.

NUTINI, H. G. (1967) "A synoptic comparison of Mesoamerican marriage and family structure." Southwestern Journal of Anthropology 23, 4: 383-404.

——— and T. D. MURPHY (1970) "Labor migration and family structure in the Tlaxcala-Pueblan area, Mexico," pp. 80-103 in W. Goldschmidt and H. Hoijer (eds.) The Social Anthropology of Latin America: Essays in honor of Ralph Leon Beals. Los Angeles: Latin American Center, University of California.

PATCH, R. (1961) "Life in a callejón: a study of urban disorganization." American Universities Field Staff, West Coast South America Series 8, 6.

PEATTIE, L. R. (1968) The View from the Barrio. Ann Arbor: University of Michigan Press.

——— (1971) "The structural parameters of emerging life styles in Venezuela," pp. 285-298 in E. B. Leacock (ed.) The Culture of Poverty: A Critique. New York: Simon & Schuster.

REDFIELD, R. (1941) The Folk Culture of Yucatan. Chicago: University of Chicago Press.

ROBERTS, B. (1970) "The social organization of low-income families," pp. 345-382 in I. L. Horowitz (ed.) Masses in Latin America. New York: Oxford University Press.

ROSEN, B. (1973) "Social change, migration and family interaction in Brazil." American Sociological Review 38 (April): 198-212.

SAFA, H. I. (1964) "From shanty town to public housing: a comparison of family structure in two urban neighborhoods in Puerto Rico." Caribbean Studies 4, 1: 3-12. (Rio Piedras, Puerto Rico)

SCHULZ, D. A. (1968) "Variations in the father role in complete families of the Negro lower class." Social Science Quarterly 49, 3: 651-659.

SWARTZBAUGH, R. G. (1970) "Machismo: a value system of a Mexican peasant class." Ph.D. dissertation. Ohio State University. (University Microfilms 70-14, 104)

UNIKEL, L. (1968) "Ensayo sobre una nueva clasificación de población rural y urbana en México." Demografía y Economía 2, 1: 1-18. (México, D.F.)

WHITTEN, N. E., Jr. (1965) Class, Kinship, and Power in an Ecuadorian Town. Stanford: Stanford University Press.

JACK R. ROLLWAGEN is Chairman of the Department of Anthropology at the State University of New York College at Brockport. He received his Ph.D. from the University of Oregon, and has done field work in Mexico. His current research includes a study of urbanization in Mexico, a study of Puerto Ricans in Rochester, New York, and theoretical work on the concept of urbanization and models used in describing urbanization. He is the founder and editor of the journal *Urban Anthropology* and has published several articles on urban growth in Mexico, including "Region of Origin and Rural-Urban Migration in Mexico" (*International Migration Review,* Fall 1971); "A Comparative Framework for the Investigation of the City-As-Context" (*Urban Anthropology,* Spring 1972); and "Tuxtepec, Oaxaca: An Example of Rapid Urban Growth in Mexico" (*Urban Anthropology,* Spring 1973).

Chapter 2

MEDIATION AND RURAL-URBAN MIGRATION IN MEXICO: A PROPOSAL AND A CASE STUDY

JACK R. ROLLWAGEN

Sufficient case study material has been presented on rural-urban migration in Latin America so that the social scientist must now begin to construct generalizations and to inquire into the conditions under which certain phenomenon are found or not found. In order to do this, however, it is necessary to formulate constructs of the rural-urban migration process that will allow us to work with more than one case study at a time. I propose that one of these constructs that will allow us to visualize rural-urban migration more clearly and to treat it as a generalizable process is the concept of "mediation." In this article, I will propose a revised definition of mediation and demonstrate that this concept can aid the social scientist to understand the processes of rural-urban migration more clearly.

THE CONCEPT OF MEDIATION

The development of a focus upon anthropological problems at the national level in the last ten to fifteen years has created many new areas of research for the cultural anthropologist. One important area is that suggested by Wolf in his article "Aspects of Group Relations in a Complex Society: Mexico" (1956). In this article, Wolf directs the attention of the anthropologist to a web of

Author's Note: This is a revised version of a paper that was read at the Northeastern Anthropological Association convention at Albany, New York, in April of 1971. The data for this article were collected during the period of September 1964 to June 1965, and during shorter visits since that time. I would like to thank Sherwood Lingenfelter and Robert V. Kemper for their comments on an earlier draft of this paper.

relationships that exists between community and nation. Building upon data extracted from the post-conquest history of Mexico, he depicts a constantly changing relationship between government, rural village, large landowner, and other elements in the nation of Mexico in general. His article illustrates that, as the basis of the economy shifts or as new political forces come into being, new relationships are created between the parts. One aspect of this process is the function performed by "brokers" who "mediate" between "community-oriented groups in communities and nation-oriented groups which operate primarily through national institutions" (1956: 1075), a function that results in the integration of these units into the larger system. Thus, as new relationships are created, new brokers arise to perform mediating functions between community and nation.[1]

Wolf's use of the term "broker" in this context pointed to a new focus for those interested in community-nation research. This new focus would be on those specific individuals or groups who mediate between community and nation. However, it is important to note that Wolf's definition is not as broad as it might first appear to be. Wolf very clearly states that he sees brokers mediating between a group from a community on the one hand and a group representing national-level institutions on the other hand. The specification that there is a definable "group" at the community level causes very little trouble to anthropologists because the communities they traditionally study are small and groups are isolable. However, when anthropologists turn their attention to the impact of the nation on the community that they are studying, they are more likely to talk about "forces" rather than specific groups. Secondly, Wolf's stricture that these national-level groups operate "primarily through national institutions" (1956: 1075) restricts the kinds of contacts by the community with the nation to those national-level groups which have a formal structure. The restriction of that which is conceived of as "the nation" to groups with formal structure may be too restrictive if one wishes to understand how community relates to nation.[2]

Silverman (1965), grappling with the same problems of community-nation relationships, suggests that Wolf's "broker" is one example of a larger class of phenomenon which he refers to as "intermediaries." He thus sees Wolf's concept as a particular configuration, a subset of the total possible kinds of relationships between nation and community, one restricted by the requirements of identifiable groups at the national level and the specification that the national group be (in most cases) representative of institutions.

Silverman then suggests a different subset of the total set of "intermediaries." This subset he calls "mediators." Mediators are defined by two formal criteria and are characterized by at least two attributes. The two formal criteria are: (1) the critical functions that they perform; and (2) the exclusivity of their roles with regard to the community that they serve. The two attributes are: (1) that mediators are usually the receivers of action initiated at the national level, a factor that we may refer to as the "direction" of mediation; and (2) there is usually a rank difference between the mediator and those "in the local system who are involved in the mediated interaction" (1965: 173), hereafter called the "mediated." In this case, as with Wolf's definition, there seems to be a restriction of an important concept by a stricture that may be disadvantageous to further investigation, that is, that the direction of the mediation be thought of as originating at the national level and then involving the community level.

In summary, the elements basic to both Wolf's and Silverman's concepts are:

(1) a specific community;

(2) a set of individuals (smaller than the total universe of individuals in the community but from that community) who:

    (a) perform critical functions for the rest of the community;

    (b) are defined apart from other elements of the community by the nature of the functions that they perform and by the fact that only they perform these functions; and

    (c) perform special functions that relate to important aspects of or forces in the nation of which the community is a part.

Wolf's use of the term "broker" permits the concept to be used for brokerage in many contexts: economic, social, and cultural as well as political. Silverman's use of the term "cultural mediation" seems to restrict the usage only to those instances of mediation in the cultural sphere. In this paper I have dropped the term "cultural" and simply refer to "mediation." This usage implies that mediation can be in any of the several spheres that Wolf's term "brokerage" covers. However, because Silverman has defined the "broker" role more precisely than Wolf, I will adopt Silverman's usage. I will term any case that conforms to the above elements a case of "mediation," the individuals who act in these critical and exclusive roles "mediators," and the function they perform the "mediating function."

The mediating function stated in this way still has the same problems of interpretation of words that is characteristic of the other definitions (for example, the interpretation of the concept of "critical" and the evaluation of the "importance" of a function). But it has the advantage of not restricting the direction of the mediation, the nature of that which is mediated to the specific community, nor of restricting that which is seen as "the nation." A definition of this sort is valuable in just those cases in which the impetus for the mediation arises in the community itself. This paper will present an example of cultural and economic mediation that conforms to the elements basic to both Wolf's and Silverman's concepts but which departs from their formulations in those areas which I have referred to as "strictures" above (i.e., the direction of the mediation and that which is conceived of as "the nation"). I view this example as a case of cultural and economic mediation. Also, I believe that the presentation of this case expands the scope of mediation without reducing the effectiveness of the concept. Furthermore, the presentation of this case of mediation in the context of rural-urban migration allows social scientists to expand their view of the processes involved in rural-urban migration. The case study will focus upon:

(1) a set of entrepreneurs who function as mediators; and

(2) a directional mediation in which the rural community and its relationships with "the nation" is examined. (In this usage, "the nation" is seen neither as institution nor as initiator but rather as a number of specified populations in the national economy who are potential consumers of a product. That which represents the "nation" in this example is the populations of nearly all the cities in Mexico above 20,000 inhabitants [and some cities below 20,000 inhabitants], since these populations are the ones which serve as the "national" market to the entrepreneurs in the case study.)

The emphasis in this case study will be on an act of mediation arising in the rural community and not, as in the general case, arising at the national level. Too often rural-urban migration is conceived in terms of "national forces" operating directly upon undifferentiated "rural populations" without any discussion of how this occurs. The idea that national involvement is a process which, at some point in some cases, is "mediated" by one set of individuals to another provides new insights into the changing relationships between rural communities and the nation in the context of rapid urbanization.

THE RISE OF THE ENTREPRENEURS AS MEDIATORS IN MEXTICACAN[3]

The rural community that is the focus of this case of cultural mediation is a village named Mexticacan, a village in the state of Jalisco, Mexico. It has a population of approximately 3,000 individuals and is thus not atypical in size of a class of county seats in counties throughout Mexico. Although Mexticacan, the county seat, is the focus of the attention, the *municipio* (county) of Mexticacan (population approximately 7,000) is the larger unit which, for some purposes, must be discussed.

Until the 1930s when the first bus and truck routes were established that connected Mexticacan with the road from Aguascalientes to Guadalajara, the economy of the municipio of Mexticacan was based primarily upon agriculture and cottage industry, the products of which were used or sold in the local area. Labor migration to the United States played a significant role in the economy of Mexticacan, as it did for many villages in Western Mexico (cf. Taylor, 1933: 1-2). At approximately the same time that the road opened linking Mexticacan to the rest of the Republic, Mexticaqueños began to market the products of their cottage industries over wider local areas and also began to involve themselves in a number of nonagricultural enterprises that depended upon a larger-than-local group of customers. The tailoring of work clothes, the making of matches, and the manufacture of candy are examples of these types of businesses. The businesses all arose in an effort by several Mexticaqueños to use the town of Mexticacan as a center for the manufacture of items that were to be sold over a wide geographical area by means of the newly constructed roads. The roads were used also for the transport of local products (such as milk and agricultural goods) to nearby collection points or to urban centers where they were to be retailed. Finally, the roads became a means of access for the sale of services as well as goods by the Mexticaqueños. All the above endeavors shared the common feature that Mexticacan was the site of the business, the central point from which goods were exported, or the home to which Mexticaqueños returned after spending varying lengths of time away from Mexticacan. Mexticacan, in short, was very central to the lives of the Mexticaqueños at this time even though they depended upon people in other towns and cities to purchase their products and services.

As a result of previous economic conditions related to the agricultural situation in Mexticacan, and as a result of this involvement in new nonagricultural enterprises, wealth differences between the Mexticaqueños began to grow. This caused greater social differentiation in Mexticacan. The older division in the municipio between the relatively wealthy, relatively large landowners and the poor, small landowners or landless took on a new dimension. Those who were the most successful entrepreneurs tended to be those who were wealthy when the opportunity arose to enter business. Not all of the landed engaged in business, nor did all those who engaged in business necessarily have large amounts of land. Nevertheless there appears to have been a strong relationship between landowning and involvement in entrepreneurship.

Because of the involvement in business and because of the economic returns from these new businesses, the structure of the town began to depart from the traditional structure of Mexican mestizo villages of the early twentieth century. (I am generalizing here from my own knowledge of Mexico, from the ethnographies of Mexico, and from such theoretical discussions of Latin American village structures as Wagley and Harris [1955] and Kunkel [1961].) The social structure of the village began to change from the characteristic form of a dual division of peasant and town type (cf. Wagley and Harris, 1955: 438, in which the town types are largely local shopkeepers) to a structure in which a third function, regional entrepreneurship, was present also.[4] The role of the entrepreneur, however, was nearly monopolized by the same people who were both the large landowners, and the local shopkeepers or cottage industrialists. The wealth division between the "have-not" peasants and the increasingly "have" town types was intensified by this additional income from a more diversified economic base. These diversified business activities allowed the entrepreneurs to accumulate capital in the form of land, equipment, goods, and money, and also to form economic relationships with business interests in the nonlocal area. By the mid-1940s, there was a large economic hiatus between the abilities of each group to engage in any economic activity that arose or might arise. Although this differential was related historically to land ownership, by this time it was directly related to previous nonagricultural involvements as sources of capital and as experience.

In 1946, one Mexticaqueño opened up a small factory for the production of popsicles and ice cream products in Aguascalientes, one of the two large cities relatively near to Mexticacan. At this time, the *paleta* (popsicle and ice cream) business in Mexico was in the hands of two categories of merchants: the merchants in various cities in Mexico who owned small businesses with largely inefficient equipment for large-scale production, and the two or three entrepreneurs located in the very large urban centers who owned large and efficient businesses but who generally only sold their products in the cities in which their factory was located. Not too long after establishment of the initial *paleta* business by the Mexticaqueño mentioned above, the owner of that business began to investigate the possibilities of making his business more efficient by increasing the volume of his output. He bought some new equipment that was just becoming available in Mexico at that time and, as a consequence of the use of this new machinery and the adoption of a work schedule that maximized the capabilities of this new equipment, began to reap sizable profits. Other Mexticaqueños followed this example in other cities in Mexico and within ten years, Mexticaqueños had established *paleterías* (factories for the production of popsicles and ice cream products) throughout Mexico and had monopolized perhaps seventy to eighty percent of the market in Mexico. Their percentage of the total market in Mexico City and in Guadalajara was not so great since they were in competition with the large-scale producers mentioned above. (In these two cities, the large manufacturers concentrated on ice cream and higher priced popsicle products. As a result, the lower priced market was still largely in the hands of the smaller producers like the Mexticaqueños.) Although the per item price of the products that the Mexticaqueños sold was low, their new machinery and their approach to production allowed them to accumulate enormous wealth in cash and equipment because they were able to sell in volume.

This national economic involvement for the *paleteros* (those who manufacture popsicles and ice cream products) from Mexticacan had a social impact on the village of Mexticacan. This social impact was related to two major aspects of the involvement of the paleteros: (1) only certain Mexticaqueños had become entrepreneurs in the process, those who had funds (or access to funds) and the desire to do so; and (2) throughout the early part of this process the entrepreneurs had remained largely based in the village of Mexticacan and had maintained close ties to fellow Mexticaqueños even though their businesses were located in urban centers throughout Mexico. These practices had repercussions for the manner of the involvement of the Mexticaqueños as businessman and as migrant and for the village of Mexticacan.

When the paleteros began to open their initial businesses, they were faced with two problems: (1) the staffing of their production centers, and (2) the staffing of their distribution apparatus. They chose two different solutions. For the staffing of their production centers, they chose people from their village and from the municipio of Mexticacan. For the distribution of the *paletas* (which are taken by vendors into the area around the factory and sold from insulated pushcarts) they chose residents of the city in which the factory was located. Their reasoning was that fellow Mexticaqueños could be trusted on the premises and also could be trusted to give a full measure of work for their hourly wages. In contrast, distributors did not work for an hourly wage but received a percentage of their daily sales. Nor were the distributors allowed access to the cash register or to the goods in the factory in general.

The results of these choices were (1) that the *paleteros* began to recruit more and more fellow villagers as workers to meet the staffing needs of the growing number of paleterías that were established in locations throughout Mexico, and (2) that those Mexticaqueños who left Mexticacan to work in these paleterías formed a peculiar relationship to the city in which they worked. These workers were limited in the amount of actual contact that they had with the city in which they worked because of the long working hours that they followed. Also, they were not involved in sales functions in any other location than the one in which the paletas were produced. In most instances, these workers ate and slept in the paletería as well. These practices limited still further the contact of the workers with the urban areas in which the paletería was located. The foregoing situation describes most accurately the arrangement during the first years of the operation of the paleterías from Mexticacan.

In terms of other social aspects of the involvement in the paleta business, it was normally only individual men that worked away from Mexticacan at first, both as owner and as worker. Later, the owners (who were already in residence elsewhere than Mexticacan) began to move their families to the city in which their business was located (or to the city in which their chief business was located if they had branch offices). As this happened, the owners' ties with the village began to diminish in number and to weaken in strength. Although they still considered themselves Mexticaqueños, they spent less of their time in Mexticacan itself and the nature of the relationship to fellow Mexticaqueños changed appreciably.

By 1965, perhaps as many as 200 Mexticaqueños (or approximately one-fifth of the total male adult population of the village) had established paleterías in urban locations in Mexico. Although not all paleterías had been successful, and although not all those Mexticaqueños who began a paleta business continued to operate that business, a majority of the paleteros from Mexticacan were still in the paleta business. Some Mexticaqueños owned only one paletería. Others owned several. One or two of the most successful entrepreneurs owned thirty or more paleterías. Economic returns were as widely varied as the number of paleterías owned. Nearly all the paleteros, however, were in a much better economic position in 1965 than at any time earlier in their lives, judging by their own statements. Several of the paleteros were wealthy by any standards. The majority of these paleteros continued to live away from Mexticacan although nearly all of them continued to own houses there for rental purposes, as family houses, as vacation houses, and as insurance in case of business loss. Land held was kept in cultivation as an additional source of income.

THE REPERCUSSIONS OF URBAN INVOLVEMENT FOR THE MEXTICAQUEÑOS

The remainder of this paper will be devoted to an examination of the role of the paleteros as mediators to their fellows from the village and municipio of Mexticacan. I am applying Silverman's term "mediation" to the role that the paleteros played in their relationship to the workers that they hired from Mexticacan because: (1) it was a critical role (in terms of the economic choices and repercussions for the workers from Mexticacan) and (2) it was an exclusive one as well (in that for all practical purposes the majority of the workers who left Mexticacan to work in Mexico at this time became workers in paleterías and to do so they had to go through one of the paleteros). I wish to focus attention on that aspect of change through time related to the role of the paleteros as mediators.

As I have indicated above, in the 1920s the amount of differentiation between the peasant and the town types in Mexticacan was probably not great. With the beginning of the involvement of the town types of Mexticacan in the economic activities described above, however, the verticality of the relationship that existed between the peasant and the town types grew and the social and economic markers that distinguished the two groups grew more pronounced. By the mid-1950s in Mexticacan there was a definite group of employers and a group of people who could be employed. Mexticaqueños who began as workers could still become owners of paleterías. In doing so, however, they normally did not become employers. They simply became owners of small, family-run businesses. The majority of the Mexticaqueños who worked outside of Mexticacan worked in paleterías. Workers who wanted to get jobs in paleterías throughout Mexico had to contact a small and definite set of employers (never numbering more than three percent of the population of the municipio of Mexticacan and probably numbering closer to two percent). This set was the paleteros who hired workers in contrast to those paleteros whose businesses were small enough to be operated by members of the immediate family. Workers could choose either of two means of obtaining these jobs: (1) the most frequent means was to seek employment by contacting a paletero in the village of Mexticacan itself, a paletero who had returned to Mexticacan for one reason or another (or for the paletero to initiate contact when he needed workers) or (much less frequently) (2) by travelling to a paletería to look for a job. Employment outside Mexticacan during this time was limited by the belief of the workers that jobs outside Mexticacan were primarily jobs in paleterías and that employment in these jobs was normally to be contracted in Mexticacan. It is in this context that the paleteros became mediators of jobs.

Although the paleteros at first only hired fellow Mexticaqueños for workers in their production centers, before long many paleteros began to move toward the policy of hiring non-Mexticaqueños in these production centers.[5] One reason for this practice was that by doing so they were able to change the relationship between themselves and their workers from a many-stranded and relatively horizontal relationship to a single-stranded and vertical relationship (which was more suited to economical business practices).[6] Perhaps equally as important was the fact that by the 1960s, the paleteros were running out of fellow Mexticaqueños who knew how to read and count well enough to be worthwhile as an employee in a paletería.

By the mid-1960s then, the situation in Mexticacan was as follows: the majority of the paleteros were living outside Mexticacan. Although they still maintained houses in Mexticacan and still retained an interest in the affairs of the town, they returned to Mexticacan with much less frequency than in years past. Their families, for the most part, had moved to the location of the paletero's business or of his major business if he had more than one. Many of the Mexticaqueños who were not owners of paleterías were away working in them. Given the process of the hiring of non-Mexticaqueños described above, it is evident that, as time passes, many of the workers would return to Mexticacan.

For the group of paleteros, this process may be described as a cycle of mediation. They began in the 1930s as relatively poor town types with few or no contacts with the greater Mexican economic, social, or political world outside of Mexticacan. By the 1960s, many of them were successful businessmen with many contacts in the national economic, social, and political world outside Mexticacan. During the period 1945 to 1965, they had served the critical and (nearly) exclusive function of mediator between those Mexticaqueños who wanted jobs outside of Mexticacan and in the national-level economy. More and more, however, they began to divest themselves of the mediator role and to consider it onerous, not especially profitable, and inconvenient. They had decided to exchange workers from Mexticacan (whom they trusted and over whom they had more control because of village ties) for workers from the city in which their factory was located (and to whom they owed nothing but wages for work performed). They began to participate more and more as national-level businessmen assimilated to urban life and less and less as villagers whose social and economic ties necessitated contact with fellow villagers. The workers, on their side, had passed through this period first as fellow villager *qua* employee, but later they had become more employee than fellow villager. Their proportion in the total work force in the paleterías owned by Mexticaqueños began to decline. Even though there were many Mexticaqueños as workers away from Mexticacan, they no longer worked for fellow Mexticaqueños in the same personal relationship. They had become employees in an urban business who were treated equally in most respects to workers hired from the local area. With this personal tie broken, the workers often returned to Mexticacan.[7] The patron-client, mediator-mediated relationship (especially as a mechanism for urban employment) was nearly gone. The cycle (defined by the mediator-mediated relationship between fellow Mexticaqueños) was coming to an end. To a great extent, Mexticacan in 1966 contained only non-paleteros and ex-workers. Although there are now more contacts in general between Mexticacan and the outside world, no new mediators that fulfill the economic function performed by the paleteros in the past have arisen recently to perform this (or any other similar) mediation function. New mediators and new functions that are mediated have entered the village of Mexticacan in the form of the various governmental officials who have come to perform services in the municipio.

DISCUSSION

The paleteros of Mexticacan acquired capital and business experience in their earlier involvements in regional entrepreneurship. When the opportunity arose to enter the paleta business, some of the paleteros had cash which they used to enter the business. Others had capital in the form of real property, cattle, or other forms that made it more difficult for them to acquire the cash necessary for the entry with the speed that their comerades did. Bank credit for entry as a paletero did not figure as a means of entry into the paleta business. Credit from equipment manufacturers was not available during the earlier years of the paleta industry. The only other source of funds was borrowing from friends or relatives. In the later stages of the paleta industry in Mexticacan, some of the paleteros who had become extremely wealthy entered into certain contractual relationships with other Mexticaqueños who wished to become paleteros. This relationship involved only two or three paleteros as patrons and perhaps ten to fifteen Mexticaqueños as clients who eventually became paleteros in their own self-owned business. Thus the entry of the Mexticaqueños into the paleta industry can be conceived of as a two-phase process: (1) the early entry of those who had money either as cash or in some form of capital that was convertible into cash with little difficulty; and (2) the later entry of an additional group as paleteros who raised money to begin business (a) by borrowing from friends or relatives, (b) by a contractual relationship with an already established paletero from Mexticacan who loaned them money to start their own business, or (c) by purchasing equipment on contract through an equipment manufacturer. Those Mexticaqueños who entered the paleta industry only as workers entered throughout the entire time period, of course.

In many of the cities in which paleteros opened businesses, the volume of their business was such that it necessitated more workers than the family of the paletero contained. It was in these cases that fellow Mexticaqueños were hired. If the original location proved profitable, branch offices were opened in the same city or in other cities. The workers who were hired from Mexticacan for these jobs were taking jobs that would not be there except for the entry into business by their fellow villagers. Furthermore, the chances were very small that those who actually did become workers in the paleterías would have become workers in any paleterías (or any other urban jobs) had it not been for the efforts of the paleteros from Mexticacan. Thus, it is a case where the entrepreneurship of the paleteros, because it was successful, enabled them to create jobs for fellow Mexticaqueños. In the context that I have provided above, this is a case of cultural and economic mediation, one in which a subset (the paleteros) of the "community" (municipio) of Mexticacan created a specific critical relationship (the provision of jobs) for another subset of individuals (the workers) from the same "community" in the context of one aspect of the nation (the populations of between 100 to 200 of the major cities in Mexico).

The control of the paleteros over access to jobs in the urban market by fellow Mexticaqueños was not exclusive. Individuals from Mexticacan had left Mexticacan before the rise of the paleteros and left after the first paletería from Mexticacan was opened. However, during the period 1945 to 1965, the number of Mexticaqueños who left to obtain employment in any position other than in paleterías owned by fellow Mexticaqueños was very small. This gave the paleteros virtually exclusive control over the access of fellow Mexticaqueños to urban jobs. Virtually exclusive control over this critical function gave them great power in the community, the power to select fellow Mexticaqueños for monetary rewards much greater than the average worker would receive by working in the municipio of Mexticacan. The income that the paleteros received from their paleterías also gave them additional power in Mexticacan because they could hire fellow Mexticaqueños to do work in the municipio of Mexticacan in agriculture or other rural activities. Money was spent by the paleteros in improving their agricultural incomes. The total of their earnings from urban paleterías and municipio agriculture and other sources elevated them to a financial power and social status unmatched by any other group in the municipio of Mexticacan.

The workers profited from their involvement as well. Since their room and board was covered in most cases by their employment agreement, all wages were net wages. The yearly income was much higher than they would have earned in

Mexticacan. In the majority of cases, however, this income was not invested in any form that created significant additional capital and thus the workers gained only that amount that they earned as wages while working for the paleteros.

ANALYSIS

The mediation that is described in this example is the mediation of employment primarily. Employment not available to the specific community at large without the efforts of the paleteros was made available by a subset of that community. In this example, the *direction* of flow can best be described as originating in the community (at least in the minds of the paleteros, since they had the choice of hiring either fellow villagers or residents of the cities in which they established their paleterías). The paleteros also chose between specifiable units (cities) that were available in the circumscribed universe called Mexico.[8] Thus they were limited in their choice to the national boundaries of Mexico but could choose any unit within that universe. The mediation performed by paleteros was thus between a subset of a particular rural community and a subset of a larger population (the purchases of ice cream and popsicle products of the specific city in which the paletería was located). The national-level unit in this case is a specific, large (but not infinite or unspecifiable) population, not an institution or a group representing that institution.

The paleteros may be seen as the channels through which funds not available to the residents of the municipio of Mexticacan were made available to certain of them. The fact that the paleteros made this money available to their fellow villagers by physically absenting themselves from the village and encouraging fellow villagers to leave to take jobs as workers with them does not change the nature of the mediation. The conceptual universe of mediation remains exactly the same as it would if that being mediated were something other than a kind of job that removed the workers from the municipio of Mexticacan. It is still an instance of a community-oriented group mediating a national-level phenomenon to another communtiy-oriented group. One departure from the formula specified in the first few pages of this article is that the mediators, as a result of their successful mediation, removed themselves in a significant way from their role as a community-oriented group. Because their mediating-function was so successful, they no longer found the original mediation role necessary or profitable. In most cases, they gradually abandoned it.

It is important to note in this example that the act of mediation was only between certain categories or groups of the municipio population even though the effects of the mediation may have been felt by the entire municipio. In terms of total numbers, those involved in the paleta industry in Mexticacan probably numbered around 900 individuals during the 25 years under consideration. This group may be thought of as being composed of three categories of individuals: those who acted only as owners; those who acted only as workers; and those who acted at one time as workers but who later became owners. In numbers, the first group may have been comprised of approximately 50 individuals; the second group of as many as 700 individuals; and the third group of approximately 150 individuals. With a very small number of exceptions, they were all males.[9] Furthermore, the acts of mediation described here were confined to individuals who at one time were residents of the municipio of Mexticacan. Thus, the defining elements of this case were: (1) a finite social universe (the population of the municipio of Mexticacan from which all the mediators and mediated were drawn—i.e., approximately 7,000 people) which we can view as the specific community; (2) a set of mediators and a set of mediated individuals who were defined as such by their participation in one of two quite specifically defined role relationships among the many that were available in the municipio; and (3) a time period which for all practical purposes can be stated to have lasted approximately 25 years. The ability to circumscribe the elements in this manner allow this example to be called a "case" of cultural and economic mediation. The configuration as defined by the elements of size and location of the population universe, the roles, and the time period would allow this set of relationships to be distinguished from any other set of relationships that one could pursue in Mexticacan or anywhere else.

The initiation of the paleta industry by Mexticaqueños resulted in rural-urban migration for many individuals from Mexticacan. Many of those who entered the paleta business became brokers or mediators who then induced others to leave the municipio to work in their paleterías as employees. Most of the paleteros who were brokers have left Mexticacan and have taken up residence in an urban location in Mexico. Many of these have become involved in businesses in addition to their paleta businesses. One, for example, bought and operates a large hotel near the central plaza in Guadalajara. Another owns a large fruit storage warehouse in the north of Mexico. Although these paleteros still own land and houses in Mexticacan, their most important economic interests are elsewhere. The mediators had power in the community while they were mediators, power that they created by assuming their role as paleteros. Now they have status in Mexticacan but they do not exercise power in the community in any except ceremonial contexts or in some unusual circumstance.[10] Money still comes to Mexticacan from those who own small paleterías and from those who are still workers in paleterías throughout Mexico. However, the amount of money that is available or expended in Mexticacan from these sources now is probably quite small and probably does not create jobs as did the money in the early days of the paleteros who served as mediators.

The cultural mediation in Mexticacan resulted in the addition of a small number of families to the upper-middle sectors of Mexico and a somewhat larger number to the lower-middle sectors.[11] Since the paleterías of the majority of the paleteros are still in operation, the money that provided the basis of their entry into the national middle sector is still there. Involvement in new businesses, if they were successful, would consolidate their position or enhance it. Thus, this case of cultural mediation is unusual in the literature in that it describes an instance of rural-urban migration in which many of the participants (of the set of paleteros) became relatively wealthy and entered the national middle sector. I would suspect that there are many more cases of this type but that they have not been described. On the other hand, the case described also depicts a large group of individuals (the workers from Mexticacan who worked in the paleterías) whose involvement in rural-urban migration did not result in many of them taking up a permanent urban residence at the time of their urban involvement, nor even learning many urban ways. Many of these workers returned to Mexticacan to continue traditional occupations there. However, I would suspect that a large percentage of the younger workers will eventually find that their past urban experiences will lead them to new urban experiences.

The above case is sufficiently different from those so far reported in studies of rural-urban migration in Latin America to indicate that there are many aspects of the migration process that remain to be described. The social relationships between migrants from one village are quite varied. The roles that migrants play in home village processes have barely been tapped. As new social elements are created in a nation such as Mexico, the mix becomes different and new combinations are created. New combinations allow new social forms to emerge. In this sense, urbanization is a process of continual creation.

NOTES

1. Wolf describes these brokers as individuals who "stand guard over the crucial junctures or synapses of relationships which connect the local system to the larger whole. Their basic function is to relate community-oriented individuals who want to stabilize or improve their life chances, but who lack economic security and political connections, with nation-oriented individuals who operate primarily in terms of the complex cultural forms standardized as national institutions, but whose success in these operations depends on the size and strength of their personal following. These functions are of course expressed through cultural forms or mechanisms which will differ from culture to culture. . . . The position of these 'brokers' is an 'exposed' one, since, Janus-like, they face in two directions at once. They must serve some of the interests of groups operating on both the community and the national level, and they must cope with the conflicts raised by the collision of these interests. They cannot settle them, since by doing so they would abolish their own usefulness to others. Thus they often act as buffers between groups, maintaining the tensions which provide the dynamic of their actions" (Wolf, 1956: 1075-1076).

2. That which is conceived of as "nation" or that which represents "the nation" can be quite varied. For some purposes, a nation is a geographical entity defined by political boundaries. At other times, a nation is a population of human beings bounded by exclusive political boundaries (as in the case of the United States of America) or included within the boundaries of another political entity (as in the case of "the Sioux Nation"). Appropriately enough, the concept of that which "represents" the "nation" is equally vague. Thus the president is said to represent the United States. An ambassador is said to represent the

United States also. In some senses, however, the Congress is said to more truly represent the nation than the president.

In Wolf's usage, "the nation" is represented by an individual or a group who operates through national-level institutions. The two questions that are suggested by the discussion above are : (1) what entity does the representative represent and for what purposes? and (2) do they represent that entity better than any other possible contender? The reason for this discussion here is that a "nation" is too often conceived of as only or primarily a political unit. In order to investigate demographic problems such as rural-urban migration, it may be more helpful to conceive of a "nation" as a large but specifiable number of human beings bound by common values (in this case, political values). This same group of individuals (because of laws that they have enacted) also constitutes a bounded economic system. By extension, then, a "nation" is a large but specifiable number of human beings bound by a common economic system. Thus, the agreed upon but unstated definition of a nation as a political entity (with formal structure) which appears to be the basis of Wolf's discussion is also too restrictive of investigation if the focus of interest happens to be economic, as in this case. It may be true that national-level political institutions represent the political life of the country better than any other entity. It may not be true that the national-level political or economic institutions represent the economic life of the country *at all levels* better than other entities. In this case, the focus is on that part of the Mexican population which is urban who are potential consumers. In light of the oftimes limited availability of products in rural areas of Mexico, this population *is* the Mexican nation.

3. A more complete description and analysis of the *paleteros* of Mexticacan and their business practices may be found in Rollwagen (1968).

4. It is interesting that Wagley and Harris, in their discussion of town types, parallel Wolf's view of the direction of mediation and imply that mediators are responsive groups rather than initiators. They state: "The existence of Town subcultures in isolated communities furnishes the key to the problem of the relationship of Peasant subcultures to lines of national political and economic integration. Local standards are set and maintained by this sociocultural segment, and it is through the upper class of the town that changes emanating from national legislation and metropolitan influences must filter before reaching the peasant stratum" (Wagley and Harris, 1955: 439).

5. Workers from Mexticacan were frequently hired for a season or for a specified period of time. There were no contracts, but there were agreements concerning lengths of employment that both paletero and worker honored in most cases. Thus, a worker might be hired for one season, or for two years or some such mutually agreed upon time period. At the end of that time, the worker would return to Mexticacan. By not rehiring a worker from Mexticacan, the paleteros could change personnel in their labor force without actually firing anyone from their own village.

6. Cf. Wolf (1966: 81-85). It is important to note that this is exactly how the paleteros viewed the situation. They expressed the feeling that hiring fellow Mexticaqueños involved too many obligations other than wages, whereas hiring non-Mexticaqueños did not involve anything but a wage payment for work performed.

7. From the beginning of the employment in the paleterías, the workers had viewed their employment as a kind of contract for a specified period of time. The paleteros contracted to take them to the paleterías and to return them to Mexticacan at the end of the unit of time agreed upon. To the workers, Mexticacan was still seen as the locus from which employment was secured whether it was employment in the municipio of Mexticacan or employment elsewhere (as in the case of work in the paleterías). This view held by the workers is the major reason why the concept of mediation is important to the understanding of what happened in this case. In the process of establishing urban businesses, the paleteros used fellow Mexticaqueños for reasons explained above. They completed the rural-urban transition themselves and induced a short-term rural-urban migration for the workers from

Mexticacan. After they had established themselves in urban locations, however, the paleteros ceased to be mediators for fellow Mexticaqueños and stopped inducing the rural-urban migration of their fellows as workers.

8. It is conceivable that Mexticaqueños could have established businesses in other countries than Mexico (e.g., the border towns of the United States or in cities in Guatemala). However, they did not. The reasons for this are probably bound up in the way that the Mexticaqueños saw the world. For them, the possibilities of establishing paleterías was limited to Mexico. This is one example of why mediation in this article is termed "cultural" mediation as well as economic mediation. The culture of the Mexticaqueños led them to believe that the universe of effort was Mexico even though in economic terms other universes might have proven equally profitable. The paleteros mediated the cultural idea that the universe of opportunity for economic effort was not limited to the municipio of Mexticacan.

It is equally interesting to note that, before the introduction of the paleta industry in Mexticacan, a major possibility for improving one's position in life was by going to the United States, legally or illegally, to work temporarily or to live permanently. During the years of the involvement in the paleta industry, this possibility was used with much less frequency than before.

9. My information leads me to believe that there were only two instances in which females became paleteros. One of these involved a woman who, upon the death of her paletero husband, continued to operate the family paletería. The second instance involved a male paletero who established his sister in a paletería business of her own.

There were also cases of females from Mexticacan who went to work in paleterías. These cases do not seem to be as clear-cut as those of the male workers, however, because it appears that they were workers in the paleterías only on a part-time basis and were hired primarily as household help for the wife of the paletero to help in the urban household and helped in the paletería only on a part-time basis.

10. See Adams' discussion of "power" and "power domain" (1967: 31 ff.) especially the example of power domains in change (1967: 44) in which the relative control of a party over the environment changes. In the case of the Mexticaqueños, this control over the environment would change because they chose not to exercise it.

11. I am using the terms "middle sectors" rather than "middle classes" in conformance with the belief that "middle classes" implies a set of economic considerations more applicable in Europe and the United States than in Latin America. A brief discussion of this terminology may be found in Johnson (1958: viii-ix).

The relationship between the development of the middle sectors and the process of urbanization is an obvious one. However, the idea that urbanization creates mechanisms that promote social and economic mobility is exactly what I am trying to illustrate in this article. Ratinoff has illustrated this relationship in the following way: "Modernization resulting from the growth of cities in the twentieth century has created an ill-assortment of families and individuals placed half-way between the traditional classes; while these middle sectors are the product of social mobility, they constitute the social area where vertical mobility produces the greatest economic and social consequences.

"*Urbanization* has brought about the recognition of the middle sectors as a social institution; the inequality it produces varies to some extent, inasmuch as it *creates machinery* and institutions *which speed up mobility*. Industry and other specifically urban economic activities require flexible forms of social inequality, so as to meet their needs in personnel and thus ensure their efficient functioning" (1967: 63, italics added).

REFERENCES

ADAMS, R. N. (1967) The Second Sowing: Power and Secondary Development in Latin America. San Francisco: Chandler.

JOHNSON, J. J. (1958) Political Change in Latin America: The Emergence of the Middle Sectors. Stanford: Stanford University Press.

KUNKEL, J. H. (1961) "Economic autonomy and social change in Mexican villages." Economic Development and Cultural Change 10 (October): 51-63.

RATINOFF, L. (1967) "The new urban groups: the middle classes," pp. 61-93 in S. M. Lipset and A. Solari (eds.) Elites in Latin America. New York: Oxford University Press.

ROLLWAGEN, J. R. (1968) "The *Paleteros* of Mexticacan, Jalisco: a study of entrepreneurship in Mexico." Ph.D. dissertation. University of Oregon. [Also available through University Microfilms.]

SILVERMAN, S. F. (1965) "Patronage and community-nation relationships in central Italy." Ethnology 4 (April): 172-189.

TAYLOR, P. S. (1933) A Spanish-Mexican Peasant Community: Arandas in Jalisco, Mexico. Berkeley: University of California Press.

WAGLEY, C. and M. HARRIS (1955) "A typology of Latin American subcultures." American Anthropologist 57 (June): 428-451.

WOLF, E. (1956) "Aspects of group relations in a complex society: Mexico." American Anthropologist 58 (December): 1065-1078.

––– (1966) Peasants. Englewood Cliffs, N.J.: Prentice-Hall.

PART II

THE

SOCIAL

AND

ECONOMIC

ORGANIZATION

OF

THE

CITY

ANTHONY LEEDS, Professor of Anthropology at Boston University, received his doctorate from Columbia University. He has held teaching positions at Columbia University, Hofstra College, City College of New York, American University, and the University of Texas at Austin, and has been a visiting lecturer at the Federal University of Rio de Janeiro, Brazil. During the 1972-1973 academic year he was a Fulbright Lecturer at Oxford University and the University of London. He has done extensive field work in Brazil, Venezuela, Peru, and the United States. His current research deals with urban squatting in West European countries. Among his principal publications are "Brazilian Careers and Social Structure" (*American Anthropologist,* Vol. 66, 1964); "The Significant Variables Determining the Character of Squatter Settlements" (*América Latina,* July-September 1969); "The Culture of Poverty Concept: Conceptual, Logical, and Empirical Problems, with Perspectives from Brazil and Peru," in E. Leacock (ed.) *The Culture of Poverty: A Critique* (Simon and Schuster, 1971); "Locality Power in Relation to Supra-Local Power Institutions," in A. Southall (ed.) *Urban Anthropology* (Oxford University Press, 1973); and "Social, Economic, and Political Effects of Producer and Consumer Orientations Toward Housing: A Systems Analysis," in F. F. Rabinovitz and F. M. Trueblood (eds.) *Latin American Urban Research, Volume III* (Sage Publications, 1973).

Chapter 3

HOUSING-SETTLEMENT TYPES, ARRANGEMENTS FOR LIVING, PROLETARIANIZATION, AND THE SOCIAL STRUCTURE OF THE CITY

ANTHONY LEEDS

As one scans the literature on cities from various disciplines, one observes that they tend to be conceived, as in architecture and urban planning, as physical entities and apparatus (buildings, open spaces, sewage systems, communication networks, etc.), or, as among the social science disciplines, as stage sets or backgrounds in front of which various categories of behavior of interest to the respective disciplines (kinship, migration, political behavior, associational life, etc.) are to be observed, or, as among the aesthetic disciplines, as expressions in form and design of major ideological orientations of a society.

My own view has increasingly moved in the direction of seeing what we call "a city," the more or less discretely bounded locality, large or small, as a combination of socio-politico-economic structures and the physical apparatus (listed above) used in their operation. The physical apparatus reflects the social and ideological order, if always in a laggard manner, because its mere physical concretization lends itself to perpetuation while the societal order is changing around it. Consequently, the primary interest in the study of cities, except perhaps for aesthetics, is not so much the physical apparatus as the social structure of the city and the societal structure which, as a whole, underlies it.

One theme of this paper, then, is to show, at least for some cases, that the physical apparatus is, to an encompassing degree, a reflection or crystallization of the societal order and its city subsystem.

A second theme is to suggest that the societal orders of capitalistically constructed societies and their social-structural manifestations in cities necessarily involve proletarianization, while proletarianization is itself a dual process in that it is largely a result of the struggle for self-maintenance of elites of the capitalist class(es) and the capitalist competition for private property as means of personal self-aggrandizement and of social control. Some secondary consequences of this total process will be underlined in the course of the discussion.

A third theme is to suggest, as a consequence of the preceding argument, that policies and plans for cities created by their own policy-making bodies or higher-level ones, as a rule, are *necessarily* ineffective, irrelevant, or even disastrous, and that urban planning can, at best, have only very limited efficacy if it does not, on one hand, deal explicitly with the global social structures of the city in the first line of attack, and, on the other, with national-societal conditions affecting the city system as pressures, constraints, and requirements.

I turn, first, to some physical aspects, especially housing, of Rio de Janeiro, Brazil, and other cities, and then to some of the social-structural aspects involved in residence and its differential location in the city.

SETTLEMENT SPECIALIZATION IN RIO

One of the striking things in Rio, as in a large number of the cities of Latin America such as Lima, Caracas, Bogotá, and Santiago,[1] is the specialization of housing settlement types. For most readers, the familiar types include "better residential areas;" the assumedly "middle- and upper-middle class" settlements of Copacabana, Flamengo, Botafogo, and certain other parts of Rio's South Zone on the beachy Atlantic shoreline, as well as Tijuca and Grajaú in the North Zone; and the *favelas* or squatter settlements.[2] Parallel differentiations are to be found in each of the cities mentioned above, though they rest on folk categories and terminologies which vary from place to place.

Favelas in Brazil, and, more generally, squatter settlements anywhere in the world, are spoken of as a "problem" in a manner analagous to the "problems" of "urban ghettos," of "slums," of "rural immigrants," of "marginalization," of "ethnic minorities," of the "culture of poverty," so often found on the minds and the tongues of concerned people all over the world. Essentially, these all refer to different aspects of the same problem—the proletarianization discussed in this paper.

Favelas are conceived of as a problem—as have been Lima's *barriadas,* San Juan's *arrabales,* Caracas's *ranchos* or *barrios,* Santiago's *callampas,* Buenos Aires's *villas miserias,* etc.—because, allegedly, their populations are comprised, at one evil extreme, of assassins, thieves, robbers, no-goods, marijuana pushers, and narcotic addicts; at another evil extreme, of communists or other kinds of politically and socially rebellious menaces; at a third, less-evil extreme, of poor, benighted, uneducated, ill-adapted, hicklike rural immigrants; or, at the best of extremes, of reasonable human beings, but sad and poverty-stricken, living in hovels, promiscuously creating a social and urbanistic cancer in the city.[3]

I have elsewhere[4] shown that almost all these conceptions are either false or drastic distortions of actualities, but I *do* want to emphasize that favelas, "shanty-towns," "squatments," unauthorized urban settlements, call them what you will, are usually the most striking *visible* form of residential settlement to be observed.

Not so visible and often difficult visually to discover or distinguish is a series of other low-income settlement types or residential neighborhoods which remain—as if they did not exist—almost totally undescribed not only in the literature regarding Rio but that respecting other Latin American cities where equivalent housing exists.[5]

First among these housing-settlement types, comprising perhaps a quarter- to a half-million people, or about five percent of the population of Rio and a much larger percentage in Lima, are the rooming houses of the types called, in the former, *cabeça de porco* or *casa de cômodo* and, in the latter, *casas subdivididas*. These terms refer to a single large building ranging from perhaps twenty to perhaps eighty or one hundred one- and two-room apartments. These are usually occupied by households composed of nuclear, subnuclear, or slightly extended-nuclear families, rarely by individuals or by what in Rio are called *"repúblicas"* —groups of unmarried persons of like sex sharing the rent or all of the household expenses. Most of this type of building in Rio originated in the last century, but some were converted from other types of buildings or enlarged at various times in this century up to the very present. They are buildings which were designed either originally or in their conversion for very low-income housing, specifically to exploit persons or sets of persons who need to be near labor markets but cannot afford other kinds of accommodations or did not, as will be argued below, have capital for squatter settlement accommodations and hence were forced to pay rents. Whether in Rio, Lima, or elsewhere, these houses have only recently begun to be studied, so we know virtually nothing about them, although impression indicates that internally each has a number of community-like features.[6]

A second settlement type in Rio, perhaps housing another five percent, is called an *avenida* or *vila* with various qualifying adjectives such as *proletária, de lavadeiras,* etc.[7] In Lima, the equivalent is the *callejón;* in Mexico, the *vecindad;*[8] in Chile, the *conventillo;* in San Antonio, the *corral* (and in the Midlands of England, where perhaps it originated, the "back-to-back"), etc. It consists of a series of horizontal one- or two-room renting units, for all of which three or four toilets and a similar number of faucets and wash-tanks serve. There is what must be a condominium area—the central, elongated courtyard and entryways. In Rio, this type is almost totally unstudied, and information is lacking from the few studies such as Patch's for Lima and Lewis's for Mexico City as to such matters as condominium work space, the internal economies, and so on.[9] In Rio, the older variant of these known as *cortiços,* left over from the last century, had a very high proportion of single-man occupancy of many of the apartments, especially on the second storey. Average household size was about 3 in contrast to the 4.6-4.7 for favelas and a roughly similar size for the rooming houses.[10] Here, as in the rooming houses, rents are paid.

A third settlement type in Rio is the *parque proletário* or, in Chile and other countries, the *vila de emergencia*—government temporary (more often "temporary"!) housing meant to supply roofs and walls to persons without shelter because of urban renewal or drastic accidents to squatter settlements such as flooding or burning. There are few or no data for Rio on this type,[11] and I know of none at all for other countries. I am not even certain whether rent is paid, although my impression is that, officially, rent is to be paid even though, in fact, often it is not. I have seen no estimate of the number of people in parques proletários. The housing units, like favelas, are occupied mainly by family groupings, but getting into them is a complex matter involving application to bureaucrats or agencies for assignment to a housing unit—a much more constraining procedure than entering a favela, although no capital is required.

A fourth type is called, in Rio, the *conjunto*, with equivalent terms in other countries. There are various types of housing arrangements called *conjuntos*, but the term always refers to a multi-unit development of some kind. I shall restrict it here to a multi-storeyed, single building or set of buildings, comprised of multiple renting units like the *unidades vecinales* of Lima or the famous (or infamous) *superbloques* of Caracas—the equivalent of the North American urban high-rise housing projects built by the insurance companies. Another sense of the term conjunto—the multi-unit, single-family occupancy, housing development—I shall return to below (see *vila*).

The conjuntos in Rio, Lima, Caracas, and other cities, have a number of features which make them particularly interesting and often confusing as a category for analysis, though here again, very little literature exists other than the study supported by the Banco Obrero of Venezuela (1959). First is that the term conjunto is *sociologically* highly misleading because the personnel resident in them are quite diverse with respect to any standard sociological category such as class, stratum, ethnic grouping, or income if one is looking at the universe of conjuntos. The conjuntos, as such, can house any kind of social category and the term *factually* denotes nothing sociologically. A study of conjuntos would have to differentiate them according to sociologically relevant categories. Interesting for purposes of this paper are the low-income conjuntos of Rio, scattered here and there, primarily in the city's industrial North Zone.

A major feature of the conjuntos populated by low-income people in Rio and, I understand, elsewhere, is their occupational specialization, because each was separately built by an agency, labor union, association, or other corporativist group catering for its membership. Thus there are the conjuntos dos Bancários (bank clerks), dos Marinheiros (sailors), da Marinha (Navy), do IAPI (the now-extinct Instituto de Aposentadoria e Pensões dos Industriários, industrial workers), do IAPC (the now-extinct Instituto de Aposentadoria e

Pensões dos Comerciários, commercial workers), do Pedregulho (public funcionaries), and so on. Thus, all over Rio and other cities are scattered occupational-residential enclaves. This fact takes on special significance in view of the scaled salaries for the entire Brazilian labor force which tend to set rather clear parameters to family income or family capital resources from which equally set amounts are subtracted by rents or amortizations. By contrast, neither the occupational specialization nor the set range of incomes holds for favelas or other housing-settlement types, a point I return to below. No estimates exist of how many people live in conjuntos generally, let alone in low-income ones. My guess would be on the order of ten percent of Rio's population.

A fifth type is constituted by the vast "popular"—i.e., proletarian—housing Levittowns (in Rio also sometimes called conjuntos, but more commonly *vilas*) delighting in such names as Vila Aliança, Vila Esperança, Vila Kennedy, Cidade de Deus, and, more recently, rather ironically in Brazil, Vila Paciência, and others in Rio; Ciudad Kennedy in Bogotá; Caja de Água and Ventanilla in Lima, and so on. The populations of these vilas have been removed from other parts of the city by act of man or God—by favela removal, urban renewal, flood, landslide, or other disaster. In these vilas, so-called "embryo" houses are sold to the residents who are selected by virtue of their alleged "capacity to pay" the calculated amortization rates based on the government's cost of building, but who are unable to afford better housing to replace the housing they lost. Thus, family capital inflows of the residents fall within rather narrow ranges, and out of them, they ostensibly pay the amortization payments. I say "ostensibly" because in Rio's vilas about sixty to eighty percent are defaulting at present. All the vilas, or a total of perhaps 250,000 or more people, comprise about five to seven percent of Rio's population. The major vilas of Rio, it should be noted, lie about fifty to sixty kilometers from the city center and the major work locations, require two or three buses or train connections, and usually one and one-half to three hours of travel each way. Virtually no labor market whatever has developed near them. In Lima, distance, transportation cost, and transportation fatigue are much less severe, but the labor market near Caja de Água and Ventanilla, for example, is virtually nonexistent. The same complaint was made about Ciudad Kennedy, certainly up to a few years ago, although it lay only eight kilometers from the city center.

A sixth type is comprised of what is locally referred to in Rio as the *"subúrbios,"* in general characterized by vast expanses of fairly humble, separate, privately owned houses on official streets which have little or no paving, often no lights, a poor water supply, few or no sewers or other urban services. They are largely in parts of the city furthest from the center, but are not properly suburbs in the North American usage of the term since they fall largely *inside* the juridical boundaries of the central city, Rio de Janeiro. Each house usually has its yard or garden with space for fruit trees, vegetables, chickens, pigs, and so on, made possible by the more or less officialized lotting, carried out by the land speculators with a greater or lesser degree of observation of the juridical norms depending only on their honesty. The subúrbio areas look somewhat like small municipal seats in the interior of Brazil which melt into the surrounding agrarian areas, but in Rio, the subúrbios are, of course, surrounded by city. Population estimates can only be guessed at since statistics are not gathered according to the category. I would hazard ten to fifteen percent of Rio's population.

A seventh type consists of the slums proper *(tugurios)*—areas of once-good but now-decaying housing and urban services; rented rooms, apartments, and houses; pensions with room and board mainly for men, cheap travellers' hotels, bordellos, and so on. There are large areas of these in all major Latin American cities, huge expanses in Rio and perhaps vaster ones in Lima—and all, to my knowledge, thoroughly unstudied. No estimates of the numbers of people in such housing exist to my knowledge; my guess would be about ten percent of the population of Rio and perhaps considerably more in Lima.[12]

The eighth type is comprised of the squatter settlements of which I shall give only a summary description here (see references given above). The single uniform criterion that distinguishes squatter settlements from other types of housing-settlement in the city is that they constitute "illegal" occupation of the land in that their occupancy is based neither on their owning it nor renting it from legal owners.

All the other criteria often used for distinguishing squatter settlements from other types of housing-settlement only apply some of the time or infrequently. Aside from occupancy, it is usually the case that they are not planned. This is almost uniformly the case in Rio, in São Paulo, and other Brazilian cities, although in Salvador, some of the *alagados* or lake invasions are known to have had a preconceived layout. Caracas's barrios also seem unplanned. Bogotá has both unplanned and planned ones. Lima, however, is remarkable for the number and size of "illegal" barriadas which were planned before invasion and some that seem to have been "regulated" after the settling took place.

Because of the developmental pattern of housing improvement to be found in them, it is highly misleading, whether in Rio, Lima, Caracas, or Bogotá, for example, to call squatter settlements "shantytowns," although many are so and others which are primarily not so have neighborhoods which are. In a number of cases, the squatter settlements, over time, are transformed into regular parts of the city with standard housing by the residents themselves.[13]

It is rarely true that their populations are primarily "true rural" migrants though many people have come from more or less rural areas, although mostly through step-migration. It is not the case that the populations are uniformly made up of marginal labor, lumpenproletariats, or mere proletariats, but, rather, display a range of stratification reaching even up to upper-middle professional, bureaucratic, and business "levels" in some of the larger and more evolved squatter settlements, like Jacarézinho in Rio and San Martín de Porras (with its banks and government agencies) in Lima. It is not the fact that they are uniform and close-knit communities even in those squatments which have fairly tight-knit residents' associations.

In sum, though squatter settlements comprise a single housing-settlement type by virtue of their origin and the common characterizing feature of illegal occupancy of land, and, consequently, their special jural status before the law and the public authority, nevertheless, as a universe, they display a much more varied range for virtually all characteristics of sociological interest than any of the other housing-settlement types and, individually, most of them are quite heterogeneous housing and social areas. Perhaps twenty percent of the jural city of Rio and twenty-two to twenty-five percent of the Rio conurbation (Rio, Niterói, São Gonçalo, Caxias, Nilópolis, São João de Meriti, etc., all except the first, which has about 4,000,000 people, having in the neighborhood of 400,000-600,000 people—a total now about 8,000,000) live in squatments at present. In Lima, today, upwards of forty percent of the total population of about 3,000,000 live in barriadas, while nearly fifty percent of Caracas's over 1,200,000 people are in the barrios.[14]

Finally, there are in Rio several minor types like the cortiço I spoke of above and the *estalagem* (equivalent to the Limeño *solar*—a kind of row house), which exist only as remnants of a past time; the *favela de quintal* or backyard favela, equivalent to the *corralón* in Lima. The latter two terms refer to shack-types of buildings or other substandard and unauthorized constructions built with the permission of the owners of the officially registered house on the street, usually as a means of his acquiring income by charging rents for the land. Still another type is the *azotea,* or rooftop shanty built on top of an officially registered house in Lima which does not have an analog in Rio. No estimates exist as to how many people live in such specialized settlements, but probably not more than one percent in Rio and a little more in Lima.

Thus, approximately seventy percent of the population of the city of Rio de Janeiro and a comparable percentage in Lima and Caracas live in housing, which, with the exception of a few more evolved squatments, is almost exclusively proletarian.

Let me emphasize that each of the settlement types discussed has a characteristic physical apparatus easily recognizable by the trained eye. These apparatuses, plus the specialized physical apparatuses of the labor structure of industry, services, transportation, etc.—that is, factories, machines, buses, car tracks, and the like—and of the administrative organization (public office buildings, airports, military installations, etc.) together comprise the physical trappings of the city which are so peculiar to it and which, in much of our thinking, tends to be *identified* with and understood *as* the city. Throughout what follows, I shall tease out the social relations which accompany and underlie these apparatuses and their spatial distribution.

From the point of view of urban form and particularly of urban social structure to be discussed at length below, the "disordered" distribution of all these types of settlements should be noted. Though, indeed, there are large patches of turgurios, nevertheless, they are discontinuous, interspersed not only with favelas, avenidas, low-income conjuntos, parques proletários, etc., but also with middle-income conjuntos, high-income residential areas, business areas, industry, and so on. Today, there is only one consistently high-income area in Rio—Ipanema-Leblon in the newest part of the coastal South Zone—and even this had, until 1968-1969 when large-scale removals were begun by the government, a number of important favelas in it. The world-famous Copacabana—an international elite playground and center of chic boutique trade, art galleries, modern furniture stores, and the like—even after the removals begun in 1968 remains an area of diversified housing-settlement types including two important favelas, two or three notorious efficiency apartment houses,[15] crowded tenements, palatial apartment houses, and so on, all interspersed. Botafogo, next to Copacabana, but mainly on the Bay of Guanabara inside Sugar Loaf Mountain which divides it from the Atlantic, has equally elite areas, interspersed with remaining favelas, some startling rooming houses, avenidas, a variety of lower-middle-income housing, some conjuntos, and the like. The next subdivision of the city, Flamengo, is even more diverse, having some of the worst rooming houses in the city, some of the most striking avenidas, favelas, conjuntos, middle-"class," and wealthy housing. Between it and the North Zone lie two major areas and the central mountain massif—the banking and public administration center of the city and of the State of Guanabara (and partly of Brazil) and the hilly, almost exclusively upper-class residential area of Santa Teresa—at one end of which are two huge favelas and, at the other, two or three small ones, and on whose lower flanks is a wild assortment of single- and multi-unit houses, both legal and illegal in their occupancy of the land and standards of building.

The North Zone is the main industrial and artesanal part of the city but also has two major upper-stratum residential areas, surrounded by and including favelas and neighboring on conjuntos, subúrbios, avenidas. To the north and east, nothing above middle-income housing is to be found, but even this is entirely interdigitated with an extraordinary array of parques proletários and emergency housing, favelas of the most varied sorts, conjuntos, vilas constructed years ago by the Fundação da Casa Popular, avenidas, favelas de quintal, subúrbios, industrial installations both great and small, agricultural plots, and so on and on.

I have given so much detail in order to impress on the reader the kaleidoscopic character of the city from the point of view not only of housing-settlement types but also of social characteristics such as income, class, even ethnicity (not important in Rio, though more so in Lima), provenience, occupation, attached to and underlying them. The kaleidoscopic aspect is clear to see in photographs taken from the air or from hilltops but is not easily recognizable by the noninitiate as *socially* kaleidoscopic in terms of the distribution of personnel *in space* according to sociological characteristics. What this kaleidoscopic dispersion and discontinuity means in terms of the social organization of the city I return to in a later section.

Lima is less multifaceted but also displays considerable interspersion. For example, in Miraflores, always thought of as one of the most elite residential and recreational centers, there is at least one barriada and several considerable corralones, as well as some callejones. La Victoria, largely a lower-middle- to low-income area, is a welter of housing projects, small barriadas, callejones, corralones, casas subdivididas, and the like. Rimac is still more complex, including some solid middle-class housing, huge numbers of callejones, some large barriadas (now called *pueblos jóvenes*), solares, rooming houses, corralones, unidades vecinales, military installations, the city's bull-ring, public gardens, etc. The only uniformly upper-income area is San Isidro.

ALTERNATIVE LIFE ARRANGEMENTS

Starting with certain models with which the field situation was approached, it was only by painful steps of extending and modifying the model, forced by the field data themselves—sometimes teased out with greatest difficulty, sometimes come upon quite by accident—that one at length discovered an order which links all the housing settlement types discussed above.[16]

Perhaps the most significant body of data in this regard is that concerning the circulation of people among the housing-settlement types, the reasons for their choices, the structure of the situations in which their decisions to move are made, and the constraints against their moving. Given the fact that the data for many kinds of cases are still extremely sketchy, I can only outline the conclusions and give tentative hypotheses.

In essence, each housing-settlement type comprises characteristic arrangements for living, elements of which have been identified above in passing. They involve varying numbers and proportions of some characteristic forms of household (an economic, corporate, budgeting unit; see Leeds, 1973b), usually, but not always, a family segment (nuclear or otherwise) combining the economic with all other ends of the domestic unit. The household, as a budgeting unit, has the task of allocating its resources—scarce, of course, for *all* the cases in the housing-settlement types I am discussing—to an array of ends in different proportions, giving priority to some, playing down others, and putting off still others altogether, if possible. Assuming that people want to live at all, some of these ends are ineluctable—food, some shelter, health; others, given contemporary society, almost unavoidable—education, clothing, etc.; and still others, more peripheral, even if felt to be necessary, like recreation.

As a rule, the pattern of weightings and content given to these ends corresponds to a given housing-settlement type as the appropriate vehicle for maximizing the pattern of ends selected. We do not yet know in detail what variables determine a household's choice of one pattern of ends rather than another, but the general outlines are clear.

The pattern of ends itself relates to perceptions, cognitions, understandings, and experiences on the part of members of the household with respect to the larger world they live in, especially to the labor market, the bureaucracy, the political system, the health system, the service and market structure, and, perhaps, especially to the cross-cutting systems of hierarchic positions which both order and link them. By the latter, I refer to both the internal formal hierarchies of offices in the bureaucratic agencies, the political parties, the hospitals, the welfare agencies, the distribution organizations, etc., and the informal networks of kin, friendship, tradeoff acquaintanceships, and patronage which cross over the boundaries of the various sectors, contributing to eliteness and to the creation of class boundaries.

The pattern of ends also relates to, and is constrained by, two other major factors. First, different states of the household moving through the domestic cycle *necessarily* determine different weightings of ends. Second, different absolute levels of income and available capital, relative to the cost of living at a given time, tend to determine patterns of ends differentially—e.g., the lower the absolute level, the greater the percentage devoted to food and to the cost of work.[17] Both of these, in addition to the external class-maintaining mechanisms, operate as constraints upon choices and limiters of strategic possibilities.

Let us delineate synoptically how these various factors operate in the selection of arrangements for living—hence, in the circulation of low-income people among housing-settlement types.

A household may choose to live in the subúrbios because it can own its own house, which maximizes its tenure security, permitting it to improve the physical living conditions; because it can raise fruits, vegetables, and animals, thus reducing food costs; because the environment is calm and familial for the appropriate raising of children. Living in the subúrbios, however, reduces travel accessibility to jobs, thus raising cost-of-work expenses; decreases accessibility to the jobs themselves, especially odd jobs (which are more frequent in the densest areas of the labor market and in elite residential areas) and better paid ones; puts one far from health, school, and recreational facilities; costs more in terms of services and retail goods; and sacrifices urban services such as water, light, sewers, paved streets, and policing. The household must also either have some original capital to pay for the land or be able to make rent, amortization, or mortgage payments, unless it can find an unwatched lot that it can invade. In general, subúrbios are advantageous for better-off households or households more advanced in the domestic cycle when the children are gone or old enough to work.

Again, a household may choose to live in a favela. Doing so maximizes savings on rents and amortizations; permits a great freedom in adapting the physical structure of the house to changing domiciliary needs; allows for a greater or lesser raising of produce, especially fruits and animals; and, above all, reduces transportation-to-work costs often to nothing and maximizes accessibility to the job-market in general—especially the better-paid jobs and odd jobs—as well as putting residents nearer to hospitals, schools, and recreational facilities.[18] Favelas also tend to allow for physical proximity of social network extensions, hence making for a more efficient social security system ready for immediate mobilization than in more fragmented low-income parts of the city. They also allow for the development of great social solidarity, a point I return to below. Disadvantages include the reduced or absent urban services with consequent possible health hazards; constraints on building because of threats from acts of God such as fire or cloudburst; tenure insecurity; the need, in order to move in at all, for capital either to buy an existing house or to build some minimal initial shelter, usually the former in crowded or supervised favelas. This last comment indicates the state in which the household finds itself at any given time in its history as an important constraint on the choice actually made, a point returned to below. The lack of an official address, too, can be an important disadvantage in terms of the communicational accessibility of a favela resident and in terms of job discrimination against favela residents, given prevailing myths (see above, pp. 72-73) about favelas.

A typical circulation of a household among housing-settlement types might be from a rooming house to a favela to a subúrbio to a vila and back to a favela, or from a rented slum room or house to a favela to a subúrbio or conjunto. However, I have no statistics as yet to indicate that there are any modal patterns of circulation, though hypothesis says that there ought to be.

The choices of housing-settlement types are equivalents analytically but not as real possibilities. What makes them unequivalent are the conditions or states of the household or the household enterprise. One major variable is the capital it has available or can mobilize, which determines, for example, whether it can purchase a house in a favela which, as standard procedure, is done in a single payment (since there is no jural way of handling time-sales in the illegal favela); whether it can project a fifteen- or twenty-year series of amortization installments or payments to a so-called housing coop; and so on. The amount of mobilizable or available capital itself depends on a series of variables:

(a) the social network extensions for mobilization of free services to reduce costs;

(b) skills of domicile members which can be used to bring in earnings or other forms of payment, such as gifts for services rendered;

(c) jobs held by domicile members;

(d) salaries received by members of the household;

(e) indemnity management by domicile members;

(f) proportion of earnings going to nonearning members of the household;

(g) health conditions of household members;

(h) the costs of job-holding for the household earners—transportation, fees, etc.

As a single example,[19] here, an abandoned mother and her children living in a rooming house at a "low" rent, given that she is a washerwoman or a domestic worker, has little or no chance to move out because she cannot get the resources to build a house, let alone make amortization payments or pay rents for a house, nor can she mobilize the services to build a house because she is isolated from any networks which might do the job for her and cannot herself do it since she cannot be *in situ* and must occupy her time working. She is too poor to escape paying rent and can only rent in places where the rents charged are exorbitant for the facilities let, however absolutely "low" the rents may be. Rents today range between about fifty and ninety percent of a minimum salary (which is fixed by the national government and was, as of mid-1973, NCr$312 or about U.S. $50/month). If the pressure becomes great enough, she may fail to pay her rent and be thrown out in the street; or she may turn to earning extra money by selling her body-services to an occasional man; or she may attempt to contract a more permanent common-law arrangement. The limitation on this last solution is that she has little to offer by way of services or capital to a man, so she is likely only to attract a man who has little to give and, often, much to take. Eventually, one of the children, if it live, becomes old enough to work, if it is in adequate health, a situation which may add enough capital intake to permit the household to make a more advantageous housing arrangement, such as buying a segment of a building or renting a room or apartment in a favela. By doing so, it saves resources which may be used to educate the younger child, thus, perhaps, raising its future job potentialities.

Hypothetical or actual case histories could be multiplied indefinitely, but suffice it, here, to indicate the crucial position of the state of the household economy. Its state is itself critically dependent on the household's relation to the labor market and the characteristics of that labor market, both controlled, in respect to its statistical manifestations and sociologically,[20] by classes and their elites external to the proletariat in which the households we are considering fall.

In brief, households whose economies depend on the wage-labor market of labor-intensive economies such as those of the neo-colonialist capitalist countries of Latin America and other "underdeveloped" areas of the world all confront a system of financial and institutional constraints (part of the structure of proletarianization) which set the parameters of the choices they can make among the arrangements for living. These choices are different from those open to households whose economies depend on capital-intensive, salarial, professional, and entrepreneurial labor markets. I return to the constraints on the former below, but first add more comment on the choices and their consequences. As a group, the choices may be looked at as alternatives allowing differential strategic and tactical advantages with respect to life goals, but all within the framework of a proletarianized way of life, created and maintained essentially by the society's holders of strategic capital resources.

Choices, as remarked, reflect changing states of households but may also reflect external conditions such as shifts in local or total labor demands in the city which themselves reflect changes in production costs, taxes, imposts, imports, costs of money, profit rates, and so on; changes in housing availability; changes in policy toward favelas (see Leeds and Leeds, 1972) or other housing types, and many other modifications of the environment.

CONSEQUENCES OF CHOICES AMONG ARRANGEMENTS FOR LIVING: SOLIDARITY AND DIVISION

Consequences of choices made, however, are not merely the changes in arrangements for living of the household *as such,* but also in that household's relation to its surrounding milieu in the direction of creating solidary relations among persons of like societal status—that is, among the members of the proletariat. In the cases of all the housing settlement types discussed here (except possibly some favelas de quintal), the relationship is to an immediate milieu, into which it goes or from which it departs, consisting of households in important ways like itself, households which are in the same set of conditions or have made the same choices it has. These households are not merely *categorically* alike, but also, by virtue of accompanying social patterns, legal conditions, elements of communitylike behavior and identity, etc., settlements, as my term indicates. Among clusters or whole aggregates of such households, there are recognitions of "we" as opposed to "they" outside—or "our interests" as opposed to "outsiders' interests," of our *gíria* ('slang') as opposed to the outsiders' in other agglomerations or classes. Crystallizations of such networks of relationship, sentiments, self-identifications, and interests are seen in the emergence, for example, of carnival groups, or soccer clubs associated with a conjunto, a subúrbio, a favela, a parque proletário—all solidary groups often with very strong articulation of their relation to the settlement-community they are attached to.[21]

Of extreme importance to this paper is the fact that changes in arrangements for living—which are, indeed, intra-city migrations—thread intra-proletarian networks of all kinds throughout the city. What becomes impressive after prolonged ethnographic work is the number, variety, multi-localization, frequency of mobilization, and utility of these networks. They are extended through kinship, compadrazco, friendship, mutual help roles, intra-class patronal ties, neighbor acquaintanceships, tradeoff relationships, and also by means of the interaction of the solidary groups, such as the *escolas de samba, blocos de samba* (respectively 'samba "school"',' 'samba bloc'; both Carnaval groups), the soccer clubs, the social clubs, the religious congregations, the mutual aid societies, and so on, which exchange visits or meet outside the settlements at federation conventions.[22] These networks serve a multiplicity of functions, although most of the time in a sporadic way—e.g., a social security, mutual aid, mutual political support in electoral, legal, or demand-making activity, etc.

What is most significant about this is the potential basis for proletarian class solidarity and even, in certain contexts, an observed tendency to create such a solidarity. I cite two examples.

After the coup d'état of 1964, elections were, for reasons of national political image, maintained in pre-coup modalities, through October 1965. In that month, gubernatorial elections were held in a number of key states of which the most important was Guanabara (more or less coterminous with the jural city of Rio de Janeiro) which was formerly the Federal District, the national capital, and remained, in 1965, despite the existence of Brasília, the major center of national administration. One candidate was Fleixa Ribeiro, the puppet (and close affinal kinsman) of the incumbent Governor, Carlos Lacerda, who had been the immediate agent of the collapse of the second Vargas Government, of the Quadros Government, and of the Goulart Government in 1964, and was a major figure in the 1964 coup, even expecting to become president. Their party, a major backer of the coup, was the conservative-reactionary UDN (União Democrática Nacional). The other candidate (aside from a couple of negligible ones from minor parties) was Francisco Negrão de Lima, one-time prefect of the Federal District (1956-1959), Ambassador to Portugal, and jack-of-all trades for ex-president Juscelino Kubitschek, a typical political hack of the center-of-the-road, pragmatic, ideologically low-keyed PSD (Partido Social Democrático). The PSD presented his candidature in coalition with the "right" wing of the PTB (Partido Trabalhista Brasileiro), Getúlio Vargas's labor-based, populist party—a coalition of long standing.

Throughout the favelas (and possibly other low-income housing-settlement types which I had not yet then come to know), with the exception of a very few residents uniformly in positions of some degree of command or exploitation over other residents, the response to this situation was consistent, paraphrasable thus: "Negrão is an evil we know—he didn't do a thing as prefect, or maybe a little something here and there, *but he is not one of Them*" (meaning the military and their supporting Lacerda forces). The vote was heavily for Negrão, most clearly so in areas of proletarian occupation.[23] The meaning of the overwhelming proletarian vote against Lacerda and his candidate was not lost on the military which, *that very night and as a direct result of the vote,* eliminated the entire party system and created by fiat the present one of a government party (largely the old UDN, plus right-wing elements of the PSD and small fascist parties) and a thoroughly emasculated "opposition" party (absorbing the rest of the PSD, the old PTB, plus various socialist parties), which has foundered in a morass of impotency in large part "legally" imposed on it by the military. This move on the part of the military rulers was not, in turn, lost on the proletariat which, in later elections, indicated their protest by a massive voting *em branco* (being legally required, or forced, to vote, they cast unmarked null votes to indicate the emptiness of the election, a fact which was censored by the military government from the news media).

The point of the case relates to networks of communication and discussion —of interpretation and understanding—linking favelas and other proletarian settlements. The mere *categorical* position of proletarianness cannot explain the opposition vote, since, atomized as they are locationally, they were also confronted by the mass media biased in favor of the government, by Lacerda's populistic representations, and other factors which tended to obscure their interest. What was striking to an outside observer was the visiting back and forth from settlement to settlement—the mobilization of communication networks— and the constant discussion of the political issues.

The second case, discussed in detail elsewhere (Leeds and Leeds, 1972; Leeds, 1973b), need only be reviewed briefly here. In 1964, a defensive and demand-making organization called FAFEG (Federação das Associações das Favelas da Guanabara) was founded. It held a "First Congress" in that year. In 1968, it held its Second Congress and was promptly crushed by the police forces of the military government. At the 1964 Congress, participants discussed rather specific favela problems—water, "urbanization," electricity, etc. In 1965, when I first attended FAFEG meetings and the radio hour of the FAFEG president, this was still the orientation. After the catastrophic rains of January, 1966, immediately followed by the calls of various "expert" elite bodies (see Leeds and Leeds, 1972) to remove favelas, FAFEG began to be more explicit in their attacks on the civil construction industry and other economic and political interests involved in the Industria das Favelas ('The Favela-Exploitation Industry' was meant, paralleling the "Industria das Sêcas" in the Brazilian Northeast—exploiting the victims of droughts). Still, however, the viewpoint was limited to favelas. After the repressive years of 1967 and 1968, FAFEG changed drastically. The documents and speeches of the Second Congress are phrased in *class* terms and in terms of *national*, other-class-generated problems such as the wage structure, inflation, the profit system, exploitation, and the like. There had emerged a clear conception of class solidarity reaching far beyond the interests of fragmentary housing-settlement areas which are, in fact, physico-social segments of a proletariat splintered partly by the very processes of coping with the urban milieu, its search for a more viable articulation with requirements and offerings of city living, and partly by deliberate action of the "upper" class.

Likewise of extreme importance to the themes of this paper is the fact that such settlements also display attitudes antagonistic to each other. If one recalls the above-mentioned kaleidoscopic locational aspects of settlement in the city, one understands also the fragmentation of proletarian or working-class solidarities by virtue of these attitudes. The occupational specialization of the conjunto, the separateness of location of the vilas, the patronalism operative in the parques proletários, the illegality and mythic criminality and marginality of the favela, and so on, all operate, each in its own way, to establish cellular identities, attached to the settlement area, at the expense of class identity as a wage-earning proletariat or an underpaid salariat. Conjunto construction, location of vilas, patronalism of parques, illegality of favelas, and the like, are aspects controlled by the society's strategic elites.

Most characteristic are the attitudes against the favelas, some of which I cited above, which pervade all classes and areas of the city. At the same time, many favela dwellers, especially in some of the more comfortable and evolved favelas, dispraise the parques, the poorer conjuntos, and especially the rooming houses abominated by all not living in them. The rooming house residents, on the other hand, say they would not live in favelas because the ambience is so bad (*pesado*, 'heavy') and the people bad people.

In other words, the low-income settlement areas, examined collectively, are, to a marked extent, organizationally centrifugal and are separated from or divided against each other. This divisiveness is strongly reinforced by the job discrimination practiced by employers against favela residents and by discriminations in services and prices; by the perjorative press treatment of favelas noted above; by the radio and television characterization of conditions in favelas, and so on. Since twenty to twenty-five percent of the total population or perhaps upwards of forty percent of the proletariat live in favelas, a major split in the proletariat is created on the grounds of settlement alone, a split and a divisiveness fostered by the nonproletarian classes in general and by the elites who control the communications system and job market in particular.

There is substantial evidence and some unequivocal proof that the physical splintering of the proletariat and lower salariat is in part intentional and often deliberately reinforced by fostering the antagonistic divisive attitudes, as, for example, by manipulation of the mass media. But much of the elites' divisive action appears not to be conscious, but, rather, occurs as an unintended consequence of their acts. For example, community development action such as that carried out by Acción in Venezuela and Lima or its Brazilian offshoot, Ação in Rio and São Paulo, by the Peace Corps, or, in Rio, by BEMDOC (Brasil-Estados Unidos Movimento de Desenvolvimento e Organização de Comunidade, an AID-sponsored community development program, run through the Guanabara State social welfare department; see Leeds and Leeds, 1972) tends to put favelas or barriadas or ranchos in competition with each other for the resources held by the community development agency: they work in their own interest instead of in the collective interest. Yet the agency looks to the improvement of both the individual settlement and, in the long run, the collectivity of settlements.[24] As another example, the conversion of an old building in a "good" neighborhood into a rooming house encysts the residents socially, whether or not such atomization was intended. Thus, the two immense rooming houses under the famous Morro do Pasmado in Rio, surrounded by Rio's elite Yacht Club, the National University, an important night club and movie house, and some upper-middle-income houses, are physically quite isolated from any other proletarian population. Together they comprise an enclave of perhaps 500 people which grows larger with the years as the landlords add new rental units to the building and its extensions up the hill. In passing, it is interesting to note that ads appear in the newspapers asking for capital to pool in rooming-house enterprises. Although, officially, this kind of enterprise is now illegal, it goes on *sub rosa*, creating, by the acts of the holders of capital, new isolated groupings of the proletariat.

Another example of such splitting is the construction of the vilas. The aim of division was at least in part deliberate and articulated, though only in private—to put the proletarians geographically out of range of the elites, on one hand, and to move large enclaves of them outside the city, separate from their former networks, neighborhoods, and communities which were sharply disrupted by the removals, on the other. The favela which used to exist on the Morro do Pasmado was torn untimely from whatever social, political, or economic ties it had with the surrounding sector of the city and put many kilometers from the center of town. All removals—whether of favelas, rooming houses, or what-not—whether for punitive reasons, for urban renewal, for public utility, for safety (real or alleged)—disrupt social networks and other links elaborated among the proletarian populations and contribute to the proletariat's atomization and divisiveness. Institutional features of divisiveness I shall return to below.

CONSTRAINTS ON CHOICE

The key constraint on choice of any given housing-settlement type is financial, whatever the state of the domestic cycle. It is not only the major constraint on specific individual choices but the one that allows no exit from the entire set of choices of proletarian arrangements for living.[25] In Brazil, today, a large proportion of the labor force officially receives only the minimum salary. A minimum income needed by a household to pay for rent, basic food supplies, clothing, transportation, and medical care comes to between 900 and 1200 new cruzeiros (3-4 minimum salaries). Perhaps a maximum of five to ten percent of proletarian households reach that level of income, the majority taking in between 300 and 500 new cruzeiros per month from wages and other sources.[26]

The results are clear. Such a wage system, with the income structure it entails, sets the parameters for the set of choices as a whole ('the choice set'). Though there is a small number of persons or households that escapes from the choice set, moving into a choice set with different parameters, yet probably an even larger number *enters* to circulate in the proletarian choice set, perhaps the lowest of the city's scale of sets, either because real wages decline since rises in absolute wages do not keep pace with rises in living costs, or because stress or disaster has pushed them out of the lower strata of the petite bourgeoisie, the self-employed, the petits bureaucrats, and the like.[27] The number of new households having to confront the choice set is also swelled by immigrants arriving from outside the city in search of employment opportunities in the wage-job market, a situation much more marked in Lima than in Rio since it concentrates a much greater proportion of the national labor market than does Rio and its growth on a large scale has been more recent. It should be noted that these immigrants become competitors in the job market, especially, supposedly,[28] for unskilled and low-skilled jobs. This competition, partly deliberately fomented by controllers of strategic resources and the job market and partly structurally induced, contributes to the fragmentation of the proletariat discussed above.

The wage-structure is maintained by national policy, national administrative acts, and national agencies, all controlled by national strategic elites. Most of the agencies have their local representations—offices, administrators, advisers, staff, and equipment—at least in the larger cities and administrative towns (*sedes de município*—'county seats'). All significant policy- and decision-making offices and administrative posts are held by elite members of the upper class[29] who are linked by blood, affinal, co-parentage, friendship, and other personal networks in bonds which create the class boundaries that exclude all members of the proletariat (see Leeds, 1957: chs. IV, V; 1964, 1967, 1973c).

Underlying the highly inequitable wage policy of countries like Brazil and Perú—the capitalist, semi-colonial dependencies of the great metropolitan capitalist countries—are the systems of capitalist-oriented private profit and private property. This is not the place to spell this out in detail; the argument has been made by others.[30]

What I wish to emphasize, here, however, is that this kind of dependent capitalist system determines a wage structure which necessarily involves proletarianization, or is indeed identical with it. Proletarianization is built into the capitalist system, as was pointed out well over a century ago, but it is even more strongly delineated, less alleviated by "affluence," less ameliorated by great masses of better-paid, highly skilled wage earners, less softened by opportunities for upward mobility, less responsive to political protest and electoral expression, and genenerally more repressive in the "underdeveloped," dependent societies than in the metropoles like Great Britain and the United States.

Insofar as proletarianization is attached to capitalism and to industrialism and insofar as it is intensified by action of the State, all three of which tend institutionally and operationally to be centered in cities, it is a peculiarly *city* phenomenon, even though its extension can be found in the agrarian sectors as well. In its mass housing and settlement aspect, it is intrinsically a part of the city in capitalistically structured societies. Insofar as housing, settlement, work, householding, and carrying out one's daily activities in the city are linked, proletarianization also involves the emergence of a *social* system or subsystem in a given city, complementing its role in the societal structure.

Since proletarianization results from the relationship with the owners and controllers of strategic resources, capital, and the State, it is, in fact, a single process which *necessarily* involves the evolution of complementary roles—a dialectic development. The complementary aspect of the process might be called "elitization," or the continuous construction of upper-class power, of self-identification, of boundary conditions to exclude the proletariat, and of the proletariat needed for its own maintenance and progress.

Put another way, the private-property and private-profit systems necessarily involve a process of complementary role set development—the evolution of the proletariats and the elites; and the city, *as an organization for production,* with all its productive apparatuses, is the primary locus of this process.

The structural underpinning of this process is the economic, social, and political exclusiveness of the elites. The elites in all these spheres evolve means for their own maintenance of which the wage-system already mentioned is perhaps the single most effective one. However, there are a large number of ancillary ones which operate together with the wage system to maintain the boundaries. In effect, they set the parameters within which the proletarian arrangements for living choices can be made.

In Rio, Lima,[31] and, in one way or another, other cities, such ancillary means include hiring and firing systems; special hiring deals; firing just before the time at which job tenure becomes obligatory, resulting in loss of accumulated retirement and pension benefits; legalized repressions of persons (if proletarian) not carrying official work cards or picked up in the streets without identification (even if they have this at home); rents and rent extortion such as double rents; low accessibility of skilled training; high cost of education at all levels, especially payments for uniforms, books, school supplies; usually, high cost of secondary education; legal reduction of wages in the form of sick-leave pay at seventy percent of minimum salary; nonpayment of benefits such as family allowance, overtime, and pay for unhealthy work; delayed payment of scheduled wage raises; housing-settlement division; breaking up of proletarian social networks by physical shifting of parts of the housing-settlement areas; partron-client relations which maintain separateness of the two classes and keep the proletarian client in a network of obligation and co-optation backed by threats of sanction such as the patron's *not* helping out in time of crisis; and so on and on.

The conjoint effect of all these is the class boundary I have been emphasizing, which itself operates as a constraint on the proletariat. With respect to the proletariat, I visualize one possible representation of this structure as involving a vast number of particles—individuals and households—in enormously varied motion, the state of which, at any given time, can only be measured statistically and whose characteristics are partly set by the elite actions which create the class boundary, and partly by the proletarian adaptation to the parameters within which they largely have to operate—set for them from outside by the elites. From this system, a few particles escape across the boundary. Others, which nearly leave the system or momentarily do so, are returned by the forces which set the parameters in the first place, while the mass of particles scarcely comes near the boundary at all.

ELITE CLEAVAGE AND COALITIONS WITH PROLETARIAN GROUPS

But, as always with social systems, the description is not so easy and does not end there. Given the capitalist system of private property, profit, and self-interest, it also follows that there is no single, common, corporate interest for the upper class as a whole or for any major part of it. The tendency is to split into ever-smaller divisions of interest, ultimately down to the individual, represented in the concept of "individualism" in Brazil and the United States and the idea of "the rugged individual" in the latter. These divisions of interest are competitive in self-aggrandizing and ego-centered ways.[32]

One can map out networks and groupings extended by single individuals in their own interest or by a member or members of a more or less stable group in the interest of both the group and its individual members when the interests are like or common (see MacIver and Page, 1949: 32). The groups themselves often have no intrinsic corporative foundation at all, or at best a rather tenuous one such as the egocentric kin ties characteristic of bilateral kinship systems such as those of Brazil, Perú, and the United States. Frequently, these semi-closed kinship networks or even personal nonkin networks are given a certain corporative formalization by creating an informal or formal charter, as, for the former, compadrazco ties and, for the latter, a corporation. Corporationalized kin networks or kin-plus-nonkin personal networks are ubiquitous among the Brazilian elites in the form of family banks, family construction companies, family industrial enterprises, family political parties.[33]

Both networks and groups compete in their struggle for the resources and rewards of the society which can be mobilized either through the economic system or through other systems which handle money and power, especially various branches of government. As will be shown, they also compete through the social system for resources whose locus is found in the proletariat but which are tactically useful in their internecine competition, for example, mass votes or (especially in Lima) cumulated savings as in popular building cooperatives. Insofar as the rewards vary in source, location, and size, and because they are so constantly and sharply competed for by the networks and groupings of the elites, the duration of these groupings is indeterminate and flexible. Persistence of the group is to be measured rather by persistence of the interest structure or, more fundamentally, by the duration of the resource, power, and policy situation lying behind the interests. Where such situations are rather jelled, as in Brazil and the United States today, the groups tend to last over relatively long periods, and the modes, directions, content, and structure of competition persist with them.

Either the resources themselves or the communications about them are located and coordinated in the cities, especially the larger ones. All the apparatuses for handling the resources, their coordination, communications, and also the paraphernalia for competing for the resources and the control of the coordination and communications tend, in capitalist society, to concentrate more and more in the city in order to cut costs, maximize benefits, and maximize power concentration. In terms of the *physical* aspect of the city, this entire *social* structure is laid out in the distribution of the apparatuses just mentioned, in the buildings which house them, and in the machinery (such as port equipment, road-building equipment, etc.) and infra-structure, such as streets, metros, airports, radio and television towers, which facilitate their use.

Another force for cleavage among the elites is immigration, especially of professional foreigners or Brazilian rural elites and professionals who enter the arena of operations of the already-present urban elites. Obviously they come in at a disadvantage since either they are not yet linked in at all or have very few ties. They therefore must compete all the harder to retain their status or to gain new status and new resources. They thus contribute to splitting the upper class into fragmentary elites.

Obviously, any elite group will gain advantage in the promotion of its interests by finding both financial and social support outside the resource domains already ordinarily accessible to it. This is done by entering into various kinds of "coalitions" with various solidary segments of the proletariat which are also working in their own interest by entering the coalition. These coalitions are, of course, even more evanescent than the coalitions among the elite groupings because they lack even the like interests characteristic of the elite parties to a coalition to hold them together. Their term is governed entirely by the extent to which both parties, and especially the elite, stand to gain: if one side no longer has any resource or reward to give, holds back in giving it, or makes overtures to other parties than the one they are in coalition with, the coalition breaks up. What is fascinating is, having discovered this aspect of urban social structure, to uncover the various situations, often not giving any 'clue as to the coalition interaction in their outward form in which coalitions between segments of both classes are occurring. Two examples of what I mean will suffice.

The Carnaval is not merely annual merry-making, but is a highly complex, perennial social structure which has been described elsewhere (Morocco, 1966). Suffice it here to say that in Rio exists a most elaborate relationship among agencies of State, especially the Departmamento de Turismo da Guanabara; large businesses, especially the Brahma Beer Company and some of the textile companies; major offices of the State such as the Secretariat of Social Welfare or even the governor; radio and television networks; important nightclubs; the phonograph record industry; the great "bankers" of the numbers racket, many of whom are major real estate owners; and the Carnaval groups themselves (see pp. 79-80 above, and note 21), especially the larger *escolas de samba* like Salgueiro, Portela, Mangueira, Império Serrano (the "Big Four") which are more or less attached to favelas or to specific proletarian neighborhoods, usually with important favelas nearby. A system of prizes given by the Departamento de Turismo is attached to this relationship and to competition among the schools at Carnaval time. The prizes involve very considerable sums of money. Major additional rewards flowing into the proletarian groups through the *escolas de samba* come from recording and television contracts and nightclub and other kinds of appearances.

One response to all this is the increasing commercialization (that is, attachment to and behavior like the values bought and sold in the capitalist market) of the Carnaval groups, a form of cooperation with the Departamento de Turismo, the beer and textile companies, and so forth, in the interest of promoting tourism, sales, consumption, or, generally, attending to the welfare of the elite-owned businesses and elite-controlled government which services the businesses.

From the point of view of the upper class as a whole, in addition to the business and income gains it may get from the Carnaval groups collectively, any given elite group may find it useful to work with a specific Carnaval group or set of such to work out deals of interest to both. Brahma, for example, has established a virtual monopoly of supply among the larger *escolas* by supplying hundreds of thousands of chairs and tables for their dance grounds which help attract both native and foreign tourists as well as members of the community and help sell more drinks to the advantage both of Brahma and the *escola de samba* which gets a few pennies from every bottle sold. Brahma thus has a monopoly in *escolas de samba* which may, at peak season, attract 30-50,000 people *a night,* each person drinking several bottles.

Much more important from our point of view, however, is that the great Carnaval groups provide large organizational nodes for political activity; for acquisition of an electorate by a politician or candidate, any one of whom is a representative of some elite fragment; for acquisition of financial resources cumulated by the Carnaval group or by some of its leading members through the group and through the *jogo do bicho,* the numbers game whose lotterylike gambling is participated in by at least half the population of the city to the great financial advantage of the bet-holders, the *banqueiros. Banqueiros* of the *jogo do bicho* and the samba group leaders often seem to reinforce each other with financial dealings at appropriate times. Some of these funds can be funnelled to the elites. It must be noted that the larger groups may have memberships or regular constituencies of about 5,000 people as represented by (a) attendance at the *ensaios* or 'practice dance sessions' almost nightly at the dance ground in the weeks before Carnaval, and (b) the number of people organized by the group in the choreography of the street presentation at Carnaval.

For the proletarian samba groups, the interest in the coalition is the payoffs—acquisition of a school or a water-system or a recreation space for the *escola de samba*, but usable by the community; getting a patron in the government who can try to funnel goods, services, jobs, or money to the favela; getting some pieces of legislation pushed through the state assembly (when it functions) for ends such as declaring some street, building, or area "of public utility," hence protected from removal by law, and so on. The samba groups continue to help deliver the vote as long as their man continues to deliver the goods.[34] Such coalitions can successfully maintain themselves against opposition, as represented, for example, by opposition candidates, for years.

Efforts at mobilizing support, at establishing ties toward a coalition, can be seen at almost any important *ensaio*. For example, we observed Governor Negrão de Lima and his secretary of social welfare at Mangueira one night; a deputy, a social scientist, and an ambassador at Unidos de Jacaré, on another; several well-known elite personnel at Salgueiro, on still another.[35]

The second example is that of favela associations. Not even the presence of FAFEG (see p. 81 above) prevented favela associations from tending to link with the extant public administrative bodies, overtly and covertly, to align themselves with one or another of the now legally "nonexistent" (or "ex" as the Brazilians would say), militarily suppressed political parties which operate underground (especially the PTB, the PSD, and the UDN) or their old coalitions (see E. Leeds, 1972). The old political parties, their divisions and coalitions, and the "sub-legendas" of 1968 and subsequently[36] themselves represent factions, maybe even *panelinhas* ('elite cliques,' see Leeds, 1964), within the upper class. Factions of the ex-PTB are operating in coalition with some of the favela associations with the aim of creating constituencies and followings which can be used in various ways, particularly in elections (if and when there are any) to gain maximum advantage for the party, especially under the restrictions imposed by the military government since 1965, or looking to the future when relatively "free" elections may be reinstated. They may also be used as groups to make public and private representation to government in such a way as to support this or that bureaucrat with whom they are in collusion. The bureaucrat returns this support by giving protection, security of tenure, goods, services, money, jobs. The politicking of these coalitions against each other in the favelas can be quite complex and cutthroat and involves efforts to get control of the favela associations, of the electricity commissions; to influence the social and soccer clubs, the churches, the recreational societies. Techniques range from flagrant manipulation of voting to complex deals among various groups, to promises by candidates and incumbents to do favors.[37] Probably parallel arrangements exist in the vilas, the conjuntos, the parques, and so on, though few data exist on this.

The result of this kind of coalition is the distribution throughout the city of a series of more or less parallel coalitions, jockeying for pre-eminence, control, leadership, and influence, but crossing *over* the elite-proletarian boundary. Other forms of such crossing over I have discussed elsewhere with specific reference to the Brazilian *oligarquias* (roughly speaking, 'situses'; see Leeds, 1964). These simply intensify the phenomenon of splits within both elites and proletariats and the competition among the coalitions.

Similar coalitions are to be found in Lima, although there appears to be no parallel to Rio's Carnaval groups there. The main proletarian solidary groups involved in such coalitions are (a) the barriada associations and/or block associations inside barriadas; (b) the cooperative building associations composed entirely of proletarian personnel; (c) the mutual building associations, more predominantly middle class, but with some working-class personnel, and, possibly, (d) regional associations. Specific groups from each of these categories become involved in elaborate negotiations with various bodies representing upper-class elites such as banks, government agencies, political office holders linked with political parties (when they were still overtly active, particularly APRA which had a large mass base in the industrial and agrarian proletariats but was not strong in the barriadas) competing with other office holders in other parties, bureaucratic offices, and, possibly, business firms such as construction goods companies. The bargaining power of the barriadas became very clear immediately after the military took over the government in 1968 because it had no clear constituency or backing. It immediately began to curry favor with the barriadas (promptly renamed *pueblos jóvenes*, 'new towns,' to wipe out the pejorative "barriada") by giving them improved services, extending roads and transportation, legalizing tenure and giving security of occupancy, giving out title, helping improve the infrastructure inside the barriadas, etc. They hoped, in turn, to be able to fuse them into the National System of Social Mobilization (SINAMOS) but the barriadas only fused insofar as was convenient to them and they continued to get rewards—and then resisted.

In sum, in both Rio and Lima, which I consider to be representative of a generic model of a class of cities and their social orders, one finds a process which divides elites from proletariats, continuously reinforces the boundary between them, and tends to generate a full-scale class organization in each. At the same time, the structure of the national economy and of the urban labor market in addition to deliberate action on the part of the elites tends to fragment the proletariats organizationally, a fact reflected in housing arrangements and in the proletariat's need to circulate among a set of housing-settlement types in order to maximize their ability to meet their goals within the narrow parameters allowed by the elites. Fragmentation is intensified by immigration. The upper class also tends to fragment because of the nature of capitalist enterprise itself and because of immigration. Its members are constantly in competition with each other, thus creating elites, that is, fragments of the class. In their competitive struggle, they seek support outside their usual sources of resources by turning to those fragments of the proletariat which can afford them resources usable in the struggle for power, wealth, and prestige. The proletarian fragments—especially their leadership—find it advantageous and convenient to enter into coalition with the elite fragments in order to pull resources from them with which they can (a) improve the life of the community and (b) solidify their own positions as leaders. In return, they deliver votes, constituencies, money, and possibly other values to the elites. The result is the linking of social groups, geographical areas, and institutions in the city into a complex social order which, to a marked degree, is coterminous with the physical city itself and represents a series of nodes, relationships among them, and multifarious exchanges based on the resources present in the city and impossible without them.

IMPLICATIONS FOR PLANNING

Put in other words, the physical city is, to a great degree, a time-linked crystallization of the *total* social order of the city—of the interactions and interests of elites *and* proletariats. The physical city, as seen on the ground, not on the planners' drawing board, is unintelligible without understanding the proletarianization process and proletarian action. Generally, certainly in capitalist societies if not more widely, proletarian process and action are either disregarded altogether, thought of with respect to specific characteristics, such as squatter settlements, as aberrations, or thought of only piecemeal, as with respect to favelas but not to other types of housing. Certainly, in Rio, most thought about the physical city has ranged between the first and second of these, while in Lima, till the last few years when it has gone much further (see Leeds, 1973b), it ranged between the second and third.

In consequence, planners, who virtually without exception are recruited from the elites, see the physical city in only a partial way. As elite personnel, they see the city as elite process. They see the future city for which planning is to be done in terms of the extrapolated future of the upper class or, more likely, those of its subsegments more closely linked with the professions and with government. Since most of them see the city only partially, they necessarily plan partially.

Planning partially means that the planning is only for some of the social roles of the city. Since the social order of the city *inherently* involves interactions with, and action by, the part(s) *not* planned for, it is necessarily the case that processes, events, and situations immediately linked with the city-as-a-social-process are not accounted for in the plans. At very worst, the accounted for and the nonaccounted for are in direct conflictual contradiction and lead to intensified social struggle and deteriorating cityscapes—as in the case of Rio today (see Leeds, 1973b) and possibly major North American cities like Washington and New York. At best, there may be an accidental coincidence of interests for a short term, as perhaps in the case of Lima, where still today, after continuous talk since the 1968 takeover of instituting an urban reform, none yet exists.

In general, then, any urban planning which does not take account of the entire social order of the city is bound to fail, just as urban plans have, in part or whole, continually failed. In societies sharply divided along class lines, where official positions such as those of planners are filled only by members of one class, the failures are likely to be of even greater magnitude—i.e., the case of Brasília (Epstein, 1973). The implication would appear to be that successful urban planning requires the elimination of class. I tend to think that this, too, would be an overly optimistic view. The problem is that a plan foresees only a range of possibilities in the future development and then only for a limited time. Once the plan is put into effect, it *literally* concretizes the state of knowledge, the conception of the possibilities, and the form of social organization that existed at the time of planning or immediately after it. But the dialectics of change do not necessarily follow the planners' vision and the unanticipated and unforeseen occur—the "over"growth of Moscow, in a supposedly classless society, is a case in point (Hall, 1966: chapter on Moscow). Possibly we shall have to come to the point of view that the social process is *itself* the planning process.

NOTES

1. These are listed in the order of my intimacy of acquaintance either by virtue of field work, extensive visits, or intensive review of the literature. I have also visited in a number of other cities, such as Salvador, Brasil, San Juan, P.R., Ciudad Guyana, Belo Horizonte, São Paulo, Curitiba, Recife, sufficiently to have a more or less detailed, if somewhat superficial, picture of each.

2. Each of the folk terms is italicized in its first usage; if used extensively in the paper, it is subsequently treated as an English word. Extensive definition and discussion of favelas appears in Leeds (1969) and will not be repeated here.

3. For documentation of such views, see Leeds and Leeds (1972), especially the appendices.

4. Ibid., also in Leeds (1969, 1970 [with E. Leeds], 1971, 1973b).

5. See Lewis (1959 and others); Patch (1961); Salmen (1971); Azevedo (ca. 1891); Eckstein (1972); Banco Obrero (1959).

6. This seems clear from a number of Oscar Lewis's writings—e.g., Lewis (1969).

7. A related type is the *cortiço,* now almost extinct, discussed later in the text. Another still found in both Rio and Lima is the *quinta,* several attached small houses or large apartments around a central garden space or yard.

8. The term *vecindad* means 'neighborhood' but is used in Lewis's works to refer to several different kinds of housing-settlement types. The one he gives the greatest amount of data on, by far, is the type described in the text. See Lewis (1959, 1969).

9. My photographs of callejones in Lima and my visits to rooming houses and avenidas in Rio, poorly documented photographically, both indicate much economic activity in these places: shops, repair shops, services, small industries like shoemakers and printers, and so on. I think that Patch's description (1961) was either distorted or of an atypical callejón. Lewis's descriptions tend to overplay the dramatic, the sorrowful, the compassion-arousing, and underplay the economy and social structures of the places he describes, but even in his sketchy references and in the textual material one finds indications of such internal economies but not enough to estimate their importance quantitatively.

10. For details on rooming houses, see Salmen (1971); average household sizes for the cortiços were worked out from statistics gotten in a survey of cortiços made by two students at the National Museum, Department of Anthropology, Rio. Virtually all favela demographic statistics show the 4.6-4.7 figures. The rooming house figure is derived from a survey of two rooming houses made by two other anthropology students at the Museum, and from Salmen (1971: 156).

11. Caldas de Moura (1969); she, too, was a student of anthropology at the Museum.

12. There are statistics for tugurios in general but they do not distinguish types other than squatter settlements as opposed to the rest. Unless one has recognized that there is a significance to the types—that is, differentiated strategies for living—there is no reason to give differential statistics for them.

13. See, in this connection, Mangin (1963); Turner (1963, 1968, 1969, 1970); Uzzell (1972).

14. These figures may seem high. However, aside from the fact that the squatter settlements in most cities grow at a faster rate than the city as a whole and much faster than the nonsquatter parts of the city, the census figures almost always underestimate the number of residents in squatments, perhaps because household-to-household censusing is most difficult for other than obsessive anthropologists, perhaps because mapping such places to do either house-to-house or sample censusing is often excessively difficult; perhaps because it is sometimes politically desirable to underplay the size of these populations. However, if one adds the estimates averaged from various sources, checks them against one's own judgment visually, the higher figures seem more than reasonable. This sort of estimating is given more support by its correspondence to figures derived for squatments by very carefully done household-to-household surveys.

15. These are known in Rio as "JKs". A pun is involved: J.K. are the initials of Juscelino Kubitschek, who was trying to build Brazil in a hurry with, sometimes, large but jerrybuilt results; they also stand for *"janela e kitchinette"*—"window and kitchenette"— which ironically described the size and facilities of the apartments. The most famous (or infamous) is known as Barrata Ribeiro 200—the street address of a building containing several hundreds of such apartments, extreme density of occupation, a constant stream of prostitutes, pimps, "hairdressers," gamblers, and policemen in chase of one or another. The place was constantly under surveillance by the police and by the building superintendent who was in the pay of the police. These data are derived from a study carried out by two students of the anthropology department at the National Museum, 1969.

16. The original model is given in full in Leeds (1973a [written in 1964]). It still presupposes that favelas are inhabited by *"favelados"*—'the favelaized' with the sense of a permanent state of being—rather than by favela residents—i.e., persons most of whom live in favelas by choice in working out life strategies (see Leeds, 1973b). When the choice and strategy aspects are at last recognized, one must ask where residents come *from* in moving to the favela. The answer is: mostly from other types of housing-settlement in the city. This is as true for Lima as for Rio, though in both places the pattern evolves with the evolution of the total residential structure of the city (see Turner's works cited above).

17. In a very large sample of intake interviews at the Foster Parents Plan in Niterói, the capital of the State of Rio de Janeiro which neighbors on the city of Rio and the State of

Guanabara, we found that, at the time of the first interviews of these very low-income cases, the average percentage of household incomes spent on food was about seventy percent. The other thirty percent *had* to be spent on clothing, transportation, and medicines. The plan gave some help both in kind and in cash up to a moderate fraction of the household income at the time of the first interview. The second interviews of the same respondents showed that expenditure for food had gone up to about seventy-five percent, that is, that all the additional income had gone for food, which had been at an absolute minimum before. No additional expenditures to speak of were made for the other needs.

18. The discussion here refers to the situation in Rio before the massive favela removals began in 1968. Up to that time, favelas displayed what might be called a "natural" distribution—that is, one that reflected the locational needs of the original settlers and subsequent immigrants. The forced removals, of course, disturb this system drastically, spewing people to the distant edges of the city far from work, hospitals, schools, recreation areas, kin and friends, and so forth.

19. Although this example is hypothetical, it is a composite constructed from a number of known cases.

20. The problem of the sociological structure of the labor market is discussed in Leeds (Ms. a).

21. The names of Carnaval groups clearly indicate this: Grémio Recreativo Paraíso de Tuiutí (Recreational Club, Paradise of Tuiutí [a favela]), which I had continuous contact with during my residence there; Unidos do Jacaré (The United Ones—referring to two or three smaller prior groups as well as its own personnel—of [favela] Jacaré [zinho]), with which I was also associated and with which two close colleagues danced; Académicos de Salgueiro (Academics of the [favela] Salguerio); Império Serrano (The Hill Top [favela] Empire); Mangueira (Mango Tree [favela])—which (except the first two) compete for national fame, recognition, honors, tours, etc., at every Carnaval. Their fortunes, successes, and failures, their politicking inside and outside the favelas, their relation to other social and political groups inside and outside the settlements, are closely followed by large numbers of the local populations. Similar groups, if less famous, are found in the parques, the vilas, the conjuntos, and elsewhere, and of course in other cities, the most famous being in Recife, a center of diffusion of nationally popular dances like the *baião* and *frevo*.

22. The various kinds of Carnaval groups, the soccer clubs, the religious congregations of different sects, and others, all belong to state-level federations and national-level confederations (although these tend to be fictions), all in accordance with Brazilian civil law of syndical organization.

23. See Leeds and Leeds (1970). Despite difficulties in assessing the vote because of peculiarities of voter-registration, there is no doubt whatsoever about the nature of the vote; see text above. See also in ibid. the poem sung by some little girls skipping rope in the favela, given at the end of that text.

24. It should in justice be noted here that some members of the elite have, on what appears to be purely ideological grounds, actually contributed to the collective organization of the proletariat by means of linking favelas or their leaders. One case is that of José Arthur Rios, discussed in full in Leeds and Leeds (1972), who brought favela leaders together in the so-called "Operação Mutirão" or 'Operation Workbee'—collectively to better their condition, receive legal information and help, material aid, guidance in organization. There is no evidence, in my opinion, that Rios was attempting to create a constituency either for himself and certainly not for Governor Lacerda, who needed at the time a popular base and who, when he got access to large sums of money through the AID-State of Guanabara Wheat Fund agreement in 1962, no longer needed an organized populist mass and fired Rios. Rios's work may have laid the foundation for the later development of FAFEG, although there is no direct connection between the two, the latter having appeared a full two years after Rios's program ended abruptly (see Schmitter, 1971: 208, to the contrary). I am certain

Schmitter is wrong, since I was at meetings of both the Operação Mutirão in 1961 and 1962 and of the FAFEG in 1965-1966. Rios continued to do the type of work he had done in 1961-1962 and in 1968-1969 in Bahia, where he was also eventually pushed out by the elites not wanting a ceding of power or control to favela residents.

25. This situation is quite as true for the United States as it is for Brazil or any other capitalist society. However, in the United States, it is more marked as a total phenomenon and made more complex by the elaborate internal stratification of the proletariat based on the ranges of skills required in the U.S. labor market, the grading of pay in accordance with skill, the attachment of racial criteria to low skill, and the general relatively higher cost of living. The first three of these do not apply in Brazil or Perú to anywhere near so significant an extent.

26. These figures are based on 1968 wages and prices but corrected for increases that have occurred in both since then and checked against figures in Salmen (1971) and Rush (1974), who, in 1973, did a summer's field work surveying a sample of persons removed from favelas. It must be recalled, in the latter case, that the lowest-income people do not get sent to the conjuntos at all, so Rush's figures are rather higher than mine.

27. For a discussion of stress, see Leeds and Leeds (1970: 243-248), with reference to proletarian populations; the same principles apply to the strata listed in the text.

28. I say "supposedly" because, in view of ethnographic evidence of various sorts, including a number of interviews with factory administrative personnel I carried out in 1968, it is not at all clear that much of the labor-intensive job market *needs* high skills; it is not clear that the skills learned in towns, villages, and on farms, which the migrants bring with them are *not* the skills most usually needed (e.g., construction and service skills); it is, further, *not* clear that employers *actually* want skilled workers because, given the technical uniqueness of each plant, the lack of other, similar plants, and the absence of standardization among Brazilian industrial installations, they must train and retrain their workers to the unique and specific technical requirements of the specific jobs, fitting into the usually unique arrangements of the specialties in each factory. The evidence suggests, on the contrary, that "unskilledness" is a rhetorical device, useful for depressing wages, maintaining a high level of competition among workers, and co-opting a few workers into clientage obligations by "generously" agreeing to give them in-house training. My evidence indicates that this is the way the system *works, not* that it is consciously organized and manipulated in this form by the elites. In any case, the procedure is a distancing one—contributing to the proletarianization and the maintenance of class boundaries. Incidentally, it is the case in the United States—contrary to much of the discussion among academics about credentialism, the need for education to train for skill, and a number of related topics—that a great part of the training for skilled jobs takes place on the job. Anyone who has worked in a factory and interviewed skilled factory workers, both of which I have done, knows this. This disagreement between how the system works and how it is supposed to work—also a difference in class views of the system—raises interesting questions and perspectives—e.g., as question: what, ideologically and socially, is the *function* of the academicians' misconception?; e.g., as perspective: even if Negroes and other ethnic minorities get credentials for jobs, the system operates to nullify them even where they are actually or supposedly being enforced by federal supervision against discrimination in the job market.

29. I have not here tried to sort out terminological problems and use 'upper class,' 'capitalist class,' or 'elites' loosely. I have discussed in the places listed in the text the foundations of the class boundary in Brazil and refer here to the aggregates there described. I think the meaning in the present context is sufficiently clear. 'Elites' in the plural refers either collectively to the upper, power-controlling ranks of the "upper class" or to a series of largely informal groups within that class who control the major resources of power; the context makes clear which usage is involved.

30. There is a large literature on dependency, most of it starting from Frank (1967, or

earlier versions of that work). Major writers have included Aníbal Quijano, Fernando Henrique Cardoso, Osvaldo Sunkel, Stanley and Barbara Stein, and a host of others. See, also, my own writings (1969; 1973b; Ms. b).

31. The picture given here for Rio is parallelled by data given in Uzzell (1972) for Lima.

32. It was notable that social workers working in various agencies, other professionals in other agencies, and even personnel at the universities–all of the "upper classes" in the sense discussed in note 29–constantly uttered the phrase "há uma falta de coleguismo aquí" ('there is a lack of colleaguism here') about their agency or work situation. It was always said with the sense that they thought there *ought* to be a collective sentiment in view of what they were doing and the aims of the agency, but that the reality was of competition and invidious backbiting among the colleagues.

33. See Leeds (1964). The interview with multiple-job holders of the elites carried out for this work made these phenomena quite clear. One interview was with a politician-industrialist-land speculator from a small Northeastern state–a classic example of *coronelismo* (see Leal, 1948) including a two-"party" system consisting of two large family networks competing with each other and trading off political rewards.

34. This was the case with the Geraldo Moreira who held various offices in the Federal District, especially *vereador* ('assemblyman'); see Leeds (1972: 50-52).

35. Each year, the *escola de samba* must choose which of several songs written by its "composers' wing" will be the theme song, marching down the avenue. The selection is carried out by a board chosen for that purpose which meets one night about six weeks before Carnaval and judges the presentation of the various songs. In the cases of the big *escolas*, nationally eminent people are asked to, and do indeed, serve–e.g., the world-famous novelist Jorge Amado, who controls (or controlled before 1964) a range of patronage in the arts which is linked with ambassadorial posts or cultural attachéships and the like. Persons of like eminence in other fields are also sought.

36. The old parties attempted to get the military government to recognize interest groups within the two-party system under the rubric of *"sub-legendas";* they were essentially the old parties attempting to regroup.

37. I give three examples all from one favela sufficiently large (two percent of the population of Rio) critically to affect the outcomes of elections in its electoral district and even in the state as a whole. First, from about 1965 on, it had a Light Commission (Commissão da Luz; LC) in the favela articulated with and recognized officially by the State Light Commission (Commissão Estadual de Energia; CEE) which created such LCs in a number of favelas over the years, starting about 1964-1965. The LC was responsible for organizing a system of electricity delivery participated in by the entire favela, often at the expense of private owners of electric supply systems used exploitatively for personal aggrandizement. In a favela of several 10,000s of people, such as this one, very large sums of money are involved from bill collections from consumers; contact with consumers also allows for the extension of patronage networks by the Light Commissioners' doing a consumer a favor (e.g., reducing installation costs). The LC was originally under the control of a favela resident closely linked with the parish priest, who had established a large church and social center in the favela, and both with the UDN through a number and hierarchy of ties. The CEE was also originally in UDN hands until the election of October 1965 brought the PSD-PTB coalition into the state patronage controlling offices. Control of the CEE, even though certain persons in the central office were retained from the previous administration, passed to the PTB, but the favela LC was still in the hands of the UDN faction. The CEE rules required periodic elections, and one came due in the favela a few months after the state election. The CEE sent in election supervisors, one of whose duties was to instruct voters unsure of procedures how to vote–a majority of them. Instructions were given in such a way as to indicate to the voter how to vote for the PTB candidates who, not surprisingly, won handily.

Second, the new LC commissioners were closely linked with or identical to the PTB clique in the favela who had at times had control of, or a strong influence in, the favela's various residents' associations (never very viable in this favela and, by CEE rules, mutually exclusive with the LC—a deliberate divide-and-rule technique on CEE's part as a means of splitting potential proletarian organization). These men appeared on the night of the *seleção* (see note 35) of the rather large, but not first rank, *escola de samba* of this favela in the company of Lutero Vargas, Getúlio Vargas's son and one of the leaders of the left wing of the PTB, who was hopeful of becoming a candidate for federal deputy (before the military government disqualified him). He addressed the very large assembly which included the selection board (of some local eminence) and about 400-500 residents joined for this important occasion. He spoke in standard populist rhetoric of the needs of the favela people, the right to self-determination of the favela which was no longer a favela but a "neighborhood" (*bairro*, a general theme song of the residents), of his desire to help the *bairro* and its associations to improve their conditions, etc., obviously attempting to win the loyalty of the *escola*.

Third, a small *escola* in a back part of the same favela offered a ceremonial dinner to which a variety of people of some importance in the favela were invited, partly to help it recapture its image and improve its fortunes again. The president of the *escola* notified a state deputy, also invited to the dinner. The *escola* had apparently been in decline, its president was elderly, and it was overshadowed by the rise of the one discussed above—the only persons who came were the faithful anthropologist and a Peace Corps volunteer. However, the deputy—expecting a crowd of favela influentials—also showed up with an extra-favela sidekick (probably a *cabo eleitoral,* or 'electoral captain'; see E. Leeds, 1972: 24-26), in the hope of making political tradeoffs in some form of coalition and finding a *curral eleitoral,* or 'voting herd,' through the influentials.

REFERENCES

AZEVEDO, A. (ca. 1891) O cortiço. São Paulo: Martins (1965). (A novel)

Banco Obrero (1959) Proyecto de evaluación de los superbloques. Caracas: Centro Interamericano de Vivienda, for the Banco Obrero de Venezuela.

CALDAS DE MOURA, M. F. (1969) "Implicações políticas na formação e desenvolvimento de um núcleo habitacional para o operariado." Rio: Museu Nacional, Programa de Pósgraduação em Antropología Social. (unpublished)

ECKSTEIN, S. (1972) "The poverty of revolution: a study of social, economic, and political inequality in a center city area, a squatter settlement, and a low-cost housing project in Mexico City." Ph.D. dissertation. Columbia University.

EPSTEIN, D. (1973) Brasília, Plan and Reality: A Study of Planned and Spontaneous Urban Settlement. Berkeley and Los Angeles: University of California Press.

FRANK, A. G. (1967) Capitalism and Underdevelopment in Latin America: Historical Studies of Chile and Brazil. New York: Monthly Review Press.

HALL, P. (1966) The World Cities. New York: McGraw-Hill.

LEAL, V. N. (1948) Coronelismo, enxada e voto: o município e o regime representativo no Brasil. Rio de Janeiro.

LEEDS, A. (Ms. a) "The adaptation of Mexican-Texans to external constraints: San Antonio and other cases." Presented at the annual meeting of the Rocky Mountain Social Science Association, May 1969.

——— (Ms. b) "The metropole, the squatment, and the slum: dependency and capitalism." Presented at the Conference on Dependency in Latin America, University of California, Lake Arrowhead, May 1971.

――― (1973a) "Locality power vs. supra-local power institutions," pp. 15-42 in A. Southall (ed.) Urban Anthropology: Cross-Cultural Studies of Urbanization. New York: Oxford University Press.

――― (1973b) "Economic-social changes and the future of the middle class," pp. 48-72 in Proceedings of the Experts Conference on Latin America and the Future of Its Jewish Communities. London: Institute of Jewish Affairs.

――― (1973c) "Political, economic, and social effects of producer- and consumer-orientations toward housing in Brazil and Perú: a systems analysis," pp. 181-215 in Volume 3 of F. Rabinovitz and F. Trueblood (eds.) Latin American Urban Research, Beverly Hills: Sage.

――― (1971) "The culture of poverty concept: conceptual, logical, and empirical problems, with perspectives from Brazil and Perú," pp. 226-284 in E. Leacock (ed.) The Culture of Poverty: A Critique. New York: Simon & Schuster.

――― (1969) "The significant variables determining the character of squatter settlements." América Latina 12, 3: 44-86.

――― (1967) "Some problems in the analysis of class and the social order," pp. 327-361 in A. Leeds (ed.) Social Structure, Stratification, and Mobility. Washington, D.C.: Pan American Union.

――― (1964) "Brazilian careers and social structure: an evolutionary model and case history." American Anthropologist 66, 6: 1321-1347.

――― (1957) Economic Cycles in Brazil: The Persistence of a Total Culture Pattern; Cacao and Other Cases. Ann Arbor: University Microfilms.

――― and E. LEEDS (1970) "Brazil and the myth of urban rurality: urban experience, work, and values in squatments of Rio de Janeiro and Lima," pp. 229-272, 277-285 in A. J. Field (ed.) City and Country in the Third World: Issues in the Modernization of Latin America. Cambridge: Schenkman.

LEEDS, E. (1972) "Forms of 'squatment' political organization: the politics of control in Brazil." M.A. thesis, University of Texas, Austin. (unpublished)

――― and A. LEEDS (1972) "Favelas and polity, the continuity of the structure of social control." LADAC Occasional Papers, Series 2, No. 5. Austin: University of Texas, Institute of Latin American Studies. (mimeo)

LEWIS, O. (1969) A Death in the Sánchez Family. New York: Random House-Vintage.

――― (1959) Five Families: Mexican Case Studies in the Culture of Poverty. New York: Basic Books.

MacIVER, R. M. and C. H. PAGE (1949) Society: An Introductory Analysis. New York: Rinehart.

MANGIN, W. (1963) "Urbanization case history in Perú." Architectural Design (August): 365-370.

MOROCCO, D. (1966) "Carnaval groups: maintainers and intensifiers of the favela phenomenon in Rio de Janeiro." Presented at the International Congress of Americanists, Mar del Plata.

PATCH, R. W. (1961) "Life in a callejón: a study of urban disorganization." American Universities Field Staff Reports, West Coast South America Series 8, 6.

RUSH, B. S. (1974) "From favela to conjunto: the experience of squatters removed to low-cost housing in Rio de Janeiro, Brazil." B.A. honors essay. Harvard College. (xerox)

SALMEN, L. F. (1971) "The casas de cômodos of Rio de Janeiro: a study of the occupations and accommodations of inner-city slums and a comparison of their characteristics with favelas." Ann Arbor: University Microfilm.

SCHMITTER, P. C. (1971) Interest, Conflict, and Political Change in Brazil. Stanford: Stanford University Press.

TURNER, J.F.C. (1970) "Squatter settlements in developing countries," in D. P. Moynihan (ed.) Toward a National Urban Policy. New York: Basic Books.

––– (1969) "Cuevas, El Ermitaño, El Agustino, Mendocita, Mariano Melgar," pp. 131-214 in H. Caminos et al., Urban Dwelling Environments: An Elementary Survey of Settlements for the Study of Design Determinants. Cambridge, Mass.: MIT Press.

––– (1968) "Uncontrolled urban settlement: problems and policies." International Social Development Review 1: 107-130.

––– (1963) "Dwelling resources in South America: urbanization case study in Perú." Architectural Design (August): 360-393.

UZZELL, J. D. (1972) "Bound for places I'm not known to: adaptation of migrants and residence in four irregular settlements in Lima, Perú." Ph.D. dissertation. University of Texas, Austin.

LISA REDFIELD PEATTIE is Professor of Urban Studies and Anthropology at the Massachusetts Institute of Technology. She received her Ph.D. in social anthropology from the University of Chicago, and has done field work among the Fox Indians of Iowa, in New York City schools, and in Venezuela, where she was associated with the MIT-Harvard Joint Center for Urban Studies Project in Ciudad Guayana. She is currently participating in a comparative study of economic dualism and sources of inequality in advanced industrial and developing nations. Her publications include *The View from the Barrio* (University of Michigan Press, 1968); "Reflections on Advocacy Planning" (*Journal of the American Institute of Planners*, March 1968); "Structural Parameters of Emerging Life Styles in Venezuela," in E. Leacock (ed.) *The Culture of Poverty: A Critique* (Simon and Schuster, 1971); and "Public Housing: Urban Slums under Public Management," in Peter Orleans and William Ellis (eds.) *Race, Change, and Urban Society* (Sage Publications, 1971).

Chapter 4

THE CONCEPT OF "MARGINALITY" AS
APPLIED TO SQUATTER SETTLEMENTS

LISA R. PEATTIE

The words we use are important, for they represent and shape the forms of thought, which is what we are all about as craftsmen in social science. When we get the wrong words I think our thought tends to take the wrong slope and may run right off into a hole in the ground. So it may be worthwhile to comment on a word which often comes into discussions of social and cultural processes in the developing nations, and which I think is a not-useful word. The word is "marginality," as applied to squatter settlements and/or technically unskilled poor people in cities.

In a recent study, otherwise a valuable monograph, this way of thinking about the situation is rather neatly summarized as follows:

> In Latin America, the growing numbers of unskilled, semi-employed and abysmally poor urbanites are often called the "marginals." The term is apt. The people to whom it is applied are economically marginal, in that they contribute little to and benefit little from production and economic growth. Their social status is low, and they are excluded from the formal organizations and associations and the informal and private webs of contacts which constitute the urban social structure. To the extent that they are rural in origin, they may also be culturally marginal, clinging to customs, manners, dress, speech and values which contrast with accepted urban patterns. They lack ties to or influence on the established political institutions. Many are marginal in a literal geographic sense, living in squatter settlements on the fringes of the cities [Nelson, 1969:5].

There are evident in this passage, as in other writings which use the word, two overlapping but at the same time distinguishable meanings. There are said to be "marginal people," and there are said to be "marginal settlements." The word is used to apply to people in cities who are unskilled, of the lowest social class, and it is also used to apply to those neighborhoods which are a conspicuous feature of cities in most of the developing world, called in Latin America *barriadas, villas miserias, favelas, colonias proletarias, ranchos* or *barrios.*

While the concept of "marginality" as it has been used most generally among sociologists probably goes back to Robert Park's (1928: 892) notion of the "marginal man" as a "cultural hybrid . . . a man on the margin of two cultures and two societies" its usage in Latin American studies has been, to a degree, historically independent. According to Gino Germani, who has written perceptively on the "marginality" concept, the term first began to be applied to settlements and was later extended to the people who inhabited those settlements.

> In Latin America the term "marginality" began to be used principally with reference to urban ecological characteristics, that is to say, to the sector of the population segregated into areas of improvised dwellings on illegally occupied land. From this point it was extended to the conditions of work and the level of life of this sector of the population. Then its marginality was perceived both in relationship to the socio-economic system of production and to the regular system of consumption of goods and services. Simultaneously it was noticed that this state of marginality included other essential aspects like political and union participation, formal and informal participation and in general its absence or exclusion from decision making whether at the level of the local community, the situation in work, or in the order of broader state and national structures and institutions. At the same time many noted that these sectors differed in a manner no less pronounced with respect to many aspects of national culture (taking as a base the patterns of the dominant centers and of the ruling and or fully participating groups) [Germani, 1972: 5; translation mine].

The two senses of "marginality" are of course interconnected. To speak of "marginal communities which are physically part of the city but which in many ways are not integrated socially, politically or economically into the life of the city" (Bamberger, 1970) is to see the residents of such communities as people who are not integrated socially, politically or economically into the life of the city, and who therefore come to manifest, or persist in manifesting, a variant subculture. To what extent is this view borne out by the facts? To what extent is it appropriate to think of squatter settlements as "marginal communities," and their residents as persons "on the margin of two cultures and two societies? "

In considering these issues, I shall draw both on the literature on Latin American squatter settlements generally, and on my own fieldwork in one such neighborhood in a developing city in Venezuela.[1]

In the first place, it turns out that the squatter settlements are not characteristically marginal in the sense of being environmental way-stations on the way in from rural areas to city. "As a general pattern," says Mangin (1967: 68), "the majority of residents of a settlement have been born in the provinces and have migrated from farms or small towns," but studies in Lima, Mexico City, Guatemala City, Bogotá, Barranquilla, Panama City, Montevideo, Rio, and in Venezuela have all dispelled the myth of people coming down from the hills and forming squatter settlements. John Turner (1969) has shown why, indeed, the physically marginal neighborhood is in fact unsuitable for people just arrived in town who need most of all to be near the jobs and who, in Latin America as in our own history, thus settle in the more developed parts of the city. Squatter settlements are more characteristically places for what Turner calls "consolidation"; places where people who have gotten an economic toehold can build themselves a permanent base in the form of a house of their own. In the city being developed in the Venezuelan interior by the Corporation Venezolana de Guayana, where I lived for some time, the planners, caught up in the myth of squatter settlements as areas of first settlement for rural migrants to town, laid out areas for the building of ranchos and called them "reception areas." Ranchos were built there, all right, but not by people who had just come to the city; indeed, the rather complex bureaucratic procedures for obtaining one of these lots ensured that incoming migrants were settling all over the city, except for these so-called "reception areas."

To what extent is it true that the residents of these settlements "contribute little to and benefit little from production and economic growth"? The very writer quoted earlier (Bamberger, 1970) as referring to "marginal communities . . . which in many ways are not integrated . . . into the life of the city" goes on to estimate that the purchasing power of the barrios in Caracas is "on the order of $200,000,000 a month." He adds that the "shanty town also provides the major source of labor for much of the city's industry and through not having to pay rent, the cost of living and, as a consequence, the cost of labor is kept down." The building of squatter housing—and such ancillary services as water lines, sewers, school buildings—is in itself a major economic input to a capital-short developing economy; it is estimated that in Caracas "the urban squatters have invested over $100,000,000 during the last twenty years in the construction of more than 125,000 houses. In addition they have built roads and water systems, installed electric lights and built schools" (Bamberger, 1970). A study in Bogota calculates the formation of capital only in dwellings in squatter and "pirate urbanization" settlements as equal to $146 million (Depto. Nacional de Planeación, 1972: 80).

It is true that unemployment rates may be high in the squatter settlements although not necessarily higher than in the central city. My little barrio, for example, at the time I censused it in 1963 had a third of adult males out of work. But the situation locally was not strikingly different from that in the city as a whole, and indeed nationally. Furthermore, my neighbors, even unemployed, were definitely in the labor market and very aware of their potential benefit from and commitment to economic growth. "Industry is the future of the worker," people said to me repeatedly. Most of the employed persons in my barrio were employed outside the barrio itself, the largest group in the new steel mill; and while I do not have figures for other barrios or other cities, I believe that generally it will be found that the squatters are part of a city or national-scale economy.

This is not to say that there may not be, in such settlements, also a more local and less monetized economy. There is likely to be a little more production for use than in the higher-income parts of town; some families will keep chickens or grow a few vegetables, and people will to some extent do their own house-building—although to an extent not generally realized, "squatter" housing is built by paid masons. In squatter settlements, as among other groups of people with low and intermittent monetary incomes, networks of mutual help develop, often of kin, within which goods and services may be exchanged outside the framework of the market.

But this "secondary economy" is, I believe, definitely a subsidiary to the general monetized economy. Although good studies of barrio economics are lacking—and much needed—the evidence in the literature and my own experience in Venezuela would suggest that even the limited part of barrio economic life which lies outside the regular market economy is quite dependent on the inflow of money represented by the wages of those employed in the "modern sector." It is these wages which are redistributed through the kinship networks, which become the payments for purchases at the neighborhood stores, and which form the capital on which local businesses are founded.

My little barrio included a substantial economic range, from female-headed families living from hand to mouth on occasional earned income and "help" from relatives and neighbors to a nurse at the social security hospital and a bookkeeper who drove his new car to work every day. One could argue that this was a result of the general shortage of housing and transitional character of institutions in a new and rapidly growing city, but there is evidence from studies elsewhere that squatter settlements are seldom one-class communities (see Mangin, 1967). It follows from this that relationships between the inhabitants of such settlements and the rest of the society vary substantially between families, and that for some, ties to "the outside" are likely to be rather more important than those to their immediate neighbors.

The people of the barrios are not particularly marginal to urban life in a cultural sense. Their clothing is urban in style; women's hairstyles follow the trends set in New York. Because ranchos are small and often built of materials like earth and bamboo, people sometimes think of them as rural in style. In fact, and perhaps remarkably, their style tends to be poor people's urban, for the traditional Venezuelan rural house with its semi-open front porch is seen only occasionally in the barrio. The people in my barrio certainly did not participate in some of the cultural life of the town; they were not members of the Rotary Club or the Chamber of Commerce; they were never seen at the Club Español, a social center for the local commercial elite, nor at the Country Club, where management from the big companies went with their families to use the swimming pool and relax together. They were not even very likely to attend services in the Catholic Church. But they shopped in the stores and market in town (one of my neighbors who tried to start a small meat business at home went broke, unable to meet the central stores' competition); they attended movies; they used the hospitals, they took their grievances and legal business to the municipal offices; they visited friends in other parts of the city. A study of the way that different sorts of people in the city saw their environment showed what was to the planners a strange phenomenon: "The lower-income groups mentioned more of the city than the educated elite, who mentioned little beyond their own residential 'ghetto' " (Appleyard, 1969: 430).

Not all children attended school regularly, but there was a general and high commitment to the value of formal education. Through newspapers, and even more through radio, my neighbors kept track of news at the city, the state and the national level. During the Cuban missile crisis, I made a trip to the capital; when I came home, walking up the dirt road to my house I saw my neighbor sitting in front of her house with a couple of her young children. "What's new here? " I asked. "Nothing, but this terrible Cuban crisis," she said. My neighbors were also quite sophisticated about making news. When they found themselves in conflict with the authorities over some issue, like the unwarranted arrest of one of the barrio residents, or the building of a sewer outlet set to pollute their beach, there would be an immediate trip into town to see the reporter of the *Bolivarense* and the staff of the local radio station in an effort to air their grievance and get some favorable publicity.[2]

Again, this cultural continuity between squatter settlements and the rest of the city does not seem to be a phenomenon unique to Ciudad Guayana or to Venezuela. In Mangin's review of the literature on squatters he summarizes:

> Not only do squatters do much of the service work of the city, but they also patronize the movies, bars, soccer games, musical tent shows, TV broadcasts and other amusements. They attend Catholic and Protestant services. . . . Without exception education ranks near the top on the list of desiderata for children in every country referred to in this survey. . . . Newspapers and magazines sell in large numbers in squatter settlements and transistor and plug-in radios are in practically every house [Mangin, 1967: 78].

What of the claim that the people of the barrios "lack ties to or influence on the established political institutions?" For those who have held this view, Talton Ray's work on the politics of the barrios should be a strong corrective, for he shows very neatly how the barrios, from their very inception, are plugged into the political structure.

> The invasion is a calculated process carefully directed by specific leadership. The outstanding credential of the leader (or leaders) is that he usually has the backing, either tacit or explicit, of one of the political parties that shares governing power in the city. . . . His connection with a ruling party situates him on the "right" side of the government which, in the final analysis, is the body that decides whether he stays on the land [Ray, 1969: 33-34].

Indeed, it turns out that the development of squatter settlements is one of those regular irregularities through which societies are able to do things which they find necessary while at the same time denying the existence of, or at least any support to, the phenomenon.

Certainly my barrio was very involved with the political institutions at the municipal level, and if they lacked "influence on the established political institutions" nationally, this seemed to have to do with the relation between political parties at the local level and nationally, rather than in the weakness of a connection between the barrio and the party in town. The little generator which provided weak electric current from six to ten each night when we first arrived was run by the local Acción Democrática *mandado,* and was part of an attempt to organize the barrio for AD; when the regular current came in later, it was through petitioning through the local politicians. The pipes for a self-help water system, the materials for the *bollas criollas* court and for the baseball field all were extracted as small-bore patronage from the party leaders in town. When an election gave the town for the first time a two-party government, at once persons in the barrio who had been in sympathy with the second party organized and came into the public view; their organization was a response to the possibility of their, too, getting concessions from downtown.

Field work investigations of squatter settlements have now shown us repeatedly that those who imagined these areas as settings of social disorganization were projecting their own anxieties about the poor. Squatter settlements, besides networks of kinship and of informal neighborhood relations, have a wide variety of more formally organized associations, most usually centering on acquiring for the area such missing services as water taps, schools or sewers. Indeed, this associational life tends to be richer in the period just after settlement formation than it is later, when some of these problems have either been solved or demonstrated insoluble (see Mangin, 1965). This does not mean that barrios are characteristically "integrated communities"—whatever that means. My little neighborhood of eighty households generated no activity in which everyone participated, nor did every resident know every other. But my barrio and others certainly do not lack "formal organizations and associations and . . . informal and private webs of contact" to use the phraseology in the discussion of "marginals" which I quoted at the outset. But when I look more closely at that passage, I see that the writer does not actually say that the "marginals" have no associations or webs of contacts, but rather that they are "excluded from (those which) constitute the urban structure." In other words, perhaps she is saying not that they do not know anybody, but rather that they do not know the right people. And here, perhaps, is the crux of the problem.

Another way of coming at this same issue is suggested by a comment made by another urban anthropologist, Walter Miller, at a meeting on anti-poverty strategies where it kept being asserted that the poor should be "brought into the mainstream." Miller said: "In the United States, there are people who go to ᴾᵀᴬ meetings and there are people who play the numbers. It's my understanding that there are many more people who play the numbers than there are who go to PTA meetings. Why do we always talk as if learning to come to PTA meetings were joining the mainstream? "

The word "mainstream" suggests a river which, as it moves along, tends always to become more homogeneous, drawing together and blending the clear water from the center with the muddy water near the bank. But a society is not like that.

To think of the American lower class or the people of the Venezuelan ranchos as "marginal" implies a misunderstanding of the nature of complex social systems. Venezuelan society is one which, like ours, involves structural differentiation of roles, and one of the aspects of this structured differentiation is structured inequality. Venezuelan society, like ours, regularly patterns inequalities of income and of opportunity, related systems of subordination, particular "subcultural" adaptations to this social and economic structure, and mechanisms for maintaining boundary distinctions between persons in the systematically related subgroups. The fact that the kinds of behavior, belief and aspirations characteristic of persons at the upper levels of the social system are generally perceived as desirable or even as "normal" should not lead us to imagine that what we identify rather loosely as a "culture of poverty" is more "marginal" to the system than the "official" or elite-carried patterns. Both are components of a single social system.

In my barrio, some patterns of behavior characteristic of rural life, like keeping chickens, still persisted in the urban setting. (Chickens are one way of saving, in a system where saving is difficult, but high unemployment makes a financial backstop desirable.) Other rural patterns, like the rural custom of communal housebuilding, were found inappropriate and did not survive. But from the fact that the people of the barrio had been losing some of their rural customs it does not necessarily follow that they were becoming like "standard" —i.e., middle-class—city dwellers.

It appeared to me that in my barrio there was a growing class differentiation going on. There were those people who had gotten a footing in the growing industrial sector of the economy—who went off to work in the steel mill, got their children education and medical care, and improved their ranchos into the little plastered concrete-block houses with window grilles and flowers in front which Venezuelans call a *quintica*—a working-class version of the upper-class *quinta*. And there were in my barrio those who had failed to get in, and who now lived in the economic fringes of unemployment and subemployment, and whose style of life tends to the kinds of adaptation around which Lewis has built his image of a "culture of poverty." Neither of these ways of life of the barrio, I would suggest, is "marginal." Both are components of Venezuelan urban society.

Here I would like to quote the strong words of Janice Perlman (1971), in her summary of an investigation of *favelados*—squatter settlement dwellers—in Rio de Janeiro, at a time when public policy was particularly unresponsive or negative toward this sector of the Brazilian population.

Our data indicate that the presuppositions and predictions of marginality theory are almost universally untrue. Brazilian society may well be divided into two sectors but ... characterizing these as "marginal" and "integrated" is deeply deceptive. It allows analysts to avoid the recognition that both sectors are integrated into society, but on very different terms. Favelados are not marginal to Brazilian society, but integrated into it in a manner detrimental to their interests. *They are not socially marginal but rejected, not economically marginal but exploited, and not politically marginal but repressed.*

We are beginning, I believe, to work toward an understanding of the new kinds of order which do develop in cities and with regard to cities as wholes—forms of order which, as in the processes we are coming to see as orderly transformations of the squatter settlements, may operate through the mechanisms of the market.

We must understand these as processes which tie various groups together, and also as processes which keep them apart through mechanisms of social differentiation and boundary maintenance. We must understand "culture" and "subculture," "social status" and "social structure" in their relationship to economic process and program, and to the structure of power and political action.

For the processes which we are looking at, as anthropologists, in these growing cities of the developing countries are the processes which are shaping the future of these countries. Policy is being made about these processes. If the way we conceive of these processes is clear and relevant, we may be able to contribute to the creation of a more humane future.

If we conceive of the city—as some Latin Americanists have done—as a kind of fortress of high culture, European and elitist, in an Indian or peasant hinterland which it dominates, we will tend to move towards certain kinds of public policy. We will tend to perceive large in-migrations to the city from the rural hinterland as an "invasion." We are led to think of dealing with the problems of urbanization basically as pacification efforts—as a problem of organizing, controlling, educating, acculturating the outsiders who have moved from the hinterland to within the fortress walls.

If we derive policy out of the anthropological tradition expressed in the conception of a folk-urban continuum which focuses on the sorts of organization developed in small rural traditional communities and on the way in which these sorts of organization tend to disappear or to become attenuated or distorted in the urban environment, our concepts will lead us another way. This tradition leads to conceiving of social processes among in-migrants to the cities as those of "cultural breakdown" and "social disorganization." We will then focus our policy efforts on the sorts of community organization effort which attempts to build up a "sense of community" at the neighborhood level within the urban setting.

Neither of these strategies I would suggest is likely to get us very far, for both are essentially marginal to the major forces shaping a new urbanized society, and both lead us away from looking at issues of inequality of economic and political power which are central to policy in developing countries.

NOTES

1. This has already been reported in some detail in Peattie (1968).
2. See "The Intellectual World of La Laja," in Peattie (1968).

REFERENCES

APPLEYARD, D. (1969) "City designers and the pluralistic city," in L. Rodwin (ed.) Planning Urban Growth and Regional Development: The Experience of the Guayana Program of Venezuela. Cambridge, Mass.: MIT Press.

BAMBERGER, M. (1970) "Acción's response to the urban challenge." (unpublished)

Depto. Nacional de Planeación (Colombia) (1972) La actividad constructora popular: análisis general y elementos para una política de apoyo. Bogotá, 24 April.

GERMANI, G. (1972) "Aspectos teóricos de la marginalidad." Revista Paraguaya de Sociología 8 (March).

MANGIN, W. (1965) "Mental health and migration to cities: a Peruvian case," in D. B. Heath and R. N. Adams (eds.) Contemporary Cultures and Societies of Latin America. New York: Random House.

——— (1967) "Latin American squatter settlements: a problem and a solution." Latin American Research Review 2 (Summer): 65-98.

NELSON, J. M. (1969) Migrants, Urban Poverty, and Instability in Developing Countries. Cambridge, Mass.: Center for International Affairs, Harvard University, Occasional Paper 22.

PARK, R. E. (1928) "Human migration and the marginal man." American Journal of Sociology 3 (May): 881-893.

PEATTIE, L. R. (1968) The View from the Barrio. Ann Arbor: University of Michigan Press.

PERLMAN, J. E. (1971) "The fate of migrants in Rio's favelas: the myth of marginality." Ph.D. dissertation. Massachusetts Institute of Technology.

RAY, T. F. (1969) The Politics of the Barrios of Venezuela. Berkeley and Los Angeles: University of California Press.

TURNER, J.F.C. (1969) "Housing priorities, settlement patterns, and urban development in modernizing countries." Journal of the American Institute of Planners 34 (November): 354-363.

PART III

THE

DEVELOPMENT

AND

ORGANIZATION

OF

URBAN

NEIGHBORHOODS

DOUGLAS UZZELL is Assistant Professor of Anthropology at Rice University. He received his Ph.D. from the University of Texas at Austin. His fields of specialization include social and cultural anthropology, social organization, and community development in Latin America. He has done field research in Peru and Mexico. His publications include "A Strategic Analysis of Social Structure in Lima, Peru" (*Urban Anthropology,* forthcoming); and (with Ronald Provencher) *Urban Anthropology* (William C. Brown, forthcoming).

Chapter 5

THE INTERACTION OF POPULATION AND LOCALITY IN THE DEVELOPMENT OF SQUATTER SETTLEMENTS IN LIMA

DOUGLAS UZZELL

Introduction

The purpose of this paper is to account for the ways particular urban localities and their populations—in this case, *pueblos jóvenes* in Lima[1] —change over time. I am concerned with developing a model that may be applied to any urban locality, not with presenting a composite or "modal" picture of the development of "typical" *pueblos jóvenes*.

What I shall attempt differs from other treatments (see, for example, Turner, 1967) chiefly in my treatment of the development of localities as the systemic product of interaction between characteristics of the locality and characteristics of its population. The original feature of this analysis is its emphasis on variations of population characteristics over time. Other authors have mentioned or implied this phenomenon,[2] but have failed to focus upon it, so that one often receives the impression that a given population comes to a locality in the beginning and, except for the effects of life cycle, remains stable. The result is a more or less linear view of the development of a locality, as it works through the possibilities of its original elements, with the emphasis on the characteristics of the locality itself.[3]

The model I shall use, which has already been presented elsewhere (Uzzell, 1972), is represented in Figure 1. The central notion behind this model is that at any given time there is a population universe (which, in this case, I arbitrarily locate in Lima-Callao) from which a set of people is attracted by characteristics of the locality and comes to live there. Next is the idea that characteristics of the

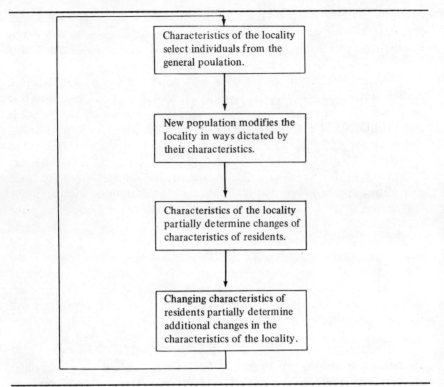

Figure 1 : INTERACTION BETWEEN RESIDENTS AND LOCALITIES

locality vary over time, and that this variation is partly determined by the characteristics of the population of the locality, how they invest their capital and labor, for example. Finally, I assume that when characteristics of the locality change, this will be reflected in changed characteristics of the people who will be attracted to it, and so on.

It appears easy enough at first glance to specify what I mean by "characteristics" of a locality: topography, location in the city (nearness to "good" or "bad" neighborhoods, industrial or commercial centers, and the like), presence or absence of urban services, including public transportation, present and potential land use in the locality, and tenure options, come quickly to mind. This grows considerably more complex, however, when we realize that it is not these characteristics themselves in any objective sense that repel or attract potential residents, but the way they are interpreted. Such interpretations must necessarily depend upon the individual actor, operating within a much larger context. That context is determined not only by such relatively accessible factors as availability and desirability of other localities (which may be thought of as competing for the population), job opportunities, and income, but also more illusive factors such as the prestige attached to living in various kinds of localities. In that sense, then, it would be conceivable that a locality not change physically at all from one time to the next and yet change in the way it was perceived by the population. Thus, when I speak of "characteristics" of a locality, I actually have in mind *perceived* characteristics.

"Characteristics" of populations are even more difficult to operationalize beyond obvious ones such as age, income, or place of origin. The elements that are relevant to the present discussion may be classed under a general heading such as "the uses people wish to make of residence in the locality." For this notion to have meaning, however, it obviously must be placed in the context of the actors' overall life strategies, expectations, limitations, and assets.[4] Neither kind of element of the model I am constructing, then, is available to my direct perception, residing as they do in the minds of individuals other than me. In the final section of this chapter, I shall discuss problems of gathering data for the kind of analysis that I am proposing.

My data were gathered during a year of field work (1969-1970)[5] focused upon four *pueblos jóvenes* in Lima. (I lived in one and regularly visited the others.) Data were gathered by participant observation, intensive interviewing, and otherwise, as well as through the collection of about 400 partial life histories of heads of households.[6] Where quantitative data are presented below, they will have been abstracted from the life histories.

PUEBLOS JOVENES IN LIMA

From the literature, one derives a picture of the typical pueblo joven in Lima as being on the outskirts of town, located on a fairly large piece of land that is originally invaded by a core group who finally receive at least implicit permission to remain, and who then bring in other settlers (who usually pay a small fee to the settlement association for the right to settle). Such settlements tend to be large, populous, and fairly orderly—streets being laid out in a grid, lots surveyed, and space left for schools, markets, and other public activities. After the initial invasion, houses are built generally as materials can be afforded, and there is a parallel (though slightly later) gradual acquisition of public transportation, water and sewage systems, electricity, garbage disposal, street lighting, police patrols, pavement of streets and sidewalks, and so on.

From the city planner's point of view, that describes the most important kind of pueblo joven. It has represented the major thrust of housing development in Lima during the past ten or fifteen years, and it is now being encouraged by the government and by various private entities. (See Collier, 1971 and Michl, 1973, in reference to the role of cooptation in the formation of pueblos jóvenes.) Because such localities tend to be large, they contain the biggest part of the population in pueblos jóvenes (which I estimate to be in the neighborhood of a million people). As settlements per se, however, that kind of settlement is not necessarily the most numerous. It is fitting, then, both because of their number and because of their relative neglect in the literature, that three of the four localities I studied are neither large, new, nor suburban.

Turner treats the localities that do not fit the description given above as a second "type, formed by the urban-born poor or rural immigrants," who have fewer resources than those who go to the suburban localities. The nonsuburban type of pueblos jóvenes, he says (along with cheap rented housing), "serve as 'bridgeheads' or urban toe-holds, enabling the very poor to live cheaply and to obtain work more easily by living within walking distance of principal markets and employment areas" (1970: 5). As will be seen in the cases to be discussed, that generalization needs stringent qualifications.

When the so-called "Law of the *Barrios Marginales*" (Law Number 13517) went into effect in 1961, it enabled many residents' associations to have their localities legally classified as *"barrios marginales"* (later pueblos jóvenes), particularly in cases where tenure was being disputed with landowners. Law 13517 and its enabling legislation (see Rueda Sánchez, 1965) have the effect of bringing the localities under the government's protection, and theoretically holding out the prospect of full title and integration into the "regular" portions of the city. Thus, for some time after the law was passed, residents of a number of localities had their settlements redefined. As we shall see, such redefinition has had the effect of changing the uses to which some of the population is putting these localities and has thus affected their development.

The Research Sites

The four localities which I studied (all designated by pseudonyms) may be described briefly as follows. *Suburbia* is one of the oldest, largest, and best developed of the modern suburban pueblos jóvenes. All but one section of it is laid out in a grid with wide streets and ample space for public structures. There is a restriction that all houses must be built of brick or concrete. Most have one story completed, many two, and some more than two. Forming the long axis of the locality is a paved avenue, which is lined with shops and retail outlets (including branches of large chain stores), branches of banks, and other commercial enterprises. There is a post office, a number of schools (public and private), several churches, government medical posts, and a police station. Off the avenue are several markets, and every block contains small-scale businesses of one kind or another (including numerous tiny groceries that appear not to show much of a profit). Piped-in water and electricity are available to all households, though a few of the poorest have not availed themselves of these services. A modest monthly tax provides public lighting, police patrols, and garbage pick-up. Several bus, taxi, and jitney lines run along the avenue and into various parts of town. The central business district may be reached by one of these conveyances in less than thirty minutes.

Hillside is the second largest of the four localities, with about 1,000 households. As the name implies, it is located on a hill. There is no overall pattern of layout, and indeed there are no internal streets negotiable by automobile, but instead, stairs and footpaths. Houses range from small cane mat shacks to large brick and concrete structures of two or three stories. Though there are few retail outlets within the locality, there is a school, a nursery, a chapel (which has no priest), and a medical post (provided by a political party). Piped-in water and electricity are available to many, but not all, sections. Hillside is within walking distance of the central business district.

Cercado (which I call such because it is enclosed) lies at the bottom of the hill that contains Hillside. It was surveyed and reorganized in 1968 so that it now is laid out in a grid. All present house construction has occurred since 1968, and by the end of my study, about half the households had begun construction of brick houses, two of which were three stories high and quite large (one containing a family-owned clothing factory as well as the family's residence). Small (225 households) and out of the flow of traffic from surrounding localities, Cercado does not have many retail enterprises, but there are a number of manufacturing activities (shoes, mattresses, and clothing), many of which are clandestine (i.e., not registered with the government). A large, modern school lies in the middle of the settlement. Water is brought in by truck or is available at a public fountain. Those households with electricity get it illegally from outside.

Though slightly farther from the central business district than Cercado and Hillside, *Shacks* is imbedded in a built-up urban area with mixed residential and industrial land use. It is the smallest of the four localities: about 80 households exist on about one half-acre of land. Houses are small and are constructed of adobe, cane mat, and a variety of scrap materials. There are a handful of very small-scale retail enterprises, a school, and a meeting hall. Water comes from public fountains, and electricity is virtually absent, except at the school. At first glance, Shacks is indistinguishable from neighboring *corralones,* the cheapest kind of commercial housing, in which a tiny lot, and perhaps a shack, is rented for a fairly small fee, all improvements being the responsibility of the renter. It is in Shacks, if anywhere, that we would expect to find the "down-and-outs" or "poor-but-ambitious" of Turner's bridgehead settlement, but upon closer inspection, this proves only partially true.

Because of its smallness, the population of Shacks is easiest to talk about. I shall treat it at greatest length below and bring in the other three localities for purposes of comparison and contrast.

THE INTERACTION OF POPULATION AND LOCALITY

Shacks

I do not pretend to know all the uses to which residents of Shacks are putting (or envision putting) their residence there. Some, however, are obvious. Others may be inferred. The history of the locality may conveniently be divided into two periods: roughly before and after 1955. Until about the mid-1940s, it was not even a single locality, but several unsold plots of land scattered about what had originally been a truck farm.[7] Gradually, those plots were sold, their residents moving to remaining plots until only the present location remained.

There must have been considerable turnover during that time. The area was diminishing constantly. It was at about that time that the city began to feel the full rush of rural-urban migration that was to transform it. Reconstruction (following an earthquake in 1940), coupled with a wartime economic boom, provided more jobs than before. By the end of the 1940s, invasion and formation of suburban irregular settlements had become an established alternative for the urban poor.[8] Surely, individuals must have moved in, taken advantage of the low rent and the nearness to work places for a time, and then moved on as their resources changed. At the same time, however, there was a nucleus of people who remained, and who saw themselves as dependents or clients of the landowners.

At least some of the regular employees of the truck farm were given lifetime promises of land to live on and assurance that their patron would intercede with local businessmen to find jobs for them. Actually, the residential portion of that guarantee was extended to children of the residents of Shacks, by the residents themselves, so long as space was available. In addition to these clients, the landowner "inherited" another group of dependents as a result of litigation to retrieve a portion of his land from an individual who was using it for agricultural purposes and also renting cheap housing to about a dozen households. A condition of the court in awarding title to the landowner was that he provide living space to the renters, some of whom were indigent. (The responsibility did not extend to finding jobs for the second group.) The merger of these two core groups and of the sense of clientage that remains is neatly symbolized by the family of the man who was president, during the time of my study, of the savings cooperative formed to purchase the land. He is the son of an employee of the truck farm and himself a former employee. His wife is from one of the households of renters from the disputed property. And their marriage sponsor *(padrino de matrimonio)* is the son of the landlord, and himself co-owner of the land Shacks is now on.

The labels "down-and-outs" and "poor-but-ambitious" might be applied to some residents, but not to the majority, particularly not to those who have shaped the locality and who promise to build substantial houses once tenure is secure. These, especially members of the savings cooperative, by and large hold steady jobs and earn as much as many residents of Suburbia.[9] They are distinguished by their conservatism, and by their continued playing of the role of client. By this last, I do not mean that all, or even most, of the present members of the cooperative are from the original truck farm. They are, however, wage laborers content to live as best they can on their wages,[10] and they are content to play the game of land acquisition by the rules of the landlord. In fact, it is in this way, above all, that residents of Shacks differ as a group from residents of the other three localities.

And yet, residence in Shacks has not always held the promise it holds today. Present-day members of the cooperative who were employees on the truck farm have been living for thirty years in conditions that they themselves describe as squalid—pointing out their cramped quarters, dirt floors, and lack of sanitation, running water and electricity. They have been assured all along of a *place* to live, but not of the possibility of living comfortably and respectably there, chiefly because only for about ten years have they seen the possibility of acquiring title to the land, without which they are unwilling to invest in improvements.[11]

That brings me to the second period of Shacks' existence. By the mid-1950s, it was clear to many of Lima's poor that irregular settlements had at least the implied approval of powerful people. President Odría had intervened on the behalf of irregular settlers on two occasions that I know of, one of which had eventuated in the development of Suburbia. Meanwhile, the population of Shacks had grown far beyond the original nucleus. In 1956 or 1957, the landowner appears to have sold the land where Shacks is located. At any rate, a work crew appeared one day with a bulldozer and began clearing. Residents physically confronted the work crew and sent emissaries to complain to the landlord. Out of this confrontation grew the organization that was to petition in 1961 for official recognition as a *barrio marginal* (later, pueblo joven), and that later (1966) formed the cooperative to buy the land. Already, by the mid-1950s, residents had themselves begun building an elementary school of brick and concrete.

The school may be a better symbol of the "new vision" of the residents of Shacks than is their resisting the bulldozer. For that new vision to evolve required both the new governmental attitude toward irregular settlements and new people who did not see themselves as clients of the landlord. The behavior of the residents makes sense if it is seen as a new aggressiveness tempered by the conservatism of the old core group. It is significant, I think, that the leader of the resistance to the bulldozer was a man who had resided in Shacks only a few years.

Once Shacks was reduced to its present location, the most significant change in it was that, beginning about 1955, residents began to gain some measure of control over it. The degree of their control has increased steadily since then and will become absolute when the landlord finally loses his claim, either through sale or through appropriation by the government. Concurrent with the increase of control over the land has been an increase of control over the population. In 1968, the government removed about forty households to clear two of the bordering streets in which houses had been built. Those households were relocated by the government in a new, large suburban pueblo joven. What criteria were used to select those who were to leave needs further investigation. I was told that those without steady employment nearby were chosen. Though that may be true, it probably needs qualification. One thing, however, is clear: those who were members of the cooperative were not removed. Once tenure is secure, there will be another removal (again of about forty households) and only members of the cooperative will remain. At that point, they will lay out lots in a grid, begin construction of new houses, and begin bringing in running water, electricity, and a sewage system.

In a sense, this will be the realization of the potential of the original organizers in the late 1950s. But the development has not been a linear one. New residents continued to move into Shacks after the leadership was established in the late 1950s, and despite the strict limitation of the number of its members, membership in the cooperative has not been closed. The reason is that any member who defaults on his payments can be voted out by the other members and replaced. When I asked the president of the cooperative whether it would be possible for me to join the cooperative, he said that it would be quite easy because there were several who were delinquent and were being left on the rolls only until somebody else sought membership.

I collected partial life histories from a random sample of nearly one-fourth (n = 18) of the heads of households in Shacks. Of these only five were currently members of the cooperative.[12] The most recent arrivals in my sample (2) came to the locality in 1964. One of these was not a member of the cooperative. The other had joined in 1970. Of the other four members, one had joined in 1967, one in 1968, and two in 1969. (One other informant, who arrived in the pueblo joven in 1958, had been a member of the cooperative in 1966 and 1967, but not thereafter.) Obviously, membership is not rigid.

In the early 1950s, something changed the way some residents (among those moving in at that time as well as among those already resident) viewed the future possibilities of living in Shacks. It was something other than the nearness of Shacks to work places and the cheapness of living there. Only three people in my sample still hold the jobs they had when they arrived in the pueblo joven, and only one of those is a member of the cooperative. Also, a considerable number of householders (about one-third) work outside the district—and these include members of the cooperative! As to the cost of living in Shacks, it is low only if one does not intend to build a substantial house there. That is, the kind of houses envisioned by members of the cooperative will be just as expensive as the houses they would build in Suburbia.

What changed, I submit, was that models were provided that demonstrated the feasibility of self-built, low-cost, but substantial housing, and the feasibility of residential development in the area of Shacks. In other words, strategies ("plays" as I call them elsewhere [Uzzell, 1974]), became available to the residents of Shacks which had not been available before—not that they had been impossible, but that nobody had thought of them. Substantial self-built housing began going up across the river in Suburbia shortly after the beginning of the decade, followed quickly by similar construction between Shacks and the river. Closer to Shacks itself, a number of moderately priced apartment projects were constructed—a far cry from the squalid downtown apartment dwellings previously available to the poor. More recently, more expensive housing developments (too expensive for the residents of Shacks) have begun, one within four blocks of Shacks. In short, the area around Shacks seems to have developed in a sequence different from the one we have grown accustomed to. Before about 1940, land use was primarily agricultural, going during the 1940s to industrial with *corralón* housing available for workers. Then, beginning a little after 1950 and continuing to the present, it has become a mixed industrial and residential area. Many *corralones* still exist, but the trend is toward more substantial residential construction.

Residents of Shacks are rural people, more so than the residents of any of the other three localities. None was born in Lima, although one immigrated at an early age. Only two are from the coast (which is generally more urbanized than the Sierra or the jungle region of the country). Only one was born in a departmental capital. The fathers of all but one were agriculturalists. The pattern of rural origins has intensified since 1955, with a growing tendency for householders to have immigrated to Lima upon reaching adulthood, and to have come to Shacks sooner after reaching the city than the older residents did. The wives of many of these later arrivals appear not to speak Spanish, or at least not to speak it well. There has been some pulling in of kinsmen and other relations of the older residents from the Sierra. How extensive this has been I cannot say. But a disproportionately large number of my sample (7) is from Cangallo Province in the Department of Ayacucho (an area predominantly of Quechua-speaking peasants), and three are from a mountainous province (Corongo) in Ancash. The later arrivals have lower household incomes (see Table 1), but the income of the heads of the households is about the same as that of the earlier arrivals—and the jobs are of essentially the same kind. Only one has a second job. This is a woman who takes in washing, and, as a second job, provides board for a few individuals. She and a man who owns a truck and does contract hauling are the only two householders in my sample who are self-employed. The rest (except for a woman who does not work) are wage laborers.

Though the sample size is too small to be accorded too much significance here, members of the cooperative in my sample seem representative of the population of Shacks. They are wage laborers. Other members of their households practically match their income. They are *serranos* (rural mountain

TABLE 1
MEAN INCOME OF HOUSEHOLDS AND OF
HOUSEHOLDERS IN SHACKS SAMPLE

| | | Income | |
Population Set	n	Householder	Household
Those arriving before 1956	9	S/. 2509	S/. 4777
Those arriving after 1955	9	S/. 2297	S/. 3097
Members of cooperative	5	S/. 2463	S/. 4702
Entire sample	18	S/. 2403	S/. 3937

people), three coming from Corongo Province in Ancash and two from Cangallo Province in Ayacucho. The only way that they differ outstandingly from other members of the sample is that they head the five largest households.

Other characteristics of Shacks householders will be mentioned as I discuss the other localities. The first of these is Cercado, which shares with Shacks a history of transformation and of the residents' eventually gaining control of the land.

Cercado

Like Shacks, Cercado began as something other than what it has become. Originally a small fruit and vegetable farm, Cercado was also the residence of those who worked there—they being allowed (as was customary) to build minimal dwellings on the grounds. With the population increase and housing shortage of the 1940s, the owner appears gradually to have found it more profitable to rent living space than to raise fruit and vegetables. During this time, he built a *callejón*[13] at the front border of the locality. By the end of the 1950s, he had decided to clear out his tenants and build an apartment complex.

When this became known to the tenants, they formed an organization, hired a lawyer, and took the landlord to court. As it turned out, he lacked legal title to his land. The former tenants were awarded control of the locality (including the *callejón*), and, soon after, the place was declared a *barrio marginal* (later, pueblo joven). In 1968, the government cleared and surveyed the land, assigned lots, and relocated in a suburban pueblo joven those households for which there was no space.

In common with the population of Shacks, residents of Cercado have gone through a process of self-selection, and the effect probably has been to make the population more homogeneous than it was before. In fact, Cercado is now at a point similar to the one Shacks will reach when the cooperative takes full control there. Selection of who was to remain (225 households) was carried out by the residents. They decided on criteria of inclusion (although some criteria probably were urged on them by the National Housing Council, which conducted the clearing, surveying, and relocation), chose a committee to rank residents on those criteria, and voted approval of the committee's actions. Nevertheless, the residents who remain appear from indicators such as place of origin, kind of employment, and income, to be more heterogeneous than the residents of Shacks.

Although mean monthly income of households in Cercado is similar to that of households in Shacks (S/. 4170 versus S/. 3937), variance within the Cercado sample is greater. Also, heads of households in Cercado earn an average of about S/. 500 more per month than their counterparts in Shacks (see Table 2). This is attributable to several factors, not the least of which is that sixteen percent of householders in Cercado hold second jobs.

Holding of second jobs, combined with widespread self-employment (thirty percent of the Cercado sample), indicate a significant difference in attitudes toward getting along in the city. A majority of residents of Cercado are hustlers, entrepreneurs, con artists. They have a lot of irons in the fire *(negocios)*. The social climate in Cercado is such that if you do not have *negocios,* you pretend to, for approval. Here at last, one might be tempted to claim, are Turner's "poor-but-ambitious."

But I do not think the Shacks people are less ambitious. The difference is not one of ends, but of means. In Shacks, you prosper by finding a good *patrón* and serving him faithfully. You may raise a few chickens, but by and large, your lot is with the *patrón.* One man in Shacks, a long-time employee of the Coca Cola bottling plant and a union official, after successfully striking the plant, was downright mournful. "We got what we wanted," he said. "But you wait. One doesn't play around with men of that level. There were strike breakers. Jobs will be lost. Loyalty is repaid, and the lack of it also is repaid." Many Cercado residents, by contrast, place faith only in themselves, living by the skin of their teeth and the seats of their pants. And some of them do very well at it.

The difference, I believe, is attributable in large part to the difference in degree of experience at living in an urban environment exhibited by the two populations. Twenty-nine percent of my sample in Cercado either were born in Lima or immigrated by age ten. Twenty-five percent of the remainder were born in other departmental capitals. But whether or not patronage is essentially a rural strategy, the question remains: Why were more urban types attracted to Cercado than to Shacks?

TABLE 2

MEAN INCOME OF HOUSEHOLDS AND OF
HOUSEHOLDERS IN CERCADO SAMPLE

| | | *Income* | |
Population Set	*n*	*Householder*	*Household*
Those arriving before 1950	25	S/. 2922	S/. 4372
Those arriving 1950-1959	24	S/. 2932	S/. 3570
Those arriving 1960-1970	7	S/. 2498	S/. 4883
Entire sample	56	S/. 2925	S/. 4170

Consider for a moment the situation of the two localities forty years ago. Shacks was part of a truck farm, in an agricultural belt between Lima and Callao. Cercado was a horticultural enclave on the edge of a part of the city that has been known for centuries as a colorful working-class section *(baja del puente)*, just across the river from the original administrative and commercial center of the city. More than a wage laborer needs easy access to his place of work, an entrepreneur needs access to buyers and sellers. The wage worker may need only to make one round trip per day. The entrepreneur may need to make many—perhaps transporting merchandise as well.

I divided my sample of householders in Cercado arbitrarily at 1950, and again at 1960 (after residents had gained control). Not surprisingly, I found that it is the earliest arrivals who most frequently have urban backgrounds (see Table 3), followed by a set with more rural backgrounds. Had I divided the sample at 1952, the contrast would have been even more extreme: the second set would have been practically indistinguishable from the Shacks sample. Then, after 1960, we suddenly see another influx of urbanites, more frequently self-employed than members of either of the other two sets.

The relative rurality of the second set may simply reflect demographic changes within the city as a whole, as it filled up with rural-urban migrants, although why precisely *these* people were attracted to Cercado remains something of a mystery to me. The attraction for the third set, though, seems obvious. In the first place, they knew that self-construction of substantial housing eventually would be possible. In the second place, Cercado had become an even more inviting place for entrepreneurs. The population and the markets of the old working-class section remained, and by 1960, the hills behind Cercado were being covered with pueblos jóvenes. Still, though near markets and surrounded by potential customers, Cercado was, and continues to be, hardly noticeable. Because of its walls and its situation relative to the hills, it is

TABLE 3
PLACE OF ORIGIN AND PERCENTAGE OF
SELF-EMPLOYED HOUSEHOLDERS IN CERCADO SAMPLE

			Place of Origin	
Population Set	*n*	*Self-Employed*	*Born in Lima or Immigrated by Age 10*	*Born in Other Departmental Capital*
Those arriving before 1950	25	36%	36%	20%
Those arriving 1950-1959	24	17%	17%	17%
Those arriving 1960-1970	7	57%	29%	14%
Entire sample	56	30%	34%	27%

paradoxically an out-of-the-way place in the middle of things—an ideal location if you are a clandestine manufacturer of cheap consumer goods.

And it also seems that these last arrivals, coming after the residents had gained control, express, like the members of the cooperative in Shacks, the gestalt of the population as a whole.

Hillside

Both Cercado and Shacks are localities where the residents are gaining control in a unitary way. That is, both populations are gaining the power to control their localities as a whole: to determine who else may live there and to make decisions in council that affect the entire locality. Hillside is a sharp contrast. It is not anarchic, but, relative to the others, it seems so. Therein may lie part of its attractiveness.

Over 400 years ago, Francisco Pizarro planted a cross at the crest of the hill on which Hillside lies. His gesture was one of thanksgiving for the apparently miraculous departure of a superior Indian army encamped there. If Hillside were to disappear as miraculously, I am sure that some citizens of Lima would plant another cross of thanksgiving. Visible from much of the central business district as a hillside jumble of houses of all kinds, facing all ways, Hillside has stubbornly refused for forty years to disappear, or to grow lovely, or even to stop growing.

For a decade and a half after its birth, its residents resisted eradication by the government. Since the mid-1950s, they have resisted gestures by political parties, philanthropic organizations, the Church, U.S. business, the National Housing Council, and the Peace Corps to bring Hillside into the civic fold.

Dividing my sample of householders in Hillside (n = 97) into three cohorts—those arriving before 1950 (n = 38), those arriving 1950 through 1959 (n = 36), and those arriving 1960 through 1970 (n = 23)—I found that

TABLE 4
PLACE OF ORIGIN AND PERCENTAGE OF
SELF—EMPLOYED HOUSEHOLDERS IN HILLSIDE SAMPLE

| | | | *Place of Origin* | |
| | | | *Born in Lima or Immigrated by Age 10* | *Born in Other Departmental Capital* |
Population Set	*n*	*Self-Employed*		
Those arriving before 1950	38	37%	47%	32%
Those arriving 1950-1959	36	39%	19%	33%
Those arriving 1960-1970	23	39%	13%	17%
Entire sample	97	48%	29%	29%

seventy-nine percent of the first cohort either were born in Lima, immigrated by age ten, or were born in another departmental capital (see Table 4). Even more strikingly, thirty percent of that set actually grew up in Hillside!

Though as conveniently located as Cercado, Hillside is not a convenient place to live. Most residents must climb to their houses. For the majority, the climb is long and strenuous. Given the permanence of many houses and the amount invested in them, that situation is unlikely to change: there is no room for streets. Property value is almost sure to increase in Cercado, Shacks, and Suburbia. In Hillside, as alternative housing continues to develop, property value may decline. At least, building a house there is a relatively poor investment.

Nevertheless, people remain. Some invest in two- and three-story homes of brick and concrete. They have built several public buildings. Most sections have, or soon will have, water, lights, and sewage systems, brought in at the expense of the residents, and often with their own hands. Why?

Hillside began as a refuge. In 1932, President Sánchez Cerro permitted people who had been flooded out of squatter shacks on the banks of the Rimac River to settle on the hill. Thirty-five years later, another administration eradicated a squatter settlement on the banks of the Rimac and some of those people went to Hillside. The cane mat shacks of some of them perch farthest up the hill.

But this is only superficially a repetition of history. The original settlers had few alternatives, no good ones. The latter-day settlers were eligible for resettlement by the government in new suburban pueblos jóvenes not too far distant. It may be that for some of these new arrivals—particularly walking vendors—the distance to the suburbs *was* too great. Others may have felt financially incapable of building a brick and concrete home. Some of these, as well as some of the earlier settlers, probably would qualify as Turner's "down-and-outs." But many more would not.

Although household income in the last cohort is below that of the first two, income of the heads of households is about the same (see Table 5). My sample includes, for example, a wholesale grocer who earns S/. 5000 per month, a policeman at S/. 5300, a shoemaker at S/. 3500. I know of a number of similar cases outside the sample among people arriving during the same period. Besides, we have seen the same pattern in the first two pueblos jóvenes: household income

TABLE 5
MEAN INCOME OF HOUSEHOLDS AND OF
HOUSEHOLDERS IN HILLSIDE SAMPLE

| Population Set | n | Income | |
		Householder	Household
Those arriving before 1950	38	S/. 2232	S/. 4304
Those arriving 1950-1959	36	S/. 2791	S/. 4420
Those arriving 1960-1970	23	S/. 2606	S/. 3015
Entire sample	97	S/. 2528	S/. 4042

tends to vary directly with the age of the household heads. Young couples lack adult offspring, and in the case of the newcomers to Hillside, the houses frequently are not big enough to accommodate other adult kinsmen. Evidently, then, extreme poverty is not a necessary condition for one's moving to Hillside at present. It may never have been.

For the early arrivals, for whom alternative housing was practically limited to downtown slums, the attraction of Hillside may have been social and aesthetic as well as economic. After three decades, those attractions have been at least diluted by the appearance, in the same area of the city, of pueblos jóvenes with the kinds of advantages over Hillside that I have already mentioned. Residence in Hillside may never have been even relatively prestigious, but even in the present era of governmental approval of irregular settlements, when coinage of euphemisms such as pueblo joven symbolizes a new drive toward respectability, Hillside remains unprestigious. Three young men of my acquaintance, two of them university students and one a city policeman, succeeded for varying lengths of time in hiding the fact from me that their parents lived in Hillside—even though I think they understood my attitude (primarily amazed admiration) toward irregular settlements, and even though I had met two of them at the homes of kinsmen in Cercado, a situation which they seemed not to find embarrassing.

And so the question remains: Why do people stay, and why do they continue to come to Hillside? Although the life histories I collected are long and detailed, providing a great deal of information about the informants and their families, I cannot find an answer to that question in my data. Nor have I been able to identify significant differences between cohorts, either using the income and place-of-origin data that I have relied upon primarily in this paper, or in the remainder of the life histories. Though successive cohorts are of increasingly rural backgrounds, the last more rural than the similar group in Cercado, I am convinced that the trend reflects little more than a demographic change in the city as a whole.

Even with all the major questions unanswered, I nevertheless believe that my model fits Hillside. Clearly, the significance of taking up residence there has changed drastically over time. Most likely, my failure to find differences between cohorts may be blamed on inappropriate data or incorrect analysis of the data that exist, but even if the cohorts are essentially identical, they have been attracted to Hillside for changing reasons.

And Hillside has been shaped by the people who have been drawn there. Obviously, topography and outside events have affected the course of the locality's development, but a different set of householders would have planned the locality as a whole, allowing for streets, markets, and other public spaces before building large, permanent houses. It is interesting to speculate that, symbolically, the spontaneous, unplanned, and essentially uncooperative physical structure seems to be replicated both in settlement organizations, which are splintered, factional, and often ephemeral, and by public projects, which have been piecemeal, one small sector at a time promoting its interests without regard to economies and other advantages of larger group actions. Once the pattern of piecemeal construction was set, it continually replicated itself as the settlement moved up the hill. This process could have been stopped at several points, but later arrivals, apparently content with the pattern, perpetuated it.

Suburbia

In many ways, Suburbia resembles the kind of settlement that has received the most attention in the literature. I shall therefore be briefest in my treatment of it, simply suggesting ways the model under discussion might be applied to it.

After a period of limited piecemeal invasion in one zone of Suburbia, a group of individuals secured from the government in 1952 permission (and support) to settle the entire locality. This act of political patronage eventuated in a settlement of some ten thousand householders. The founders—the government as well as the "Family Fathers" organization—clearly set the physical pattern of Suburbia by surveying and by enforcing regulations governing such things as building materials and size and disposition of lots. The physical pattern, as well as official sanction (which implies security of tenure), have from the outset made construction of a house in Suburbia an attractive long-term investment for people who are not quite in a position to make more conventional kinds of investments. The size of the locality probably has been important from the beginning, making its population (or originally, its prospective population) a constituency for politicians to reckon with, and a market to be exploited by merchants. This has assured a series of inputs such as government aid for the installation of water pipes and towers on the one hand or the recent establishment of local branches of banks on the other.

Many residents did not occupy their lots immediately, but remained in the city for several years until their houses were fairly well advanced. Others who could not afford that double expense moved directly to their lots and, in the pattern made familiar by Turner, Mangin, and others, lived in their houses as they built them. A critical change took place in the mid-1960s, when the government paved the central avenue. This removed the last major unpleasantness associated with life in Suburbia. Water, lights, and a sewage system had already been installed, but the trip to town was time-consuming and difficult. Pavement of the avenue not only established the commercial focus of the settlement, but also brought the merger of the homesteaders and those who had remained in town. Increase of publicly and privately owned mass transportation rendered access to other parts of the city almost as easy as it is, say, from Shacks.

Those building while remaining in the city moved to Suburbia. Many of the homesteaders began to appreciate the potential of their property for renting. It was too early to be sure in 1970, but the number of second- and third-floor apartments under construction suggested that the next significant population input would be renters. Though the majority of householders are from the provinces, the Suburbia sample was the most urban of all. In 1970, a large number of their children were enrolled in universities and were otherwise being trained for employment as remunerative as, or more so than, that of their parents. I would expect that within a few years, when many of that generation begin to inherit the homes of their parents, they will have moved elsewhere. These being, for the most part, children of the "investor" contingent, the "homesteaders" and their heirs will be left in Suburbia, together with people renting from nonresident owners.

CONCLUSION

If anything is obvious at this point, it must be that my model requires different kinds of data than I have. Also, changes in sampling techniques are indicated. Mistrustful of surveys in general, I consciously limited the schedule of the life history interviews to questions that referred to fairly concrete objects and events: I asked for names, dates, places, hours, and amounts. The data generated, though more intelligible in one sense than, say, attitudes and opinions, are skeletal. Uninformed by a participant observation, these data would have been virtually uninterpretable. Though useful, perhaps essential, this kind of information needs enrichment.

I think that the best way to correct this would be to proceed with the life history interviews much as before. But then, after studying each interview, the investigator personally should do a follow-up interview that would focus on certain critical events in the informant's life, particularly the conditions surrounding his decision to come to the locality, build a house, or, in Shacks, to join the savings cooperative. Analysis of such accounts would, of course, be more cumbersome than manipulation of numerical data, but ultimately more fruitful. Sampling probably should not be done randomly, but should be controlled to assure equal representation of cohorts. Perhaps the greatest weakness in the entire scheme is that former residents cannot be included. This may be corrected partially where large groups have been relocated in one or two settlements, as happened to former residents of Shacks and Cercado.

Even with inadequate data, though, I consider this kind of analysis to have been fruitful. The careers of the four localities (even treated programmatically, as was Suburbia's) have been demonstrated to be very complex, affected by external events as well as by interaction of elements within the localities themselves (for another formulation of this complexity, see Leeds, 1969). Particularly interesting to me is that serious questions are raised as to the validity of establishing "types" of localities on the basis of physical characteristics and then associating with each type of locality one or two social types, represented by slogans such as "down-and-out" or "poor-but-ambitious." It may be that the four localities I chose to study are peculiarly untypical. That is an empirical question, but not one that can be resolved with census data or opinion surveys. Until the reverse is demonstrated, I must assume that each locality, together with its population, presents as unique a pattern as each of the four discussed here. In fact, I am sure that with better data and more sensitive analysis, my own generalizations will appear as crude as those I have questioned.

All of this applies to other kinds of localities than irregular settlements. Writing about Lima, for example, we are in the habit of lumping all *callejones* together, but even from my own limited observation, it is apparent that *callejones* vary tremendously.

My objection is not to generalization, but to generalization on the basis of physical appearance of buildings and grounds and a superficial knowledge of their inhabitants. I realize that the kind of small-scale, intimate study required would pose problems for the urban designer with large programs, budgets, and proposals to implement. But that need not concern anthropologists, for whom social engineering may be a proper subject but not a proper objective of study. Even the anthropologist who wishes to "apply" his information to pragmatic concerns may serve best here as critic.

There is nothing novel about the notion that different places attract different kinds of residents, or about the idea that people change the places where they live. Putting the two concepts together in a systemic model does, however, seem to provide a useful framework for studying and describing the development of an urban locality.

NOTES

1. *Pueblo joven* is the official and locally preferred term for what is better known in the literature as *barriada*. The more general term, "squatter settlement," I would prefer to replace with "irregular settlement," because not all residents of *pueblos jóvenes* are "squatting," in the sense of occupying land illegally.

2. For example, Turner (1970) contrasts "auto-selection" of residents with selection by government agency and considers the latter's possibly deleterious effects on the settlements. Deitz, considering an attitude survey made in three pueblos jóvenes, says, "the *barriada* populace is a self-selected universe and questions which deal with the attitudes and opinions of people over time run the risk of being invalid. For example, satisfaction expressed with the site might increase over time simply because those who are dissatisfied with the *barriadas* will leave" (1969: 3-4).

3. The best such study I have seen on irregular settlements in Lima was done by Rodríguez, Gianella and Jaworski (1969), who do make a factor analysis of various characteristics of pueblos jóvenes.

4. Consideration of the uses to which people put residence in various kinds of localities has been made by Turner (1967). As an urban planner, however, Turner is concerned with more general (and hence weaker) theory than I need be as an ethnographer. His four types

of uses do not go far enough for my purposes. Mangin (personal communication) has criticized one of my earlier treatments of Turner (contained in Uzzell, 1972) as being an exercise in debunking for its own sake, charging that I do not understand what Turner is saying. In that work, I rejected the implicit evaluation of irregular settlements in Peru by Turner, Mangin, and many others, including Peruvian government officials, on the ground that it serves to perpetuate the existing socioeconomic structure. To that extent, I may have been debunking. Happily, there is nothing to debunk in the present paper. This treatment, if it relates to Turner's model (which is not terribly difficult to understand) at all, stands as an extension and possibly a refinement.

5. Field work was funded by a Fulbright-Hays Graduate Fellowship and by a research grant from the Institute of Latin American Studies, University of Texas, Austin.

6. Collection of the life histories made use of an interview schedule and was done by trained interviewers, usually during more than one visit and over a period of more than two hours. Households were selected at random. In the locality here called Suburbia, the sample was taken from two of a total of seven subdivisions; samples were taken from entire localities in the other three. A more complete discussion of the collection of these life histories appears in Uzzell (1972: 255-267). The interview schedule is Index 2 of the same work.

The life history data have been partially recoded and further refined since the earlier report was written. That is the reason for minor conflicts in numerical data presented there and here.

7. I consider Shacks to have been a single entity, even while it was scattered. Present residents who were there during the earlier period speak as though they considered it that way. At least, there is a basic continuity of residents. The effect is like that of moving from house to house in a small urban neighborhood. The sense of having resided in the same locality is unaffected by the removals within the borders of the locality.

8. I should stress that it is the large-scale, planned occupation of suburban land that was new, not "squatting," which appears to be virtually as old as Lima. At least, it was the object of complaints by very early authors (Cobo, 1935).

9. It is difficult to operationalize notions such as "down-and-out," which in my mind implies attitudinal factors. Only slightly less difficult to operationalize is "poverty." Obviously, nobody in Shacks is wealthy. Yet very few are so poor that food, for example, is inadequate. Mean household income in Shacks, Hillside, and Cercado is close to S/. 4000 per month. In Suburbia, it is about S/. 6000 per month. It was my observation that a household with about six members (an average household) that did not have extraordinary expenses could be fed adequately and clothed decently for about S/. 4000, and that a substantial house (of brick and concrete) could at the same time be built over a period of ten or fifteen years. At that level, though, entertainment, travel, and manufactured goods were difficult to come by. At what point poverty leads to malnutrition, I cannot say, much depending upon kinds of expenditures. I should think, however, that a household with six members whose monthly income fell below S/. 3000 would have a difficult time building a house, and that below S/. 2000, members of such a household would be hard pressed to get enough food to eat.

Three households in my sample reported monthly earnings appreciably below S/. 3000. The lowest earnings were reported by a 39-year-old woman, who lived alone—S/. 1400. Two others were just above and below S/. 2000, and one of these was a member of the cooperative. He had apprenticed himself to a mechanic the year before and had a reasonable expectation of increasing his income in the near future. (It was he who had joined the cooperative in 1970.) It is important to remember that I am speaking of *household* income. Income of the head of the household averages about S/. 2400 per month in Shacks. This tends to tie household income to household composition, the older householders with resident adult children generally enjoying higher household incomes.

10. I have argued elsewhere (1972) that wage labor without entrepreneurship is a social and economic dead-end in Lima, and that it is, symbolically, a continuation of the old structure of patron-client relations.

11. Residents of larger localities do make such investments with less secure tenure. One resident of Shacks told me that the difference is that the population of Shacks is too slight to make an effective bargaining force—in other words, that there is safety in numbers, and they lack numbers. Also, because the Shacks people plan to buy the land, they fear that improvements would raise the price.

12. The number of members of the cooperatives in my sample is disappointingly small. The only explanation I can think of is that some members are clustered in kin groups. I know of one case in detail in which four households, headed by two brothers, their mother, and the son-in-law of one brother, are adjacent to each other. All are members of the cooperative. My sampling technique in Shacks—taking every fourth house—caught only one of these, whereas it should have included two. I believe that there are at least two other such clusters, and possibly more. In the other localities, I used a table of random numbers to select households within subdivisions, and so avoided this problem.

13. A *callejón* is an alleyway with apartments opening onto it. See Patch's (1961) account of the life of a young resident of a downtown *callejón*.

REFERENCES

COBO, B. (1935) "Historia de la fundación de Lima." (Republished by the Provincial Council in Lima; original copyright 1882.)

COLLIER, D. (1971) "Squatter-settlement formation and the politics of co-optation in Peru." Ph.D. dissertation. University of Chicago.

DEITZ, H. (1969) "A study of integration, social mobility, and political attitudes in a migrant population in Lima, Peru." (unpublished)

LEEDS, A. (1969) "The significant variables determining the character of squatter settlements." América Latina 3: 44-86.

MANGIN, W. (1967) "Latin American squatter settlements: a problem and a solution." Latin American Research Review 2 (Summer): 65-98.

MICHL, S. (1973) "Urban squatter organization as a national government tool: the case of Lima, Peru," pp. 155-178 in Volume 3 of F. F. Rabinovitz and F. M. Trueblood (eds.) Latin American Urban Research. Beverly Hills, Calif.: Sage.

PATCH, R. (1961) "Life in a *callejón:* a study of urban disorganization." American Universities Field Staff, West Coast South American Series 8, 6 (June).

RODRIGUEZ, A., J. GIANELLA, and H. JAWORSKI (1969) "Vivienda en barriadas." Cuadernos Desco, A4 (August). Lima: Centro de Estudios y Promoción del Desarrollo.

RUEDA SANCHEZ, G. (1965) "Ley de las barriadas No. 13517 y su regalmentación (Decreto Supremo No. 23 de 21 de julio de 1961), concordancias y modifatorias." Lima: Editorial "Thesis," S.A.

TURNER, J.F.C. (1970) "Barriers and channels for housing development in modernizing countries," pp. 1-19 in W. Mangin (ed.) Peasants in Cities: Readings in the Anthropology of Urbanization. Boston: Houghton Mifflin.

––– (1967) "Four autonomous settlements in Lima, Peru." Paper for the Latin American Colloquium, Brandeis University, Waltham, Massachusetts.

UZZELL, D. (1972) "Bound for places I'm not known to: adaptation of migrants and residence in four irregular settlements in Lima, Peru." Ph.D. dissertation. University of Texas, Austin.

——— (1974) "A strategic analysis of social structure in Lima, Peru, using the concept of 'plays'." Urban Anthropology 3 (Spring): 34-46.

LARISSA LOMNITZ is Professor of Social Anthropology and Urban Planning and a staff member of the Center for Applied Mathematics and Computer Sciences (CIMAS) at the Universidad Nacional Autónoma de México. She received her doctorate from the Universidad Iberoamericana, Mexico, and has done field research in Mexico and Chile. Her current interests include models of social interaction, networks of reciprocity and mutual assistance, and the influence of power structures on human creativity. Her publications include "Patterns of Alcohol Consumption Among Mapuche Migrants" (*América Indígena*, 1969); "Reciprocity of Assistance among the Urban Middle Class of Chile," in George Dalton (ed.) *Studies in Economic Anthropology* (American Anthropological Association, 1971); and "Structure and Scientific Productivity in a Research Institute" (UNAM, 1973).

Chapter 6

THE SOCIAL AND ECONOMIC ORGANIZATION OF A MEXICAN SHANTYTOWN

LARISSA LOMNITZ

Introduction

A common prejudice found in the sociological literature on poverty consists in portraying the urban poor as people bedevilled by a wide range of social pathologies, amounting to a supposed incapacity to respond adequately to social and economic incentives. More social scientists have directed their attention toward the material and cultural deprivation that meets the eye than toward the sociocultural defense mechanisms which the urban poor have devised. My work in a Mexican shantytown, as summarized in the present chapter, deals with a basic question: How do millions of Latin Americans manage to survive in shantytowns, without savings or salable skills, largely disowned by organized systems of social security?

The fact that such a large population can subsist and grow under conditions of extreme deprivation in Latin American cities has important theoretical implications. Obviously, the members of such a group can hardly be described as "unfit" for urban life in any meaningful sense. On the contrary, the proliferation of shantytowns throughout Latin America indicates that these forms of urban settlement are successful and respond to some sort of objective social need (Mangin, 1967; Turner and Mangin, 1968). My own work in Mexico City tends to support this view, by providing evidence that shantytowns are actually breeding grounds for a new form of social organization, which is adaptive to the

Author's Note: I would like to thank my husband, Professor Cinna Lomnitz, for his continuous encouragement and support, as well as for his help in editing the English version; Professor Richard Adams for his guidance and comments; and the Wenner-Gren Foundation for Anthropological Research for financial support.

socioeconomic requisites of survival in the city. In this paper, I show that the networks of reciprocal exchange among shantytown dwellers constitute an effective standby mechanism, whose purpose is to provide a minimum of economic security under conditions of chronic underemployment.

This study is the result of two years of field work in a shantytown. There is an abundant literature on shantytowns in Latin America (Bonilla, 1961; Leeds, 1969; Mangin, 1967; Matos Mar, 1968; Nichamin, 1968; Safa, 1964; Roberts, 1973; Peattie, 1968; Portes, 1972). Like most of these authors, I have used participant observation and unstructured interviews in the anthropological tradition. However, I have also made a number of quantitative surveys covering the totality of households in the shantytown, in order to substantiate the major conclusions. This eclectic approach works better in the urban environment, where the homogeneity of the unit of study cannot be taken for granted. Statistical results are not presented for their own sake; rather, they are used to fill out the conceptual model based on direct observation.

The Research Site

The shantytown of Cerrada del Cóndor sprawls over a ravine in the southern part of Mexico City, facing a cemetery on the opposite slope. The ravine represents the natural boundary between two residential middle-class neighborhoods of fairly recent development. This area makes up the hilly outskirts of the ancient township of Mixcoac, a part of urban Mexico City since about 1940. Prior to that time, a few small entrepreneurs raised flowers and tree seedlings on the hills and worked the sand pits in the ravine.

The earliest settler bought a tract of barren land about 1930, at the location of the present shantytown. There he settled with his family and began to manufacture adobe bricks. He was later joined by a caretaker of the sand pits. Within ten years, there were about a dozen families living in Cerrada del Cóndor, all of them workers in the adobe industry. Around that time the owner decided to sell fifteen small lots to new settlers, who immediately started to build their own homes.

By the end of the 1940s, the whole surrounding area was being urbanized. The southward growth of the city had begun to swallow up the towns of Mixcoac and San Angel. The shantytown, however, was unfavorably located on the slopes of the ravine and was bypassed by developers. During the 1950s, thirty new families arrived. These included workers in the sand pits, the adobe works, and in the housing projects of the neighboring hills, particularly the suburb of Las Aguilas. A considerable number of relatives of the original settlers also came directly from rural areas. After 1960, the shantytown began to grow very rapidly: 111 families arrived during this period, plus around 25 families who left during the period of the study (1969-1971) and are therefore not included in the survey.

As both the adobe factory and the sandpits closed down, their owners became the slumlords of the shantytown; yet they did not move away. The settlers pay rent for their houses or for plots of land on which they erect houses of their own. At present the shantytown of Cerrada del Cóndor includes about 176 households, most of which were surveyed during the study.

Origins of the Settlers

A full 70 percent of the heads of families and their spouses (hereafter referred as the "settlers") are of rural origin, having migrated to the Mexico City metropolitan area from localities of less than 5,000 inhabitants. The remaining 30 percent were born in the Federal District, either as sons or daughters of rural migrants, or as inhabitants of the small towns which are now part of the southern residential area of the city.

Eighty-six percent of the rural migrants moved directly to Mexico City, without intermediate stops. This high proportion applies to all age groups. In fact, about 70 percent of all migrants moved in family groups, and only 30 percent were single. The rural migrants came from the most impoverished sectors of the Mexican peasantry. Eighteen states are represented in the shantytown, but the states of Guanajuato, México, and San Luis Potosí account for 56.6 percent of all migrants. Veracruz, Zacatecas, and Hidalgo come next, with about 6 to 7 percent each. In discussing their reasons for migrating, nearly all migrants declared that they had been landless field workers, or that their land holdings had been too poor for subsistence.

Thirty-five percent of the migrant heads of families and their spouses were illiterate; another 9 percent had never been to school but knew the rudiments of reading and writing. Another 33 percent had had one to three years of schooling. It is probably fair to say that more than half the settlers of rural origin were functionally illiterate at the time when they reached the Federal District. They had neither savings nor skills of any value in the urban labor market.

Among those born in the Federal District, the illiteracy rate was significantly lower. Only 17 percent had never been to school, and nearly half of those had taught themselves the rudiments of reading and writing. We shall see later that there is a significant correlation between schooling and economic status, as measured by income and material possessions.

When migrants reach the city, they normally move in with relatives. The presence of a relative in the city is perhaps the most consistent element within the migration process. The role of this relative determines the circumstances of the migrant family's new life in the city, including place of settlement within the metropolitan area, initial economic status, and type of work. There is no escaping the economic imperative of living near some set of relatives: the initial term of stay with a given kinship set may be variable, but subsequent moves tend to be made with reference to pre-existing groups of relatives elsewhere.

Unattached nuclear families soon manage to attract other relatives to the neighborhood.

The Villela Group: An Example of Kin-Mediated Migration

Among the thirty-odd households from the state of San Luis Potosí, twenty-five came from the *hacienda-ejido* Villela near Santa María del Río. These families are related through consanguinal and marriage ties. The experience of the Villela group will serve as an example of the process of kin-mediated migration as observed in Cerrada del Cóndor.

The settlement of migrants from Villela goes back to the early 1950s, when two young men from the village decided to try their luck in Mexico City. They found work in the adobe factory and settled in Cerrada del Cóndor. One year later, one of them brought a sister and two nieces with their offspring to Mexico City. These nieces later brought their mother and brothers, and other relatives in successive waves. Two other Villela families also migrated to Cerrada del Cóndor and became related to the first family group by marriage or *compadrazgo* (fictive kinship).

After working at various trades, one of the migrants was fortunate to find work as a carpet-layer. Later migrants were lodged, fed, and counseled by those among their kin already in residence, with the result that practically all men now work in the carpeting trade. This pattern can be observed quite generally among family networks and is by no means unique to the Villela network. Thus, all the men in one network polish tombstones; in another, they work as bakers; still others are members of bricklayer crews, and so on.

Villela settlers in Cerrada del Cóndor maintain a closely knit community within the shantytown. They founded the oldest functioning local association, the Villela football club, with three teams in constant training which participate in league tournaments in Mexico City. Social contact among Villela families is intense, and there is a great deal of mutual assistance among them. All migrants express satisfaction at the positive results of their move to Mexico City, and not even the grandmothers show any nostalgia for Villela, where, they say, "we were starving."

Moves Within the City

It has sometimes been assumed that migrants to Mexico City initially tend to gravitate toward the crowded tenements in the old downtown area (Turner and Mangin, 1968). Our research in Cerrada del Cóndor does not confirm this hypothesis. Instead, the place of initial residence is determined by the residence of pre-extant cores of relatives in the city. In general, the migrants continue to move within the city, but always in the same general sector. Thus, the settlers of Cerrada del Cóndor were born in or migrated initially to the southern part of the metropolitan area, and few of them have more than a very superficial acquaintance with other parts of the city, including the downtown area. Few of the men venture farther into the city than their jobs require. Women and children barely know anything of the city beyond a church, a market, or the home of some relative.

The mechanism of moves within the urban area was studied in some detail. In general, a family moved once every five years on the average for the first ten or fifteen years of married life; some families never seemed to settle down. Moves seemed to be caused largely by displacement due to the southward growth of the city, coupled with a desire to seek better work opportunities and more congenial kin. There is an important turnover in Cerrada del Cóndor: during the period of my study, about twenty-five to thirty families moved away, and some forty new families moved in. As previously noted, Cerrada del Cóndor has been bypassed by developers and represents an area of refuge for those displaced by urban growth.

Most of the new settlers in Cerrada del Cóndor, however, merely follow the pull of relatives who already live in the shantytown. These relatives have told them about cheap available housing and have offered the exchange of mutual help, without which life in a shantytown is extremely difficult. Thus, kinship is also the determining factor in the process of residential mobility within the city. When job opportunities seem sufficiently bright for a nuclear family to move into a new area, they soon bring in other relatives from nearby areas or directly from the countryside. New migrants may be recruited during trips to the village, as migrant families keep in regular contact with their place or origin. Visits occur normally on festive occasions, such as holidays and celebrations.

In conclusion, it may be said that each migrant helps several new migrants to settle in the city, or to move from another part of the city to this shantytown. This he does by providing temporary or permanent lodging, food, information, assistance in job-hunting, moral support, and the basis for a more permanent form of exchange to be discussed later.

Economics of Shantytown Life

The general economic setting of Cerrada del Cóndor is one of extreme poverty. A typical dwelling consists of a single room measuring ten by twelve feet, containing one or two beds shared by members of the family. There may also be a table, a chair, a gas or petroleum stove, and sometimes a television set—33 percent of all households own one. There are three public water faucets in the shantytown, which are used by most of the population (a few clusters of dwellings have a faucet of their own). There is little public sanitation and drainage; more than four-fifths of the population use the bottom of the gully for a latrine. Sanitary conditions are made worse by the presence of a large public garbage dump next to the shantytown. There is no regular electric service; power is obtained by illegal hook-ups to the power lines. There are no paved streets, only alleys and gutters left between residential units.

Families residing in Cerrada del Cóndor can be classified according to the following levels of living:

Level A. Three or more rooms, running water, bathroom or privy, brick construction, cement or tile floor; dining-room furniture, living-room, electric appliances such as sewing machine, washer or refrigerator; gas stove.

Level B. Two rooms, cement floor, no running water, some furniture such as a trunk or closet, table and several chairs, some electrical appliance(s), gas stove.

Level C. The same as level B but no electrical appliances (except for radio or television), lower-quality furniture, petroleum-burner for cooking.

Level D. One room with or without small lean-to for cooking; no furniture (except beds and an occasional table or chair); clothing kept in boxes or under the bed; no appliances (except for radio or television); petroleum cooking only.

Analysis by means of contingency tables showed that the four criteria used (housing, furniture, type of cooking, and electrical appliances) were highly intercorrelated.

The distribution of levels of living within Cerrada del Cóndor was found to be as follows:

Level A	7.8%
Level B	8.9%
Level C	23.8%
Level D	59.5%

The level of living was also found to be highly correlated with other economic indicators, particularly the occupational status of the breadwinner. Table 1 shows that the total of unskilled laborers, journeymen, servants, and petty traders corresponds closely to the total of families classified in levels C and D.

Unskilled laborers or apprentices include hod carriers and other construction workers (foremen excepted), house painters, sandpit workers, brickmakers, bakers' helpers, truckers' helpers, carpet-layers, electricians, gardeners, and other unskilled laborers paid by the day who earn the minimum legal wage or less. Semi-skilled or skilled journeymen or craftsmen include independent or freelance workers such as bakers, carpet-layer foremen, construction foremen, electrician foremen, truck drivers, tombstone polishers, carpenters, cobblers, blacksmiths, potters, and so on. These may earn higher wages, but their job security is usually as low as that of the unskilled workers. Some of them have

TABLE 1
OCCUPATIONS OF HEADS OF HOUSEHOLDS IN
CERRADA DEL CONDOR

	Men		Women	
	n	%	n	%
Unskilled laborers or apprentices	51	32.0	1	4.5
Semi-skilled or skilled journeymen or craftsmen	48	31.0	–	–
Industrial workers	16	10.3	–	–
Service workers	5	3.2	12	54.6
Traders	7	4.5	4	18.2
Employees	8	5.1	1	4.5
Landlords	5	3.3	1	4.5
Unemployed	15	9.7	–	–
Housewives	–	–	3	12.7
TOTAL	155	100.0	22	100.0

developed a steady clientele and work with their own assistants, usually relatives. Industrial workers are those who work in an industrial plant, usually with the lowest wages and qualifications: watchmen, car washers, janitors, and unskilled laborers. The service workers include waiters, water carriers, watchmen, icemen, and domestic servants. Traders include all kinds of street vendors. None of these has a steady income or social security. The employees are unskilled workers who earn fixed salaries: municipal workers (street sweepers, garbagemen), and a few similarly employed with private corporations. These have a relatively high job security and other benefits. Finally, there are six households whose income is mainly derived from rentals of property in the shantytown.

About 10 percent of the household heads were out of work at the time of the survey. However, more than 60 percent of those who said they were working consider intermittent joblessness for variable periods of time to be normal. Thus, the majority of the working population in the shantytown are underemployed ("eventuales"), and have no job security, no social security, and no fixed income. They exist from day to day, as urban "hunters and gatherers." Members of level-of-living D belong to this group. More than half the settlers in level D were illiterate. None owned both his home and the lot it was built on; nearly two-thirds paid rent for both. All lived in a housing unit consisting of a single room. The average number of people per room was 5.4, if the cooking was done inside, and 6.2 if there was a lean-to for cooking. Of all acknowledged cases of problem drinkers, more than 75 percent belonged to level D.

In contrast, members of level A were practically all owners of their homes and lots. Most of them were either born in the Federal District or have lived in town for many years. There was practically no illiteracy, and most settlers had completed third grade. They tended to belong to the upper types of occupations: landlords, employees, traders, and industrial workers; their most distinctive trait was job security. More than half the households in this group included two or more breadwinners. The men were either abstemious or moderate drinkers.

Levels B and C are intermediate, but they can be sharply distinguished. Level B is urban in type of dwelling, furniture, and life style, while Level C is still rural in most of these respects. Households of either type can usually be recognized by a glance at their belongings. The transition from C to B is not determined so much by gross income as by the degree of cultural assimilation to urban life: hence, time of residence in the city is a significant factor. Even the highest income in Cerrada del Cóndor could easily be used up by a single heavy drinker. Wives receive a weekly allowance and have no direct knowledge of their husbands' income. Working wives contribute their total income to household expenses; likewise, sons and daughters hand their earnings to the mother. The husband's contribution to raising the economic level of the household is largely limited to major appliances which are purchased on the installment plan. However, if the husband enjoys a steady income and has a tolerant view of a working wife, the economic improvement of the family may be rapid by shantytown standards. Nevertheless, the transition from level C to level B is rarely accomplished before a household has completed ten years of residence in the city.

Social Organization

The pattern of social organization which prevails in the shantytown can be described as follows. Most nuclear families initially lodge with kin, either in the same residential unit (47 percent), or in a compound arrangement (27 percent). Kinship compounds are groups of neighboring residential units which share a common outdoor area for washing, cooking, playing of children and so on. Each nuclear family in such a cluster forms a separate economic unit. Compound families are related through either consanguinity or marriage ties; each compound household contains at least two nuclear families.

Extended families—e.g., two brothers with their wives and children—may share the same residential unit temporarily; in the case of newly married couples with the parents of either husband or wife, the arrangement may be more permanent. Any room or group of rooms having a single private entrance is defined as a residential unit: this excludes tenements of the *"vecindad"* type, consisting of a series of rooms opening on an alley with a public entrance gate, which may contain several independent family groups. Extended families contain at least two nuclear families; these share the rental expenses or own the property in common. Sometimes they also share living expenses.

Extended households are more unstable than compound households. Nuclear families in an extended household tend to move into a nearby room of their own, or to join a different set of relatives elsewhere. However, those who move away in search of independence and privacy eventually return for security or assistance. In the case of compound households, the rate of desertion is much lower. Of forty-four nuclear families who joined a compound arrangement since the beginning of married life, only seven moved away in an attempt to form an independent household.

Thirteen couples began their married lives as independent households within the Federal District; these represent the major exception to the pattern of social organization described above. The heads of these households had all been born in Mexico City or had lived there for many years. Yet even these households do not remain independent for long, since they tend to attract other kin who join them in an extended or compound arrangement. The complete data for household types is summarized in Table 2.

Independent nuclear families are in the minority; those who live within walking distance of relatives are usually waiting for a vacancy to move into a compound-type arrangement. In this case, there is much visiting, mutual assistance, and other types of interaction even though the related nuclear families are not yet fully integrated into a compound household. The term "nuclear family" is used in a broad sense here, as each nuclear family may include one or more individually attached kin. Most of them are older persons or young children of unmarried recent arrivals from the country. Nuclear families may also include the offspring of a previous union of the mother; in two such cases, there was no offspring from the present union.

Thus, the social organization of the shantytown may be described as a collection of family networks which assemble and disband through a dynamic process. There is no official community structure; there are no local authorities or mechanisms of internal control. Cooperation within the family networks is the basic pattern of social interaction. There is a pattern of movement from the extended toward the compound household type, as illustrated by a survey tracing the moves of each household over the past years. The results show that there is an increase of 29 percent in compound household arrangements, against a decrease of 46.7 percent in extended household arrangements, as compared with the initial state of residence.

This pattern can be viewed as the outcome of a dynamic process, which

TABLE 2

TYPES OF HOUSEHOLDS IN CERRADA DEL CONDOR

Extended families	29
Nuclear families in a compound-type arrangement	68
Independent nuclear families:	
(a) without kin	30
(b) with kin in Cerrada del Cóndor	28
Other unknown	7
Total households in survey	162

depends on economic circumstances, the stage in the life cycle, the availability of housing vacancies, personal relationships with relatives, etc. The initial choice of moving in with the family of either spouse is usually an economic one. Since young husbands or wives often do not get along with their in-laws and conditions in an extended family may be very crowded, the couple tends to move out. However, new circumstances, such as the arrival of children, desertion of the husband, loss of employment, and so on frequently compel the family to return to the shelter of relatives. The preferred arrangement is the compound household, which combines proximity of kin with an adequate amount of independence and privacy.

Kinship Relationships Outside the Shantytown

A pattern of residential moves such as we have described, sometimes over large distances, implies a substantial amount of contact among kin extending beyond the physical boundaries of the shantytown. The existence of such contact was confirmed initially through personal observation and later by means of a kinship census covering all households in the shantytown.

Contact with relatives within the Federal District depends on kinship distance and on physical distance. Informants tend to list first their nuclear family of orientation, then other relatives by order of spatial proximity: first those who live in the shantytown, then those who live in a nearby shantytown such as Puente Colorado, and so on. If a relative is not particularly close and lives as much as two hours away by bus from Cerrada del Cóndor the contact is unlikely to be significant, and may be lost after a generation. The mother is often the only nexus between such relatives, and contact vanishes after her death. Of course, if there exists a true closeness of relationship each set of relatives will exert a great deal of "pull" on the other, in order to encourage them to move into as close a neighborhood as possible.

Changes in socioeconomic status become a factor which influences the intensity of contact between kin. A female informant commented that she hardly ever saw her sisters, who were married to skilled industrial workers: "To tell the truth, I don't like to go and see them because they can dress very nicely and I can't afford to and so . . . I feel ashamed." The informant is the daughter of a skilled worker, who married a man who "never finished grade school and is worse off" than her sisters' husbands. Her parents were opposed to the match because her husband had no skills, "not even that of a truck driver, a barber or a carpenter," but she was in love and they went to live with his parents. At first they lived in the same residential unit in Cerrada del Cóndor; now they have a room nearby, because "each on his own is better."

Contact between migrant families and their relatives in the countryside usually takes the form of visits to the village on festive occasions, such as Mother's Day, All Saints' Day, and the festival of the patron saint of the village.

Unmarried migrants often return to the city accompanied by a smaller brother, sister, or cousin whom they help out until they find a job. Married migrants frequently maintain a share in a small plot of land which they own jointly with a brother, and they time their occasional visits to coincide with harvest time, and so on. Most migrants send money home to their parents or close relatives. Through word of mouth or correspondence, they keep up with village gossip; eventually they are instrumental in promoting the migration of their close kin from the village. For years there is a steady stream of relatives from the country, who are lodged and fed for indeterminate periods of time depending on resources and needs.

Contact with the village gradually wanes over the years. About one-fourth of all informants said they had relatives in the country but had lost all touch with them: "I haven't seen my folks since I got married and moved to the city eighteen years ago" . . . "I never went back home since my mother died—my father married again and I don't get along with my stepmother" . . . "My brothers have moved to the city; I used to visit them and bring them money; now I don't go any more" . . . "I never went back since my grandparents and parents died." Other migrants, however, said they maintained significant contact through visits to and from the village; through economic interests (land owned in common); through correspondence; through remittances of money; through sentimental pilgrimages (visiting Mother's grave on All Saints' Day), and so on.

Local Groups

The shantytown is not organized around central institutions of any kind. Instead, there are several types of groupings, of unequal importance: (a) the family network; (b) football teams; (c) the medical center; (d) temporary associations.

The family networks will be discussed in greater detail below, as it is our thesis that they represent the effective community for the individual in the shantytown. They are composed of members of an extended or compound family, but may include neighbors who are assimilated through fictive kinship. We shall see how these networks have developed into systems of reciprocal exchange of assistance, which provides an important explanation for the fact of survival of large numbers of people under the severe economic handicaps of shantytown life.

Other forms of organization at the community level are relatively rudimentary. There are four football teams in Cerrada del Cóndor. Three of these teams belong in effect to a single large family network, the Villela network described above. The fourth is a more recent team whose membership is recruited among young people of the shantytown irrespective of family origins. Football teams represent one of the few vehicles of social contact between men of Cerrada del Cóndor and men who live in other parts of town. After a game, there are drinking sessions which reinforce the team spirit and friendships among members of the team.

The shantytown's medical center was organized and financed by a group of middle-class ladies from the neighboring residential district, with some assistance from a nearby church. Later, the national Children's Hospital agreed to staff the center, but this help has recently been withdrawn. In spite of the modest assistance offered, the center has become an important part of shantytown life. It is a place where children are welcome during most hours of the day, and where many girls and women can receive guidance from an understanding social worker.

There is no local organization for solving the common problems of shantytown life. Groups of neighbors may band together for specific issues; this has happened three or four times in the existence of Cerrada del Cóndor. The first time was to request the installation of a public water outlet. Another time, a group of women jointly requested an audience with the First Lady, in order to lodge a complaint about spillage of oil from a refinery that was causing brush fires in the ravine. These exceptional instances of cooperation merely serve to highlight the absence of any organized effort to solve community problems.

The residents of Cerrada del Cóndor have little contact with citywide or national organizations. Articulation with Mexican urban culture occurs mainly through work and through mass media such as radio and television. School is, of course, very important among the children's population. Adult reading is limited to sports sheets, comics, and photo-romance magazines. Only about one-tenth of the men belong to the social security system. About 5 percent are union members. In general, extremely few people belong to any organized group on a national level, such as political parties, religious organizations, and so on.

Social Networks

According to Barnes (1954), a network is a social field made up of relations between people. These relations are defined by criteria underlying the field. While Barnes saw a network as essentially unbounded, Mayer (1962) showed how certain types of migrants encapsulate themselves in a bounded network of personal relationships. In the case of Cerrada del Cóndor, we find networks defined by criteria of neighborhood social distance and exchange of goods and services.

Each network is constituted of nuclear families, not individuals. Initially we shall use an operational definition of networks as clusters of neighboring nuclear families who practice continuous reciprocal exchange of goods and services. A total of forty-five such networks were identified in Cerrada del Cóndor. The social relationships which form the basis of these networks are as follows: thirty are networks based on consanguineal and marriage ties, seven are based on kinship but included also one or more families not related by kinship, and eight are formed by families not related by kinship. The number of nuclear families per network is shown in Table 3. The average network contains four nuclear families. Of course, the number of families in a network is not static but changes with time. Initially, the network may be composed of two or three families; it may grow until a part of the network is split off because of lack of room or facilities. Table 3 does not include unattached nuclear families (estimated at less than ten).

It is possible for several networks to be interrelated through kinship. Thus, the Villela macro-network includes about twenty-five nuclear families grouped into five networks. Each of these networks internally displays a high degree of reciprocal exchange of goods and services on a day-to-day basis. The resources of the macro-network are used more on ritual occasions, in important matters such as job placement, in the expression of kin solidarity (football teams), and drinking. Reciprocal exchange does occur between families belonging to different networks within a macro-network system, but the recurrence of such exchanges is less frequent, because no single nuclear family in the shantytown has enough resources to maintain a generalized day-to-day exchange with such a large group of families.

All nuclear families in a network practice reciprocal exchange among each other on an equal footing. In addition, a nuclear family may maintain dyadic exchange relations with families outside the network, or belonging to other networks. These dyadic ties are important because they provide the mechanism through which an outside family can be attracted to join the network, or by which a network which has outgrown its optimal size may split.

A network constituted as an extended family practices a generalized exchange of goods and services, which includes the informal pooling of resources for rent and entertainment, joint use of cooking facilities, communal child care, and many others. Each nuclear family contributes according to its ability and receives according to the availability of resources within the network. There is no accounting of any kind among the members of such a network. In a compound household, on the other hand, each nuclear family has a roof and an

TABLE 3
NUMBER OF NUCLEAR FAMILIES PER NETWORK

Nuclear Families *n*	Cases *n*
2	9
3	13
4	10
5	6
6	5
uncertain	2
TOTAL	45

economy of its own; yet there is an intense exchange of goods and services in the form of daily borrowings of food, tools, and money. Reciprocity here is not openly acknowledged, but it is definitely expected; each member family is supposed to provide assistance in proportion to its economic ability. Thus, if a nuclear family within a compound network becomes economically more secure than the rest, it may find its resources taxed beyond the actual returns which it can expect from the network. As a result, the more prosperous families may stop asking for and offering services.

Case History

The network is of the compound type and includes two sisters A and B, who married two brothers. A nonkin neighbor is also included in the network. A third sister, C, brought in from the village to live with A, soon found work as a maid living in the house of their employer. On her days off, she visited A. A niece from the country has now joined the network with her husband. At first they lived with A, who obtained work for the husband and a room adjoining hers. All men in the network are currently working as tombstone polishers. When C became pregnant, she quit her job and went again to live with A. After she had the baby, she went back to work and left the baby in A's care during the day.

Meanwhile, B's economic status had been rising steadily. Her husband did not drink and invested in home furnishings. He also found advancement at work and became a skilled worker (in the placement of tombstones). B began to refuse to lend (or ask for) favors within the network, claiming that she had no money. Her sister, niece, and neighbor gradually stopped requesting assistance, and so did their respective husbands. After a while, B found a room just beyond the limits of the shantytown, two blocks away from her former room but with urban services. Her economic level is rated "B."

Sister C found a husband and moved in with him. The husband lived several blocks away from the sisters' compound, outside Cerrada del Cóndor. Yet C practically continued to live at A's place whenever her husband was away at work. When she works she leaves her child with A; when she needs money she borrows from A or from her niece. Her interaction with the nonkin member of the network is less intense; yet these neighbors have become double *compadres* in the meantime, and their exchange with both A and the niece and their respective husbands is very active. When a room became available, C began to convince her husband to move in with the network. In that case, an active exchange between C and the nonkin neighbor is anticipated.

What Is Exchanged?

The following items represent the most important objects of exchange in the networks, according to my observation:

(a) *Information,* including directions for migration, employment, and residence; gossip; and orientation about urban life.

(b) *Training and job assistance,* including the training and establishing of a relative as a competitor. Thus, a carpet-layer or a building contractor would take his newly arrived brother-in-law along as an assistant, teach him the trade, share earnings with him, and eventually yield some of his own clientele to set him up as an independent worker.

(c) *Loans,* of money, food, blankets, tools, clothing, and other goods.

(d) *Services,* including the lodging and care of visiting relatives, widows, orphans, old people; care and errand-running for such neighbors; and minding children for working mothers. Assistance among men includes help in home construction and in transporting materials. Children must lend a hand in carrying water and running errands.

(e) *The sharing of facilities* such as a television set or a latrine (which the men may have built jointly).

(f) *Moral and emotional support* in ritual situations (weddings, baptisms, funerals) as well as in day-to-day interactions (gossip among the women, drinking among the men). It is essential to recognize that much of the socializing in the shantytown is based on network affiliation. This constant interaction generates an overriding preoccupation with each other's lives among the members of a network. There is little opportunity for privacy.

The ubiquity of these forms of exchange provides important evidence in support of our interpretation of shantytown networks as economic structures which represent a specific response of marginal populations to economic insecurity in the city.

Reinforcing Mechanisms

The exchange of goods and services serves as the underpinning of a social structure: the network organization. When this exchange ceases to exist, the network disintegrates. The social structure which is erected on the basis of exchange depends on physical and social proximity of network members. Ideally, the networks are composed of neighbors related through kinship.

Actually, many networks contain nonkin members whose allegiance must be reinforced by means of fictive kinship *(compadrazgo)* and other means which will be analyzed presently. Even among kin, relationships are far from secure: economic and personal differences arise frequently under conditions of extreme poverty and overcrowding. The reinforcing mechanisms to be discussed are therefore present in all networks.

Compadrazgo is widely used to reinforce existing or prospective network ties. In Cerrada del Cóndor, the *compadres* have few formal obligations toward each other as such. An informant says: "When choosing a godfather for one's child one should look for a decent person and a good friend, if it's a couple, they should be properly married. They should be poor so no one can say that you picked them out of self-interest." Among 426 compadres of baptism (the most important type of compadrazo in the shantytown), 150 were relatives who lived close by, and 200 were nonkin neighbors. Another 92 were relatives who lived elsewhere in the Federal District or in the countryside—i.e., prospective network affiliates. In most cases of compadrazo, the dominant factors were physical proximity and kinship. This equalitarian pattern is at variance with the frequently observed rural pattern of selecting a compadre above one's station in life (Forbes, 1971).

The great importance of compadrazgo as a reinforcing mechanism of network structure is also reflected in the variety of types of compadrazgo that continue to be practiced in the shantytown. These types are, by order of decreasing importance: baptism (426 cases), confirmation (291), communion (79), wedding (31), burial (16), Saint's Day (13), fifteenth birthday (10), Divine Child (8), Gospels (8), grade school graduation (4), habit (3), sacrament (2), scapulary (1), cross (1), and St. Martin's (1). All these types of compadrazgo mark ritual or life-cycle occasions. The formal obligations among compadres can be described as follows: "They must treat each other with respect at all times, and must exchange greetings whenever they meet." Ideally some compadres should fulfill economic obligations, such as taking care of a godchild if the father dies; but these obligations are no longer taken very seriously in the shantytown.

If compadrazgo formalizes and legitimizes a relationship between men and women, *cuatismo,* the Mexican form of male friendship, provides the emotional content of the relationship. *Cuates* (a Nahuatl term for "twins") are close friends who pass the time together, talking, drinking, playing cards or football, watching TV, treating each other in restaurants, and having fun together; above all, they are drinking companions. Women are totally excluded from the relationship. A wife "would never dare" to approach a *cuate* of her husband's to request a favor.

Assistance among cuates is ruled by social distance. Among relatives, there will be more unconditional help than among neighbors. In general, the cuates borrow freely from each other, help each other in looking for work, give each other a hand in fixing their homes, and stand by each other in a fight. Like compadrazgo, cuatismo is practically universal: the man who has no cuate and no compadre is lost indeed. Among a total of 10 percent of households headed by men, the circle of cuates of the family head was recruited as follows: 86 were groups of cuates who lived in the immediate vicinity, 9 were mixed groups (some cuates living close by and some far away), and 11 were groups whose members did not live in the immediate neighborhood. Two heads of households had not yet made any cuates in the city.

It is clear that these groups of cuates are based primarily on the male sector of the networks described above, even though neighbors, work companions, or friends not affiliated with one's special network may be included. The existence of cuatismo to reinforce network affiliation is evidence that the networks are not simply built around the wives and mothers, as might be supposed from a superficial analysis. On the contrary, many networks appear to be male-dominated. If networks were based exclusively on the more visible forms of daily exchange of goods and services practiced by women, the substantial overlap between networks and groups of cuates would be rather puzzling. Networks are constituted by nuclear families as entities; all members of each nuclear family participate actively in the relationship.

Drinking relationships among cuates are exceedingly important and usually take precedence over marital relationships. From a psychological point of view, drinking together is a token of absolute mutual trust which involves a baring of souls to each other (Lomnitz, 1969; Butterworth, 1972). From the economic point of view, cuatismo implies a mechanism of redistribution through drink which ensures that all cuates remain economically equal. And from a social point of view, it reinforces existing social networks and extends the influence of networks in many directions, since a drinking circle may contain members of several networks.

The *ideology of assistance* is another important factor in network reinforcement. When questioned, most informants are reluctant to describe their own requests for assistance; yet they are unanimous in claiming to be always ready to help out their own relatives and neighbors in every possible way.

The duty of assistance is endowed with every positive moral quality; it is the ethical justification for network relations. Any direct or indirect refusal of help within a network is judged in the harshest possible terms and gives rise to disparaging gossip. People are constantly watching for signs of change in the economic status of all members of the network. Envy and gossip are the twin mechanisms used for keeping the others in line. Any show of selfishness or excessive desire for privacy will set the grapevine buzzing. There will be righteous comments, and eventually someone will find a way to set the errant person straight.

Reciprocity and Confianza

The types of reciprocity between shantytown members are determined by a factor which I have called *"confianza"* (Lomnitz, 1971). Confianza depends on cultural factors (social distance) and physical factors (closeness and intensity of exchange, as when a close friend or "cuate" enjoys greater confianza than a relative who lives elsewhere and is met only occasionally).

The formal categories of social distance are culturally determined. They imply a "series of categories and plans of action" (Bock, 1969: 24) which dictate expected behavior between individuals. These categories and plans of action can only be described ethnographically: they represent an essential part of the culture or subculture of a group or subgroup. In Mexico, within the national culture, there are subcultures of each social class, each state or region, and so on down to the level of family subculture which may imply strongly particularized sets of behavior. Two individuals are close in the scale of confianza to the extent that they share the same set of behavior expectations. These expectations include a specific type of reciprocity, extending from unconditional sharing to total lack of cooperation and distrust. The scale of confianza measures, among other things, the extent to which these expectations are actually fulfilled. Hence, the degree of confianza is not rigidly determined but may vary during the evolution of the relationship.

Social Networks in the Context of Marginality

Residents of shantytowns such as Cerrada del Cóndor are often counted among the "marginal" sector of the urban population in Latin America. The emergence of urban marginal populations is not, of course, exclusive to underdeveloped societies. In advanced industrial nations, such populations result from the displacement of certain social strata from the labor market through mechanization and automation of the means of production. These growing population sectors have no expectation of absorption into productive occupations, and become increasingly dependent on welfare. They represent *surplus* population (rather than a labor reserve) and are, therefore, an unwanted by-product of the system.

According to Quijano (1970), this situation is considerably aggravated in underdeveloped countries, because the rate and pattern of industrial development are imposed from abroad. Economic dependence introduces a factor of instability, because of the hypertrophic growth of large industrial cities at the expense of the countryside. Accessibility of sources of raw materials and cheap labor attract an overflow of hegemonic capital into formerly pre-industrial societies. As a result, (1) there is an increasing gap between "modern" cities and "traditional" rural areas on the verge of starvation; (2) new skills required by industrial growth are monopolized by a relatively small labor elite, while the great mass of unskilled peasants and artisans is displaced from their traditional sources of livelihood; (3) superficial modernization has caused a sudden population explosion, which increases the rate of rural-to-urban migration, thus offsetting any efforts at promoting the gradual absorption of surplus populations into the industrial labor force. Thus, the process of marginalization is not transitional, but, rather, intrinsic to the system.

Quijano specifically identifies the capitalistic system in general, and the dependent industrial development observed in Latin America since 1945 in particular, as responsible for the phenomenon of marginality. Adams (1970: 89-94, 1972) generalizes this analysis to apply to any large society which is subject to a process of economic development and technological change.

According to Adams, any increment in social organization is achieved at the expense of disorganization among sectors of the same society, or of dependent societies. Dialectically speaking, order is the source of disorder: work creates entropy. Starting from an undifferentiated labor force, we may build up an industrial proletariat with highly differentiated skills and a centralized form of organization; but this will generate marginalization of those populations which can no longer be assimilated or successfully utilized by the more advanced system.

In Latin America, the urban marginal strata share the following economic characteristics, which are also found among the settlers of Cerrada del Cóndor (a) unemployment or underemployment; (b) lack of stable income; (c) generally the lowest level of income within the urban population. Most settlers of Cerrada del Cóndor are rural migrants, or the offspring of migrant parents. Most of them are unskilled workers, such as construction workers, who are hired and fired on a daily basis; journeymen and artisans who are hired for specific jobs and have no fixed income; petty traders; and people who work in menial services. They may be described as urban hunters and gatherers, who live in the interstices of the urban economy, where they maintain an undervalued but nevertheless well defined role. They are both a product of underdevelopment and its wards.

If this vast social group lacks any economic security and has no significant support from organized welfare, how does it survive? This question was posed by Quijano (1970: 87-96), who surmises that there must be some mechanism of reciprocity operating among marginal groups, which has not been described. It is the purpose of the present section to analyze this mechanism in some detail, as a function of the socioeconomic structure.

According to Polanyi (1968: 127-132) and Dalton (1968: 153), there are three forms of exchange of goods and services: (1) market exchange, in which goods and services circulate on the basis of offer and demand, without any long-term social implications attached to the exchange; (2) redistribution of goods and services, which are first concentrated in a single individual or institution from whence they flow out toward a community or society; and (3) reciprocity among social equals. Reciprocity defined in this manner is an integral part of a permanent social relationship.

The urban marginal population of Mexico is estimated at four million, a considerable part of the total urban population. While the dominant mode of exchange in the cities is market exchange and is afflicted by the internal contradictions described by Marx and Polanyi, no adequate systems of public or private redistribution have been created in response to the needs of a growing mass of urban marginals left to their own devices. Economic dependence aggravates the problem, because capital gains tend to be transferred abroad instead of becoming available for redistribution within the country.

Thus, the marginal individual cannot rely on the social system for his elementary needs of survival. He has nothing to offer the market exchange system: no property, no skills except for his devalued labor. His prospects for absorption into the industrial proletariat are slim, since marginality grows faster than the number of industrial job openings. He has nothing to fall back on: no savings, no social security of any kind. His chance of survival depends on the creation of a system of exchange entirely distinct from the rules of the marketplace, a system based on his resources in kinship and friendship. This system follows the rules of reciprocity, a mode of exchange between equals, imbedded in a fabric of social relations which is persistent in time, rather than casual and momentary as in market exchange. The three basic elements of reciprocity are: (a) "confianza," an ethnographically defined measure of social distance; (b) equivalence of resources (or lack of resources); (c) physical closeness of residence.

Characteristically, reciprocity generates a moral code which is distinct, and in some ways opposed, to the moral code of market exchange. In a reciprocity relation, the emphasis is less on receiving than on giving; the recipient is preoccupied with reciprocating, rather than with extracting a maximum personal benefit from a transaction. Both systems of exchange may be used simultaneously in different context: a member of a reciprocity network may sell his labor as worker or servant on the urban market. Yet it is the reciprocal exchange among relatives and neighbors in the shantytown which ensures his survival during the frequent and lengthy spells of joblessness. Market exchange represents the ultimate source of livelihood; but it is a livelihood at the subsistence level, without any element of security. Through sharing these intermittent resources with another six or ten people, the group may successfully survive where as individuals each of them would almost certainly fail. The networks of reciprocal exchange which we have identified in Cerrada del Cóndor are functioning economic structures which maximize security, and their success spells survival for large sectors of the population.

REFERENCES

ADAMS, N. R. (1970) Crucifixion by Power. Austin: University of Texas Press.
––– (1972) "Harnessing Technology." (mimeo)
BARNES, J. A. (1954) "Class committees in a Norwegian island parish." Human Relations 7: 39-58.
BOCK, P. (1969) Modern Cultural Anthropology. New York: Alfred A. Knopf.
BONILLA, F. (1961) "Rio's favelas: the rural slum within the city." American Universities Field Staff Reports (East Coast, South American Series) 8, 3.
BURLING, R. (1962) "Maximization theories and the study of economic anthropology." American Anthropologist 64.
BUTTERWORTH, D. (1962) "A study of the urbanization process among Mixtec migrants from Tilaltongo in Mexico City." América Indígena 22: 257-274.
––– (1972) "Two small groups: a comparison of migrants and non-migrants in Mexico City." Urban Anthropology 1, 1.

COOK, S. (1968) "The obsolete 'anti-market' mentality: a critique of the substantive approach to economic anthropology," in E. E. Le Clair, Jr. and L. Schneider (eds.) Economic Anthropology. New York: Holt, Rinehart & Winston.

DALTON, G. (1968) "The economy as instituted process," in E. E. Le Clair, Jr. and L. Schneider (eds.) Economic Anthropology. New York: Holt, Rinehart & Winston.

FIRTH, R. (1970) Themes in Economic Anthropology. Edinburgh: T. A. Constable.

FORBES, J. (1971) "El sistema de compadrazgo en Santa María Belén Atzitzinititlán, Tlaxcala." M.A. thesis. Universidad Iberoamericana, Mexico, D.F.

FOSTER, G. (1969) "Godparents and social networks in Tzintzuntzan." Southern Journal of Anthropology 25, 3.

GOULDNER, A. (1960) "The norm of reciprocity: a preliminary statement." American Sociological Review 25, 2.

LEEDS, A. (1969) "The significant variables determining the character of squatter settlements." América Latina 12, 3.

––– and E. LEEDS (1970) "Brazil and the myth of urban rurality," in A. J. Field (ed.) City and Country in the Third World. Cambridge, Mass.: Schenkman.

LOMNITZ, L. (1969) "Patrones de ingestión de alcohol entre migrantes mapuches en Santiago." América Indígena 29, 1: 43-71.

––– (1971) "Reciprocity of favors among the urban middle class of Chile," in G. Dalton (ed.) Studies in Economic Anthropology. Washington, D.C.: American Anthropological Association.

MALINOWSKI, B. (1961) Argonauts of the Western Pacific. New York: E. P. Dutton.

MANGIN, W. (1967) "Latin American squatter settlements: a problem and a solution." Latin American Research Review 2, 3.

MATOS MAR, J. (1968) Urbanización y barriadas en América del Sur. Lima: Instituto de Estudios Peruanos.

MAUSS, M. (1954) The Gift. London: Cohen & West.

MAYER, P. (1962) "Migrancy and the study of Africans in town." American Anthropologist 64: 576-592.

NICHAMIN, J. (1968) "Shantytowns in Latin America: prospects for political change." Papers of the Michigan Academy of Science, Arts and Letters 53, 2.

PEATTIE, L. R. (1968) The View from the Barrio. Ann Arbor: University of Michigan Press.

POLANYI, K. (1968) The Great Transformation. Boston: Beacon Press.

PORTES, A. (1972) "Rationality in the slum: an essay on interpretive sociology." Comparative Studies in Society and History 14, 3: 268-286.

QUIJANO, A. (1970) "Redefinición de la dependencia y proceso de marginalización en América Latina." Santiago, Chile: CEPAL. (mimeo)

ROBERTS, B. (1973) Organizing Strangers: Poor Families in Guatemala City. Austin: University of Texas Press.

SAFA, H. (1964) "From shantytown to public housing: a comparison of family structure in two urban neighborhoods in Puerto Rico." Caribbean Studies 4, 1.

SAHLINS, M. D. (1968) On the Sociology of Primitive Exchange. London: Tavistock.

TURNER, J. and W. MANGIN (1968) "The barriada movement." Progressive Architecture (May).

VALENTINE, C. (1968) Culture and Poverty. Chicago: University of Chicago Press.

MICHAEL B. WHITEFORD is Assistant Professor of Anthropology at Iowa State University. He received his Ph.D. from the University of California at Berkeley and has done field work in Mexico, Costa Rica, and Colombia. His fields of specialization include migration and urbanization, changing peasant societies, and applied and medical anthropology. He is currently engaged in a comparative study of self-help community development activities in Bogotá, Cali, and Popayán, Colombia. He has published "Barrio Tulcán: Fieldwork in a Colombian City," in G. M. Foster and R. V. Kemper (eds.) *Anthropologists in Cities* (Little, Brown, 1974); and a monograph on the same low-income Colombian neighborhood, *The Forgotten Ones: Colombian Countrymen in an Urban Setting* (University of Florida Press, forthcoming).

Chapter 7

NEIGHBORS AT A DISTANCE:
LIFE IN A LOW-INCOME COLOMBIAN BARRIO

MICHAEL B. WHITEFORD

Introduction

Anthropologists in Latin America increasingly are turning their attention from rural to urban settings. Their studies generally focus on low-income groups, and are often neighborhood studies (e.g., Peattie, 1968; Mangin, 1967a, 1967b, 1970a, 1970b; Lewis, 1959; Roberts, 1970, 1973) or investigations of urban migrants from a specific rural area (e.g., Butterworth, 1962; Lewis, 1952; Kemper, 1971). Most deal with large, industrialized, cosmopolitan, often capital, cities, resulting in quite a large body of material for those areas.[1] The effect is that many statements and generalizations about the nature of urban life are based on information from places like Bogotá, Mexico City, Lima, and Buenos Aires.[2] The importance of these cities cannot be ignored, but numerically they constitute only a fraction of the total number of urban centers in Latin America. Comparable data are not so abundant for smaller, provincial, intermediate cities (e.g., A. Whiteford, 1964; Rollwagen, 1973; Reina, 1973). Often such cities are regional capitals with little or no industry and populations ranging from 10 to 20,000 to 200,000. Knowledge about these secondary cities is therefore important to the conceptual and theoretical framework of urban studies and the processes of urbanization.

Like many Latin American urban areas, the provincial city of Popayán,

Author's Note: The research here described was conducted in 1970-1971 and was made possible by National Institute of General Medical Sciences Grant GM-1224 to the Department of Anthropology, University of California, Berkeley. The author would like to thank George M. Foster, Steffen W. Schmidt, Andrew H. Whiteford, and Scott Whiteford for reading all of, and parts of, an earlier draft of this paper.

Colombia, is growing. In 1970 it had an estimated population of 77,000 (DNP, 1969: 57), a considerable increase from 58,500 (DNP, 1969: 21) in 1964. While this growth is not of the same magnitude as that of Colombia's largest cities, it is nevertheless a healthy increase,[3] one result of which is an expanding city surrounded by new barrios. In Popayán's case, this growth has been rather orderly, and its outskirts do not have the hodge-podge appearance which characterizes so many other Latin American cities. While some of these new neighborhoods are being built by private contractors for Popayán's upper and middle classes who are moving out from the city's center, most of the construction is being done by the Colombian government's housing and urban development agency, the *Instituto de Crédito Territorial* (ICT) to accommodate the influx of rural migrants.

In this chapter, I will discuss selected aspects of life in Barrio Tulcán,[4] a low-income neighborhood with a population of 1,780, located on the outskirts of Popayán. Specifically, I will describe Tulcán and then will look at how the people earn a living and at social organization and social relations among the barrio's inhabitants: how they perceive their own situation; to what extent they interact and cooperate with others whom they feel to be in a similar situation; what adaptive strategies are apparent in their relations with one another; and whether they feel they have common interests and goals with people in other socioeconomic situations.

BARRIO TULCAN

Situated about half a mile from the edge of town, Tulcán looks like a country village with its narrow dirt streets and large plots of *yuca* (sweet manioc), bananas and plantains, coffee, corn, and other garden vegetables.

It is a low-income barrio: both its inhabitants and people living in Popayán agree that it is the poorest of the city's barrios. Officially, ICT and the municipal government classify it as a slum. Tulcaneses call themselves "humble people," "poor people," or members of the "lower class," and they call Tulcán a "poor barrio," "popular barrio," or "worker's barrio." These terms also are used by other Payaneses when referring to Tulcán, and they are the designations for Tulcán which appear both in the local newspaper and in the official literature.

Tulcán is a barrio of the young: fifty-four percent of its population is fifteen years old or younger, with twenty-nine percent of Tulcaneses being under the age of ten. There are few "senior citizens"; less than one percent (n = 14) of the residents are sixty-five years old or older. Of the 275 households, the nuclear family—a married or unmarried couple with or without children—is the ideal and most prevalent (fifty-three percent) form. However, due to a high number of free unions, strict bilaterality is not common among Tulcaneses. Truncated families—an absent father or mother—account for twelve percent of these households; nearly three-quarters of these are households headed by women, most of whom are unmarried, but some of whom are widowed or abandoned. The remainder are extended families (twenty-one percent)—families with married children and perhaps grandchildren—and households composed of two unrelated nuclear families, or parts of families, living together (fourteen percent). Tulcán is less than ten years old, and unlike most of the city's present expansion programs, was not built by ICT. Instead, it was developed by a private individual who had used the land for digging clay for one of the small brick factories in the area, and who, after abandoning the unprofitable brickmaking business, subdivided the land himself into 164 irregularly shaped lots, selling many of the lots to his former employees. Because 80 percent of the barrio's household heads were born outside of Popayán and since most of these families migrated to Popayán within the last fifteen years, it can be described as a barrio of migrants.

Migration

Tulcaneses move to Popayán for a number of reasons, often described in the literature as "push-pull" factors (cf. Herrick, 1965: 13-15; Matos Mar, 1961: 182-190; Germani, 1961: 212-214). A general desire to improve their economic situation heads the list. The majority of Tulcanés migrants were peasant farmers before leaving for the city, cultivating a number of crops which, along with their supply of animals, kept them relatively self-sufficient. Population increases, primarily due to a drop in infant mortality in recent years, and an inefficient traditional agricultural technology work together to create land shortages, forcing them to migrate (Camacho de Pinto, 1970: 62). Declining prices for coffee, their cash crop, has made the situation even worse. Some individuals expressed boredom with life in the country and moved to the city for "its many diversions." Others came in order to educate their children, to obtain medical care for some member of the family, or for other, less frequently cited reasons. Although Colombia's two decades of internal strife have been cited in the literature as factors creating considerable internal migration (cf. Guzmán Campos et al., 1962: 295-296; Pineda, 1960; Lipman and Havens, 1965: 244; Flinn, 1966: 8-9), no Tulcanés suggested it as a cause for leaving the rural area.[5] In fact, most of the migrants came from areas not badly affected by the violence.

After arriving in the city, Tulcaneses note that the transition from life in the country to life in the city is really quite easy, for several reasons. To a certain extent, the migrants know what to expect when they arrive in the city. For most of this century, national market systems have focused their attention on peasant farmers; the construction of roads has improved travel; and the building and staffing of rural schools have produced literate peasants. In addition, many migrants came from areas less than a day's bus ride from Popayán, and some lived as close as fifteen or twenty miles away. For years before moving to Popayán, they sold their cash crops in Popayán and traded in its stores. Furthermore, people who have migrated to cities return to the country to visit relatives, and to attend baptisms and local saint's days fiestas; during these times, they derive considerable pleasure from explaining the ways of the city to their curious friends and relatives. In many respects, then, the migrant experiences no real surprises when he steps off the bus.[6]

Tulcán itself has a rural, villagelike atmosphere, and people find security in its small size. Relatively self-contained, with its own stores, school, government, and health center, it probably differs little from the villages where its residents were born.[7] Finally, most of the migrants living in Tulcán had some assistance upon their arrival in Popayán. Many had friends and relatives already living in Popayán when they arrived, who often provided them with housing and, less frequently, found them jobs.

EARNING A LIVING

Finding adequately paying stable employment is an omnipresent problem for Tulcaneses, migrants and native-born alike, because Popayán is not an industrial center. The absence of industry is not due to oversight by large companies, but rather to the conscious efforts of leading Payanés families. These families derive their incomes from cattle ranching and for years have actively discouraged industry from settling in the city, suggesting instead that they locate in nearby Cali (Crist, 1950: 137). This lack of industry greatly reduces the number of jobs available, resulting in a swollen labor force.

Tulcaneses' lack of marketable skills also adds to their difficulties in finding work. The great majority of migrant household heads originally were peasant farmers, and thus most have no nonagricultural training. Consequently they are in a poor position to compete for the few skilled or semi-skilled jobs which occasionally are available. Payanés-born residents are scarcely better off, for their levels of education and job training experience are similarly low.

Even with job training, people often are unable to find employment in fields for which they are prepared. Héctor Arias, for example, spent nearly three years going nights to the Don Bosco trade school learning to be an accountant. He finished the course but was unable to get a job where he could utilize his new skills. Not one to give up easily, he enrolled a year or so later in the government-sponsored trade school *Servicio Nacional de Aprendizaje* (SENA) and completed a course in farm machinery maintenance. Much to his chagrin, Héctor once again was unable to find a job where he could put his learning to use, so he now divides his time between salting skins brought in from the municipal stockyards and helping his father cultivate a large garden plot.

Tulcanés Occupations

Thus, Tulcaneses must rely on their own ingenuity to make a living, and consequently they have developed a wide variety of occupations. I have classified these jobs into thirteen categories, with an additional one for the unemployed (see Table 1).

Small-scale commerce accounts for almost a quarter of the jobs of household heads. This is by far the broadest category, and in it one finds the widest spread of economic returns and possibilities, ranging from four households where each head earns $50 or less per month to two households where the heads make

TABLE 1
JOBS AND INCOMES: HOUSEHOLD HEADS ONLY

Job and % of Household Heads Represented	Lowest Income ($)	Average Income ($)	Highest Income ($)
Small-scale commerce 22.5 (n=62)	0- 50	384	1001-1500
Construction 16.7 (n=46)	101-200	450	1001-1500
Hauling[a] 9.8 (n=27)	0- 50	248	801-1000
Government 9.8 (n=27)	0- 50	674	1001-1500
Agriculture[b] 8.4 (n=23)	0- 50	162	601- 800
Unemployed 7.6 (n=21)	–	–	–
Other 7.3 (n=20)	0- 50	464	1501-2000
Housewife 4.7 (n=13)	–	–	–
Wash clothes 4.4 (n=12)	0- 50	145	401- 500
Stockyard personnel 3.6 (n=10)	101-200	470	801-1000
Industry 2.2 (n=6)	401-500	800	1501-2000
Clerks and waiters 1.8 (n=5)	51-100	365	601- 800
Tailors and seamstresses 0.7 (n=2)	51-100	163	201- 300
Maid 0.4 (n=1)	101-200	150	101- 200

a. In hauling, as in most other categories, response is based on the assumption of ideal full-time and continuous employment.

b. Agriculturalists' incomes are misleading. They often have no idea what they earn and produce for themselves what others have to buy.

between $1,000 and $1,500 per month. (The exchange rate was approximately 19.50 Colombian pesos to the U.S. dollar. All prices will be written in pesos.) Included in this group are the women who sell cooked food in the barrio and in the city markets, the produce vendors in the markets, and the people who sell candy and cigarettes from sidewalk stands around town. Similarly, the families that buy three-pound bundles of herbs and spices from the large food cooperatives in Popayán and carefully repackage the ingredients into small cellophane envelopes for resale are classed as small-scale merchants. Bakers, who work half the night preparing their wares and the following morning selling them, likewise come under this heading. The category also includes the numerous (n = 41) small store owners in the barrio, whose goods range from a few commonly used items to practically everything Tulcaneses will need for any occasion.

TABLE 2

JOBS AND INCOMES: ALL HOUSEHOLD MEMBERS COMBINED

Job and % of Household Heads Represented	Lowest Household Income ($)	Average Household Income ($)	Highest Household Income ($)
Small-scale commerce 22.5 (n=62)	0- 50	607	2000 and up
Construction 16.7 (n=46)	201-300	645	1501-2000
Hauling 9.8 (n=27)	51-100	419	801-1000
Government 9.8 (n=27)	301-400	875	1501-2000
Agriculture 8.4 (n=23)	0- 50	452	1501-2000
Unemployed 7.6 (n=21)	0- 50	351	1001-1500
Other 7.3 (n=20)	0- 50	576	1501-2000
Housewife 4.7 (n=13)	0- 50	483	1001-1500
Wash clothes 4.4 (n=12)	0- 50	308	601- 800
Stockyard personnel 3.6 (n=10)	201-300	550	801-1000
Industry 2.2 (n=6)	401-500	1108	1501-2000
Clerks and waiters 1.8 (n=5)	51-100	455	601- 800
Tailors and seamstresses 0.7 (n=2)	301-400	400	401- 500
Maid 0.4 (n=1)	101-200	150	101- 200

Construction work accounts for the employment of 16.7 percent of Tulcanés household heads. Since most building in the city is done with bricks and mortar, these men usually are masons or masons' helpers; they are freelance workers who, when one project is finished, must search for work elsewhere. In the construction trade, an individual earns between $10 and $35 a day for an average of approximately $450 per month.

The general category of "hauling" is the third most common occupation, with approximately 10 percent of household heads engaged full-time in this work. The terms *cotero, tersiador,* and *bultiador* are used to describe the men (and less frequently, the women) who push two-wheeled carts loaded with produce through the streets of town, or who work unloading cargo from buses and trucks. Three horse-drawn carts used for transporting freight are also based in Tulcán. Hauling, too, is freelance; men leave their houses at six or six-thirty in the morning and head for the markets and warehouses in the city where they stand around, talking and smoking, as they wait for customers. It is exhausting, heavy work with little financial reward (about $250 per month). On good days, José Luís Muños may make $15; other times he brings home only $5, not unusual for men in this line of work. People age quickly in this profession; after working eight years as a hauler, José Rivera is permanently crippled and hunchbacked from the heavy loads with which he struggles daily.

Another 10 percent of household heads work for branches of either the municipal or departmental government. Their occupations include road maintenance, garbage collection, and street sweeping. Any government job is highly desirable, for the work pays well, averaging between $650 and $700 per month, and it includes many fringe benefits unavailable in other types of work.

TABLE 3
PERCENTAGE IN EACH INCOME GROUP

Income Group[a] ($)	Households %	Household Heads %
0-50	7.3 (n=20)	16.7 (n=46)
51-100	2.2 (n=6)	5.1 (n=14)
101-200	8.7 (n=24)	12.7 (n=35)
201-300	12.0 (n=33)	14.9 (n=41)
301-400	8.0 (n=22)	11.3 (n=31)
401-500	12.0 (n=33)	14.2 (n=39)
501-600	11.6 (n=32)	9.1 (n=25)
601-800	16.4 (n=45)	10.2 (n=28)
801-1000	9.1 (n=25)	2.5 (n=7)
1001-1500	8.0 (n=22)	2.5 (n=7)
1501-2000	4.4 (n=12)	0.7 (n=2)
2000 and up	0.4 (n=1)	–

a. These income divisions were derived from responses recorded during my census of the 275 households in the Barrio Tulcán. The divisions were made as they were because of the large number of low incomes in the barrio.

Agriculture is the primary occupation of 8.4 percent of household heads, and a secondary occupation of *most* Tulcaneses. Men like Jaime Arias, Jaime Istuasi, and Olimpo Castellanos are urban farmers who cultivate their plots of yucca, plantains, coffee, and a variety of garden vegetables. By selling herbs and vegetables to their neighbors and by supplementing their incomes with wood brought down from the hills to be sold for cooking fuel, these men are able to make a living. Other agriculturalists work land outside the barrio. Some commute daily to small farms and return in the evening. Others, like Luís Martínez, leave their homes in the barrio early Monday morning and spend the week working of their farms, returning late Friday evening or early Saturday morning for the weekend. Still others, like Ever Astaiza and Jesús López, work nights in Popayán, but try to spend at least one day a week on their farms, which are located in small villages within walking or cycling distance of Popayán. These agriculturalists should not be confused with other families whose primary source of income is derived outside agriculture, but who have large gardens. A certain amount of farming is common to most Tulcaneses, and almost every family raises some produce for its own consumption.

The remaining household head occupations are scattered among rather diverse jobs, such as clerks and waiters (1.8 percent), a tailor and a seamstress (0.7 percent), people who wash clothes (4.4 percent), and stockyard personnel (3.6 percent). The final category, "other," includes drivers, shoeblacks, night watchmen, prostitutes, and the like.

No professionals such as lawyers, medical doctors, or teachers live in the barrio, nor are there skilled craftsmen and petty artisans, occupations which would seem like natural possibilities in a city with little industry. Although Popayán's city fathers are interested in attracting tourists, at present there is not enough demand for crafts to support a sizable number of artisans. Tulcán does have a few tinsmiths and cobblers, but they are not really craftsmen and do not consider themselves to be such.

Unemployment[8] levels are difficult to estimate for several reasons. First, data from my interviews, casual conversation, and observations indicate that both the jobs and incomes reported in the census sometimes reflect wishful thinking calculated on full-time employment and based on optimum earning levels, when actually the people involved were without jobs at the time. Second, since most occupations are freelance, employment is not steady for many, and nearly everyone spends a certain amount of time unemployed. And finally, most people not working at their chosen professions find piecemeal jobs, tend their gardens full-time, or chop wood to sell to their neighbors. Thus, while they are unemployed as far as their nominal profession is concerned, they manage to keep busy and bring in at least some income. Hence, the job situation is more accurately characterized by underemployment[9] than by unemployment. For example, Pablo Arboleda said he was a mason, yet for over a year, he did nothing but repackage herbs and spices with his wife and mother. Another individual described himself as a driver when he could find openings in that line of work. Between times, however, he kept himself busy by running a very successful bicycle theft ring, in which he and a couple of cohorts stole bicycles from town, painted them, and trucked them south to the city of Pasto for sale there.

Work-Related Problems

There are serious problems that relate to the whole complex of work. One of these is the common practice among employers of underpaying their workers. Because of the relatively large labor force, employers can pay very low wages and still find people willing to work. Most Tulcaneses feel they are lucky to get any type of job, regardless of how small the financial benefits are. Thus it is not unusual for a person to work thirty days a month, twelve hours a day, and to bring home less than half of what the Ministry of Labor of the Department of Cauca has designated as the minimum wage for his category of work.[10]

The use of child labor is also common, and because many families find it necessary to send their children off to work, Tulcaneses tacitly accept this form of exploitation. Judith Ramírez, a thirteen-year-old girl, works a seventy-two-hour week carding wool in a small store where *ruanas* (the Colombian poncho) are woven. For this, she earns $5 a day. Her family sees this as a necessary addition to the family income, and they are not willing to have her quit in protest over poor wages and working conditions.

Tulcaneses also cite numerous cases of nonpayment for work done. Joaquín Saldarriaga's case is typical: he worked ten days as a mechanic and driver for a teamster, and when he finished, was paid $15, a sum which did not even cover the cost of food on the trip. He was told that that was all the boss had and to return in a few days for the remainder. Joaquín went back twice, and after being sent away both times, he realized he was never going to get his money.

Few receive the *prestaciones sociales* (employment social services), such as hospitalization and medical care, to which they are legally entitled, and which should be paid for by monthly joint employer-employee contributions. Included in these services are the family subsidy in which the worker receives an extra percentage of his earnings for each child, the transportation subsidy which defrays some of the cost of getting to work, a retirement fund to which the employer pays one month's wages for every year the employee has worked, and a paid vacation based on the amount of time the individual has worked. Government-sponsored construction work, the local and regional government offices, and *Empaques del Cauca* (a factory which manufactures hemp sacks) provide some of these benefits. However, most employers do not, and they are rarely considered as possibilities by employees. In some cases, the lack of these services is due to employer disregard for the law. In other instances, and this is true also in paying the minimum legal wage, many small concerns—as most are in

Popayán—would find it impossible to remain operational if they were to comply with the law.

The Ministry of Labor occasionally makes spot checks to determine if employers are obeying the law, but this produces mixed results. María Cruz was making $100 per month working a seventy-two-hour week in a small candy factory which employed three girls. After what María believes was a visit by someone from the government, the establishment's owner announced that henceforth they were going to receive social security medical benefits, usually the first item employers will pay for. The following month, María had $19 deducted from her pay. Calculated on what her minimum wage should have been ($312 per month), this would have been the correct amount, but because she was not making it, the deduction amounted to a fifth of her salary. Medical service was not worth that much, and María's parents made her quit and look for work elsewhere.

Tulcaneses view legal recourse against labor injustices as totally unrealistic. When asked if complaints can be lodged against employers, Tulcaneses just shrug their shoulders and ask what good it would do. If the employee protests, he is likely to be fired; there are always people waiting for jobs. Manuel Calderón maintains if the employee tries to make a complaint to a municipal official, he "would be called a Communist and thrown in jail." Colombia's two powerful labor unions, the *Unión de Trabajadores Colombianos* (Union of Colombian Workers) and the *Confederación de Trabajadores Colombianos* (Confederation of Colombian Workers), which should provide protection against labor abuses, are regarded by Tulcaneses as organizations which are not concerned with their plight, and which, at least tacitly, are in league with the upper class. While both the unions and the upper class probably would object to such a description, as far as most Tulcaneses are concerned, this might as well be the case.

Rather than helping them, the poor feel many government regulations discriminate against them. There is resentment at what they feel is unnecessary legal paperwork often needed just to apply for a job, such as blood tests and X-rays required at employee expense to prove good health. Employees also need a $10 identification card and a $40 police good conduct certificate. If a job applicant has been in trouble with the police, he must pay additional money to lawyers and officials to get the card. "Poor people like us," lamented Faustina de Arias, "can hardly afford all of these expenses." In addition, job seekers generally need two letters of recommendation from *personas honorables* (citizens in good standing who are known in the community) attesting to their character and trustworthiness. These are difficult for poor people to obtain, especially if they are new in the city, and generally require influence with someone in the barrio who knows a third party who will write the letters. All of these items cost money, and although this may amount to only $100, it may prevent people from competing in the job market. Some may be able to get jobs where the various documents are not required by the employer, but this means they will not be paid very much.

Licensing of small businesses and sidewalk stands presents still another problem to Tulcaneses. Permits are required by law and may be revoked without warning for what Tulcaneses consider to be unfair, capricious, and illogical reasons. Micaela de Miranda felt discriminated against because the city made her close her *cantina* (bar) since it lacked adequate sanitary facilities. Even though most of the barrio is without a sewer, and even though the existing sewerline does not run by her establishment, the health inspector closed the bar due to a violation of the city health regulations. Micaela fumed at this directive, feeling it was just another example of how the poor are mistreated and abused. Furthermore, she was upset because she was one of the few cantina owners in the barrio who did pay the municipal tax, and for that reason the authorities were able to locate her cantina and close down her operation. She felt the inspector would have settled for a bribe, but she said she was too poor to pay off officials. Eventually her problem was solved when her husband spent two days digging a long trench and installing a urinal that was connected to the sewer line of a nearby street.

Thus, the Tulcanés worker sees himself as a pawn in the work structure. He is ignored by the labor unions, underpaid, exploited by his employers, cheated of his earnings, and denied his rights. As far as he is concerned, the government does not care about the plight of the poor; on the contrary, Tulcaneses feel that not only does it fail to enforce regulations established to protect the poor, but it appears to enforce only those ordinances which will serve to harass them.

Although poor people feel they are abused and exploited, it is important to note that Tulcaneses have limits beyond which they will not allow themselves to be mistreated. There are several cases of people giving up good jobs for reasons of personal dignity. Jorge Cruz was on Popayán's police force for six years, a job he liked, with good pay and benefits. One day, after he was humiliated unjustly by an officer in front of his entire unit, Jorge quit. He was unhappy at having to give up the benefits of being a policeman and says his present job not only pays less, but also has an element of instability in it; nevertheless, for reasons of honor, he felt he had no choice but to resign. Four years later, he is still bitter about the episode. Perhaps quitting for matters of principle is good for the personal pride of Tulcaneses who feel abused, but these are moves of consequence as they must find other jobs, often not as good, in a flooded labor market.

Working Women

As bleak as the labor situation appears for men in Tulcán, it is even gloomier for working women. Largely unskilled and more poorly educated than men, they must make a living for themselves, often while supporting a large brood of children. Some receive aid from kinsmen or have offspring who are old enough to make financial contributions, but these instances are more the exception than the rule. Widowed, abandoned, or otherwise single women have very few job opportunities. Because of their financial difficulties, most of them share homes with other families, often having only a single room into which they must crowd with their children. As means of support, they generally take in laundry or sell *arepas* (a Colombian tortilla), *masamora* (a corn and sugar broth), or other cooked foods. Some make their living bringing firewood down from the hills and selling it to barrio stores. Others manage to keep going by picking raspberries and cutting flowers which they sell in the markets and on the streets in Popayán. Most do a combination of these things and send their children to beg in Popayán. Some turn to prostitution.

Margarita Chávez is single, and although she is only twenty-nine years old, she looks forty. Life has not been easy for her. At the age of fifteen and unmarried, she had her first child. Now, fourteen years later, she has eleven children living with her. They survive on what the children bring home from begging and what she makes washing clothes and as a prostitute.

Luz Benavides is eighteen years old and unmarried. She lives with her two daughters, ages four and two, and four half-brothers and sisters, ranging in age from thirteen to six, in a one-room dirt-floored hovel. Luz and her thirteen-year-old half-sister make tamales and in this manner, earn approximately $150 a month. The other children bring in what they can by begging. The plight of the urban poor is thus accentuated in the case of women.

Attitudes Toward Work

It should come as no surprise that a considerable gap exists in Tulcanés attitudes between real and ideal work situations and types of employment. Tulcaneses would prefer to have nonmanual labor jobs, for they are more prestigious and almost by definition carry with them higher monetary rewards than does manual labor. Tulcaneses also see what appears to them to be a correlation between Payaneses who work in offices and those who at least appear to have financial comfort and security. They believe that nonmanual labor is far less taxing on the body and that, because of this, life is made easier.

Tulcaneses say people should work at whatever they want. The general attitude among adults of both sexes is summed up by Hernán Sánchez: "People should learn work they like. If they do not like it, they will not learn and will not work." It is significant that residents feel this way since they are at the lower end of Popayán's socioeconomic continuum, their occupational roles for all intents and purposes are ascribed, and their possibilities for change are minimal.

When asked how they feel they can improve their situation, they admit that their only chance for improvement would be to move from a lower-paying job to a higher-paying job, but only within the range of occupations which members of their community presently share. That is, they feel they could never become lawyers, teachers, or clerks in the local banks. Tulcaneses believe that their chances for any kind of real improvement are negligible because those in power need an abundant supply of cheap labor. Thus, they believe the system purposely holds them where they are.

Tulcanés children regard the situation somewhat differently, as revealed in short essays on career aspirations written by the twenty-six third graders (seven girls, nineteen boys) of the Barrio Tulcán elementary school. Both sexes wrote about the importance of helping support their poor families and beseeched assistance from the Almighty in doing this. The girls all mentioned wanting to become either nuns or teachers. For most boys, being a truck-driver was the favorite choice, reflecting a preference for "nonmanual" labor, while most others indicated a desire to work in construction. In these essays, the belief was expressed that it takes money to make money, which probably is a way of saying, "This will never happen to me." A common essay read like Pedro Londoño's: "If God gives me life, and if I am able to make money, I would like to be a driver in order to help my family which is so poor."

In spite of their difficulties in obtaining work, Tulcaneses have a very explicit work ethic. Except for the very young and very old, the physically and mentally infirm, and those going to school, everyone is expected to make a contribution to the household. While residents express sympathy for themselves and their neighbors who have particularly difficult or unpleasant jobs, they do not feel sorry for anyone who does not work and who complains about not finding a job. Tulcaneses are convinced that anyone can find some kind of work if he is determined to. People who use a difficult job market as an excuse simply are dismissed as irresponsible.

SOCIAL RELATIONS

Tulcaneses take a jaundiced view toward the society which they feel has either forgotten them or has intentionally held them down. In looking at overall social structure, Tulcaneses do not see a continuum of social classes; rather, they view society as polarized, consisting of "them"—referring to anybody who is not as poor as they—and "us"—the residents of Tulcán and Popayán's other poor barrios. Tulcaneses view life as a continuous struggle, one in which people must "defend" themselves and must "fight" the myriad forces of life in a constant effort to survive, a conception which is carried over to their model of social classes. The poor, they feel, have little or no control over their destiny.[11] Naturally, this realization produces discontent, a feeling which is far from new among the poor but which has increased in recent years because many of the poor no longer are convinced that their position in life is something willed by God; it is now therefore subject to change. This new attitude is due to improved media communications, which expose the poor to new thoughts and ideas, prompted in part by a changing attitude of the ruling aristocracy (cf. A.

Whiteford, 1970). This in turn has served to create a sense of frustration and resentment among the poor at their inability to make what they feel is sufficient headway toward meeting these now-rising expectations.[12]

Under these circumstances, it is not surprising that Tulcaneses feel life is a fight against a conscious conspiracy perpetrated against them by the "oligarchy" which wishes to maintain its power and can do so only by keeping the "common people" from ever really asserting themselves. To Tulcaneses, the term "oligarch" means anyone they believe has a vested interest in maintaining the status quo; obviously it is not a complimentary or endearing term. This feeling of being restrained or held down by the rich extends to every area of their lives. Thus, when Tulcaneses talk about their plight, which they refer to as *la lucha* (the fight), they frequently use a gesture like a basketball dribble to illustrate how the oligarchy keeps them down.

Further, they say their poverty forces them into situations they would not have to face if they were rich, and they assume that both directly and indirectly their lives are controlled by the rich. Hence, when Lupe de Martínez' son-in-law was jailed on charges of robbing a drunk, she was very perturbed. After a trip to the jail, she decided that it was a clear case of harassment of the poor. If her son-in-law had been rich, she argued, he never would have been arrested, or if by some remote chance he had been, a few well-placed pesos would have settled the issue quickly and quietly. Even after Ernesto confessed to the crime, Lupe was undaunted. This would not have happened in the first place, she maintained, had they not been so poor, and after all, their poverty essentially was the fault of the rich. In this way, Tulcaneses believe they are completely at the mercy of those with more resources.

The poor also resent the patronizing and condescending attitude which they believe the wealthy have regarding their situation. One day when talking about the problems of being poor, Faustina de Arias said, "The rich say we poor spend all our money on soda pop. But, I ask you, where do we get the wherewithal to pay for these soft drinks?" No, she continued, the poor are not poor because they have frivolous spending habits or because they are not able to save what little they earn. They are poor because they are not permitted to live any other way. Tulcaneses harbor no doubts that they are just as capable as the oligarchy and, given the chance, many feel they could run the country in a better, more equitable manner than does, as Héctor Arias puts it, "the rotating oligarchy which does nothing but eat, fornicate, and sleep while the people slave to support them." I heard this statement, with variations, many times.

Yet in spite of their vitriolic denunciations of the oligarchy as a whole, Tulcaneses speak fondly of various members of this group whom they know personally. The man who subdivided the land on which the barrio is built is always referred to in the most complimentary and glowing terms. Several medical doctors and dentists also are praised for their skill and humanitarian concerns. Tulcanés women sometimes describe particular upper-class women they know as "magnificent people," as do their husbands in talking about men of the oligarchy for whom they have worked. It is almost as if they are saying: "Oligarchs are exploitative people, and we would be very much better off without them. Nevertheless, I have never met one whom I did not like and admire."

Although Tulcaneses believe that an unscrupulous oligarchy takes advantage of them at every turn, they can see ways in which their situation might possibly improve, even though they admit their plans may never be realized. Luck —coupled with divine intervention—is seen to be the most important way for improving their situation. As one resident rather philosophically observed, "God helps you or he doesn't." Praying to the right saints, Tulcaneses note, also helps.

Education is another way in which Tulcaneses feel they can get ahead for they realize that many jobs require at least an elementary knowledge of reading and arithmetic. Be they candidates for positions in large stores or night watchmen, they usually wind up taking tests the primary aim of which is to reduce the number of contenders by eliminating the less educated.

Many Tulcaneses see change coming through political processes. While for some the belief in the inevitability of a revolution in the near future permits them to remain patient a while longer, others feel that peaceful political and social evolution will advance their cause.

Tulcaneses see themselves as a unit vis-à-vis the outside world, and they all claim membership in the lower class, but no one seriously would claim that everyone is equal within the barrio. Speaking for many, Jaime Torres notes, "We are not all equal, naturally, but we are all poor." Rather than speaking of "richer" or "poorer" when conversing about themselves and their neighbors, Tulcaneses talk in euphemistic terms. Hernán Granada stated, "Some say we are equal, that we all suffer the same. That isn't true. I, for example, suffer less than my neighbor here, but I suffer more than others. They have an easier life." Or, says another, "Some individuals in the barrio have better 'proportions' than others." Still others speak of some people in the barrio as being "better adapted" than others.

I asked Adolfo Samboni if the barrio has people living in it other than those from the lower class. No, he replied, the first thing someone with enough money to be considered other than lower class would do would be to move to another neighborhood. There are no lawyers, bank tellers, medical doctors, or engineers in the barrio. Still, barrio residents agree that those of their numbers who are the most "comfortable" have steady, salaried jobs, preferably with the local or departmental governments.

When I asked friends to name the five richest families in the barrio, there was very little consensus; they had trouble deciding who the wealthiest in the barrio were. Further, in spite of saying they believed that salaried, steadily employed people were the richest, the Tulcaneses generally named were families where the household head worked in construction or owned a store in the barrio.

Proximity also played an important role, for people tended to name individuals or families who lived close to them. Perhaps the lack of consensus may be explained by the simple fact that movement in and out of the barrio, plus a lack of any real community cohesiveness, prevents inhabitants from getting to know each other well, and contacts often are limited to immediate neighbors. Also, in asking people to list the wealthiest residents in the barrio, I asked them to speculate on a subject about which they previously had not given much thought. In any case, no one named the families who were, according to my data, the wealthiest.

When asked who the five poorest were, most Tulcaneses would not even attempt a choice. They replied there were so many needy people in the barrio that they had no idea who were the poorest. Those who did list fellow residents almost inevitably included themselves. When I inquired among the others who did not list themselves among the poorest families if they considered themselves to be among the richest or the poorest, they generally placed themselves among the poorest, even if it should have been clear to them that this was not the case.

Social Interaction

In spite of professed pride in Tulcán, there is very little community cohesiveness, and the desire of inhabitants to remain aloof from social entanglements is evident in several ways. For instance, residents say they have few good friends living in the barrio, and know the names of very few of their neighbors, calling them "neighbor" or "fellow-countryman." Tulcaneses always address one another as *usted* (the formal Spanish "you"), and insist on calling each other by the formal, respectful *don* for men, and *doña,* or its equivalent, *mísia,* for women before their given names, even if they have known each other for years.

When Tulcaneses meet on the street, greetings are short, verging on being curt; men rarely shake hands and women do not embrace. They do not inquire about members of each other's families, perhaps as if not wanting to get involved even at that level. In comparison, whenever higher class Payanés friends meet, they shake hands and exchange embraces, even if they have seen each other recently. And when Tulcaneses interact with people of a higher social class, they too shake hands and are very genteel and cordial, exhibiting a type of behavior not demonstrated among lower-class social equals.

Tulcaneses remain aloof even in their drinking behavior, for drinking is usually a solitary experience. In the barrio's cantinas, men sit by themselves, listening to music and sipping their beers or staring at their shot-glasses of *aguardiente* (an anise-flavored liquor). No social pressures are placed on drinking and, in fact, excessive drinking is not widespread, and spending money on intoxicants is frowned upon. Yet, on certain occasions, men do drink together. Weddings, baptisms, certain religious holidays, and the arrival of a friend or relative from the countryside result in the consumption of copious quantities of *guarapo* (fermented sugar cane juice), beer, and aguardiente. In these instances, residents may invite neighbors or a few kinsmen to celebrate with them. There are virtually no barrio-wide associations in Tulcán. While the *Pro-Barrio Junta de Acción Comunal* (the barrio's elected governing council) is set up as such, its leaders receive little cooperation from barrio residents, and, at present, not much benefit is derived from it. The organizations which are supposed to govern the school and build the barrio chapel in large part consist of the same individuals who are leaders in the Junta, and neither group is very effective, nor do they receive much community support. There are no mutual aid societies in the barrio, and voluntary associations are limited to a barrio soccer team and to a group of men who compete for Tulcán in the city *tejo* (a game similar to quoits) championships.

At the same time, on an individual basis, Tulcaneses can be quite generous and helpful. While Jaime Saturino never participates in the occasional Junta-run community work projects, he willingly helped his neighbor, Jaime Torres, to remove tree stumps from his back yard. Tulcaneses will take in homeless old people who can no longer make a living, and many make small, periodic financial contributions to church charities or give a few centavos to beggars. They are sympathetic to the plight of others, and, if asked, will give vegetables from their gardens or rice or a few sticks of wood to a neighbor in need.

In spite of their desire to live independently, help and assistance occasionally are necessary in every family, and Tulcaneses periodically are obliged to call on friends and neighbors for aid. Most Tulcaneses have loose-knit networks of individuals with whom they exchange gifts and on whom they can rely in times of need (cf. Wolf, 1966; Mitchell, 1969). In discussing dyadic contracts in Tzintzuntzan, Mexico, Foster states, "A very important functional requirement of the system is that *an exactly even balance between two partners never be struck.* This would jeopardize the whole relationship since, if all credits and debits somehow could be balanced off at one time, the contract would cease to exist" (1967: 219). In Tulcán, just the opposite is true: a gift or favor by Party A is repaid by Party B as quickly as possible. In this way, the individual satisfies his need and at the same time remains free of entanglements by repaying his benefactor within a very short time. The system functions because of the ease and availability with which such contracts can be established.

For example, one morning I was watching Jaime Torres make a window frame when Carmen de Aguirre came in with vegetables for Jaime's wife Victoria. Half an hour later, Carmen left, taking with her the empty vegetable basket and a bowl of fresh *sancocho* (a local stew) covered neatly with a cloth napkin. The gift was given and repaid within that short time, and while the families were building a tradition of exchanging with each other, each remained free of obligations to the other.

In some instances, the flow of exchanges between families is almost continuous. Thus, one neighbor uses the water of another on a regular basis to wash his clothes, repaying his friend each time by bringing over some scraps for the family dog. Perhaps Faustina de Arias expressed the concept best when a neighbor boy came over with a large pan filled with vegetable scraps for Jaime's and Faustina's pig. After Faustina had emptied the pan into a nearby pail, she gave Juan a handful of sticks from the woodpile. "It was a gift," she told me, "but you have to give something in return so they do not forget you."

Conflict Resolution

Tulcaneses feel it is desirable to avoid any form of direct physical or verbal confrontations which might result in a loss of temper or face for someone, and thus the person who fights (physically) is considered undesirable, as is the person who argues. People go out of their way to avoid conflicts even if it means not rectifying a situation that is unjust. Darío Ramos was very pleased when a municipal "fence inspector" arrived in the barrio one day to check for property line transgressions. Tulcán's roads are very crooked, and in most cases, anyone moving his fence out a yard or two would go unnoticed, but Darío was distressed at the number of violations he knew about, and he wanted action. The Junta, he noted, would not consider the issue, and he could not directly intervene himself because he did not want a confrontation.

The desire to avoid verbal confrontations appears in speech. Tulcaneses often preface remarks with "as the saying goes," even when it is obvious the speaker is not repeating a common saying or belief but is expressing his own opinion. By stating the opinion as a general belief, he avoids the possibility that the person to whom he is speaking will disagree and ask him to defend his statement. When talking about future action they plan to take, Tulcaneses are likely to say, "if God wills it," or "if the Virgin permits." In saying this, the speaker acknowledges the possibility that he might not take the action in the end and, in that case, wishes to remain blameless.

At times, disputes occur which cannot be avoided, and then it is up to the parties involved to work out a satisfactory settlement among themselves. Perhaps the difficulties inherent in such action emphasize the reasons for wanting to avoid conflicts in the first place, for, in Tulcán, there is neither tradition nor mechanisms for handling disputes. Neither is there an outside agency which can aid them in conflict resolution: the Junta has no powers to settle disputes and Tulcaneses look upon the courts and the judicial process as not designed to help them.

The general rule for resolving disputes is simply to reestablish the status quo. For example, after drinking guarapo all night, José López broke an empty bottle over Pedro Aleman's head, and Pedro had to have twelve stitches taken in his head and face. The neighbors agreed that José's actions were very "anti-social" and eventually, without legal sanction, José agreed to pay the hospital bill and the equivalent of two days of work for the time Pedro was unable to operate as a hauler.

Envy and Gossip

Because of the limited number of jobs available to unskilled workers in Popayán, Tulcaneses tend to look upon their environment as fixed or closed, offering them few opportunities for immediate change (cf. Foster, 1965, 1971).[13] The limited economic possibilities in turn restrict options in other areas, and people without some financial resources find it difficult to obtain reasonable health care or education for their children. Thus, there is a great deal of competition for the few opportunities which do exist, and each person worries that his neighbors will get ahead at his expense, perhaps taking a job with the municipal government which he had applied for a few days earlier. There is also resentment toward those who, for no apparent reason, manage to get ahead. Samuel Méndez notes that if someone in the barrio has good fortune, other barrio residents will stop greeting him in the streets, and, after a while, they will start talking behind his back, saying that he did not deserve such good luck and that he is no good. Manuel Calderón echoes this feeling when he says:

> Referring to myself, I know that my neighbors are envious of me. They see this house. It is not very elegant, but it is large. They say, "How can a poor man who sells sweets for a living have a house that large? " I know there are rumors about me. They probably think I sleep by day and work by night as a thief. If you work hard and better yourself, people will think you are a thief, or they will say you have found a pot of treasure. Everybody has heard stories about people making pacts with the devil in the mountains over there and getting rich that way.

The fear of envy does not keep people from trying to get ahead, but they hope to avoid envy in other ways. When Tulcaneses entertain guests, the normally shuttered windows are opened and neighbors are free to drop by for a bite to eat and a small glass of rum or aguardiente. When anyone gets something new, he explains that it is the property of anyone who desires it. When I commented on David Narváez's new horse, he replied, "I got it last week and it is yours," thus symbolically saying, "Do not be envious of me because I have something you do not have. I offer it to you."

Tulcaneses seek to control the actions of their neighbors through gossip. When someone allows the façade of his house to fall into disrepair, his neighbors will not confront him directly with their dissatisfaction about this, but will gossip about him. Manuel Calderón feels that gossip is endemic to the poor. "You cannot do anything without having everyone comment," he says. "If you have a drink, or see a woman, maybe dance a little, people tell your wife. We lower class people talk too much. It is impossible to enjoy yourself without someone telling your wife, 'Oh, your husband was drinking'."

It is through gossip that Tulcaneses can impose the stronger social sanction of ostracism. In a barrio with so much anonymity, this is effective only in sections where people have known each other long enough to exchange gossip and be upset when it is directed at them. After leaving her common-law husband, María Molina was forced out of the house into which she had moved because of rumors and gossip about her loose behavior, and she went to live with her half-sister on the other side of the barrio where she was unknown. Eventually she mended her ways and came back to live with Pedro, but she continued to be a social outcast among the women in that section of the barrio.

Although gossip usually has a derisive effect, it is perhaps the only effective means available to Tulcaneses to keep a modicum of social order in their world.

Expectations: The Ideal Person

After many conversations with residents, a picture emerges of how the ideal Tulcanés behaves. Within the family, the most important quality of the adult is a sense of responsibility toward his dependents; he must care for his offspring by feeding them, dressing them properly, educating them, and making them respectful. A man who drinks while his children go hungry or a woman who neglects her brood is deemed irresponsible. At the same time, children reflect on their parents, and people talk if they do not contribute actively to the betterment of the household by working or studying, or if they go undisciplined and have no manners.

Working hard is a virtue, and although some men work only half days and appear to relax the rest of the time, holding down a job or working to support the family in one way or another is highly important. In an area where there is so little work available and so much un- and underemployment, there seems to be surprisingly little sympathy for those individuals who cannot find work of some kind or who allow members of the family who are potential breadwinners to remain idle. Once I mentioned to Miguel Agredo that I had talked with many people who were unable to find work. He answered angrily that those who say things like that just do not want to work. He felt there was work to be had if the individual really wanted it, but too many people put forth their own specifications for jobs and would not accept what was available. When Lupe Martínez asked Jaime Arias to help her two teenage sons find jobs, he suggested taking them with him to cut wood, something for which there is a considerable market in the barrio. The boys went twice and then stopped going. Jaime concluded that they were being irresponsible because they were not making use of an opportunity to earn money and that Lupe also was to blame for permitting her sons to do this.

Finally, the ideal Tulcanés should be *formal* (reliable), not *vulgar* (coarse or common), and not *egoista* (selfish). A selfish person invites envy, and this is something to be avoided at all cost.

ON THE FRINGE

Elsewhere (M. Whiteford, 1974) I have described Tulcaneses as marginal urbanites—based not only on a geographic separateness from Popayán, but also on their degrees of economic, political, and social detachment. Economically, as we have seen, residents are concerned with survival, and many families operate on a day-to-day basis with little or no cushion of insurance. Politcally, while not disenfranchised, they are nowhere close to being power brokers and have no say in nominating or appointing local officials. In this regard, Tulcaneses say they are a forgotten lot. They call the municipal government a "centralist" regime, which they believe is concerned only with the needs of the rich. When a change of national as well as local administrations occurred in 1970, Tulcaneses hoped they would benefit from new governments. When early promises of assistance to the barrio were not immediately forthcoming, Tulcaneses shrugged and responded by saying this was nothing new and that the poor were used to such unfulfilled promises.

Socially, too, Tulcaneses are on the fringe. They do not play integral roles in Popayán's major activities, and on occasions when they do participate, they do so in minor roles, as individuals, and not as residents of Tulcán.

Although barrio residents see themselves as sharing a corpus of similar problems with other poor in Popayán and elsewhere, they do not see any prospect of joining forces in an attempt to resolve them. Instead, they feel they must face life's various obstacles by themselves. This theme of independence as a strategy for survival appears repeatedly in various forms. It is apparent in the living situation where they discourage family ties which might compromise them financially, and in the manner in which Tulcaneses assign little importance to kinship ties (real as well as fictive). That everyday social networks are kept on a short-term, temporary level, yet carefully reciprocated, so the relationship can be renewed when either party desires, stresses independence. They also avoid close personal friendships with their neighbors and seem unable to or uninterested in cooperating in a meaningful way in any large-scale barrio projects.

Thus, their concern is with themselves and their immediate families and not with implementing change on a large scale. While they might regard their situation as precarious, they are not revolutionaries: their feelings of neglect have not led them to violence. They are intimidated by the power structure, but do not fatalistically accept their present situation as static. On the contrary, many—particularly those who have moved in from the countryside—feel their lives are improving, albeit slowly. Furthermore, they are convinced that the natural forces of social and political evolution are on their side, and if patience is what is needed—well, it is something they possess in abundance.

NOTES

1. Some recent investigations of urban life in Colombia demonstrate the heavy emphasis in studying the country's largest cities (see Calle Restrepo, 1964; Neglia and Hernández, 1970; Flinn, 1968, 1971; Flinn and Converse, 1970; Usandizaga and Havens, 1966, on Bogotá; Ashton, 1972, on Cali; Mesa Valásquez, 1960, on Medellín; and Foster, 1972, on Barranquilla).

2. Rollwagen makes a similar point in discussing "city life" in Mexico. He notes how the majority of studies are on Mexico City, followed by investigations of Guadalajara and Monterrey (1972: 70). These cities "comprise only 3/256th of all cities in Mexico and their combined populations total 1/3 (33.63%) of the total number of the inhabitants of cities in Mexico" (1972: 70). He calls for studies of other smaller urban centers in an effort to more accurately understand the urban character of Mexico (1972: 80).

3. Between the 1951 and 1964 censuses, Popayán's population increased by 46 percent. During the same period Bogotá grew by 70 percent, Medellín by 66 percent, and Cali by 72 percent (DNP, 1969: 21).

4. The names of the barrio and its inhabitants are pseudonyms.

5. McGreevey writes that rural violence, although often mentioned as one of the principal causes for rural-urban migration, with few exceptions, has not played a significant role in total interdepartmental movement of people (1968: 213-214). Cardona Gutiérrez's study of two squatter settlements in Bogotá supplies similar data (1968: 63).

6. The Leeds write that a rural background in fact is good preparation for life in the city (1970: 233-234). Lisa R. Peattie also notes in her study of migrants to the barrio of La Laja in Ciudad Guayana, Venezuela, that by the time migrants reach the city, they are "in some senses preadapted to urban life. One observer has called them a 'protoproletariat' " (1968: 118-119).

7. Lewis points out that, in Mexico City, "The *vecindad* acts as a shock absorber for the rural migrants to the city because of the similarity between its culture and that of the rural community" (1959: 400). This seems to be true of Tulcán.

8. Urrutia reports that, compared to the United States, unemployment is high even in Colombia's industrialized cities. From 1963 to 1965, the average minimum rate of unemployment in Bogotá was 7.1 percent. In Medellín, for the same period, it was 10.7 percent, and in Cali, records kept for March through September 1965 showed an average minimum rate of 11.8 percent unemployed (1968: 3). He points out that because Colombia is a "developing" nation, at present its structural set-up makes it literally impossible to obtain the goal of 3 percent or 4 percent unemployed which the United States sets as a healthy level for its economy. Urrutia feels Colombia would do well to reach a goal of 6 percent or 7 percent unemployed (1968: 38).

The following table presents figures on the general levels of unemployment and underemployment in Colombia.

NATIONAL LEVELS OF UNEMPLOYMENT (in percentages)

Sex	Unemployment		Underemployment		Disguised Underemployment	
	Urban	Rural	Urban	Rural	Urban	Rural
Male	8.8	2.9	1.7	0.9	1.8	2.7
Female	12.2	10.4	3.8	4.8	4.3	11.6

(DANE, 1971: 83).

9. The Colombian Council on Economic Development, working from the explanation used by the Colombian government's bureau of statistics, defines the underemployed as "those persons, even though working, who worked during the week (when the study was conducted) less than 32 hours and have been looking for more work" (CEDE, 1968: 302).

10. The Ministry of Labor of the department has drawn up guidelines for minimum pay, which ranges from $10 per day for people engaged in agriculture to $15 per day for those individuals working on construction sites with capital value of over $200,000. These guidelines were issued in September 1969 and, by June 1971, had not been revised even though inflation had caused the cost of living to spiral upward in the interim.

11. This is not an unusual reaction from members of the lower class. Referring to lower-class coastal Colombians, Whitten notes a similar feeling to powerlessness among them. "[The] power of lower class persons over the events influencing their well-being is minimal vis-a-vis other groups" (1969: 228-229).

12. Whiteford noted a change in attitude among urban lower-class individuals from Barrio Alfonso López between 1952 and 1962. There was "considerably more tension, frustration, and expressed antagonism toward the status quo than I ever encountered before" (1963: 17).

13. In describing the "Image of Limited Good" Foster states, "I mean that broad areas of peasant behavior are patterned in such fashion as to suggest that peasants view their social, economic, and natural universes—their total environment—as one in which all of the desired things in life such as land, wealth, health, friendship and love, manliness and honor, respect and status, power and influence, security and safety, *exist in finite quantity* and *are always in short supply,* as far as the peasant is concerned" (1965: 296). A corollary to the Image of Limited Good is "if 'Good' exists in limited amounts which cannot be expanded, and if the system is closed, if follows that *an individual or a family can improve a position only at the expense of others*" (Foster, 1965: 296-297). This model is by no means exclusive to behavior in peasant society (Foster, 1965: 311, 1971: 3), and I have found it helpful in explaining and interpreting actions and attitudes of urban Tulcaneses.

In contrast, in her study of social mobility and industrialization in Uzice, Yugoslavia, Denitch states residents operate according to an "image of unlimited good" (1969: 144). Rather than seeing their environment as limited and fixed, *Uzicani,* who live in a rapidly industrializing area in a socialist country, see themselves with essentially unlimited opportunities for improvement.

REFERENCES

ASHTON, G. T. (1972) "The differential adaptation of two slum subcultures to a Colombian housing project." Urban Anthropology 1, 2: 176-194.

BUTTERWORTH, D. S. (1962) "The study of the urbanization process among Mixtec migrants from Tilantongo in Mexico City." América Indígena 22: 257-274.

CALLE RESTREPO, A. (1964) Conflictos familiares y problemas humanos: la familia en zonas de rapida urbanización, estudio sociológico en tres barrios populares de Pereira (Colombia). Madrid: Escuelas Profesionales "Sagrado Corazón."

CAMACHO DE PINTO, T. (1970) Colombia: el proceso de urbanización y sus factores relacionados. Tunja: Universidad Pedagógica y Tecnológica de Colombia.

CARDONA GUTIERREZ, R. (1968) "Migración, urbanización y marginalidad," pp. 63-87 in Urbanización y marginalidad. Bogotá, D.E.: Asociación Colombiana de Facultades de Medicina, División de Estudios de Población.

Centro de Estudios sobre Desarrollo Económico (CEDE) (1968) Empleo y desempleo en Colombia. Bogotá, D.E.: Ediciones Universidad de Los Andes.

CRIST, R. E. (1950) "The personality of Popayán." Rural Sociology 15: 130-140.
DENITCH, B. S. (1969) "Social mobility and industrialization in a Yugoslav town." Ph.D. dissertation. University of California, Berkeley.
Departamento Administrativo Nacional de Estadística (DANE) (1971) Boletín mensual de estadística, No. 238 (Mayo). Bogotá, D.E.: Imprenta Nacional.
Departamento Nacional de Planeación (DNP) (1969) La población en Colombia: realidad, perspectivas, y política. Bogotá, D.E.: Imprenta Nacional.
FLINN, W. L. (1966) "Rural to urban migration: a Colombian case." Research Paper 19, Land Tenure Center, University of Wisconsin, Madison.
——— (1968) "The process of migration to a shantytown in Bogotá, Colombia." Inter-American Economic Affairs 22: 77-88.
——— (1971) "Rural and intra-urban migration in Colombia: two case studies in Bogotá," pp. 83-93 in Volume 1 of F. F. Rabinovitz and F. M. Trueblood (eds.) Latin American Urban Research. Beverly Hills, Calif.: Sage.
FLINN, W. L. and J. W. CONVERSE (1970) "Eight assumptions concerning rural-urban migration in Colombia: a three shantytown test." Land Economics 46: 456-466.
FOSTER, D. W. (1972) "Housing in low-income barrios in Latin America: some cultural considerations." Presented at the Seventy-First Annual Meeting of the American Anthropological Association, Toronto, November 29-December 3.
FOSTER, G. M. (1965) "Peasant society and the image of limited good." American Anthropologist 67: 292-315.
——— (1967) Tzintzuntzan: Mexican Peasants in a Changing World. Boston: Little, Brown.
——— (1971) "A second look at limited good." Presented at the Seventieth Annual Meeting of the American Anthropological Association, New York, November 18-21.
GERMANI, G. (1961) "Inquiry into the social effects of urbanization in a working-class sector of greater Buenos Aires," pp. 206-233 in P. Hauser (ed.) Urbanization in Latin America. New York: International Documents Service.
GUZMAN CAMPOS, G., O. FALS BORDA, and E. UMANA LUNA (1962) La violencia en Colombia, Tomo I. Bogotá, D.E.: Ediciones Tercer Mundo.
HERRICK, B. H. (1965) Urban Migration and Economic Development in Chile. Cambridge, Mass.: MIT Press.
KEMPER, R. V. (1971) "Migration and adaptation of Tzintzuntzan peasants in Mexico City." Ph.D. dissertation. University of California, Berkeley.
LEEDS, A. and E. LEEDS (1970) "Brazil and the myth of urban rurality: urban experiences, work and values in 'squatments' of Rio de Janiero and Lima," pp. 229-285 in A. Field (ed.) City and County in the Third World. Cambridge, Mass.: Schenkman.
LEWIS, O. (1952) "Urbanization without breakdown: a case study." Scientific Monthly 75: 31-41.
——— (1959) "The culture of the *vecindad* in Mexico City: two case studies," pp. 386-402 in Actas del 33 Congreso Internacional de Americanistas. San José, Costa Rica: Lehman.
LIPMAN, A. and A. E. HAVENS (1965) "The Colombian violencia: an ex post facto experiment." Social Forces 44, 2: 238-245.
McGREEVEY, W. P. (1968) "Causas de la migración interna en Colombia," pp. 211-221 in Centro de Estudios sobre Desarrollo Económico (CEDE), Empleo y desempleo en Colombia. Bogotá, D.E.: Ediciones Universidad de los Andes.
MANGIN, W. P. (1967a) "Latin American squatter settlements: a problem and a solution." Latin American Research Review 2, 3: 65-98.
——— (1967b) "Squatter settlements." Scientific American 217, 4: 21-29.
——— (1970a) "Tales from the barriadas," pp. 55-61 in W. Mangin (ed.) Peasants in Cities. Boston: Houghton Mifflin.
——— (1970b) "Urbanization in case history in Peru," pp. 47-54 in W. Mangin (ed.) Peasants in Cities. Boston: Houghton Mifflin.

MATOS MAR, J. (1961) "Migration and urbanization—the 'barriadas' of Lima: an example of integration into urban life," pp. 280-293 in P. Hauser (ed.) Urbanization in Latin America. New York: International Documents Service.

MESA VELASQUEZ, J. (1960) "Las zonas urbanísticas irregulares en la ciudad de Medellín." Ciencias Sociales 1, 4: 318-327. (Medellín, Colombia)

MITCHELL, J. C. (1969) "The concept and use of social networks," pp. 1-50 in J. C. Mitchell (ed.) Social Networks in Urban Situations. Manchester, Eng.: University of Manchester Press.

NEGLIA, A. and F. HERNANDEZ (1970) Marginalidad, población y familia: estudio de un barrio de invasion de la ciudad de Bogotá (el Barrio "Quindío"). Bogotá, D.E.: CELAP-CEF, Instituto de Desarrollo de Comunidad (INDEC).

PEATTIE, L. R. (1968) The View from the Barrio. Ann Arbor: University of Michigan Press.

PINEDA, R. (1960) "El impacto de la violencia en la tolima: el caso de el Líbano." Monografías Sociológicas 6, Bogotá , D.E.: Universidad Nacional de Colombia.

REINA, R. E. (1973) Paraná: Social Boundaries in an Argentine City. Austin: University of Texas Press.

ROBERTS, B. R. (1970) "The social organization of low-income families," pp. 345-382 in I. L. Horowitz (ed.) Masses in Latin America. New York: Oxford University Press.

——— (1973) Organizing Strangers: Poor Families in Guatemala City. Austin: University of Texas Press.

ROLLWAGEN, J. R. (1972) "A comparative framework for the investigation of the city-as-context: a discussion of the Mexican case." Urban Anthropology 1, 1: 68-86.

——— (1973) "Tuxtepec, Oaxaca: an example of rapid urban growth in Mexico." Urban Anthropology 2, 1: 80-92.

URRUTIA, M. (1968) "Métodos para medir los diferentes tipos de subempleo y de desempleo en Colombia," pp. 23-38 in Centro de Estudios sobre Desarrollo Económico (CEDE), Empleo y desempleo en Colombia. Bogotá, D.E.: Ediciones Universidad de los Andes.

USANDIZAGA, E. and A. E. HAVENS (1966) Tres barrios de invasión. Bogotá, D.E.: Tercer Mundo.

WHITEFORD, A. H. (1963) "Social change in Popayán," pp. 12-17 in Land Reform and Social Change in Colombia. Land Tenure Center Discussion Paper 4. Madison: University of Wisconsin.

——— (1964) Two Cities of Latin America: A Comparative Description of Social Classes. Garden City, N.Y.: Doubleday.

——— (1970) "Aristocracy, oligarchy, and cultural change in Colombia," pp. 63-91 in A. Field (ed.) City and Country in the Third World. Cambridge, Mass.: Schenkman.

WHITEFORD, M. B. (1974) "Barrio Tulcán: fieldwork in a Colombian city," pp. 41-62 in G. M. Foster and R. V. Kemper (eds.) Anthropologists in Cities. Boston: Little, Brown.

WHITTEN, N. E., Jr. (1969) "Strategies of adaptive mobility in the Colombian-Ecuadorian littoral." American Anthropologist 71, 2: 228-242.

WOLF, E. R. (1966) "Kinship, friendship, and patron-client relations in complex societies," pp. 1-22 in M. Banton (ed.) The Social Anthropology of Complex Societies. A.S.A. Monograph 4. London: Tavistock Publications.

DOUGLAS BUTTERWORTH received his Ph.D. from the University of Illinois at Champaign-Urbana, where he is presently Associate Professor of Anthropology. His field of specialization is cultural anthropology, with emphasis on urbanization and migration. He has conducted field research in Mexico, Puerto Rico, Cuba, and the United States. His current research interests include urbanization in Mexico, Mexican-American migration in the Southwest, and culture change in post-Revolutionary Cuba. His publications include "From Royalty to Poverty: The Decline of a Rural Mexican Community" (*Human Organization,* Spring 1970); "Two Small Groups: A Comparison of Migrants and Non-Migrants in Mexico City" (*Urban Anthropology,* Spring 1972); "Squatters or Suburbanites? The Growth of Shantytowns in Oaxaca, Mexico," in R. E. Scott (ed.) *Latin American Modernization Problems* (University of Illinois Press, 1973); and *Tilantongo: Una comunidad mixteca en transición* (Instituto Nacional Indigenista, Mexico, D.F., forthcoming).

Chapter 8

GRASS-ROOTS POLITICAL ORGANIZATION IN CUBA: A CASE OF THE COMMITTEES FOR THE DEFENSE OF THE REVOLUTION

DOUGLAS BUTTERWORTH

The Committees for the Defense of the Revolution (CDR's) represent an attempt to involve the Cuban masses in active participation in government. Originally established in response to the need for security, the CDR's have over the years greatly expanded their functions. Although their principal task remains neighborhood vigilance, their overall goal is to integrate, socialize, and mobilize the masses (Fagen, 1969: 80). The purpose of this paper is to describe and analyze how this major Cuban revolutionary institution functions in a community of former slum dwellers in Havana, Cuba.

The research upon which this paper is based was carried out as part of the Oscar Lewis Cuban Project (funded by the Ford Foundation) which began in 1969 and, despite Lewis' untimely death in 1970, continues today under the direction of Ruth M. Lewis. I spent February through June, 1970 in Havana coordinating research on the population of a new housing project.

THE COMMITTEES FOR THE DEFENSE OF THE REVOLUTION

The Committees for the Defense of the Revolution were formed following a speech by Fidel Castro on September 28, 1960, in which he called upon the Cuban people to "establish a system of collective vigilance." Each block would have a CDR whose primary duty would be to know who lived there, what they

Author's Note: I wish to thank Ruth M. Lewis for comments on this paper. I am indebted to the late Oscar Lewis for the use of his field notes.

did, what their relations with the Batista government were, what kinds of things they were involved in, and with whom they met (Castro, 1968: 17).[1] Thus the founding of the CDR's was directly related to national security, and vigilance duties have remained a primary task to this day.

As Fidel Castro asked in his rhetorical style on the twelfth anniversary of the CDR's: "Who can make a move without the CDR's knowing about it? Not even an ant! Why? Because there are four million activists" (Granma, 1972: 2). In the same speech Castro pointed out that, although vigilance was the initial task of the CDR's, they went beyond that task long ago. Almost immediately, these organizations were assigned numerous other duties, and they rapidly became the main vehicles for administration and political indoctrination at the local or "grass-roots" level.[2]

Unfortunately, most accounts by journalists and scholars about the CDR's have stressed almost exclusively the "spying" nature of the Committees. For example, in an article entitled "Case Study of a Police State," Max Frankel of the New York *Times* talked of "the ugly emergence of neighborhood spies" and the appearance of concierges and janitors in government service "to report on the psychological as well as the physical conditions of tenants" (New York *Times Magazine*, 1961: 7, 88). Another New York *Times* writer, R. Hart Phillips, related that "to spy on one's neighbors and denounce them to the authorities is a 'patriotic duty' " and that Castro keeps his enemies under surveillance by the CDR's, "which are composed of voluntary spies for the government" (New York *Times*, 1961).

It is true that these articles appeared following the abortive Bay of Pigs invasion at a time when the Castro regime did employ repressive measures against its suspected enemies; nevertheless, a decade after the CDR's had ramified their interests to embrace activities as diverse as collecting old bottles and taking censuses, the press continued to view the Committees as little more than spy rings. An article in the *Wall Street Journal* on the eve of the tenth anniversary of the establishment of the CDR's, while mentioning some of the multiple facets of these organizations, stressed the vigilance functions of the Committees; the article was entitled "Comrade Spy" (*Wall Street Journal*, 1970: 1, 15).

Scholarly works on Cuba have, for the most part, been equally remiss in their coverage of the CDR's. Many do not even mention the Committees, or, if they do, they usually dismiss the CDR's in cavalier fashion. Karol (1970: 457) concludes that the CDR's "now have a purely repressive function." Thomas' monumental study offers an exception to the neglect of the CDR's. His treatment of the Committees is brief, but Thomas does not reduce them to mere spy organizations. In fact, he maintains that "these committees are really the core of the new Cuban society, creating a new culture of propaganda, participation, conformity and labour in a country which in the past was such a curious mixture of private endeavor and private suffering" (Thomas, 1971: 1457).

The best and most comprehensive treatment of the CDR's has been by Fagen (1969). He concludes that the CDR's are the most innovative and far-reaching of all the mass organizations in contemporary Cuba. "One has only to compare the situation in 1960 with the situation eight years later," he points out, "to be convinced that the CDR have contributed very significantly to protecting the institutions and property of the revolution, to teaching citizens what is expected of them in the new Cuba, to mobilizing the population for participation in revolutionary activities, and to bringing together under a common organizational umbrella persons of the most diverse political and social characteristics" (Fagen, 1969: 99-100).

Operations of the CDR's

The first important undertaking of the CDR's followed the Bay of Pigs invasion of April 1961. Fidel Castro called upon the Committees to sort out potential counter-revolutionaries and denounce them to the appropriate authorities. Reports and eyewitness accounts leave no doubt that this operation was at best thorough, and at worst overzealous to an extreme.[3] With the aid of the CDR's, perhaps 100,000 or more suspects were rounded up, many of whom were held incommunicado for days.[4] Castro himself admitted that injustices did occur, but he justified them on the grounds of national security (Revolución, 1961: 11). Nevertheless, the proposal put forth in the New York *Times* (1961: 1) that "the mass arrests following the invasion brought a personal taste of terror to 1,000,000 Cubans" is hardly credible.[5]

Shortly after the Bay of Pigs invasion, it became necessary to ration lard and oil in Cuba. For this, it was essential to know how many Cubans there were. A national census had not been taken since 1953, so the government considered it urgent to take another. There was no existing bureaucratic structure which could effectively do it on short notice, so the revolutionary regime turned to the CDR's.

Since each Committee was supposed to have already taken a census of all residents in its block, it was relatively easy to utilize these figures for the new rationing program. Within twenty-two days the Committees had enumerated six and one-half million Cubans (Dirección Nacional de los CDR, 1965a: 12). The following year, when fullscale rationing began, Castro called upon the CDR's to cooperate with the Ministry of Interior Commerce to issue and control the ration books (Obra Revolucionaria, 1962: 24). In Havana alone, the Committees distributed 450,000 ration books in five days (Dirección Nacional de los CDR, 1965a: 13).

In the literacy campaign of 1961—one of the most successful undertakings of the Revolutionary government—the CDR's contributed 100,000 voluntary literacy workers. They scoured the countryside and inner-city slums, helping to teach workers, farmers, and housewives to read and write (Dirección Nacional de los CDR, 1965a: 12).[6]

The CDR's are active in other areas of education as well. They try to ensure that children enroll in school and attend regularly; if there are problems, CDR representatives visit the children's parents. They sort out exemplary students and "exemplary parents" and recruit thousands of people to help in adult education (Granma, 1972: 2).

Whenever possible, new political study groups are organized by the CDR's. These groups meet once a month and, according to a speech by Fidel Castro to the Committee members, they are attended by some two million people (Granma, 1972: 2). Instructors in these schools are trained in special cadre schools of political indoctrination. The cadre schools (Escuelas de Cuadros de los CDR's) were established following a speech by Premier Castro commemorating the second anniversary of the founding of the CDR's (Castro, 1968: 76). In the same speech, he called upon the CDR's to help in the campaign to establish night schools for retraining some twenty thousand former domestic servants (Castro, 1968: 67). Ex-prostitutes were also retrained as part of a social rehabilitation program.

The National Bank of Cuba purchases gold and silver objects that can be sold abroad for foreign exchange. People who are reluctant to go to the bank with their goods may use CDR officials as middlemen. CDR's are authorized to receive these articles. The Committees encourage people to open and maintain savings accounts, but so far appear to have had very limited success in this campaign, especially in rural areas (Foreign Area Studies, 1971: 412-414).

The Committees are responsible for the administration of housing confiscated by the government or left by departing citizens. The Committees inventory the contents and keep charge of the building until it is reassigned to a new tenant (Foreign Area Studies, 1971: 433).

They have also played a key role in public health. They operate Popular Schools of Public Health. There were 1,294 of these "schools" reported in 1966, giving neighborhood instruction in sanitation, first aid, and trash disposal (Foreign Area Studies, 1971: 433).

The CDR's were instrumental in the national polio immunization campaign in which over two million children were vaccinated (Dirección Nacional de los CDR 1965a: 13). The campaign eliminated polio from the island; a similar effort has practically eliminated tuberculosis (Granma, 1972: 2). Although yellow fever has long since ceased to exist in Cuba, the Committees are still required to direct programs of eradication of the mosquito which carries the disease (Bohemia, 1968: 112). Collaborating with the Ministry of Public Health, the CDR's have undertaken campaigns to enjoin women to submit to cytological tests in order to detect uterine cancer (Bohemia, 1970b: 68). They also urge and organize citizens to donate blood for local and international needs. During the earthquake in Peru in 1970 the CDR's were responsible for 100,000 donations in just ten days (Granma, 1972: 2).

The Committees have been instrumental in the "Emulation Campaigns" which began in 1963. Laborers in the work centers *(centros de trabajo)* are encouraged to outdo each other, "emulate" the best performers, and set an example for others. Outstanding workers are distinguished as "vanguard workers" *(obreros vanguardias)* and honored in national ceremonies. Fagen (1969: 78) considers the "Emulation Campaigns" to be "perhaps the most important of all the management devices used in the CDR system."

With the assistance of the work centers, the CDR's have organized voluntary labor projects—unpaid labor performed beyond regular working hours (Bohemia, 1970a: 64-65; Dirección Nacional de los CDR, 1965a: 13). Unpaid labor is also supplied by nonemployed women, students, prisoners, and military recruits (Mesa-Lago, 1969: 354). During the 1970 sugar harvest, the CDR's were extremely active to prevent sabotage and report failure of workers to perform as they should. They cooperated closely with the Ministry of the Interior and the armed forces in that job, as well as in guarding state property and frontier areas against invasion (Nelson, 1972: 179).

The Committees have been intimately involved in the functioning of the Popular Tribunals or People's Courts of Cuba. CDR officials may make up a list of nominations for judges, help collect evidence, and sometimes serve as witnesses during the trials (Berman, 1969: 1317-1354).

A major task of the Committees for the Defense of the Revolution has been the collection of raw materials for re-use or reprocessing by government industry. Old bottles, newspapers and cardboard, scrap metal, and other materials collected by volunteers are sent by the CDR's to one of the processing plants of the Empresa Consolidada de Recuperación de Materias Primas (Consolidated Enterprise for the Recovery of Raw Materials). In 1972 alone, the CDR's collected eighty-eight million glass containers of various kinds and thirty thousand tons of raw materials for the paper industry. The Cuban government estimates that through their campaigns to collect raw materials, the CDR's have saved Cuba more than thirty-seven million pesos in foreign exchange in the past twelve years (Granma, 1972: 2, 11).

On March 13, 1968, Premier Castro declared a "revolutionary offensive" against small enterprises, petty self-employed businessmen, gamblers, speculators in foreign currency, and other individuals who carried on activities forbidden by the revolutionary regime (Bohemia, 1970c: 52-53). Many enterprises such as bars were closed permanently or placed on a two-day-a-week schedule. In cases where it was decided to continue the services, the establishments were turned over to the CDR's (Nelson, 1972: 104). Finally, the CDR's clean and beautify the cities and help in the construction of public works.

In the field of foreign relations, Committee members have visited national fronts in friendly socialist countries and obtained the cooperation of technicians for projects on the island. And in Peru, the military government organized Committees for the Defense of the Revolution based upon the Cuban model (New York *Times,* 1971: 24; Palmer, 1973: 85-88).

Organization of the CDR's

The Committees for the Defense of the Revolution are organized hierarchically in pyramidal form.[7] At the bottom are the Neighborhood or Block Committees. Each block or its equivalent has a CDR with locally elected officers. Immediately above the block level are the Sectional (or Zonal) CDR's. The Sectionals have the responsibility of "orienting" the Block CDR's (mainly political education and indoctrination), assigning them specific tasks, and reviewing complaints and recommendations of the base-level organizations. Sectionals generally comprise no more than twenty Block CDR's, and in rural areas of dispersed population, may include as few as seven base-level organizations (Dirección Nacional de los CDR, 1965b: 11).

Ascending in the hierarchy, next is the District or Municipal level. The number of Sectionals supervised by the Municipal Committees depends upon geographic and demographic features of the area. The Municipal CDR's are subsumed beneath Regional and Provincial Committees. There are six Provincial Committees, one for each province in the nation. Finally, there is the National Direction of Committees for the Defense of the Revolution, with administrative control over all the levels below it.

Initiative is encouraged at the "grass-roots" level—the Block and Sectional CDR's. The higher levels prefer to limit their direction to major policy decisions. The Neighborhood and Zonal Committees are run by elected citizens who do not receive pay for their CDR work. The four highest levels—National, Provincial, Regional, and Municipal—where organization consistency is required, are staffed by full-time, salaried workers (Direct from Cuba, n.d.: 4).

There may be as many as sixteen officers at the block level heading different "fronts." At a minimum, there would usually be a president and officers in charge of vigilance, finances, public health, and voluntary labor. Frequently there are also "fronts" of education, organization, supplies, propaganda and culture, and sports and recreation.

Ideally, block meetings are held once a week, but often they convene less frequently. Officers are expected to attend all meetings, which are usually held late in the evening, and members of the organization are urged to attend. At the meetings, problems of the block or neighborhood are discussed and needs and recommendations are forwarded to the Sectional Committee. The meetings also serve as clearing houses for policies and propaganda handed down from the upper levels.

Membership in the CDR's is voluntary, but pressure is exerted on everyone over fourteen years of age to join. Token dues are collected monthly from each member; a percentage of the receipts is employed by the block CDR's for local expenditures and the remainder is forwarded to the next higher level. In 1972, the CDR's were reported to have 4,236,000 members, about half the total Cuban population and close to seventy percent of the adult population (Granma, 1972: 2).

Although the Committees have the same basic structure wherever they are found, three geographical variations may be distinguished. There are the urban CDR's, located in the blocks of cities and towns; the CDR's which operate in Work Centers, to which almost every non-agriculturally employed Cuban belongs; and the rural CDR's. Depending then upon the geographical area and population density, CDR membership at the block level runs from a minimum of about ten persons per committee to over one hundred (Dirección Nacional de los CDR, 1965b: 11).

THE CDR's IN ACTION:
THE CASE OF BUENA VENTURA

In practice, how efficiently do the CDR's operate? Our study of the Buena Ventura (pseudonym) housing project was illuminating in this respect. The housing project, located in a rather remote area on the south edge of Havana, consists of one hundred pre-fabricated cement houses inhabited by somewhat over four hundred people. The only immediate neighbors of the project are middle-class residents of the *reparto* (community or neighborhood) living above them on a hillock to the north. All the people in the *reparto* share such service facilities as a grocery, a bakery, a school, and a bus line to the center of the city.

The project homes were provided with furniture, running water, and electricity. Sidewalks were installed and most of the illuminated roadways were paved. Each structure faces a small front yard where flowers, fruits, and vegetables are raised. Also scattered about the periphery of the settlement are communally owned garden plots which families may cultivate for their own use. A Community Center and public park were constructed for social and educational activities.

Buena Ventura is one of seven settlements built by the Revolutionary Government to house former residents of a Havana slum known as Las Yaguas. Las Yaguas was the most infamous slum in pre-revolutionary Cuba. Over a decade after its eradication, the reputation of the slum lives on and its mark remains indelibly impressed upon its former inhabitants. Located in the Luyanó district of Havana, at the time of the Revolution Las Yaguas claimed some 3,500 residents, the majority Negro.

García Alonso (1968) carried out a survey of the slum as it was in the process of being razed. She painted a dismal picture of life in Las Yaguas, a portrait reflected in the accounts of many of our informants. In general, this pattern included most of the traits of what Lewis (1968) called the "culture of poverty." Illiteracy was widespread; contagious diseases, especially tuberculosis, were endemic; infant mortality seems to have been especially high. Most marriages were consensual and of short duration; it was commonplace for children to be born from casual liaisons. There was a great deal of unorganized prostitution. Wages were low and there was chronic unemployment and underemployment. Most importantly, there was a lack of effective participation and integration of the people in the larger society.

The houses were mostly flimsy structures with dirt floors and a single room, sometimes divided by cardboard partitions. Furniture was sparse and limited to a few bare essentials. Modern sanitation facilities were absent.

Violence, drunkenness, and drug addiction are reported to have been widespread in Las Yaguas. With perhaps some exaggeration, García Alonso (1968: 13) relates that the principal economic activities of the slum dwellers were theft and the sale of marijuana. Many of the women worked as domestics or laundresses. There seems to have been a rather strong in-group feeling; strong hostility was directed toward the out-group, particularly the government.

Into this scene stepped the Revolutionary Cuban Government. Shortly after the triumph of the Revolution, government officials visited Las Yaguas to advise the people that they were to be relocated. The initial reaction among the families was one of consternation. They were fearful that when their homes were razed they would be thrown out on the street with no provision for shelter. However, the officials assured the populace that no one would be deprived of a place to live and promised new homes to those who were willing to help build them.

A census was taken in which all adults were asked if they would be willing to participate in the construction of new public housing. The majority volunteered to help. Those who did were given receipts stipulating the number of labor hours contributed. After these hours had been converted for each family into monetary units, they were applied toward the cost of the new dwelling. Household heads were to pay monthly installments until the home and furniture were paid for.

Social workers were brought into the slum in an attempt to rehabilitate those citizens who were deemed not to possess a "revolutionary indoctrination." Then revolutionary organizations were established: Popular Defense (Defensa Popular), Federation of Cuban Women (Federación de Mujeres Cubanas), and Committees for the Defense of the Revolution (Comités de Defensa de la Revolución).

At first there was widespread skepticism and distrust. For a people who had been plagued by government harassment for decades, the idea of joining forces with "the enemy" seemed absurd. García Alonso related that when some of the residents began working on government projects, a few joined the Popular Defense, but more out of fear of losing their jobs than from civic consciousness. "To belong to the CDR's was something humiliating, since their members were judged to be informers" (García Alonso, 1968: 14).

By the spring of 1963, Las Yaguas had been razed and its populace relocated in the seven new housing settlements in Havana. Despite the fact that CDR's (and other organizations) had been established in Las Yaguas several years earlier, it became clear that few of the relocated individuals had any idea of the history or purpose of these organizations. The government took great interest in the relocation experiment and, at least in the beginning, went to considerable length to imbue the people with revolutionary ideology.

Social workers were introduced into the community. In addition to political indoctrination, they made sure that the children attended school and tried to teach them appropriate behavior there and in the home. They fetched medicine and treated illness. They passed out a few sewing machines and organized a short-lived class in dressmaking in the Community Center. They arranged for families to be given cradles for the youngsters but balked at providing other furnishings because of their dismay at the rapid destruction and deterioration of other furniture the people had been given.

The Sectional assisted Buena Ventura by sending representatives frequently to the community, encouraging adults to attend night school, showing films in the Community Center, and giving small parties there. In all, the people of Buena Ventura were rather flattered by these attentions and many responded by cooperating with the Sectional officials. They participated in the Militia for People's Defense of the Sectional. They helped the social workers by making a census of school-age children in the community and talked with parents who kept their children home from school. Several CDR members attended a course on polio vaccination and vaccinated children in the housing project. They also vaccinated local dogs against rabies. Others received training in cytological tests and administered these to women in the community.

The Committees of Buena Ventura collaborated with Sectional officials in organizing "voluntary" and "productive" labor. At agreed-upon days (usually Sundays), the Sectional would send trucks to the *reparto* to pick up volunteers to spend the day working in agricultural activities. The CDR's also instigated a campaign to collect old bottles and used postage stamps. This enterprise was so successful that one of the Block Committees in Buena Ventura was awarded a pennant in recognition of its diligence.

The Sectional (or Zone) Committee responsible for Buena Ventura set up four Committees for the Defense of the Revolution in the housing project, one for each block. Nicholás Salazar, one of our informants, recalls the circumstances surrounding the founding of the CDR in his block:

> One night the people from the Sectional showed up in the *reparto*. They stopped on every block and called on the neighbors. They asked if we'd cooperate and said, "Anybody who agrees with the Revolution can be a CDR member, and if we organize a Committee on each block, there will be a great number of Committees. So let's do it that way." It was after 9:30 when they got to my street, and most of the neighbors were in bed. It wouldn't have been right to bother them. So we got fifteen or sixteen people who were awake, instead of thirty or forty from the thirty houses on the block.

"Well, comrades, who do you think we should name President of the Committee? " the Sectional comrades asked. Everybody called out, "José Dávalos, because he's the oldest." Dávalos could tell us who met the qualifications because he knew everything that went on in the *barrio*. Comrade Alejandra agreed that Dávalos was the right person for the job.

Dávalos said, "No, no. Not me! I don't want to take on any responsibilities. I don't want to be Committee President. Anybody who has that job is bound to get into twenty thousand kinds of trouble with the neighbors."

Comrade Alejandra reassured him, "You won't get involved in any problems. When something comes up all you have to do is report it to the Sectional and we'll come right away to deal with it." Minerva Ruz and others chimed in, "Calm down, there's nothing to worry about."

I kept my mouth shut, except to say, "Why don't you wait till tomorrow? Then maybe all the residents of the block will come." But the Sectional comrades couldn't afford to delay. They had to submit a list of the organized CDR's to the District Coordinators. Those were the orders they got from above and they couldn't wait. They had to obey the orientation handed down to them.

Actually, they almost forced Dávalos into the job. "All right," they said, "you are going to be President. Does everybody agree? " And pam! they wrote his name down in the blank beside the word, "President," Then they asked his age, address, and so on to fill in the rest of the form. "We'll drop in at your house tomorrow to talk with you about the CDR," they told him.

Minerva Ruz was elected CDR Organizer the same way. Dávalos proposed her name. "The comrade is really good for this," he said. "She knows politics and she knows everybody here. She's the best candidate we have."

"No, no, not me! " Minerva protested. But Alejandra told her, "Yes, Minerva, you know more than Dávalos and you know a lot about politics. You're the best candidate for Organizer." Minerva and Dávalos asked me to be in charge of Public Health. "This guy can help Dávalos with any task that has to be done," one of the Sectional leaders explained. So I accepted.

The neighbors sure grumbled when they heard José Dávalos was CDR President. "How can they name somebody who runs an illegal workshop in his house? " Marcelo Quintana said to me. "That guy is not integrated in any way and he doesn't care about the tasks of the Revolution. He doesn't have one single revolutionary quality." Edelberto said the same thing. Dávalos never even listened to Fidel's speeches. The first time he went to the Plaza of the Revolution was after he was in the Committee.

I thought he was the worst person they could've picked. Why, he was downright opposed to the Revolution. He made no secret of it. "I've always worked on my own and been my own boss," he'd say. "I've always earned enough to keep myself fed with my pottery workshop no matter what government is in power." But who else was there? Most of the neighbors are too old for the job. The rest don't want the resonsibility.

The CDR started to function but none of us knew what a Defense Committee was. We reçeived notices from the Sectional and attended meetings but we didn't understand the orientations. We could only carry out the simplest tasks. We cleaned up the *reparto* Community Center and cut the grass and weeds in the park. The Sectional saw we were in trouble. Alejandra and then Guido Jerez lent us a hand. "Well comrades," he told us, "your Committee is a bit disorganized. The tasks are hardly ever done. The censuses are left incomplete. Let's see if we can't straighten things out. I'm going to explain to you how to go about running this Committee right." He'd meet with us in Dávalos' house or mine and teach us how to fill in forms. "Look, you are responsible for the CDR here," he said. "When an orientation is sent, you work on it thus and so."

The twenty-eight members we had weren't enough, he told us. He explained all the requirements for CDR membership. The person should agree to belong, he should not have any terribly bad qualities, like being effeminate, or exploiting people through *santería*, or selling things above the legal price. He shouldn't have a negative attitude toward the Revolution. A negative attitude means to criticize the Revolution, to protest at the grocery, the butcher shop or anywhere. He should not criticize the CDR. It was our duty to speak up and refute a person who did any of those things. But aside from people like that, every neighbor should be given an opportunity to join.

Guido Jerez went with us to ask people to join. For instance, we went to Ramiro Ortíz, Hernán's brother. "Comrade," we said, "we've come in the name of the Revolution to ask whether you're willing to join the CDR."

"No, no, I don't want to belong to the CDR or anything else. I belong to my work, that's all," he answered.

Guido told him, "Look, this is an orientation I was given by the Coordinators of the Party. They said that if somebody doesn't want to join the CDR, they've got to give their reasons."

"I don't have any reasons to give. I just don't like that sort of thing. Write down anything you like." It was plain we wouldn't get him to join and there was no point trying anymore. We didn't take action against him or anyone like him. We simply wrote down their names and addresses. If there's any trouble in the *barrio*, we know where to look first—among the individuals who are not integrated.

I don't think it's right to apply pressure to get people to join. "If you don't want to join," I tell them, "you stay out under your own responsibility. But nobody is going to pressure you into it." Then I explain the consequences of not joining. If you don't belong to the Block Committee, they won't resolve any of your problems for you. And if anything happens, the people who are not integrated are the first to be picked up and taken to some faraway place until the crisis is past. If he agrees to join, I fill out a form for him. After a while we had sixty-eight CDR members on our block.

The procedures described by Nicolás were typical of those followed by the other three Committees in Buena Ventura. Confusion and ignorance surrounded the organization of the Committees and, despite good intentions by the Sectional, communication and understanding between the new housing project and the Sectional directors were at a minimum. No records were kept by the Buena Ventura CDR's; as a consequence, today few agree upon or remember details of the early days of the Committees in the *reparto*.

Elections were only nominally democratic and just a few of the offices or "fronts" were filled by popular vote. Other officers were named by the Sectional without consulting the residents of Buena Ventura. A few influential individuals in each block made their views prevail; they operated to ensure that the most important posts were taken by themselves or their hand-picked followers. In Nicolás' block, Minerva Ruz and a handful of others met before the elections to decide on the nominations. Reportedly, Minerva insisted that José Dávalos, a weak and ineffectual man, be nominated as President. She would take a lesser position, manipulating Dávalos from behind the scenes. According to informants, Dávalos was acceptable because the people preferred a weak President to someone who would wield a heavy hand—and Minerva was very heavy-handed.

Where did Minerva, a woman now in her sixties, get her power? One can trace the origins of her influence to the early days of Las Yaguas. Her family was one of the most important in the slum. Her mother was a renowned spiritist and Minerva followed in her footsteps. In addition to religious powers, Minerva acquired some influential political ties. She was a left-wing radical and political organizer for the Communist Party from 1935 to 1952.

Further, Minerva possessed a strong, domineering personality and did not hesitate to resort to violence when it fit her purposes. Thus, through a combination of political connections, force and persuasion, and a knowledge of the occult, she emerged as a powerful figure in Las Yaguas. After the move to Buena Ventura, she attempted to use the CDR structure to dominate her neighbors.

Minerva was not the only person to use the CDR's for personal aggrandizement. One of the Committee presidents saw to it that three of his relatives were named to posts. He and other officials arrogated many of the communally owned plots of land for their exclusive use and otherwise abused their power.

In view of the confusion and conflict surrounding the formation of the CDR's in Buena Ventura, it is surprising that the Committees functioned at all there. Yet they achieved, albeit in a somewhat limited way, a number of the goals set by themselves and by the Sectional.

It became apparent very early that one of the blocks, designed largely for single elderly people, could not support its own CDR. The initial recruiting drive succeeded in registering only five members of the block, the youngest of whom was sixty-four years of age. Three of these became officers. However, the President of the Committee moved from Buena Ventura and his replacement went to work permanently in agriculture, leaving only three members and no president. As a result, this CDR merged with a neighboring one.

With the new structure of three CDR's in the four blocks, the Committees introduced nightly vigilance in the housing project. Guard duty was kept from midnight to dawn. Usually there were two shifts; a pair of women kept guard from midnight to 2:30 a.m. and were replaced by a couple of men until dawn. The purpose of the vigilance was twofold—that is, to maintain security from outside counter-revolutionary actions and to guard against robberies and other anti-social acts from both within and without the housing settlement. The Sectional did not allow those on guard duty to carry firearms. The people of Buena Ventura, former inhabitants of Las Yaguas, were judged not to be of sufficient revolutionary caliber to carry arms; they might use them in personal feuds or turn them against real revolutionaries in the *reparto*. There was some resentment of this in Buena Ventura, both on the practical grounds that a man without a weapon is of limited security value, and on the emotional grounds that here was one of the first indications that outsiders were never going to let the people of the community forget their origins.

The Committees for the Defense of the Revolution in Buena Ventura seem to have reached their peak of efficiency in 1965, two years after their formation. This is not to say that they were ever very efficient or carried out tasks to a degree where the revolutionary government might cite them as "exemplary CDR's." Indeed, they never really "got off the ground." But to paraphrase Fagen (1969: 98) in his resumé of CDR operations in the nation, despite evidence of disorganization and incompetence, in the main the suspects did get reported, the children did get vaccinated, the consumers did get counted, and the evening classes did get taught. It would be difficult to imagine that any of these tasks would have been handled nearly as well without the CDR's.

About 1966, the CDR's in Buena Ventura began to cease to function, and by the time of our study they had become completely paralyzed. The fronts still existed in name, and most of the old officers retained their titular positions, but not a single task was being performed. All guard duty had stopped; health, recuperation of raw materials, and other campaigns had long since ceased to be undertaken; block meetings were no longer held, and local CDR officers did not attend the Sectional meetings. And at a time when the Cuban nation was emotionally and economically geared to reach its goal of harvesting ten million tons of sugar cane, only a scattering of individuals from the housing project turned out sporadically for voluntary labor.

What were the causes of the demise of the CDR's? There were several intertwined factors. For one thing, personal feuds and animosities, which always had put a brake on proper CDR functioning, eventually became incompatible with any effective action whatsoever on the part of the Committees. For another, there was a total breakdown in communication and cooperation between Buena Ventura and the Sectional Committee. Underlying these was the large cultural gap between the former residents of Las Yaguas and the people with whom they had to interact—their neighbors, the Sectional officials, and, on occasion, higher-echelon bureaucrats. "The people from below" were never allowed to forget their origins. One woman residing in the middle-class neighborhood above the housing project told us:

> I've lived here since 1967. When I arrived those people were already here, but we didn't know about them at first. We still have very little contact with them, only in the store. Just imagine the impact! Their educational level is so low. They feel discriminated against, and when you mention Las Yaguas to them, they jump. For that reason, I never mention it.

Through a combination of revolutionary zeal, pressure from above, and a genuine desire to form a viable, congenial community, most people in Buena Ventura had tried to forget old rivalries and prevent new ones from emerging. A supposedly democratic, egalitarian organization like the CDR, in which everyone would have an equal voice in the future of his community, seemed an ideal structure to alleviate friction. Ultimately, almost the opposite appears to have happened. The dilemma was expressed by Lucía, the mother-in-law of one of the CDR presidents:

> I don't know why, but now my old friends and I don't visit each other anymore. I ask myself if something has happened here to make the people so distant. I don't know if it's the Committee, but many people don't treat you as they did before. People here get along worse than when we lived in Las Yaguas. After they installed the CDR here, everybody turned their backs on us. Your closest neighbors are those who are the most remote. I believe that it's because almost everyone here has something up his sleeve so he doesn't want to have friends or visitors. And the best way to hide what they're up to is to withdraw and not allow visitors so they can't see what's going on. Everybody's afraid, and since they don't want to find out what's going on, they turn their backs on us.

Her son-in-law, Abelardo, the President of the CDR, said:

> People here don't want the Committee because then they would have to spend time in agricultural work, concern themselves about vigilance, and do

something about preventing delinquency and theft. They hate me here and have done things to hurt me. They've robbed me of 150 pesos worth of chickens and ducks thinking they would make me take the Committee out of here. At first I didn't say a word, but no longer. When you get right down to it, I don't care what happens any more. I'm sixty years old and have lived long enough.

It might be pointed out that this man is reputed to be a small-time black marketeer and has antagonized his neighbors by preempting some of the best communally owned plots in the settlement for cultivation of his fruits and vegetables. So at least some of his unpopularity was based on his personal actions. Nevertheless, by virtue of his official position he was a figure to be avoided by those who indulged in extra-legal activities.

There is no question that illicit enterprises were carried on in Buena Ventura. Several homes were known gambling dens; a few petty artisans continued to ply their trade after the 1968 prohibition; a thriving, though minor, black market existed; several girls were suspected of being prostitutes; it was said that some drug traffic occurred. Naturally, the practitioners of these counter-revolutionary activities were anxious to hide their dealings from the local CDR officials.

While the CDR officials complained about their fellow residents hiding things from them, the people, in turn, accused the officers of using their political posts to protect their own kith and kin. An informant talked about Minerva Ruz:

In Minerva's block there are a number of problems which she does nothing to resolve, because if she did she'd have to take steps against her friends and relatives, people under her jurisdiction who do nothing but play bingo, dominoes, and *bacará,* day and night. Minerva will tell you she struggles for law and justice. Why, so she does, but for her relatives. Now let's tell the hard facts about Minerva. What she does isn't any struggle for justice. It's a struggle to defend the nephews who give her three or four *pesos* now and then, the friends she can count on for a free meal and a couple of *pesetas* when she's broke. Her nephews are a bunch of hooligans, marijuana smokers and thieves, every one of them. [Barrera]

The failure of the CDR's in Buena Ventura cannot be attributed solely to the internal situation in the housing project. An important factor was the lack of attention by the Sectional Committee. The block CDR's looked to the Sectional for guidance and assistance only to be disdained or rebuffed. Naturally, this created resentment on the part of the local CDR's toward the higher echelons of the organization.

As noted earlier, this was not always the case, and one of the prime reasons that the Buena Ventura CDR's functioned reasonably well at first was because they received cooperation and support from the Sectional Committee. The

Sectional officers used to pay frequent visits to the Buena Ventura, hold meetings, and provide entertainment. But, as if familiarity bred contempt, the Sectional grew increasingly distant from Buena Ventura. One local CDR President commented:

> This Zone [Sectional] Committee we have isn't worth a cent. They say dirty things, obscene things—that we used to live in Las Yaguas, that we're thieves and the women here are prostitutes. The Sectional President is the one who has run down this neighborhood in every way, and she even had the nerve to accuse me, a man who's never set foot in a police station in my life and never had a brush with the law, of the worst things you can think of. She went so far as to say that we're a bunch of crooks in Buena Ventura. She said *that* because we live in such a poor neighborhood. This *reparto* is excluded from all organizations, from everything. [Abelardo]

Why did the Sectional cease to give succor and instruction to the Committees of Buena Ventura? One reason was that it apparently felt that it had done its job. The people had gotten their new homes, and most of the men were employed. The Sectional had subordinated other tasks to devote a large amount of time and energy to rehabilitating the former slum dwellers and indoctrinating them with revolutionary ideals. After several years of this, the Sectional felt that it had to divert its energies in other directions.

Beyond this, Sectional officials had become disheartened at the lack of progress in Buena Ventura. They felt they had done their best and, as tasks increasingly went undone in the housing project, the Sectional eventually stopped assigning them. As for the people of Buena Ventura, they interpreted the actions, or want of them, on the part of the Sectional as one more indication that they were simply not worth bothering with. The feeling of exclusion and neglect was probably the most pervasive sentiment among the residents of Buena Ventura. A typical comment was made by a teenage girl:

> This *reparto* has always been abandoned. They've regarded it as something apart from everything else, from all other people. At first there was a lot of talk and they helped us cut grass, clean up the neighborhood, and that sort of thing. But afterwards everything was neglected and nobody comes to help us anymore.

DISCUSSION

The Committees for the Defense of the Revolution in the Buena Ventura project experienced a limited degree of success for approximately two years after their founding, but gradually became paralyzed. At the time of our study in 1969-1970, they were moribund and represented virtually a total failure at the grass-roots level of perhaps the most important of all revolutionary organizations in Cuba.

It is not claimed that Buena Ventura is a typical case, nor is it implied that the demise of CDR's is probable or inevitable in contemporary Cuba. Indeed, the record offers us some striking successes. The Cuban government has published numerous accounts of Committees that function at a high degree of efficiency.[8] Most of these reports have a Pollyannic quality about them, but independent observers such as José Yglesias, in 1968, and Robert Keatley (*Wall Street Journal*, 1970) leave little doubt that many CDR's have performed remarkable tasks.

An example of an efficient Committee is found in a Cuban government publication on CDR's (Dirección Nacional de los CDR, 1965a). The Committee in question, "Luis Sera,"[9] won the National Model award for Committees for the Defense of the Revolution in the Emulation Campaign of 1963. The CDR "Luis Sera" is one of the Committees of the *reparto* Arquímedes García, located on a *batey* (premises of a sugar mill) on the north coast of Oriente Province.

The *reparto* was nicknamed "El Basurero"–the Garbage Dump–because of the huge mounds of offal deposited there by the sugar *central*. The trash heaps–some higher than the forty houses composing the *reparto*–consisted of old metal, construction and production waste, paper, meal refuse, and even dead animals. According to reports, the president of the "Luis Sera" CDR received a letter one day from the district-level office addressed to the "Garbage Dump CDR." Offended at this indignity, the president met with the officers who head the dozen or so "fronts" of his Block CDR. The officers first decided to rechristen the *reparto*, naming it "Miramar" (Seaview). They then convinced the sugar *central* to stop dumping garbage there and immediately set to work to clean up their neighborhood. In seventy-six days, the eighty-seven members of the CDR had cleared all the garbage and converted the former offal site into an attractive communal fruit orchard.

The clearing of the garbage dump not only eliminated a health hazard and eyesore, but resulted in the recovery of important raw materials for use in industry. Among these were twenty thousand tons of scrap iron, four hundred pounds of bones, twenty-five thousand bottles, and quantities of copper, zinc, and plastic.

Now aware that they had the ability to organize and carry out a joint undertaking, members of the "Luis Sera" CDR took on a more ambitious project. For years, the *reparto* had suffered a water shortage because the pipes from the water system of the *batey* did not reach the settlement. The officers of the "Luis Sera" CDR turned to the sugar *central* for assistance, requesting pipes to extend the water system. The *central*, however, had only seventeen pipes, not enough to expand the system to any significant extent.

During a meeting of the CDR, one of the members recalled hearing of an old system of underground pipes on the *batey* and asked the administrator of the *central* for permission to search for it and, if found, to extricate it for use in a new water system. The CDR received permission and recovered some sixteen thousand feet of tubing, enough to not only set up a water supply system for themselves but for neighbors as well.

Encouraged by their success in community enterprises, the CDR members began building a road to the nearby sea and another to the school. The school, incidentally, had been constructed through the cooperative effort of all the block CDR's in the zone. Records were kept of the labor contributed by each person, the amount of primary material he recovered, and similar data.

The CDR "Luis Sera" then undertook new tasks. They asked for materials to build a park for the children and persuaded the *central* to donate lights for it. The CDR holds periodic sanitation meetings, cultural and political rallies, operates a "family circle," and instructs adults in evening classes. Everyone participates in guard duty, the collective orchard is flourishing, and they have even removed the pigs to a distant area of the *reparto* (Dirección Nacional de los CDR, 1965a: 65-74).

What lay behind the success of the CDR in the "Garbage Dump"? It was something more than the revolutionary fervor which swept the island. Residents of the "Garbage Dump" were employees of the sugar *central* on whose *batey* they lived, and Cuban sugar workers have had long experience with organization, particularly unionization. In fact, the most influential leaders of the Confederación de Trabajadores de Cuba (Federation of Cuban Workers) were officers of the Federación Nacional de Trabajadores Azucareros (National Federation of Sugar Workers) (MacGaffey and Barnett, 1962: 152).

Zeitlin (1967: 277) states that Cuban sugar workers were probably the island's most politically conscious and militant workers before the Revolution and are the outstanding base of the Revolution itself.

> These very workers, moreover, have been in constant contact with and drawn to a great extent from rural wage laborers, who were themselves politicized and well organized before the revolution despite the seasonal nature of their employment. Thus in spite of the sparsity of manufacturing industry outside greater Havana, the working class formed a *national* class whose local struggles tended to take on the character of a national class struggle; the centrals tended to link up industrial with rural workers; and their employment in the same industry, subject to the same seasonal cycle allowed them, nay, compelled them, to coordinate local strikes into an industrywide, therefore nationwide, effort [Zeitlin, 1967: 272].

It was thus a relatively easy matter in the "Garbage Dump" to harness this organizing spirit and experience to revolutionary political structures. The former dwellers of Las Yaguas, in contrast, had no history of organization, no feeling of class identity. Shortly after the triumph of the Revolution, various committees —block, educational, party—were established in Las Yaguas. But they were little more than formal trappings; most people in Las Yaguas were unaware of their existence.

Residents of Las Yaguas were prime examples of persons living in the "culture of poverty." There was a lack of effective participation and integration of the people in the larger society, and a minimum of organization beyond the family. As Lewis (1968: 9) said, it is the low level of organization that gives the culture of poverty its marginal and anachronistic quality in highly complex, specialized, organized societies. Buena Ventura and its sister settlements faced problems common to other Committees in Cuba.[10] As Fagen (1969: 100) put it:

> Among the problems associated with the performance of the CDR, one stands out above all others: the cost to the legitimacy of the revolution. The committees have been plagued from the beginning by various forms of arbitrary, officious, self-serving, and corrupt behavior on the part of some of their members, behavior that has cost the revolution dearly in the coin of support and thus of legitimacy. Many citizens' most direct and frequent contact with any revolutionary institution is with the local committee; and when committee members are arbitrary, uninformed, opportunistic, or corrupt, the popular image of the revolutionary movement suffers accordingly.

However, along with this, the people of Buena Ventura were expected to make the difficult transition from thought and behavior patterns illustrative of the culture of poverty to those idealized by the new society. The generation of men and women who grew up in Las Yaguas could not do this. Perhaps the younger generation can. As an old man told me on my last visit to Buena Ventura, "The Committees may be dead, but I believe in life after death. When you return, you will see our 'new men and women' running Committees we can be proud of."

NOTES

1. Castro's call for the CDR's was supposedly a spontaneous reaction to the explosion of several petards during his speech. However, some months before he had spoken of the need for increased vigilance and formation of civil defense teams (see Fagen, 1969: 69-70).

2. José Matar, first coordinator of the National Directorate of the CDR's (and later expelled from the Party), insisted that it would be a mistake to think of the CDR system as an administrative appendage of the government. He said that the CDR's are, above all, political and social (or politicizing and socializing) organizations. "The CDR's are inculcating in hundreds of thousands of their members a feeling of civic responsibility toward the Fatherland, a feeling that the apparatus of the state is not abstract and distant, but close and respected, because it is *their* state" (quoted in Fagen, 1969: 86).

3. Lee Lockwood (1967: 248) comments: "Many [prisoners], it appears, were the victims of overzealous revolutionary tribunals which, in the aftermath of the Bay of Pigs invasion, meted out justice with a vindictive severity reminiscent of the Reign of Terror in revolutionary France."

4. Estimates of the number of people apprehended at this time vary. Fagen (1969: 73) says that by April 19 tens of thousands had been detained. He adds that the total number was probably in excess of 100,000 and cites an estimated of 200,000 by an Italian journalist

(Fagen, 1969: 247). Thomas (1971: 1365) says: "Between the raids on 15 April and the evening of 17 April, perhaps 100,000 were arrested, including all the bishops . . . many journalists and the vast majority of the real underground, including most of the CIA's 2,500 agents and their 20,000 suspected counter-revolutionary sympathizers."

5. This estimate is based on the assumption that each of 200,000 Cubans arrested had an average of four close relatives who were affected.

6. The CDR's were but one of the dozen or so organizations under the *Comisión Nacional de Alfabetización* which participated in the literacy campaign. Fagen (1969: 39) mentions that "some organizations such as the Committees for the Defense of the Revolution were themselves being formed in the autumn of 1960 and thus did not participate fully in the work of the *Comisión* until somewhat later."

7. For details of the organization of the CDR's the reader is referred to Fagen (1969).

8. See, for example, Pueblo Organizado, and Los CDR en Granjas y Zonas Rurales (Dirección Nacional de los CDR, 1965a, 1965b), and issues of Bohemia, Con la Guardia en Alto, and Revolución.

9. Committees for the Defense of the Revolution are traditionally named after Cuban martyrs.

10. We made cursory investigations of the CDR's in the six other *repartos* where Las Yaguas residents had been resettled. In general, it seems that they experienced the same initial successes and suffered the same decay as the Committees in Buena Ventura.

REFERENCES

BERMAN, J. (1969) "The Cuban popular tribunals." Columbia Law Review 69, 8: 1317-1354.

Bohemia (1968) (July 5, supplement): 112.

––– (1970a) Number 13 (March 27): 64-65.

––– (1970b) Number 26 (June 26): 68.

––– (1970c) Number 38 (September 18): 52-53.

CASTRO, F. (1968) Discursos de Fidel en los aniversarios de los CDR 1960-1967. Havana: Instituto del Libro.

Dirección Nacional de los CDR (1965a) Pueblo organizado. Havana: Ediciones con la Guardia en Alto.

––– (1965b) Los CDR en granjas y zonas rurales. Havana: Ediciones con la Guardia en Alto.

Direct from Cuba (n.d.) "Committees for the defense of the revolution."

FAGEN, R. (1969) The Transformation of Political Culture in Cuba. Stanford: Stanford University Press.

Foreign Area Studies (1971) Area Handbook of Cuba. Washington, D.C.: Government Printing Office.

GARCIA ALONSO, A. (1968) Manuela la Mexicana. Havana: Casa de las Américas.

Granma (1972) (October 8): 2-3, 11.

KAROL, K. (1970) Guerrillas in Power: The Course of the Cuban Revolution. New York: Hill & Wang.

LEWIS, O. (1968) A Study of Slum Culture: Backgrounds for La Vida. New York: Random House.

LOCKWOOD, L. (1967) Castro's Cuba: Cuba's Fidel. New York: Macmillan.

MacGAFFEY, W. and C. R. BARNETT (1962) Cuba, Its People, Its Society, Its Culture. New Haven: HRAF Press.

MESA-LAGO, C. (1969) "Economic significance of unpaid labor in socialist Cuba." Industrial and Labor Relations Review 22, 3: 339-357.

NELSON, L. (1972) Cuba: Measure of a Revolution. Minneapolis: University of Minnesota Press.

New York Times (1961) "Castro's repressive acts awaken Cubans to reality." (June 12): 1; (June 13): 18.

––– (1971) "Peruvian regime woos the masses." (April 16): 24.

New York Times Magazine (1961) "Case study of a police state." (April 30): 7, 88.

Obra Revolucionaria (1962) Number 7 (March 14): 24.

PALMER, D. S. (1973) " 'Revolution from above': military government and popular participation in Peru, 1968-1972." Latin American Studies Program (Cornell University, Ithaca, N.Y.) Dissertation Series,47, January.

Revolución (1961) (April 24): 11.

THOMAS, H. (1971) Cuba, the Pursuit of Freedom. New York: Harper & Row.

Wall Street Journal (1970) "Comrade spy: how a Cuban worker helps keep 'revolution' alive." (August 20): 1, 15.

ZEITLIN, M. (1967) Revolutionary Politics and the Cuban Working Class. Princeton: Princeton University Press.

PART IV

THE

RURAL-URBAN

INTERFACE

BRYAN R. ROBERTS is Senior Lecturer in Sociology at the University of Manchester, England. He received his Ph.D. from the University of Chicago, and has been a visiting professor of anthropology at the University of Texas, Austin. He has done field work in Guatemala and Peru, most recently as co-director of a three-year research project on regional development in the Central Sierra of Peru. His major fields of interest are urban anthropology, educational sociology, and rural development. Among his recent publications are *Organizing Strangers: Poor Families in Guatemala City* (University of Texas Press, 1973); "Education, Urbanization, and Social Change," in R. Brown (ed.) *Knowledge, Education, and Cultural Change* (Tavistock, 1973); and "The Social Structure of Guatemala: The Internal Dynamics of U.S. Influence," in E. de Kadt (ed.) *Patterns of Foreign Influence in the Caribbean* (Oxford University Press, 1972).

Chapter 9

THE INTERRELATIONSHIPS OF CITY AND PROVINCES IN PERU AND GUATEMALA

BRYAN R. ROBERTS

Introduction

A striking contrast between Peru and Guatemala is the more evident persistence and strength of rural ties and cultural practices in the towns and cities of Peru as compared to Guatemala. In Guatemala City, the activities and relationships of migrants are not evidently organized by their rural origins. Social and sporting activities are organized by neighborhood or workplace; political activity, both formal and informal, is not carried out by groups of fellow villagers. Cultural events, such as local fiestas, religious and administrative ceremonies or personal celebrations, rarely reflect the practices of people's place of origin and are rarely stimulated by events in such places. Migrants do not make a custom of visiting their place of origin; nor do they incorporate it or its inhabitants as part of their strategies of economic survival in the city. All these aspects of rural-urban interrelations are considerably more evident in Peru. A substantial section of the population of Lima organizes its social and sporting activities in terms of associations based on place of origin (Mangin, 1959; Doughty, 1972). Fiestas that are organized in forms customary in provincial villages and towns are common in Lima among fellow migrants and among urban occupational groups, such as, for example, market traders, chauffeurs or policemen. Migrants return home frequently and especially to celebrate local fiestas; they also exchange produce with friends and relatives in the village and establish trading links there.

Data reported from other Latin American cities indicate further variations in the strength and nature of migrant organization: in Mexico City, provincial migrants do not formally group themselves into associations to the extent of migrants in Lima; but their degree of cohesion and residential concentration appears to be higher than is the case among migrants in Guatemala City (Lomnitz, 1973, and the study included in this volume; Butterworth, 1970; Roberts, 1973a: 155-156). In contrast, there is little reported evidence in Rio de Janeiro that place of origin plays any significant part in organizing the lives of the city's inhabitants (Leeds and Leeds, 1970).

My aim in this paper is to use data from Guatemala and the central region of Peru to analyze the sources of these variations in the urban behavior of migrants.[1] The comparison between Guatemala and Peru is a useful one because there are many similarities between the two countries in social and economic factors affecting the urban identities of provincial migrants. Both countries have large indigenous populations and a long-standing, well-developed provincial culture. Both countries have been economically dependent on foreign powers and are experiencing rapid urbanization, in which the growth of the largest cities is disproportionately higher than that of other places. These cities have relatively little industry and the increase in the number of jobs available in the formally organized sectors of the economy is not sufficient to meet the increase in the adult urban population.[2]

There has been an increasing interest among anthropologists and political scientists in comparative analysis of urban behavior in Latin America. Some accounts have stressed characteristics of the political and economic organization of different cities which elicit different economic and political "responses" from inhabitants. In talking about shantytowns in Brazil, Leeds and Leeds (1972) stress government structure and the nonavailability of political party organization in determining the strategies and relative success of shantytown dwellers in organizing to obtain benefits. Cornelius (1974) extends this focus to consider the nature of administrative and political organization in Mexico and Peru as limiting and channelling the political and material demands of underprivileged sectors of the population. In the economic sphere, Balán (1969) has argued that the occupational position and mobility of migrants is to be understood in terms of the type of economic development occurring in the city and in terms of the type of place from which cities draw their migrants.

The present account differs from those mentioned above by stressing that the interrelationships between city and provinces represent additional, significant variables in the comparative analysis of urban behavior. An important factor in whether migrants maintain a distinctive identity in the city is the extent to which urban life involves continuing social and economic relationships with the provinces.

The set of relationships in which an urban resident is involved forms a field of activity that often cuts across the physical boundaries between provinces and city; this field of activity constitutes the significant social environment of an individual and the content and scope of this field is more important in influencing the orientations of urban residents than their spatial location. When urban residents' fields of activity include both city and provinces, their behavior is less likely to be influenced by the character of the political or economic organization of their city than in those cases where fields of activity are restricted to the city. I develop this argument by showing that, in the case of Peru, urban residents have operated within activity fields that include city and provinces, whereas in Guatemala, a greater proportion of the activities of city residents are confined to the city.

Focusing on the effective field of relationships of urban migrants means that I emphasize the element of choice open to city dwellers in interpreting and creating their urban situation. This approach has become familiar through the studies by urban anthropologists of the behavior of African tribesmen in urban industrial settings (Mitchell, 1966; Epstein, 1958). Though these commentators have differed over the importance to be attributed to tribal culture in influencing migrants' urban behavior, they agree that migrants exercise considerable initiative in selecting those forms of behavior appropriate to the particular situations with which they are confronted.[3] From this perspective, a city is not usefully analyzed as a single social system, but must be broken down into the variety of situations which confront its inhabitants.

Studies in Latin American cities have also shown how city dwellers create their own situations in terms of finding and making jobs and housing and in terms of organizing with others (Mangin, 1967; MacEwen, 1972). The control of political and economic resources by government and powerful individuals effectively limits the range of innovatory behavior by less privileged urban inhabitants; but jurisdictions are rarely so compelling or so clearly defined as to make predictable the behavior of the mass of the urban population.[4]

The differences between Guatemala and Peru in the salience of provincial identities in urban situations is a product of the choices exercised by migrants. It is a choice that significantly affects the emerging urban organization in both countries. The relative cohesion and distinctive identity of urban migrants in Peru has enabled them to be more effective in organizing their urban environment than is the case among their counterparts in Guatemala. Both Leeds[5] and Cornelius (1974) comment upon the greater sense of group organization among low-income families in Lima as compared with other cities in Latin America. We shall see that the activities of urban migrants in Peru as compared to those in Guatemala have also had a greater influence on provincial organization.

In discussing these topics, my aim is to consider those processes that enable city dwellers to maximize the resources at their disposal and gain a greater control of their own environment. My focus on migrants leads me to consider only one of these processes; those economic and political developments in the provinces which enabled migrants to take advantage, in an organized way, of the opportunities presented by urbanization and the growth of cities. The significance of provincial developments in shaping the character of urban organization is often overlooked because provincial regions are depicted as dependent on political and economic forces originating in the national capital or in foreign countries. This emphasis on the structure of dependency provides useful insights into the character of urbanization in Latin America, but it is an emphasis that runs the danger of giving an overdetermined view of the evolution of provincial society.

I restrict my account to considering the general characteristics of provincial life in Guatemala and in the central region of Peru that are associated with differences in the local sense of development. My comparisons are illustrative, and I use case studies to suggest the implications of these provincial characteristics for the strategies of migrants in the large cities of both countries. I devote special attention to the development of regional associations and to the operation of fiestas. My account has a historical emphasis because I feel that synchronic and functionally oriented accounts of urban life have ignored the possible influence that the origins of urban institutional forms have on subsequent urban behavior. One important difference between Peru and Guatemala is that city dwellers in Guatemala have little sense that their origins are significant for their present identities.

THE DEVELOPMENT OF PROVINCIAL ORGANIZATION IN PERU AND GUATEMALA

In this section, I detail the major social and economic processes that have contributed to a sense of difference between the patterns of social organization in the provincial settings of Peru and Guatemala. In Guatemala, I shall be referring mainly to the *ladino,* or non-Indian, areas of the country and to developments occurring in the last forty years.[6] It is from these ladino areas that most recent migration to Guatemala City has come (Zárate, 1967). In Peru, I refer to the development, in this century, of villages in the Mantaro valley. The comments apply, though to a somewhat lesser extent, to the villages of the pastoral highlands above the valley. Other areas of Peru, such as the coastal plantation economy and parts of the southern Sierra have had different patterns of landholding and land exploitation, and a different sequence of development. It is those provincial areas whose organization is similar to that of the Mantaro area that appear to have had the greatest cultural impact on the emerging urban organization.[7]

The Sense of Difference in Provincial Social Organization

I begin with the distinctions I detect in the ways provincial households in Peru and Guatemala have characteristically organized their relationships and understandings to cope with their environment. I characterize these differences in organization by labelling the pattern of organization in Guatemala a conservative one and that of the Mantaro area of Peru as an aggressive one.

In Guatemala, those households who own the larger extensions of land make a practice of renting out parts of this land to poorer families and regard the rent, in money or in kind, as an important element in their social as well as economic position (Gillin, 1958: 73; Méndez, 1967: 101; Adams, 1964: 71-75). In the Mantaro area, certainly until the last few years, larger village farmers were more likely to seek additional land to farm than to rent it out.[8] This difference extends to the forms of mutual aid customary within the villages. In the Guatemalan situation, there is little evidence of even kinsmen helping each other in agriculture. Additional labor was given or obtained through direct payments in cash and kind (Adams, 1964: 86). In Peru, a highly elaborated system of mutual aid developed which included exchange of agricultural labor, often of highly specific kinds, and aid in house construction and the other activities (Adams, 1959: 124). These transactions extend over a large sector of a village population and are often used to build up a social and economic credit that an individual might call upon several years later. These patterns of mutual aid appear to have been one basis for extending the economic activities of households, enabling them to engage in more complex activities than would otherwise be possible. Household members absent in labor migration would have their land farmed for them; they might repay in goods, in labor at a later date, or in favors such as providing accommodation for a child wishing to study, or providing help in obtaining a job.

These transactions formed a well-established pattern of cross-cutting obligations within a village; active membership of a village and the ownership of land within it, meant access to these relationships and a means to carry on activities based on the village but dispersed in time and place. In contrast, in Guatemala, social relationships are less likely to extend economic opportunities than to reinforce economic differences. Tumin (1952) and Gillin (1958) report the ways in which ladinos segregate themselves socially from Indians and the ways in which social differences among ladinos are reinforced by marriage within social groups and by different patterns of interaction. Social custom protects the economic status quo of families: Established families are oriented to protecting rather than expanding their position (Méndez, 1967: 164, 193). Gillin (1958: 155-156) reports how the richer ladinos of the town he studied see income from property as a means of "escaping" from the village. Similarly, the social relationships of *compadrazgo* (fictive kinship) among ladinos are reported to reflect and reinforce social position. In the Mantaro area, such relationships cement social and economic alliances (Long, 1973b).

This contrast can be generalized to understand the meaning of ethnic and social differences in the villages and towns of the two countries. In the Peruvian situation, there have been evident differences in the economic resources of villagers, but these differences do not appear to have resulted in a rigid social separation (Adams, 1959: 82-92). Through subdivision upon inheritance and differences in economic fortunes, family groups have not retained a dominant economic position from generation to generation: families with less land could, by work and labor migration, build up their resources. There is little evidence from our data on the economic position of the parents of present-day farm men and women that a practice has been consistently maintained of marrying into families of similar land resources.

Above all, it appears that even ethnic categorization of families within villages could change over time. Throughout the valley there has been a consistent decline in the last two hundred years in the proportion of Indians in each village reported in the census. Today, villages which originated as Indian settlements are regarded by observers, and by themselves, as entirely mestizo. At the same time, these valley farmers have acquired a sense of indifference to ethnic identities that is very different from that of their counterparts of ladino Guatemala. It is hard to imagine Guatemalan ladinos presenting themselves as "poor Indians" in the official petitions they present to government authorities, as do the eminently prosperous and mestizo municipal officers of the valley towns.

There is no evidence from the villages and small towns of Guatemala of that confidence in local development that commentators have seen as long characterizing the Mantaro area (Whyte and Williams, 1968; Adams, 1959; Tschopik, 1947).

Excerpts from the municipal records of Sicaya—a large village in the Mantaro area—illustrate the content of this interest in local development. The officers of the municipality are the middling and larger farmers of the locality. From the end of the last century, statements and decisions make clear the confidence of municipal officers in local social and economic progress: The word "progress" is frequently employed and from the early part of the century several associations on behalf of local progress emerged among different age and sex groups. The local market is sponsored and regional fairs are promoted in which there are competitions for the finest breed of animal, for the best varieties of different crops, and for good examples of local crafts. The municipal officers petition for, and obtain, a postal and telegraph service as early as 1900. They are constantly improving and enlarging municipal buildings; they obtain a town clock by voluntary contribution; they also secure, through contributions and through pressure on the government, a printing press, a local radio and a police station. Somewhat like the small towns of Midwest America in the heyday of their expansion, they lobby for the "promotion" of their village to the higher status of provincial capital.

The spirit of these activities appears in the frequent denunciations of the license and inefficiences associated with customary religious practices. They see the administration of land by religious *cofradías* as a waste of resources and eventually secure these lands for municipal administration and municipal revenue. Customary ritual and ceremonial practice, such as the period of mourning for the dead or the traditional street dances, are either prohibited or restricted by municipal ordinance. The reason given is always the same—that they make for licentiousness and unnecessary expense. They even succeed in the 1930s in prohibiting the bullfights customary during the more important festivals. The practices that are now seen by observers and participants alike as most typical of village life in Peru were once seen by influential villagers as undesirable.

This "progressive" emphasis on the part of some villagers from the Mantaro area provides a further contrast with Guatemala. Ladino contempt for Indian custom has been described by commentators as emphasizing alternative social activities such as beauty queen contests or cavalcades, and not reform to stimulate local economic rationality (Gillin, 1958: 201).

The impression that the different commentators give of ladino culture in rural Guatemala is that it reflects an undynamic, socially stratified situation. It is an impression that was substantiated by the reports that ladino migrants in Guatemala City gave me of their villages. It contrasts with the interest and pride with which many city dwellers from the Mantaro area spoke to us of their villages. The view of rural ladino culture in Guatemala is biased by an overevaluation on the part of observers of the virtues of the more cohesive and picturesque organization of Indian life; but observers working at very different levels of analysis appear to agree that local ladino society has little hold over the allegiances of its members (Adams, 1970: 169).

The Development of Provincial Society

The contrast between Guatemala and the Mantaro area of Peru indicates a crucial source of difference: The Peruvian case reflects a situation in which rural people perceive that many more economic opportunities are available locally than appears to be the case in Guatemala. The origins of this difference in perceptions lie in ecology, political structure, and societal differences in economic development.

To understand the organization of life in the central Sierra of Peru, it is necessary to juxtapose two sets of conditions: the differentiated ecology of the region and the particular pattern of colonial settlement and domination. Social and political organization has long been characterized by activities designed to extend the domain of individuals and groups to include the variety of climates and soil types that lie within a relatively short distance of each other (Murra, 1968, 1972). The creation of larger political units and the generation of economic surpluses have been closely related to conscious attempts to dominate this ecological variation. These practices exist elsewhere, but acquired special salience in Peru, within a territory divided by river valleys and sharp differences in altitude. These activities provide a dynamic for change and differentiation as individuals and groups extend their domains to include those of others. Internal population movements brought about by the search for new resources or by the power of dominating groups have been characteristic of Peru both before and after the Spanish conquest.

Within this framework, there developed a set of possibilities for local existence. Small cultivators, based in villages, farmed land with family labor and the occasional help of friends and neighbors. They took advantage of ecological variations to cultivate different types of crops and to pasture animals. Farmers with larger extensions of land began early to produce crops for market, employed labor (often on a sharecropping basis), and dominated local administrative units. In the highland pastures, large cattle haciendas developed that encroached on village land, but required the labor of shepherds. These shepherds, other hacienda laborers, and often their relatives in the villages, were able to use hacienda lands to graze their own animals or to cultivate. The proportion of permanently landless agricultural laborers was very small, but many small farmers complemented their agriculture with wage labor. Trades and crafts also developed, especially in the larger villages.[9]

This situation meant that there existed a diverse set of local opportunities for making a living. On the basis of these opportunities, and as a result of land subdivision and accumulation through inheritance and purchase, social and economic groupings of changing composition developed in the Mantaro area. This dynamic reflects the ecological patterns described earlier; modes of farming did not permit close supervision, and shepherds were able to exploit the land to their advantage. Likewise, the careful combining of plots in different zones, trading and craft activities could make one family's fortunes while another by careless management of large holdings courted disaster. Other opportunities existed in the accumulation of lands reserved by decree and by testament to the Church and to the cult of its saints. Enterprising farmers could often rent these lands or quietly usurp them.

In contrast, Guatemala does not have such a varied ecology. This is especially true in the predominantly ladino areas of the country, where there are few extensive pasturing opportunities. An indication of the lesser differentiation both within and between ladino villages is the relative absence of a regional marketing system. Crops needed for subsistence are grown locally and other items for consumption are purchased in local stores or in stores at provincial centers (Durston, 1972). An extensive marketing system did, however, develop in the Indian highlands (Tax, 1953). The significance of the ecological variations in Peru is clearer when it is remembered that they include within a municipal boundary many different soil types and sometimes as many as five micro-climates significant for agriculture. There are many risks attending agriculture in the Sierra of Peru, especially through frost and hail; soils and micro-climates are differently affected by these risks. Much of the pattern of mutual aid mentioned earlier represents one means of distributing these risks more evenly among a population whose land is dispersed in different parts of the municipality. This incentive for the development of social obligations is not present in the more uniform climate and soil types of most Guatemalan villages.

At the beginning of this century, the differences between Guatemala and the

Mantaro area of Peru were accentuated by the local implications of the development of an export economy based on the large-scale cultivation of cash crops and, in the case of Peru, on mining. These developments created important markets for agricultural produce from the central Sierra of Peru in mining centers and, indirectly, in other urban centers as coastal land previously used to grow crops for the coastal cities become converted to export crops (Bonilla, 1967-68). These market opportunities did not appear in Guatemala due to the absence of mining centers and of any large urban centers, and the relative self-sufficiency of plantations in providing food for their workers. The labor opportunities provided by economic development in Guatemala were also less attractive than those of Peru. In Peru, wages in the mines and coastal plantations were high relative to the income that could be obtained from farming. In the Mantaro valley villages, it was the members of households with middling to large farms who took most advantage of these opportunities (Roberts, 1973b).[10] Illiteracy and a greater urgency to provide support for dependents meant that members of poorer families engaged in temporary unskilled labor on construction projects and other short-term labor activities. Labor opportunities in the Mantaro area also tended to reinforce ties to the village or small town: miners often left their families in the village and expected to eventually settle there. Most of the coastal migration which, from 1920 to 1950, employed yearly some 4,000 workers, lasted for three months; these were the slack months of the local agricultural cycle.

In Guatemala, labor in the expanding plantations has not been well paid; this labor often involved permanent migration as families colonized small plots and new villages sprung up in the plantation lowlands (Adams, 1970: 155-164, 369-372). The absence of economic opportunities in their villages of origin undoubtedly encouraged migrants to remain permanently away from home. Also, the different political complexion of Guatemala and Peru is an important factor. Government decrees in Guatemala instituted what was, for a period, forced labor on the plantations. Subsequently, labor was tied to plantations by having to pay off debts incurred through advance payments and purchases in company stores (Tax, 1953: 105-108). Such measures kept down the wages that plantations needed to pay to keep workers. In Peru, labor was more strongly and consistently organized in mines and plantations, obtaining wage increases and social benefits.

By the early twentieth century, there existed in many parts of highland Peru a more developed economic and social basis for making use of local agricultural opportunities than was the case in Guatemala. These opportunities were restricted in Peru by customary jurisdictions that often had no direct commercial interest in the land. The Church did not directly benefit from its estates; remaining communal land was farmed inefficiently; even the haciendas often controlled more land than they could effectively farm (Martínez Alier, 1972). Between villages also, similar restrictions were apparent: Villages which were municipal capitals held land in other villages or held rights to the labor of people from constituent smaller villages.[11] These lands and rights were often of more annoyance to the subordinate villagers than they were economically beneficial to those who controlled the municipal capitals. They did diminish the possibilities of local people taking control of their resources and using them to their own ends.

Different social groupings had different interests in these situations. Small, independent farmers sought opportunities to farm Church or communal land, to obtain lease or ownership of hacienda land, and to irrigate for commercial farming. Larger farmers also wished to expand their farming, to retain their rights to the labor of others, and to secure ample sharecropping labor for their estates. Workers on the haciendas or sharecroppers on the lands of larger farmers also perceived opportunities for themselves in their existing situation. To complicate matters, villages and their constituent social groups sought independence from other villages. These strategies cross-cut any uniform class or economic interest; village cultivators were not uniformly hostile to the haciendas nor were sharecroppers to owners. These strategies were directed against jurisdictions that were mainly locally based and that did not use their rights in an economically efficient manner.

The political structure of Peru encouraged these villagers to pursue these economic opportunities. Factors such as the size of the country, geography, and the foreign and civil wars frequent in the latter part of the nineteenth century meant that considerable regional autonomy developed in Peru. Provincial and departmental authorities existed and were responsible to the central government; but the supervision was not close and there were few civil service employees to provide permanent links with the government bureaucracy. Instead, provincial political organization was characterized by the existence of municipalities left to their own devices with ill-defined jurisdictions, few responsibilities for government taxation, and little revenue from the government. The central government had a small budget, and ministries did not, until recently, maintain branches in the provinces. Moreover, for many years the political system gave the patronage of government funds available for work in the provinces to elected provincial political representatives, semi-permanently established in the capital.

In this situation, municipalities and their sub-units, led by the middling and larger farmers of the locality, found it to their advantage to lobby the courts and central government to redefine boundaries or change political jurisdictions. Provincial authorities of all levels were frequently bypassed, and government officials, politicians and legal authorities were directly approached in Lima. Without commitments to a strongly established provincial chain of command or to revenues based on existing jurisdictions, government was ready to receive and evaluate the often conflicting requests made by local people.

In contrast with Peru, the political and economic structure of localities in Guatemala was more rigidly defined. Partly this was due to the absence of "reserved" land resources that offered possibilities to enterprising farmers. Church or *cofradías* did not control important extensions of village lands, and there were no extensive, underexploited pastoral lands. In Guatemala, as in Peru, there is very little truly communal land. Also, the organization of provincial life in Guatemala has been more tightly organized by the central government than in Peru (Adams, 1964: 163-166).

In Guatemala, except for brief periods of democratization such as the Arévalo-Arbenz period from 1944-1954, village and small town officials have been appointed by the central government and its provincial representatives. Furthermore, in the different municipalities of the nation, there existed a group of full-time public employees appointed by, and responsible to, the central government. These included a municipal secretary, whose occupational experience would often consist in moving from one small town to another at the behest of the central government. Furthermore, municipalities had responsibility for collecting taxes for the central government and received, under tight budgetary supervision, smaller amounts for their own local needs. The civil hierarchy was complemented by a military one that descended from the army command in the capital to provincial garrison commanders and to *comisionados militares* who at municipal level were responsible for recruitment to the army (Durston, 1972: 81-109).

MIGRATION AND REGIONAL ASSOCIATIONS

These patterns of provincial organization in Peru and Guatemala are expressed in differences in the organization of migration in the two countries. Migration is not simply a movement of individuals responding to economic opportunities in their place of origin and at their destination, but an organized movement based on social and economic arrangements at both local and national levels. Migration from villages often coincides with stages in the agricultural cycle, or with stages in the life cycle, as young, unmarried people leave, earn money, and return to marry and take over land. These same people may subsequently leave again when their family is growing and cash is needed to complement their farming activities. Village life takes account of such movements in the arrangements that exist to cultivate land in the absence of able-bodied members of the village, or through the expectation that local projects or celebrations be financed by earnings from migration.

Migration becomes in these ways a regular part of village organization. The pattern of farming that develops as well as the encouragement of education and of skills in particular crafts may be based on the expectation that the economies of households will be complemented by some of its members migrating to trade, to obtain ready cash, or to "represent" the household enterprise in another economic or political niche. When this happens, migration is an extension of the social and economic fields of activity of a village. This is the pattern of migration which I have described as occurring in the Mantaro area of Peru. This pattern was encouraged by the existence of local economic opportunities that cash or political contacts, made during migration, could help exploit. Guatemala shows a different pattern: Migration is more frequently a final resort of people who cannot make a living in a village, and it often entails the severance of social and economic ties with the village. Even for those families with larger landholdings, out-migration represents the abandonment of provincial life for a different mode of existence elsewhere.

Social and economic arrangements at the national level contribute to this process through the types of labor opportunities available and through an increasing economic concentration in the capital city. In the Peruvian case, the village continued as a focus of migrants' activities during the first half of this century because labor opportunities in mines, plantations or construction work did not encourage permanent out-migration. Subsequently, with the decline of these labor opportunities relative to those available in Lima, migrants shifted the focus of their activities from village to city, as they were required to commit their resources to making a place for themselves amid the competition for jobs and housing in the city. This subsequent pattern of migration affected the villages of the Mantaro area from the 1950s onwards (Roberts, 1973b). Migration to Lima and to the other large cities of Peru increasingly drains the villages of their economic and social resources, but continues to be an extension of their social and economic fields of activity. To find or create work in the city, to obtain housing or secure other forms of assistance, migrants use kinsmen or fellow villagers previously established or with work experience in the city. Migrants receive agricultural produce from villages to meet the high cost of foodstuffs in the city.[12] Aged kinsmen and other dependents are provided for within the social and economic arrangements of the village. In these ways, village organization remains important to the ways in which migrants cope with their environment. Likewise, villages continue to be organized on the expectation that migrants finance celebrations and other projects, supply city-produced consumer goods, or serve as essential elements in extended economic enterprises.

In Guatemala, village organization appears to have been little affected by the replacement of labor opportunities on plantations by migration to seek work in Guatemala City which has occurred since the 1950s. Among the migrants I interviewed in Guatemala City, very few had continuing economic and social relationships with their place of origin, whether in the form of rights to land, of economic enterprise, or of receiving or sending produce (Roberts, 1973a). Whereas in Peru migration to the city occurred as a member of a household took up urban residence, followed over a period of months or years by other household members, in Guatemala whole households left their villages, selling their land and ceasing to rent. As noted in the previous section, there were no readily available mutual aid systems to allow the remaining members of a family to farm land in the absence of its able-bodied members.

In the Peruvian migration process, the social and economic practices of migrants include both city and village and are often common to both locations. It is not a question of these migrants deciding between a provincial culture appropriate to provincial situations and an urban culture appropriate to urban situations: The life situations that are relevant to migrants in Peru are likely to encompass village and city locations and village and city residents. In contrast, in Guatemala, villages and the city present very different situations which are not meaningfully linked by common or interdependent enterprises. In Guatemala City, relationships with kin or with fellow villagers are frequent among migrants and do assist in coping with urban life; but the social situation of these migrants is more restricted to the city than is the case in Peru, and is closely related to features of urban economic and administrative organization (Roberts, 1973a: 77-89). Under these conditions, relationships with kin or fellow migrants have few advantages over those that can be developed with other urban dwellers in the course of daily life or through participation in different kinds of urban association.

The Development of Regional Associations

The earliest migrants to Lima and to the other parts of the coast were drawn disproportionately from the sons and daughters of village families who held the large- and medium-sized landholdings. They gained cash, experience, and contacts in the labor centers; they retained their rights to land in the village and were interested in developing the economic possibilities of their villages. It was under these conditions that the first village-based associations appeared in work centers and in the cities of Peru, as early as 1910.[13]

We can distinguish two features of these early clubs. They were set up by resident traders or professionals from the village, and they provided a temporary means of organization for the circulatory labor migrants who came to the town or labor center. On one large cotton hacienda, for example, it was the *enganchador* (labor contractor) who established a village club and organized its sporting and other activities. He persuaded this club to donate a large clock to the village. In Lima, professionals practicing in the capital likewise often sponsored a village club. To obtain access to reserved lands, to obtain independence from other jurisdictions, or to obtain improvements that could raise productivity, villages required access to central government. In this situation, the associations were a channel by which enterprising elements in villages and small towns could gain access to governmental resources and obtain the decisions needed to facilitate the development of local opportunities. The work of clubs, especially in Lima, responded to the needs of villages, the perspectives of migrants whose interests remained focused provincially, and to the structure of political authority in Peru.

That the clubs originated from the coincidence of these factors in the social field of migration, rather than simply the desires of city residents to institutionalize their common provincial origins, is evident in the timing of the foundation of the clubs. As local political issues became salient as a result of boundary conflicts or efforts to secure independence of other jurisdictions, so clubs were formally established in Lima. Many villages with migrants in the capital have not been represented by formally organized clubs; in these cases it is likely that there is no coincidence of economic possibilities and of political issues at the village level. Organizing a formal association enables migrants to represent their village before government authorities and to claim a formal say in village deliberations. In the case of Huayopampa, for example, it is only when the economic possibilities of the village change substantially for the better that there is talk of migrants organizing a formal association in Lima. Previously, the dominant groups in the village secured needed services by sending delegations and through the personal intervention of influential migrants residing in Lima and in the provincial centers (Fuenzalida, 1968).

This process is illustrated by data on the foundation in Lima of an association for migrants from the southern Sierra town of Ongoy (Altimirano, 1971). The southern Sierra is a less economically dynamic area than the Mantaro valley, and migration to Lima began later and has been less extensive. The Ongoy club, formally recognized in 1923, was the first club of its department to be organized in Lima. An explicit reason for its foundation was to give more formal backing to its members' activities on behalf of their community in its conflict with neighboring haciendas. From 1925 onward, the club lobbied the government for restitution of village land.

The village succeeded in obtaining hacienda land, and the lobbying activity of the Lima club on behalf of the village has continued until the present. These political activities led Altimirano to estimate that the club effectively determined the political strategies and priorities that were adopted by the village. The Lima club also provided recreational opportunities for the village's Lima residents—who were concentrated in three of the city's barriadas—by organizing several football teams and by holding social evenings. The club became an important point of contact for the many Ongoy residents who migrated to the coastal plantations for seasonal work. Through these visits, the return visits of the more stabilized migrants, political activity and sports, the capital and the village became part of the same field of action for migrants and residents.

Similar activities occur in the regional associations whose members are drawn from the villages of the Mantaro valley. The clubs of the larger villages were informally established in Lima by the first decade of this century. The villages with the most extensive out-migration have associations in hacienda, mine, provincial capital and national capital; villages with a more restricted migration experience have correspondingly fewer clubs (Adams, 1959; Long, 1973a).

The recorded activity of the Lima club of Sicaya, a village of some 7,000 people, illustrates the extensive participation of regional associations in village life. As early as 1903, Lima residents from Sicaya were lobbying in Lima to obtain postal service for the village, working in concert with one of the elected representatives of the Mantaro area in Lima. Club members active in Lima during this period were later to return to Sicaya to farm and to hold political office. The Lima club figured most actively in Sicaya affairs in the 1920s, 1930s, and 1940s. In this period, the Lima club was the source of important financial contributions, especially for the local school system; it was used in lobbying activities to improve the village's supply of water and light, and to extend irrigation; its advice was also sought on technical matters. The club also took action independently, writing to the village council to draw its attention to abuses of local jurisdictions or to needed action. The club served as a watchdog over the administration of communal lands. It replied sharply to a village project for the installation of a water supply system, on the grounds that it had been insufficiently planned or estimated financially. At one stage (1929), the village council justified its constant referrals to the club in Lima by contending that "the residents in Lima have the same rights as those of Sicaya."

The Lima club of Sicaya included many professionals and could rapidly mobilize other professional expertise when needed. Members of the club were also used to dealing with government departments and politicians, and occasionally the Lima club reminded Sicaya of the need to pay homage to a particular political figure. A composite picture of this field of activity is provided by one Sicaya delegation sent to Lima in the 1940s to lobby for improved services. It included two village council members, the labor contractor who, for many years, had contracted Sicaya labor to work on the cotton harvests of the coast, the area's political representative in Lima (with whom the labor contractor had business relationships), and two delegates from the Sicaya club in Lima.

The activity of villages and their migrant associations bypassed the regional population centers: These offered few economic opportunities to villagers and did not contain significant centers of power (Roberts, 1973b). In this way, migration contributed to the direct penetration of metropolitan society by the villages and small towns of the more developed areas of the nation. The direct articulation of villages with the capital did often mean that local developments were not coherently organized; absent migrants, in encouraging village projects, were often responding less to local needs than to their own perspectives and possibilities. This feature of the articulation of villages with national centers became more apparent from the 1950s onward. A study evaluating communal projects initiated in Muquiyauyo, for example, shows how these projects came to be increasingly concentrated on prestige items such as ornaments and public buildings rather than on the development of the economic infrastructure of the village (Grondin, 1973). Likewise, the Sicaya club in Lima has taken a less active interest in village affairs, and contact with government offices is now often initiated by villagers without consulting the Lima club or seeking its aid. In part, this change in the relationship of migrant club and village has occurred because the government has strengthened its provincial presence, establishing branches of different ministries which villages can, and often must, approach.

This development responds to the change in the pattern of migration in Peru that was earlier described. Migration from the Mantaro valley villages is increasingly to Lima and on a permanent basis; Sicaya, for example, now has as many adult citizens resident in Lima as it does in Sicaya. These people still retain an active economic interest in Sicaya, but their primary concerns are now focused on establishing themselves in the capital. Under these conditions, the Lima-based clubs cease to be organizations that reflect the problems and social organization of the village; instead they reflect the problems associated with living in the city. Previously a village club in a city or mine might be divided by factions representing the different economic interests of the village and its constituent parts. Recently, divisions in these clubs reflect city-based occupational differences. The Sicaya club has been split in the last ten years by the rivalry between the many Sicaya butchers in Lima and the professionals and white-collar workers from Sicaya who work in the city. Similar divisions have been observed in clubs based on other Mantaro valley villages.

Despite these changes in the focus of activities of migrant clubs, the villages continue to be important parts of the field of activity of migrants. The implications of this situation for village organization are illustrated by Long's account of the Lima associations of the Mantaro valley village of Incahuasi (Long, 1973a).[14] The village has a population of some 4,000 people and has had substantial out-migration to labor centers and to Lima. From the early part of the century, the migrants to Lima formed a succession of associations, the first being formally registered in 1925. An association would be formed, flourish for a number of years, and then lie dormant until replaced by another. These early associations were sponsored by migrants with professional occupations, but they explicitly catered to workers and traders whose migration was often temporary.

In 1970 a group of migrants with professional occupations split from the existing Lima club: They disagreed with the village policies of the dominant faction in the club. Their own policy toward Incahuasi was that of improving the public appearance of the village. For example, they sponsored a project to restore the ruined village church. They identified themselves with the existing village authorities and with the existing military government of Peru. These professional migrants had few active economic interests in the village; they retained homes there and returned for holidays and festivals. The established club was dominated by a group with occupations such as owners of small workshops, traders, office workers, construction workers, and factory technicians. Some members of this group alternated their residence between Incahuasi and Lima, and had active economic interests in the village. This dominant faction allied itself with a group of larger farmers and traders in the village, and appointed two members of their group as their representatives in Incahuasi. The dominant club faction and their allies were opposed to the existing village authorities and, by using the pool of influential contacts available to them, secured their replacement by individuals drawn largely from their own group. Politically, the dominant group and its allies were sympathetic to the Aprista party (APRA) and suspicious of the military government's intentions with respect to agrarian reform and the possible collectivization of agriculture.

The Incahuasi case illustrates the extent to which the political, as well as the economic, field of activity of Peruvian migrants includes both city and provinces. A village is often a more accessible arena for the political strategies of urban residents than is the city itself, in which the proliferation of small-scale enterprises and an ill-defined administrative structure make collective action on behalf of particular economic interests more difficult. Note, for example, that the breakaway Incahuasi faction includes people whose occupational interests might well be favored by the expansion of government bureaucracy; in contrast, many of the leaders of the dominant club faction have jobs which have often been associated with opposition to the centralist tendencies of Peruvian government.

As Long (1973a) points out, these clubs are but part of an elaborate institutional network located in both city and provinces. Sporting and social clubs that are based in the villages we studied in the Mantaro area include migrants who reside permanently outside the village. Of the seventy-four members of one Incahausi sporting club, twenty-five live permanently outside the village; the leaders of the club are a mixture of residents and nonresidents, and are disproportionately drawn from people in higher-status occupations and with the most economic resources. Cross-cutting memberships link clubs with different locations and different purposes. These linkages are extended to higher-order associations such as provincial and national sporting associations.

The change in the focus of club activity suggests one way of resolving the controversies concerning the importance of these clubs in city and national life (Doughty, 1972; Jongkind, 1971). Evidence for the relative lack of importance of these clubs is drawn from the contemporary period when, with the extension of government agencies into the provinces, local needs can be answered by local strategies. Many clubs lose their places as channels of communication and, consequently, one of the dynamics of the establishment and continuation of clubs disappears. Clubs have always experienced fluctuations in their activities, in response to a number of factors varying from time to time and from place to place. The fortunes of clubs have recently fluctuated with government policy toward land reform in the provinces. Some Lima-based clubs, representing villages that are presently affected by agrarian reform, have become active as lobbying groups.

The significance of these clubs in urban life is much broader than that of socializing people unaccustomed to city ways. They have been important in this respect, and in providing a point of organization for sporting and other recreational activities (Doughty, 1972). Their significance as social foci was greater, I suspect, in the case of those villages like Ongoy where migration included both temporary and more stablized migrants to the city. The distinct contribution that migrant clubs have made to the emerging urban organization of Peru is that they have provided one of the means by which a metropolitan society became sensitive to local-level provincial politics. Subsequently, these clubs acted as an additional channel by which provincial society was exploited from the metropolis.

In Guatemala City, there are some four or five active regional associations which represent the important provincial capitals; this compares with the more than 1,000 clubs identified in Lima (Doughty, 1970; Jongkind, 1971). The Guatemalan associations organize social gatherings attended by high-status families. They are markedly similar in character to the association that represents the whole Mantaro area in Lima—the Huancayo club. Unlike the village-based clubs, the Huancayo club plays little active part in the politics of the region; it organizes social gatherings attended by prominent people from the region and organizes receptions when regional officials visit Lima. At this regional level, in both Peru and Guatemala, policies and economic resources are effectively pursued by direct personal contact with goverment. Given the concentration of economic resources in the capital in both countries, there has been little opportunity for distinctive and cohesive regional economic interest groups to develop among influentials, either in the provinces or in the capital.

Among the low-income groups I studied in Guatemala City, there was little interest in formalizing their social relationships with fellow migrants. Opportunities for recreation were provided by neighborhood-based football associations, often organized by government social workers. Religious groups, local community associations, consumers' cooperatives, and even political parties were additional, accessible means of establishing relationships in the city (Roberts, 1973a: 150-192).

The Fiesta System

In this section, I present some cases of fiesta activity in Peru, taken from both "rural" and "urban" situations, as examples of the contemporary activities by which city and provinces are interrelated. Other evidence suggests that contemporary fiesta organization is a useful means of understanding the present state of rural-urban relationships in the Andean region (Buechler, 1970).

I begin with a condensed description of fiestas in honor of a village's patron saint. In the central region of Peru, these fiestas occur most frequently in the months from June through September. Depending on the size and wealth of these villages, the fiestas extend from two days to over a week. A typical fiesta in Chongos Bajo, extending over a period of eight days, included the following activities: High school students organizing a program of talks, music and plays; several marches by local school children; six solemn masses attended by villagers and the municipal authorities; an official meeting of the municipal council; a football championship competition; at least a dozen banquets given by the different organizers of the fiesta; an extended program each day of traditional dances, including parades, charades and fights; a fireworks display; several processions of the image of the saint; public dancing; and bull-fighting, with bulls dedicated to the major political authorities of the region, local authorities, a regional radio station, the president of the regional football league and important commercial figures such as the president of a city-based trucking cooperative which handles the village's produce. This village is unusual in that the expenses of the fiesta are partly met from the profits of land attached to the cult of its saint, but the major officials of the fiesta still spent large sums of their own money, amounting to approximately $250 (U.S.) each. The officials were helped in their expenses by contributions from kin, friends and business acquaintances. Though there was extensive local participation in the fiesta, most of the ceremonial activities, including the traditional dances, were undertaken by migrants now resident in the nearby city of Huancayo or in Lima. This pattern is evident in other villages, and in some of these, such as Sicaya, migrants have for many years assumed the major responsibility for financing and undertaking the fiesta (Escobar, 1964; Long, 1973a).

The organization of these fiestas is a product of the urbanization of the Mantaro area. Until the early part of this century, religious fiestas were based on the communal exploitation of lands tied to the cult of the saints and expressed customary devotional practices of local people. It was this type of "folk" celebration that the more "progressive" villagers sought to restrict and even eliminate. Contemporary fiestas are now actively encouraged by these same "progressive" villagers and by their descendents; they have become one means by which resident and nonresident villagers attempt to organize an environment that includes different social and geographical loci. The organization of fiestas provides certain "solutions" to the dispersal of the economic and political power affecting village life.

The fiesta provides a situation in which the various participants in villagers' fields of activity are present at the same time: Absentee landowners, city-based merchants, political authorities, and small farmers seek each other out and consolidate contracts and arrangements for the coming year. In the Sicaya fiesta, the returning migrants used the occasion of the fiesta to oversee the administration of their lands. Farmers interested in renting land from them chose a good opportunity to approach them with ready cash. The fiesta facilitates these activities because its structure allows for diverse forms of public participation in which obligations are visibly contracted and repaid.

The fiesta also provides an opportunity for people to establish their identity with respect to various others on whom they depend for making a living. To sponsor a fiesta indicates that a man has sufficient position to call upon a variety of social and economic resources; it also means that he is sufficiently interested in the village to spend his resources there. In these ways, a sponsor establishes his credit worthiness both to the outsiders he invites and to those who reside in the community. He depends on community residents to farm his land, administer property, or to prevent political trouble over his absentee landownership. The fiesta structure suits the strategies of others as well: Poorer farmers and landless laborers sense out likely patrons. Arrangements are made with an influential migrant to obtain work in Lima. Local small traders make large profits from their sales during the fiesta. Village authorities have an opportunity to display to a large audience their position and to use the regional press and visiting dignitaries to lobby for more attention for their village.

The organization of the fiesta involves spatially extended relationships. Musicians are often recruited from professional bands, and one of the most desired of these is the army band; villagers extend contacts to the neighboring city to obtain its services. The provision of beer and other refreshment often means the establishment of contact and credit with nonlocal distributors. Similar processes occur in obtaining bulls, bullfighters, and other facilities. Outsiders interested in establishing commercial contacts with the village sometimes use the fiesta as an opportunity to do a favor by underwriting some of these needed facilities or by sponsoring part of the fiesta.

In contrast, village fiestas in Guatemala are less socially and economically complex affairs. They are financed by contributions, often from the wealthier villagers, but the personal expenses involved are not so heavy as in Peruvian case, nor do they involve calling upon a set of extended social and economic relationships (Adams, 1964: 188-189). In the ladino areas they appear to be viewed as mainly for the benefit of Indians or the poorer elements of the population. Richer families have their own dances which are restricted by invitation and entrance fee. Elements of social differentiation are present in fiestas in Peru also; but the organization of the fiesta in Peru maximizes the participation of all those present.

The case of a fiesta in Incahuasi studied by Norman Long (1972) demonstrates how the fiesta structure reflects the particular economic relationship that has developed between city and provinces in the Mantaro area. This fiesta is organized by a group of some forty residents who call themselves the San Sebastián Club. This group includes truckers engaged in transporting agricultural and other produce from the valley to Lima and to other areas of the country. In Long's analysis, the San Sebastián Club and its fiesta provide a situation in which members exchange favors and help each other to organize the activities from one year to the next. This organizational framework emphasizes the equality among members and binds them to each other. Other members of this fiesta club have occupations, such as traders and industrialists, that complement the activities of the truckers.

Long shows how truckers, who work over a wide region, with many uncertainties attending their operations, require a large pool of people to draw upon for help and information. At the same time, they need to keep their options open in terms of possible cargo and not to commit themselves to any one set of relationships. The club and fiesta provide them with this flexibility; kinship relationships would be too constricting. The San Sebastián group has in effect developed into a large and complex economic enterprise, but without the inflexibility and administrative costs entailed in establishing a formal enterprise. The form of organization provided by the San Sebastián Club is one explanation why a village like Incahuasi should be able to sustain an economic enterprise of this size. In addition, high out-migration has provided an extended set of contacts which resident entrepreneurs use to their advantage.

At this point, our argument can be extended. Fiestas and their organization provide flexibility in choosing and consolidating relationships which an individual must combine over different locations and among different social groups. They are pre-eminently an expression of rural-urban interrelationships and not rural practices adapted to urban situations. This is especially clear in the fiesta activity of the wholesale traders of the market of Huancayo—my example of an urban situation. Their celebration extends over five days and is organized by four sponsors, all migrants from small villages. During the fiesta, much of the wholesale activity of the market comes to a standstill, and large sums of money are expended. In 1972, the sponsors calculated they would spend close to $1,000 (U.S.) each on the fiesta. They also received help from over one hundred other people who donated beer, presents, decorations, fireworks, and toy bulls. The majority of those who gave this help were themselves wholesalers. Another category of support came from the employees and business associates of fellow wholesalers. Finally, kin from villages came especially to the city to prepare the meals of the fiesta and help with arrangements.

The pattern of interdependency that is fostered by the fiesta is one that is recognized by the participants themselves. Meetings are held to plan and coordinate the fiesta. The participants talk about how the fiesta helps identify their true friends and associates and enables them to recognize people who might be untrustworthy. One wholesaler explicitly linked sponsoring the fiesta and helping others to sponsor it with the task of establishing oneself as a reputable merchant in the market. Those merchants who were seen by others to be marginal to the organization of the market made some effort to support a sponsor who traded in the same branch of produce as themselves. In certain cases, the fiesta served to consolidate family and friendship enterprises: Associates among the fruit and potato wholesalers made a practice of taking over the sponsorship of the fiesta from each other. These associates were two groups of migrants from the same villages.

These wholesalers are busy and successful merchants. That they should be prepared to invest large amounts of money and time in the fiesta and its preparation indicates the value that it has for them. Part of this value is the satisfaction they derive from fulfilling customary religious and social obligations. Through public participation in the fiesta, sponsors acquire prestige and establish their trustworthiness. It is also clear that the fiesta aided them in their everyday enterprises. All these wholesalers operated under conditions in which their constant preoccupation was that of securing supplies and finding markets in the face of hazardous communications, price fluctuations, and competition from other traders in the city and region. Each wholesaler in the market tended to specialize in a certain area and clientele for his activities; this area of operation was often that of the wholesaler's home village. They often had to call on each other for loans of trucks when their own were held up or had broken down. They needed to borrow money to pay off an especially big consignment, and they needed access to market information. Under these conditions, a wholesaler's capacity to call on the help of associates constitutes a social capital vital to the success of his enterprise. Under the unpredictable and uncoordinated economic conditions of Peru, this social capital is a more flexible means of operating an enterprise than trusting to fixed capital assets.

The fiesta structure is important for these enterprises because it represents an organizational technique suited to an informally organized urban economy. Also, it is based on the continuing interrelationships of city and countryside. In all the fiestas, regardless of their location, city dwellers and village residents participate together and are interrelated by their interests in an extended field of economic and social activity. A village's particular pattern of migration gives it "representatives" that villagers use to extend their enterprises; the regions from which a city draws its inhabitants constitute "resources" upon which city dwellers build their enterprises.

This process occurs in the political as well as the economic field. Migrants from the Mantaro area colonized various labor centers, and some of them became active in union organization and political organization. The mass political party, APRA, was strong in these labor centers, and many valley migrants became prominent in APRA politics. Since migrants, especially the politically active ones, were drawn from the middling and larger farmers, village authorities and politically active migrants were often kinsmen. In the Mantaro area, APRA politicians from different sectors of the economy and different areas of the country could often be seen sponsoring village fiestas. In one valley village, for example, among the migrants attending a fiesta were people who had been officials of a mine union, a textile union, and a peasant league. Village-level politics became part of wider national issues; also, the politics of different economic sectors, such as the mines and the textile industry, were influenced by considerations external to that sector. Mine union officials and textile union officials, for example, retained land in their villages, kept up economic exchanges with their kin, sponsored fiestas, and held community office.

CONCLUSIONS

The organization of the provinces in Peru and the economic opportunities that some areas have offered to their inhabitants result in an urbanization process that does not give rise to distinctive "urban" and "rural" ways of life. The pattern of life in both city and provinces reflects the interrelationships of these locations; the social context that is significant to many inhabitants of city and provinces is a shared one, and similar cultural practices have developed in these different locations. By cultural practices, I mean the set of understandings and activities that are habitually used and developed to cope with everyday life. In the course of the development of these practices, elements of traditional provincial culture have been adopted and transformed both in provinces and city; this is a societal transformation and not the adaption of rural culture to an urban situation. In Guatemala, people living in city and provinces are weakly interrelated by social and economic ties. In Guatemala City, the cultural practices of city residents reflect the urban environment and include few evident transformations of provincial culture. There are few social situations or frames of common reference which facilitate the development of understandings and of activities with people who reside in different locations within the city and provinces, and who occupy different social positions.

I am not referring to the elaboration of detail in cultural practices. The poverty of culture in both Guatemala City and in ladino provincial areas of Guatemala is often remarked upon, and differs from the color and ceremony of traditional Indian life. I find it more useful to focus on the range of understandings and activities that people are able to develop with others. Even the poorest inhabitants of Guatemala City develop sufficient relationships with others to cope with a very difficult urban environment. The difference between city residents in Guatemala and Peru is that in Guatemala, city residents have a more restricted range of possibilities open to them in attempting to organize their environment. The fiesta examples indicate that many Peruvians have readily available means of developing reliable and economically useful sets of relationships, despite a mobile social environment and an uncertain economy. The continuing interrelationships of city and provinces means that these relationships can be developed consistently, as people living in different locations and occupying different social and economic positions are brought together through fiestas and clubs or through the business of daily life. Irrespective of their social and economic position, residents of Guatemala City find considerable difficulty in combining their relationships consistently to achieve a given purpose. Instead, subject to the uncertainties of urban residential and occupational mobility, Guatemalans develop relationships with distinct sets of people and in situations which often expose them to contradictory expectations for their behavior.

The contrasting situation in Guatemala and Peru is illustrated by considering local-level politics among poorer families. There are many ways in which the poor in Guatemala City can manipulate the existing urban power structure to their advantage. The groups and organizations which control the political and economic resources of the city do not have clearly defined jurisdictions and are eager to extend their patronage and to assess, whether defensively or otherwise, the political potential of the mass of the urban population. In this situation, poor people make use of the resulting competition among the powerful to obtain needed urban services. They ensure that their situation is defined by other groups in ways that maximize the possibility of their obtaining further services and minimize the possibility of sanctions. In recent field work in Peru, I found similar instances in which skillful, local-level politicians were able to manipulate the apparently monolithic structure of the present military government by taking advantage of the ambiguities in jurisdiction among the various dependencies and authorities of the state.

These manipulative strategies, which have been frequently reported and assessed by other observers of urban politics in Latin America, have little lasting impact on the existing structure of power or on the distribution of resources.[15] Manipulative strategies are merely palliative if they are not sustained and built upon by the creation of a more extensive and enduring organization among poor people. This organizational failure reflects factors in the economic and political structure of cities in both Guatemala and Peru, and underlies the persistent failure of poorer people to secure significant access to social and economic resources. This failure is absolute in Guatemala; it is a qualified one in Peru. In Guatemala, poorer city residents are constantly being organized from above in recreation, in politics, and in welfare; their attempts to organize among themselves in residents' associations or in cooperatives have been failures. The shantytowns in Guatemala show neither improvement nor legal recognition after fifteen years of existence. City residents in Peru have been more successful in generating an organization that has extended their participation in urban life. The material and political development of Lima barriadas is one result of this; another is the elaboration of economic enterprises in commerce and transport, controlled by provincial migrants, which have considerable economic and political influence.[16] I suggest that the greater organizational capacity of poorer people in Peruvian cities as compared to those in Guatemala City is partly due to the continuing strength of rural-urban interrelationships and to the long tradition of provincial development in Peru.

NOTES

1. The data on which this paper is based are drawn from field work in Guatemala in 1966 and 1968 (Roberts, 1973a), and from a three-year study (1970-1973) of the Mantaro region of Peru, financed by the British Social Science Research Council and directed by Norman Long and myself. The study of the Mantaro valley area included sample surveys,

interviews and participant observation. We collected extensive data on nine villages, one town, the regional capital, Huancayo, and several cooperative enterprises and large-scale businesses. Norman Long helped considerably in the writing of this paper with his comments and field material. Carlos Samaniego was another valuable source of comment and information.

2. The intercensal growth of Lima from 1961 to 1972 has approximated 7 percent a year, to a total population of three and a half million. In 1961, 47 percent of Lima's total population was classified as migrant; the majority of adults were migrants (Gianella, 1970). In Guatemala, during the intercensal period 1950-1964, there was a 53.5 percent increase in the total national population; in the same period, the population of Guatemala City increased by 101.5 percent to 572,937 people; and, of this 1964 city population, 38.4 percent were migrants (Termini, 1968). In both Lima and Guatemala City, increases in the economically active population have been absorbed by small workshops, personal services, and trade. In both cities, there is little evidence of a significant expansion in employment possibilities in large-scale manufacturing or in formally organized trading and service concerns (Gianella, 1970: ch. 2; Roberts, 1970).

3. There are differences in the emphasis that urban anthropologists working in Africa have given to the significance of tribal origins for urban behavior. Mayer (1961) emphasizes that some tribal migrants to town are tradition-oriented and remain encapsulated in relationships with fellow villagers. In contrast, Mitchell (1966) gives priority to the analysis of the urban situation in saying "the tribal origins of the population, in so far as they imply tribal modes of behaviour, must . . . be regarded as of secondary interest." Both these commentators emphasize that migrants situationally select appropriate modes of behavior in town.

4. Despite the ability these urban dwellers demonstrate in taking advantage of the ambiguities in the urban power structure, they are not well enough organized to affect significantly the distribution of resources in the city. The major impact of these local-level political activities on the urban power structure is that of creating a state of political uncertainty for those who control political and economic resources.

5. Leeds is preparing a comparative analysis of Lima, Santiago, and Rio de Janeiro in which he indicates the greater success that Lima barriada dwellers have had in manipulating the political structure than those of Rio have had; the situation he describes for Rio is similar in many ways to that of Guatemala City.

6. *Ladino* is the cultural and situational definition of a person who does not evidence by his speech, dress, and location, membership in the Indian group. Many *"ladinos"* in the city are undoubtedly of Indian origin. The social distance maintained between Indians and Ladinos depends on such factors as their relative proportions in the local population and the economic relationships between one another (Adams, 1964: 53-63).

7. The Mantaro area is one of the most important regional sources of migration to Lima. Several departments of Peru which have also contributed substantial numbers of migrants to Lima, such as Ancash, have characteristics (e.g., the predominance of independent, small farmers; access to diverse labor opportunities; the development of a market economy) that are similar to those of the Mantaro area.

8. The data on the Mantaro area are drawn from our field work in the area. They were obtained by extensive interviewing among village populations, including the gathering of life history material. We also obtained municipal records and data on land transfers from the beginning of this century. Other accounts of the Mantaro area are found in Tschopik (1947), Castro Pozo (1946), Arguedas (1957), Adams (1959), Escobar (1964) and Tullis (1970).

9. I define the Mantaro area to include the Mantaro valley, located at approximately 11,000 feet in the central Sierra of Peru and some five hours by road from Lima, the pastoral highlands above the valley, the high jungle on the eastern side of the mountains,

and the extensions of the valley that include the mining center of Oroya. The valley is some forty miles long, by three or four miles wide. The total population of the Mantaro area is approximately 500,000. The regional capital is Huancayo, with a population of 125.000, located at the southern end of the valley.

10. Other associates have been working on the historical pattern of migration in the Mantaro area. Laite (1972) has documented the pattern of migration for the northern end of the valley, including Oroya. Samaniego (1974) has worked on the southern end, including the highland pastoral villages.

11. There are basically four levels of regional political administration. There is the department headed by a prefect and, at one time, having a departmental council; below the department are the provinces headed by a sub-prefect and by a mayor and provincial council. The provincial council is also the council of the city which is the provincial capital. Below the provincial council, and responsible to it, are the districts of the province, each with a mayor and council. Each district includes one or more population centers; those outside the municipal capital are called annexes and are headed by an assistant mayor. To complicate the situation, villages, including the annexes, are also likely to be officially recognized as "peasant communities." Each peasant community represents a corporation with rights to land and labor and deriving revenue from these. The peasant community is headed by a president and various councils. At the district level, there is also a governor who is directly responsible to the sub-prefect and prefect. The nature of these jurisdictions is not clearly defined to participants and has changed over time. Annexes could obtain a considerable measure of independence by being declared a peasant community; additionally, they could petition for district status. By this process, the numer of districts in the Mantaro area has increased in the last hundred years from less than ten to over eighty.

12. Though we do not have exact figures on the amount of foodstuffs remitted to relatives in the cities, our interviews indicate that the majority of village households send some produce. Our informal estimate is that the amount remitted is almost equal to the amount sold on the market. Since this valley supplies about a quarter of Lima's total market consumption in items such as potatos, certain vegetables and cereals, the remittances form an important part of Lima's household economy.

13. The characteristics of regional associations are more fully treated in Mangin (1959), Doughty (1970, 1972) and Jongkind (1971). There are different levels of regional association, representing departments, provinces, districts and annexes. Jongkind (1971) provides data indicating that the higher the level, the more active members there are, and the higher is the occupational status of these members. There are also different levels of legal organization, from clubs with full juridicial recognition to informally organized gatherings notified by press or radio. Many of these clubs are sporting clubs.

14. Norman Long (1973b) is preparing a more detailed analysis of this sequence of events as part of his general study of patterns of local-level social organization and economic development.

15. This analysis is comparable to that of Leeds (1972) and Cornelius (1974) in which the palliative nature of much local-level politics is stressed.

16. There is little available evidence of the direct relation between these examples of urban organization and rural-urban interrelationships. Mangin (1959) reports that the stimulus for the founding of some barriadas came from existing regional associations. Barriadas present more complex residential patterns than those of the settlement of a single provincial group, though there are concentrations of people from the same villages within barriadas (Matos, 1966). Matos's (1966) data also indicate the versatility of these barriada dwellers in seeking out the possibilities in the political and administrative structure of the city.

REFERENCES

ADAMS, R. N. (1970) Crucifixion by Power. Austin and London: University of Texas Press.
——— (1964) Encuesta sobre la cultura de los ladinos en Guatemala. Guatemala City: Seminario de Integración Social.
——— (1959) A Community in the Andes: Problems and Progress in Muquiyauyo. Seattle: University of Washington Press.
ALTIMIRANO, T. (1971) "El cambio del sistema de hacienda al sistema comunal en un área de la sierra sur del Perú: el caso de Ongoy." M.A. thesis. University of San Marcos, Lima.
ARGUEDAS, J. M. (1957) "Evolución de las comunidades indígenas en el valle del Mantaro y la ciudad de Huancayo." Revista del Museo Nacional (Lima) 26.
BALAN, J. (1969) "Migrant-native socioeconomic differences in Latin American cities: a structural analysis." Latin American Research Review 4, 1: 3-29.
BONILLA, H. (1967-68) "La coyuntura comercial siglo XIX en el Perú." Revista del Museo Nacional (Lima) 35: 159-187.
BUECHLER, H. C. (1970) "The ritual dimension of rural-urban networks: the fiesta system in the northern highlands of Bolivia," in W. Mangin (ed.) Peasants in Cities. Boston: Houghton Mifflin.
BUTTERWORTH, D. S. (1970) "A study of the urbanization process among Mixtec migrants from Tilantongo in Mexico City," in W. Mangin (ed.) Peasants in Cities. Boston: Houghton Mifflin.
CASTRO POZO, H. (1946) "Social, economic, and political evolution of the communities of Central Peru," in Volume 2 of J. Steward (ed.) Handbook of South American Indians. Washington, D.C.: Smithsonian Institute.
CORNELIUS, W. A. (1974) "Urbanization and political demand-making: political participation among the migrant poor in Latin American cities." American Political Science Review 68, 3 (September).
DOUGHTY, P. (1972) "Peruvian migrant identity in the urban milieu," in T. Weaver and D. White (eds.) The Anthropology of Urban Environments. Boulder, Colorado: Society of Applied Anthropology Monograph 11.
——— (1970) "Behind the back of the city: 'provincial' life in Lima, Peru," in W. Mangin (ed.) Peasants in Cities. Boston: Houghton Mifflin.
DURSTON, J. W. (1972) "La estructura de poder en una región ladina de Guatemala." Estudios Centroamericanos 7. (Guatemala: Seminario de Integración Social.)
EPSTEIN, A. L. (1958) Politics in an Urban African Community. Manchester, Eng.: Manchester University Press.
ESCOBAR, G. (1964) "Sicaya: una comunidad mestiza de la Sierra central del Perú," in L. Valcarcel (ed.) Estudios sobre la cultura actual del Perú. Lima: San Marcos University.
FUENZALIDA, F. et al. (1968) Estructuras tradicionales y economía de mercado: la comunidad de indígenas de Huayapampa. Lima: Instituto de Estudios Peruanos.
GIANELLA, J. (1970) Marginalidad en Lima metropolitana. Lima: Centro de Estudios y Promoción del Desarrollo (DESCO).
GILLIN, J. (1958) San Luis Jilotepeque. Guatemala: Seminario de Integración Social.
GRONDIN, M. (1973) "The problem of community development during urbanization: the case of Muquiyauyo." México, D.F.: Universidad Iberoamericana. (unpublished)
JONGKIND, C. F. (1971) "La supuesta funcionalidad de los clubes regionales en Lima, Perú." Boletín de Estudios Latinoamericanos (CEDLA—University of Amsterdam) 11 (January): 1-14.
LAITE, J. (1972) "Industrialisation and land tenure in the Peruvian Andes." Presented at

the Symposium on Landlord and Peasant in Latin America and the Caribbean, Department of Sociology, University of Manchester, Manchester, England.

LEEDS, A. and E. LEEDS (1972) "Favelas and polity: the continuity of the structure of social control." LADAC Occasional Papers, 2, 5. Austin: University of Texas.

——— (1970) "Brazil and the myth of urban rurality," in A. J. Field (ed.) City and Country in the Third World. Cambridge, Mass.: Schenkman.

LOMNITZ, L. (1973) "Supervivencia en una barriada de la ciudad in México." Demografía y Economía 7, 1: 58-85.

LONG, N. (1973a) "The role of regional associations in Peru," in M. Drake et al. (eds.) The Process of Urbanization. Bletchley: The Open University.

——— (1973b) "Commerce and kinship in the Peruvian Highlands." Presented at 1972 Annual Meeting of the American Anthropological Association, Toronto.

——— (1972) "Kinship and social networks among transporters in rural Peru: the problem of the 'local' and the 'cosmopolitan' entrepreneur." Department of Social Anthropology, University of Durham. (unpublished)

MacEWEN, A. M. (1972) "Stability and change in a shantytown: a summary of some research findings." Sociology 6, 1: 41-57.

MANGIN, W. (1967) "Latin American squatter settlements: a problem and a solution." Latin American Research Review 2, 3: 65-69.

——— (1959) "The role of regional associations in the adaption of rural population in Peru." Sociologus 9, 1: 23-35.

MARTINEZ ALIER, J. (1972) "Los huacchilleros en las haciendas de la sierra central del Perú desde 1930: algunas hipótesis preliminares." Presented at the Second Symposium on the Economic History of Latin America, Rome, Italy.

MATOS, J. (1966) Estudio de las barriadas Limeñas. Lima: University of San Marcos.

MAYER, P. (1961) Townsmen or Tribesmen: Conservatism and the Process of Urbanization in a South African City. Cape Town: Oxford University Press.

MENDEZ, A. (1967) Zaragoza. Guatemala: Seminario de Integración Social.

MITCHELL, J. C. (1966) "Theoretical orientations in African urban studies," in M. Banton (ed.) The Social Anthropology of Complex Societies. London: Tavistock.

MURRA, J. (1972) "El 'control vertical' de un máximo de pisos ecológicos en la economía de las sociedades andinas," in I. Ortiz de Zuniga, Visita de la Provincia de León de Huánuco, Tomo II. Huánuco: Universidad Nacional Hermilio Valdizán.

——— (1968) "An aymara kingdom in 1567." Ethnohistory 15, 2.

ROBERTS, B. R. (1973a) Organizing Strangers: Poor Families in Guatemala City. Austin and London: University of Texas Press.

——— (1973b) "Migración urbana y cambio en la organización provincial en la sierra central de Perú." Ethnica 6.

——— (1970) "Migration and population growth in Guatemala City: implications for social and economic development," in B. Roberts and S. Lowder, Urban Population Growth and Migration in Latin America: Two Case Studies. Liverpool: Centre for Latin American Studies.

SAMANIEGO, C. (1974) "Location, social and economic differentiation and peasant movements in central Peru." Ph.D. dissertation. University of Manchester.

TAX, S. (1953) Penny Capitalism: A Guatemalan Indian Economy. Washington, D.C.: Smithsonian Institution. Institute of Social Anthropology Publication 16.

TERMINI, D. L. (1968) "Socio-economic and demographic characteristics of the population of Guatemala City with special reference to migrant–non-migrant differences." M.A. thesis. University of Texas.

TSCHOPIK, H. (1947) Highland Communities of Central Peru. Washington, D.C.: Smithsonian Institution. Institute of Social Anthropology Publication 5.

TULLIS, F. LaM. (1970) Lord and Peasant in Peru: A Paradigm of Political and Social Change. Cambridge, Mass.: Harvard University Press.

TUMIN, M. (1952) Caste in a Peasant Society. Princeton: Princeton University Press.

WHYTE, W. F. and L. K. WILLIAMS (1968) Toward an Integrated Theory of Development: Economic and Non-economic Variables in Rural Development. Ithaca: Cornell University.

ZARATE, A. (1967) "Migraciones internas de Guatemala." Estudios Centroamericanos 1. (Guatemala: Seminario de Integración Social.)

BILLIE JEAN ISBELL holds a doctoral degree from the University of Illinois at Champaign-Urbana, and is presently Assistant Professor of Anthropology at the State University of New York, Albany. Her principal interests lie in the fields of social and urban anthropology, language acquisition, kinship, and structuralism. The focus of her field research has been Peru, and her current research deals with the acquisition of social structures in the Andes and the transformations of such structures resulting from cityward migration. Her publications include "Acquisition of Quechua Morphology" (*Papers in Andean Linguistics,* University of Wisconsin, Vol. 1, No. 1); and "Kuyoq–Those Who Love Me: An Analysis of Andean Kinship and Reciprocity within a Ritual Context," in D. Maybury-Lewis (ed.) *Andean Kinship* (Harvard University Press, forthcoming).

Chapter 10

THE INFLUENCE OF MIGRANTS UPON TRADITIONAL SOCIAL AND POLITICAL CONCEPTS: A PERUVIAN CASE STUDY

BILLIE JEAN ISBELL

Introduction

The literature on migration and squatter settlements in Peru has focused upon cityward migration rather than the return of migrants to their places of origin and the resultant impact upon the traditional culture from which they have come. Elsewhere (Isbell, 1972a, 1972b, 1973), I have analyzed the traditional culture of Chuschi, a Central Highland Peruvian village in the department of Ayacucho. This paper will examine the transformation of certain aspects of village culture among migrants from Chuschi who have resided in one of Lima's squatter settlements, and the impact of these transformations upon the village.

I view urban and rural places as existing in a dynamic relationship in which mutual influences occur. The focus of the present study is the dialectic between the urban and rural ideologies within the domain of social and political concepts. I have utilized the methodology of structuralism (Barthes, 1972: 148-154) to dissect concepts in order to discover discrete units. The concepts have been rearticulated in model form to discover the relationships between the units. We might say that the structuralist method is one in which structures are "taken apart" and then "put together again" to clarify facets and relationships that eluded explanation before the analysis was performed. I am of the conviction

Author's Note: This paper is based upon fieldwork in the village of Chuschi in the Central Highland department of Ayacucho, Peru, and the squatter settlements of 7 de Octubre and San Cosme during the years 1967, 1969-1970. I wish to thank my assistant, Justa Vilca M., for her untiring persistence and patience. I also wish to acknowledge the hospitality of the

that the structuralist method will give us new insights into the dynamics of migration, by leading us to take the position that one must understand the concepts which people use to interpret events in order to understand the events themselves. Maranda (1972: 338) argues that, in order to communicate, people must share common mythic conceptions. He also argues that: "In essence structuralism seeks to understand how societies preserve their identity over time. Structuralism emphasizes therefore not the study of inertia as a cultural fact but, by analogy with information theory, the study of negentropic processes" (Maranda, 1972: 330). In other words, structuralism is concerned with how societies are able to abate the entropic effects of history. Societies do so by constructing structures and mythic conceptions of history and events. What better laboratory have we than the rapid phenomena of migration, urban land invasion, and the return to one's place of origin, to study how such structures and mythic conceptions come about, are transformed, or disappear? It is possible to observe structures in the making as migrants construct urban identities; it is also possible to witness the struggle between traditional and urban ideologies as migrants return to their places of origin. The migrant might be called the "bricoleur" (Lévi-Strauss, 1966) of concepts and symbols; he takes the elements at hand and rearranges them for his own purposes. However, he is constrained by the structural elements available to him, and the interplay between the migrants' collective experiences and the transformation of key traditional concepts gives rise to the formation of new structures. As the random and chaotic events of history impinge upon a society, the members construct a "mythic conception" of those events to coincide with their ideologies. This case study provides an example of how an Andean society made the chaotic events of migration and illegal invasion orderly and how they utilized these experiences to modify their shared traditional social and political structures.

Before proceeding, there are four terms that I must define: structure,

village of Chuschi and the migrants who spent so much time helping me to understand their points of view. My fieldwork was supported by the National Institute of Mental Health, Doctoral Dissertation Grant 1-F01-MH-40-565. My gratitude goes especially to the Museo do la Cultura Peruana in Lima and its Director, Rosalia Avalos de Matos, for their sponsorship and assistance. Florence Sloane, of the State University of New York, assisted in the tabulation of data, and Jan Townsend drew the diagrams. A graduate seminar at the State University of New York at Albany in social organization provided helpful criticisms of an earlier draft of this paper. I especially thank Ted Bradstreet for his critical comments. My husband, William H. Isbell and his colleague, Owen Lynch, of the State University of New York at Binghamton, provided many helpful criticisms. Elizabeth K. Hewitt, also at Binghamton, read the manuscript and made many helpful suggestions. Kenneth David of Michigan State University provided me with many stimulating ideas. Finally, I wish to thank Salvador Palomino (1970, 1971), for helping me unravel many of the traditional concepts discussed in this paper. However, the interpretations presented here are my own and only I am responsible for possible errors.

concept, symbol and ritual. Jean Piaget (1971: 5) defines structure as a self-regulating transformational system. This means that any input or change to any one of the elements of the system results in rearrangement or change in the other elements. A structure is a whole whereby the elements exist in regulated relationships to one another; structures are not mere aggregates, they are transformational systems. Piaget (1971: 10) concludes that structures are transformational systems capable of self-regulation; they are constantly in a dynamic state.

A concept is defined in the Random House Dictionary as an idea of something formed by mentally combining all of its characteristics or particulars. I assert that concepts are also structures; concepts are self-regulating, transformational wholes; I have studied the process of construction of concepts in the context of performances. A ritual can be defined as a series of formalized actions which are obligatory and standardized. These actions form a pattern of symbols which are statements in action (Leach, 1965: 13-14) dramatizing important shared values and beliefs (Wilson, 1954: 241) about the natural and social environment in which the participants operate (Turner, 1969: 6). A symbol is a motivated, nonarbitrary entity such as an image or an object which has a complex of meanings shared by a collective. Symbols are perceived as having inherent value separable from that which is symbolized. Symbols are utilized in rituals to unambiguously construct concepts basic to interaction and activity.

The Village

Chuschi is located 120 kilometers southwest of the department capital of Ayacucho via a dirt road that was completed in 1961. Prior to that time, the only communication the village had with outside points was via footpaths and llama trails. The completion of the road has facilitated a steady flow of migrants between Chuschi and Lima. During the dry season, May to September, two bus lines communicate between the village and Lima once a week. The trip is an arduous one, taking three days of continuous travel over dirt roads. However, migrants are able to arrive in Lima and walk to the invasion settlement where 250 co-villagers have settled.

Chuschi, designated an independent Peasant Community by the 1970 Agrarian Reform Law, has never experienced hacienda domination. The nearest haciendas are about fifteen kilometers away, and villagers judiciously guard their boundaries and their independent status from the encroachment of all foreigners. Chuschi represents one of the negative extremes of land tenure in the department of Ayacucho, where eighty-three percent of agricultural units are less than five hectares in size, and thirty percent of agricultural units are less than one hectare (Instituto Nacional de Planificación, 1969: 403). Chuschinos hold on the average one and one-half to two hectares of agricultural land per family. However, they hold herding land communally and control extensive areas of *puna* (high tundra grasslands) where cattle, sheep, alpacas and llamas are maintained. As is true elsewhere in the Andes, the scarcity of land and the low level of subsistence have stimulated cityward migration.

The 1970 Agrarian Reform Law

The 1970 Agrarian Reform Law abolished the existing bureaucratic structures in recognized indigenous communities such as Chuschi.[1] The law states that these communities are now designated Peasant Communities governed by an administrative council and a vigilance council. In 1970, the first councils in Chuschi were presided over by returned migrants. The law establishes two statuses for membership in a Peasant Community:

(1) Full *comunero*—one who resides at least six months of the year in the community, derives fifty percent of his income from agricultural activities, and complies with the membership criteria set by the community (usually birth and inscription).

(2) Associate *comunero*—one who is not a member of the community but whose income is derived equally from agriculture and some other enterprise and whose residence is within the community.

The 1970 law also abolished private property and has instituted a system of usufruct in plots of three to five hectares. A lottery system will be established when there is not sufficient land, as will be the case in Chuschi. If the law is applied implacably, many villagers will not have access to agricultural plots nor will they be able to diversify production by maintaining plots in the three major zones—the high *puna* or *sallqa* where root crops are grown, the corn producing *qichwa* zone, and the river bottom which produces fruits, squash and other temperate crops. The residence specifications of the law require that a *comunero* reside near or adjacent to his one plot. The law is contradictory to a thousand-year-old agricultural system which minimizes crop failure by diversifying in the various altitudinal zones.[2] The persons heading the two new bureaucratic councils are in particularly powerful positions; they will interpret the law and enforce the inscription and lottery systems. Migrants are returning to the village to retain usufruct of their land, and they are integrating themselves into the new political structure imposed by the 1970 Agrarian Reform Law.

BASIC TRADITIONAL CONCEPTS

A Basic Opposition of a Closed Corporate Community

Probably the most fundamental opposition found in human societies is that which segregates "My Group" from "The Other Group." In Chuschi, this concept is integrated and manifest in ritual performances, in physical and social space as well as in social and political concepts. Quechua-speaking villagers who participate in the communal life of the village supported by reciprocal exchanges and the traditional civil religious hierarchy live in the two *barrios* of the village designated upper and lower. They refer to themselves as *comuneros*, meaning members of the commune. Comuneros refer to all "foreigners," outsiders, and mestizos, as *qalas*, which literally means peeled or naked. In the past, the term has been applied to returned migrants, and it is said that the migrants "have peeled off their true identity."

Qalas do not live in the two barrios; they reside on and around the village plaza. The village church, the schools and the bureaucratic governmental buildings are located on the village plaza as well as eight small general stores *(tiendas)*. Among the qalas are the village shopkeepers, a health worker, an agronomist, seven primary and three secondary school teachers, four arts and crafts teachers, the priest, and descendants of the first teacher who arrived in Chuschi three generations ago. Qalas identify themselves as Peruvian nationals; comuneros identify themselves as Chuschinos. Qalas participate in the national polity and economy; comuneros do not. Qalas speak Spanish and wear western dress; comuneros traditionally do not. In fact, an informant claims that the term *qala* was first applied to migrants who returned wearing leather shoes instead of the traditional rubber tire sandals.

During rituals several foreign elements are portrayed vividly. The priest is burlesqued as a greedy, vulgar sort with an idiot for a sacristan. Army officers are characterized as cigarette-smoking, whip-brandishing bullies wearing sun glasses and high boots. Another traditional portrayal is the dreaded *naqa*, the supernatural form which foreigners assume to eat babies, castrate men, and steal the body fat used as fuel to run foreign industries. Depictions of two indigenous foreigners are enacted as well: lowland tropical forest Indians and herb traders from Lake Titicaca. The priest symbolizes spiritual domination and his idiot sacristan the comunero duped into servitude. They perform mock marriages and baptisms, blessing passersby with mock holy water which is aged urine. The army officers symbolize the real threat of governmental domination and conscription into the army by force. The naqa is the most dreaded of all for he symbolizes foreign invasion by supernatural powers. The Quechua-speaking comuneros clearly see themselves opposed to the entire outside world. Their narrow definition of "My Group" serves to maintain the closed corporate nature of Chuschi.[3]

Two Basic Structures

The closed corporate nature of comunero society is reinforced by both the sociopolitical structure and the economic structure of the village. These structures are superimposed onto spatial organization. As illustrated in Figure 1,

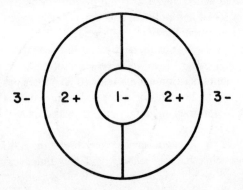

Legend:
(1) The *qalas* localized in the center of the village.
(2) The *comuneros* localized in the two traditional barrios.
(3) The threatening outside world.

Figure 1: THE SOCIO-POLITICAL STRUCTURE OF THE VILLAGE

the sociopolitical structure expresses the concentric dualism of Chuschino society: Comuneros live in the two traditional barrios while the threatening qalas, the "foreigners," not only surround the village but have penetrated comunero social space and are localized around the village plaza.

The economic structure excludes the qalas, and in the conception of the comuneros the village is viewed as a civilized whole opposed to the savage part of their economic world. The *sallqa* literally means *puna* or tundra grasslands, as well as savage or uncivilized. The village, where civilized activities occur, is separated from the savage tundra by a corn-producing zone, the *qichwa*.

The village, the adjacent agricultural zone, the qichwa, and the root crop-producing sallqa all have definite boundaries delineated by the location of chapels. Members of each barrio of the village maintain fields in both the qichwa and the sallqa. The two major economic zones are subdivided into upper and lower subzones, also delimited by chapels. The village is located at 3,154 meters. The upper qichwa reaches about 3,300 meters, which is the upper limit of corn production. The lower sallqa, and root crop agriculture, begins at the border of the upper qichwa and continues upward for some 300 meters where the "true" savage part of the world is found, the upper sallqa which extends beyond 4,000 meters in altitude. Nothing is grown on the upper sallqa, but the region is extremely important for grazing llamas, alpacas, cattle, sheep and goats. Herders are called savage, uncivilized men, *sallqa runa.* The upper sallqa is not only dangerous and uncivilized but also the dwelling place of the powerful mountain deities, the *Wamanis,* who control water and all animal life (Isbell, 1972a, 1972b, 1973).

Both the economic structure and the sociopolitical structure described above

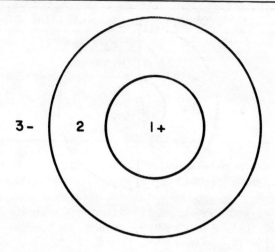

Legend:
(1) The civilized village.
(2) The corn-producing *qichwa* zone as mediator.
(3) The savage tundra or *sallqa.*

Figure 2: THE ECONOMIC STRUCTURE OF THE VILLAGE

are concentric and dual. However, they differ in one important aspect: The economic structure has a mediator, corn agriculture, which has resolved the antithesis between the savage and civilized parts of the world (see Figure 2). The sociopolitical structure does not contain a mediating element, and the antithesis between comuneros (insiders-members) and qalas (outsiders-nonmembers) has intensified. This difference helps to explain why the economic structure is more stable and resistant to change at this time, while the sociopolitical structure is more sensitive to change.

The village church is the residence of 14 saints, called *santos mayores* (major saints). Each saint "owns" a corn plot two or three times the size of the average comunero holdings. The produce from each of the fields is used to celebrate the saint's day with great quantities of *chicha* (corn beer). Two of the female major saints are said to have "daughters" who reside in the sallqa; the "daughters" are small replicas of their mothers and they are called *santas menores* (minor saints). Twice a year the daughters journey into the civilized village to "visit their mothers." The concept of major and minor saints denotes political domination and subordination. Those localities presided over by minor saints are politically and religiously subordinate to another, more powerful locality. The sallqa or tundra of Chuschi is under the dominion of the village. This concept extends to larger political units as well. During the Incaic and colonial periods, Chuschi was the bureaucratic center for seven other villages. Some of the subordinate villages continue to pay homage to Chuschi as an ancient political and religious center, even though these villages are now in different provinces and districts.

TABLE 1
ELEMENTS OF BASIC TRADITIONAL CONCEPTS

Positive Elements	Negative Elements
Inside	Outside
Member	Non-member
Comunero	Qala
Civilized	Savage
Major saint	Minor saint
Superordinate	Subordinate

Chuschinos appear to be concerned with representing basic concepts spatially and physically, and we would therefore expect to find migrants utilizing basic concepts to orient themselves spatially in their new urban environment. Furthermore, we would expect migrant "bricoleurs" to choose from the same sets of elements around which villagers organize their concepts of "We—My Group" versus the "Outside World" (see Table 1).

The maintenance of the closed corporate structures discussed above is perpetuated by the civil-religious prestige hierarchy, whose major function is the care of the chapels and the observance of fertility and fecundity rituals. The civil-religious hierarchy has undergone a series of reductions and pressures during the past fifty years, but the organizations representing the two traditional barrios and another representing the sallqa herding area have resisted pressures (Isbell, 1972b). A mutual dependence exists between the spatial structures and the civil-religious prestige hierarchy. Membership in the prestige hierarchy demands that one reside in one of the traditional barrios, become initiated into the hierarchy at an early age, and advance through a series of positions until retirement as an esteemed elder of the village. I found that those who migrate out of the village, learn Spanish, and then return are not incorporated into the prestige system but rather become eligible for a bureaucratic position as an appointed or elected official. As we will see, returned migrants, who are considered qalas, are occupying bureaucratic positions; but they identify themselves as "sons of comuneros, not qalas." These events will have far-reaching effects on the traditional structures and concepts of the village as migrants attempt to mediate between the opposing elements of the sociopolitical structure.

THE MIGRATORY PROCESS

The population of the city of Lima tripled during the twenty-year period of 1940 to 1961, and the projected population for 1980 is 5,800,000 if the present rate of growth continues (Delgado, 1971: 120). Much of this growth is due to rural-urban migration. The volume of migration to the metropolitan capital increased over 300 percent during the five years between 1956 and 1961 over the period between 1941 and 1946 (Delgado, 1971: 122). In 1967 alone, an estimated 75,000 persons migrated to Lima (Delgado, 1971: 125). The major thrust of rural-urban migration in Peru has occurred since World War II, with a mass exodus of highland peasants to the major cities, predominantly Lima and Arequipa. Paul Doughty has aptly stated:

> The situation facing the individual migrant in Peru is complex, and one must be startled not by the fact that there is apparent social chaos and anomie at times, but that so many individuals and families are indeed able to retain their integrative structure or to reorganize their lives in meaningful ways [1970: 32].

Doughty offers an analysis of migrant clubs or regional associations as integrative structures facilitating adaptation to the urban environment. Similarly, Mangin (1967) has emphasized the positive functions served by squatter settlements in helping migrants to cope with potentially adverse urban situations.[4]

A Brief History of Migration from Chuschi

In the late 1930s, the first villager to journey to Lima was a young monolingual Quechua speaker, with no formal education, who had been one of the early conscripts into the army. He returned to Chuschi and convinced a male first cousin to join him in Lima. The two found lodging in one of the inner-city's densely populated block slums *(tugurios),* and established a small commercial business in the major market. The first migrant never married. He returned to the village in his advanced years and died there. Several of the subsequent migrants were widowed women who preferred to set up small enterprises in the major market of Lima or as ambulatory venders rather than remain in the village and try to remarry.

By 1941, there were perhaps fifteen to twenty Chuschino migrants residing in Lima in various inner-city *tugurios.* These early migrants had organized a religious society dedicated to *El Señor de los Temblores* (the Lord of Earthquakes), patron saint of Chuschi. A small effigy of the saint was passed from household to household, where small shrines were constructed. The small effigy was believed to be the son of the major patron saint housed in the village church, and every year someone was responsible for taking "the son" home to "visit his father." The Society of El Señor de los Temblores still flourishes today.

In 1941, the migrants organized a second religious cult, the Progressive Society of Santa Rosa of Lima, with Santa Rosa as its patron saint. The declared purpose of the Society was to promote and safeguard the welfare of the village. In the same year the members presented the petition and documentation necessary to obtain the legal status of Indigenous Community for the village. With that action, the Society was recognized as the legal representative of

Chuschi, and it has continued to handle legal matters, supervise elections, audit books, and inspect records in the village. The Society also raises funds for the village schools, buying such items as sports equipment, uniforms, and band instruments. Over the years, the Society of Santa Rosa has been transformed into a political body; the Society of El Señor de los Temblores has remained a religious cult.

In 1946, the members of the Society of Santa Rosa participated in the squatter invasion of San Cosme, presently one of the largest *"pueblos jóvenes"* or "young communities" (formerly known as barriadas) in Lima, located on the central highway about five kilometers from the central city. Matos Mar (1966: 19) estimates that in 1955 the population density of San Cosme had reached 857 inhabitants per hectare (about 343 persons per acre). The population in San Cosme continued to expand, and the original migrants from Chuschi sponsored newcomers from their village of origin by offering temporary housing to those who wanted employment during the period between November and April, the interval between planting and harvest. With the concentration of Chuschi migrants in San Cosme, two types of migration emerged:

(1) cyclical migration, whereby migrants seek employment in Lima only during the period between November and April;

(2) permanent migration, whereby migrants decide to become permanent residents of Lima when their economic situation becomes stable enough. They retain control of their lands and provide cash for seed, often returning to the village to supervise the harvest. A relative agrees to plant the migrant's fields for one-half the harvest.

Chuschi has suffered a decline in population during the past two decades. The census of 1940 lists a population of 1,310; and by 1961, the population had dropped to 1,099. A survey completed in 1967 by the Ministerio de Trabajo (Bolivar de Colchado, 1967: 16) tabulated out-migration from the village between January and August of 1967. It was found that forty villagers migrated to Lima, ten to Ayacucho, the department capital, and ten to a cocoa plantation in the department of Jauja. The study did not determine whether these migrants were seeking temporary employment or whether they intended to remain permanently at their destinations. However, it is common for villagers to migrate to Lima and to the department capital to seek temporary wage employment during the period between planting and harvest. During the dry season, a Chuschino can catch a weekly bus to Lima and arrive two days later within walking distance of the squatter settlement called "7 de Octubre," where his fellow villagers are now clustered. He can make his way back and forth between the rural and ruban places without speaking Spanish, adopting western dress, or crossing the Plaza de Armas in the center of Lima. He can work for relatives in the principal public market or find employment near the 7 de Octubre settlement.

The Invasion of 7 de Octubre

On October 7, 1963, twelve migrant families from Chuschi residing in San Cosme participated in a "spillover" invasion across the central highway into an unpopulated area owned by a housing cooperative comprised of 600 market vendors. One of Lima's leading papers, *La Prensa,* reported that 2,000 people took part in the invasion. The police and the Guardia Civil successfully expelled all but 200 of the invaders the following day. The police and Guardia suffered eleven wounded and the invaders many more. The twelve Chuschino families were among the 200 entrenched squatters. They reported that they defended their position by fortifying the upper entrance of a double-mouthed cave. On October 9, 1,000 squatters returned to the site, and the authorities did not contest their claim to the area. The first activities of the squatters were to delineate plots with stones, to construct mat shelters, and to level paths up the steep hillside. The invaders of 7 de Octubre followed closely the formula for a successful land takeover in Lima (Mangin, 1970), except that the area they chose to invade was private rather than public property. The market vendors' cooperative has attempted to reclaim their land legally, but no action hass been taken.

During the first months of occupancy, a seven-man junta elected by the squatters instituted a defense system whereby each household was responsible for one day of guard duty at the entrances to the settlement. Failure to comply resulted in a fine imposed and collected by the junta. This effort was not totally effective in keeping out latecomers to the area, and informants say that the first few months saw many new squatters pouring into the area. If a mat shelter was left unattended, informants report that it would be immediately occupied. One of the original invaders left his plot for two weeks in order to participate in the village harvest, only to return to find his plot occupied by persons he called "foreigners," a family not from his village.

The first months of occupation in 7 de Octubre saw not only the creation of a quasi-military-political organization, but the emergence of territorial division, strife and fraud as well. Six zones became differentiated in the settlement, with the migrants from Chuschi living in the third zone. Squatters in the first and second zones complained to the junta that their plots were smaller than those occupying zones four through six. They attempted to take over areas adjacent to their zones, causing open hostilities. Informants relate that they were compelled to carry straw shields to and from work to protect themselves from the barrage of stones as they passed through the first and second zones. A mat shelter could not be left unoccupied even for a period of a few hours for fear of takeover by those of the first and second zones. Anxiety over possession of individual plots heightened, and the squatters were ready prey when one of the members of the junta fraudulently sold titles to the land. Complaints were brought against him; he was tried and sent to prison for fraud. However, in spite of the territorial strife and fighting, the settlement united in order to construct a primary school. They were successful only after battling government forces and suffering casualties in the fracas.

The New Community in 7 de Octubre

At the time of my field research (1969-1970), the migrant population from Chuschi included approximately 275 persons residing in 55 households in 7 de Octubre, and 45 persons residing in 9 households in San Cosme. A household typically includes someone from the village, usually a relative, who is in Lima temporarily. These persons generally have minimal facility in Spanish and rely upon their relatives for aid in seeking temporary employment. They often work for their relatives in the market as street vendors or as construction laborers. They are the cyclical migrants discussed above.

Out of a sample of fifty-nine unions of persons residing in 7 de Octubre and San Cosme, only eighteen were with persons other than co-villagers. Of these eighteen "foreign" unions, five were with persons of the same district or province, and the remaining thirteen were with other migrants of highland origin. The preferred pattern is to marry someone from Chuschi after a period of residence together. One informant had not known her husband, a young man who had established himself in Lima with wage employment, prior to her arranged marriage at the age of fifteen. The man returned to the village and, after the two families successfully negotiated the marriage, he brought his fifteen-year-old bride-to-be to Lima. They lived together for a year, after which they returned to the village to be married in the church and by civil law. The custom of "a year together" *(watanakuy)* has been almost eradicated in the village by the priest, but it has reemerged in Lima where church influence is remote. Migrants explain their preference by saying they prefer to marry "our people." A further important consideration is that land and animals can be consolidated when a propitious marriage is contracted with a fellow villager.

Migrants prefer *compadres* who reside in Chuschi, or fellow migrants from Chuschi residing in 7 de Octubre or San Cosme. Essentially the same forms of *compadrazgo* are practiced in the squatter settlement as in the village. Changes in both marriage preferences and compadrazgo selection will probably occur during the next generation, when the descendants born in Lima consider themselves Limeños rather than villagers. They will prefer to intensify their urban identity at the expense of their rural ties. However, one wonders whether the traditional reciprocity that has aided in adaptation to urban life will be abandoned.

I have identified two different types of village reciprocity—public work days for community projects, and private reciprocity which is kin-based and directed toward individuals or families (Isbell, 1973). The latter is repaid in kind, and the former guarantees membership in the community. In Lima, both public and private reciprocity are utilized, and mutual aid has been a key factor in the success of the migrants' adaptation to their self-constructed community. House construction is usually carried out over a period of years; both wage labor and mutual aid are utilized. Turner (1970) estimates that self-construction of housing by Lima squatters extends over a twenty-year period. The priorities established by Chuschino squatters parallel those outlined by Turner: First they erected temporary mat constructions, followed by one-story cinder block shells without roofs, flooring, plumbing or electricity. Adequate living space is the first consideration; a second story is added as the migrant family is able to pay for the materials. Mutual aid is utilized for part of the construction labor, but wage labor is used for special skills such as bricklaying. Communal labor is essential for the later priorities—sewers and electricity. Presently, electricity in 7 de Octubre is obtained illegally by hooking up to lines from a commercial urbanization project below the settlement. Communal labor is being utilized to construct the social and ceremonial center of Chuschino urban life—the club house.

The Club House: A Symbol of Identity

The club house was begun under the auspices of the Progressive Society of Santa Rosa of Lima in 1966. They held dances, sports events, and lotteries to finance the materials, and public work days were called on Sundays with the Society providing beer for all workers. The club house has been built around the lower entrance of the double-mouthed cave which was crucial to the defense of the migrants' newly occupied territory.

The building is a three-sided structure, with the cave serving as the back wall, and the upper entrance closed off. Thus far, the building has not been roofed, so the cave itself is the place where public meetings are held, often accompanied by the retelling of the invasion story. The club house is the physical, self-constructed icon of migrant unity and identity. The recounting of the invasion story is the manifestation of the creation of a modern urban origin myth or "mythic conception." The choice of the cave as the site for the club house is not coincidental, but rather demonstrates the influence of Andean concepts. One of the Inca origin myths describes the emergence of the founders of the Inca nobility out of the mouth of a cave (Rowe, 1963: 316). The migrants' new urban origin is symbolized by the construction of their community club house at the mouth of the cave.

THE TRANSFORMATION OF ANDEAN CONCEPTS

The traditional village is organized around the basic concept of "We—My Group," whose definition includes the positive and negative elements described above. The concept is reinforced by annual ritual reenactments, a spatial organization that is bounded and closed, and the traditional civil-religious prestige hierarchy. We have seen that two spatial structures operate: (1) the sociopolitical structure, and (2) the economic structure. In the first, the dominating foreigners, represented by the government and the church, are localized in the center of the village. Their presence serves to remind the comuneros of the dangerous outside world, which must be dealt with cautiously. The economic structure relates the civilized village to the high tundra lands (the sallqa) which is conceived of as savage, potent and threatening. The two opposing sectors are mediated by a region dedicated to corn agriculture. I have said earlier that the economic structure is more stable due to the presence of this mediating element. Furthermore, this structure does not take into account the presence of foreigners. It is indigenous; it expresses Andean economic traditions of long standing. Chuschinos have made both these structures conform with their spatial conceptions, which are closed, concentric and dual patterns.

The Structure of Space in 7 de Octubre

In Lima, neither of these dual structures is appropriate. However, the Chuschino migrants have organized themselves spatially. The members of "my group of squatters" are localized around the club house, and the most threatening element to their social space is the presence of other squatters around them who covet their territory. The migrants do not see the entire world as foreign and threatening. They are upwardly mobile and desire integration into the national culture. Most often this is expressed in terms of the possibilities for their children to become professionals or bureaucrats. Their notion of social space is still concentric and dual, but the organization has been rearranged (see Figure 3). The values have been reversed, and there has been a transformation from the concept of the closed, corporate, bounded "We" versus the foreign, threatening "They," to a conceptualization of the unified members clustered together around the club house versus the threatening squatters adjacent to their territory. The outside world is viewed positively in terms of opportunities for membership and national urban identity. The transformation is illustrated in Figure 4.

The village structure expresses the presence of threatening, confining, negative forces; the squatter settlement structure expresses potential expansion and integration into the national culture.

A New Cult and New Rituals

When the migrants organized the Progressive Society of Santa Rosa of Lima, with the major saint, Santa Rosa, as their patron, they were expressing a growing identification with the urban center of Lima. But, more importantly, they organized the Society as the legal and political representative of Chuschi.

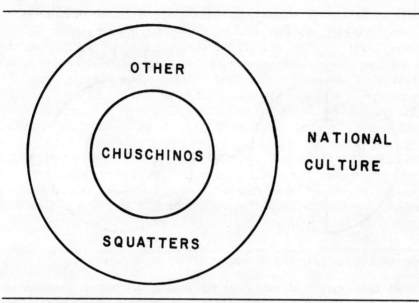

Figure 3: MIGRANTS' CONCEPTION OF SOCIAL SPACE

Through the years this group has grown in power and sophistication. The village of origin now depends upon the Society for representation as a recognized Peasant Community. The Society transacts all the village's bureaucratic business, sends representatives to audit the village's books (resulting in the imprisonment of the municipal mayor on several occasions), and submits lists of candidates for village elections.

The Chuschi squatters in Lima no longer consist of colonists who are subordinate to Chuschi, the political and religious center; rather, the squatters in Lima exercise a substantial degree of control over village affairs. The first migrants journeyed to Lima with the "son" of the patron saint of the village, a small effigy of El Señor de los Temblores. The "son" continues to make pilgrimages once a year to the village to "visit his father." However, this cult has decreased in importance as the Society of Santa Rosa has grown. It is likely that, as the migrants strengthen their conception of themselves as leaders and urbanites, they will give up the practice of carrying the small effigy of El Señor de los Temblores to "visit his father" in Chuschi, and the cult to Santa Rosa will grow in pomp and importance. Already, the migrants have adopted a new ritual not native to Chuschi.

There are two diametrically opposed rituals celebrated in the 7 de Octubre settlement by the Chuschino community. One is traditional in character and recalls the "old life in the village"; the other is an adopted ritual reflecting urban prosperity. The celebration dedicated to Santa Rosa of Lima is derived from traditional comunero rituals. A *mayordomo*, or sponsor, gains prestige and

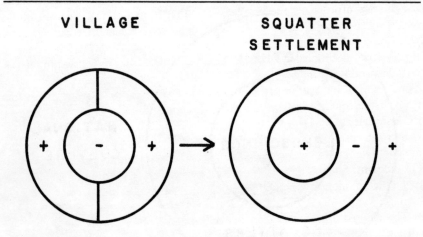

Figure 4: RURAL-URBAN TRANSFORMATION OF SPATIAL CONCEPTS

esteem in the eyes of his fellow migrants when he sponsors the fiesta. Several informants told me that they planned to sponsor the celebration three to five years hence. They calculated that it would take that long to save the necessary cash and amass the necessary goods to give a successful fiesta, "that people would remember." An urban prestige system is being formed in 7 de Octubre with the same function as the complex of positions in the village—to increase one's prestige through generosity. Both of the new rituals have this function. However, the forms of generosity manifested for the two rituals are somewhat different. The celebration of Santa Rosa is accompanied by the heavy, obligatory drinking which has traditionally accompanied all Chuschino rituals. Corn beer *(chicha)* is brought by the mayordomo's kinsmen from Chuschi, along with meat and agricultural products from the fields. The mayordomo sponsors a public celebration in the club house for the entire community of migrants. But he also holds a private celebration for "those who love him" (see Isbell, 1972a) by helping with his ritual obligations through contributions of labor, goods or money. A sponsor of a ritual cannot fulfill his obligations without calling upon a wide network of kinsmen, friends and compadres.

The changes in the ritual formula are most enlightening. I participated in the festivities dedicated to Santa Rosa in August 1970. The sponsors of the fiesta were the members of a sports club claiming a membership of 200. All the members share a common surname. The membership is distributed in both the squatter settlement and the village. Twenty-three young men residing in Lima shared the expenses of the celebration, utilizing the large network of kinsmen mentioned above. Collective rather than individual sponsorship of the fiesta is a reflection of urban influence. The other major change was the total absence of the dramatizations of religious, political and supernatural dominators (the priest, the military officers and the dreaded *naqa*) that form an integral part of village rituals. The omission of these icons of oppression exemplifies the migrants' changing view of the outside world. Chuschinos in Lima appear to be stressing the positive, traditional symbols of identity, rather than the conception of the outside world as threatening. Traditional musicians from the village were commissioned by the sports club to accompany the traditional procession through the squatter settlement's streets. A mock bullfight was staged with a papier-mâché bull. Two small children, a boy and a girl, were dressed in traditional costumes and garlaned with the items customarily offered to the mountain deities, the *Wamanis*. These two children are said to be the sponsors of the bullfight. Such is the custom of the village. The celebration of Santa Rosa functions to intensify group identification and recall the migrants' Andean heritage.

The adopted ritual of the Chuschi migrants is called the *Corta Monte*, or "tree cutting." It has none of the trappings of a traditional comunero ritual and is unknown in the region around Chuschi. Only the most affluent migrants had sponsored the ritual since its adoption from migrants in a neighboring settlement in 1967. The fiesta calls for one male and one female sponsor. The male is responsible for buying and transporting a grown tree into the settlement. Once the tree arrives, the migrants proceed to "plant" the tree in front of the club house. The female sponsor is responsible for gifts that are tied to the tree. These gifts include small bottles of wine and alcohol, small bags of coins, plastic household items, candy and other small articles. All of the gifts are specially purchased. Sponsorship of this fiesta requires an outlay of a considerable amount of cash by both sponsors. Only those wishing to sponsor the next year's celebration participate in the festive cutting of the tree, which takes all afternoon and night. As the group dances around the tree, each couple taking a turn cutting with the ax, the less successful watch and wait for the gifts to fall. The last couple to wield the ax when the tree falls must sponsor next year's celebration.

During the 1970 celebration, I observed that the participants were costumed in the dress common to the landholding *hacendado* class. The men were wearing cotton ponchos, large straw hats, bright-colored neck scarves, and sunglasses. They appeared to be emulating the hacendado class; actually they were emulating the prosperity and success of the landholding class. The *Corta Monte* has been adopted by the most successful, affluent migrants as a means to display their prosperity and success. They wish to differentiate themselves from the mass of migrants, but they also wish to gain prestige by displaying generosity in the traditional manner. However, they have chosen a form of generosity that requires cash that cannot be supplied by the mutual aid of one's kin network. The *Corta Monte* is, therefore, an individually sponsored ritual, whereas the Santa Rosa ritual has become the domain of a collective—the sports club. The former reflects urban prosperity, while the latter reflects the positive aspects of traditional life. Both function to gain prestige and display generosity.

THE IMPACT OF MIGRANTS UPON THE VILLAGE

I would like to turn to the question of the impact of the transformed concept of "We" versus "They," upon the villagers' traditional ideas. I have stated that migrants have played an important role as legal representatives and "cultural brokers" for the village. However, their position has been extra-legal in that they often sought solutions to village problems outside the law. For example, the Progressive Society of Santa Rosa tried for several years to remove the director of the schools from office. The director, who is a prominent *qala* descendant of the first school teacher who arrived in Chuschi four generations ago, was charged with neglect of office due to his attention to his store and truck businesses. He was also charged with attempting to cheat comuneros out of their land by plying them with alcohol and then buying the land at low prices. In 1970, a delegation of members from the Society returned to Chuschi and distributed fliers denouncing the director. Charges and counter charges proliferated. The migrants were jailed repeatedly, but each time the officials of the national government's agrarian reform program had them released. The migrants continued their attack on the director until he was transferred in 1971. Their second focus of attack was on the rich holdings of the Catholic Church.

An Aggressive Plan

The members of the Progressive Society formulated a plan to confiscate the Church's holdings in land, cattle and sheep and to convert these into a cooperative in the name of the community. Again, after several stormy attempts resulting in repeated arrests, the migrants were able to instigate a court action whereby a village cooperative would be formed from the Church's herds, made up of 250 head of cattle, 1,500 head of sheep and 13 large, highly desirable corn plots dedicated to specific saints. One of these *cofradia* corn plots equals the total amount of agricultural land owned by the average comunero family (about one to two hectares). Agrarian reform officials supported the migrants' efforts by coming repeatedly to their defense and releasing them from jail. The dispute with the Church was placed under the jurisdiction of the 1970 Agrarian Reform Law; the priest was transferred to another locality, and the matter is currently before the courts.

Two neighboring villages have had similar histories of efforts instigated by migrants to form cooperatives utilizing Church possessions. The migrants were not only opposed vigorously by the Church; they also had to deal with the apathy of the villagers. Over the years, the villagers opposed the migrants' efforts because, as they said, "you come from Lima and stir up trouble and then you return to Lima and leave us with the trouble." However, due to the pressure of the 1970 Agrarian Reform Law, some migrants have returned to the village to retain usufruct rights of their land, and their return has legitimized their efforts for reform. It is highly probable that the majority of migrants from Chuschi hold agricultural plots, and the migrants who have returned to the village to comply with the residence requirements of the law are doing so to maintain comunero status. Two migrants have been elected as Presidents of the newly created Administrative Committee and Vigilance Committee. These committees are charged with implementing the new Agrarian Reform Law. Both migrants are members of the Progressive Society of Santa Rosa of Lima and have been active in the movements to take over the Church's holdings and to remove the director of the schools. Their efforts and position are no longer extra-legal; they have reintegrated themselves into the political and social fabric of the community.

The Structural Position of the Migrants

Returned migrants now occupy the positions of authority in the district and village. They have learned to deal with bureaucracies through their urban land invasion experience. Labor union membership has enabled them to develop political sophistication and organizational skills. Yet they identify themselves as "sons of comuneros," and they value the cooperative and reciprocal bases of the village social structure. The migrants have dual identities; they see themselves as members of the national culture as well as members of the village community. They are, in short, the mediators between the urban ideology of the national culture and the traditional ideology of the village. Their position as legal representatives and interpreters of laws affecting the village has been legitimized. I predict that the rate of change in the village will increase due to the presence of the returned migrants. The migrants' success as mediators between urban and rural ideologies depends, in part, upon historical events beyond their control. It also depends upon the degree of resistance which they encounter among the comuneros.

In structural terms, the returned migrants now occupy the position in the center of the village traditionally occupied by the foreign, savage, threatening qalas (see Figure 5). I have not assigned positive or negative values to their position. The degree of acceptance or resistance to them as vehicles of reform will determine in part the value of their position in the village's sociopolitical structure. The logical possibilities include: (1) the comuneros standing opposed to the migrants and the outside world; (2) the migrants and comuneros uniting in opposition to some element of the national culture such as government bureaucrats, the national police, or the church; or (3) the villagers losing their closed corporate attitudes and perceiving the possibility of integration into the national culture. They would still define the outside "They" as neighboring villages, with whom continous conflicts over land boundaries persist.

Whether any one of the above possibilities becomes the dominant pattern in the village will depend upon historical events and accidents; however, it is possible to outline some of the conditions which would impinge upon the

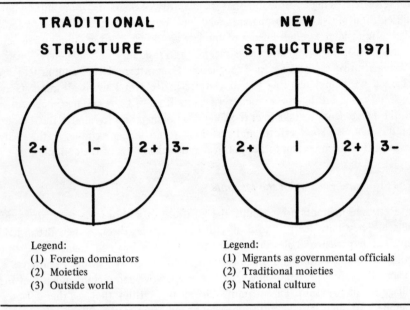

Figure 5: TRANSFORMATION OF THE SOCIO-POLITICAL STRUCTURE OF
THE VILLAGE

conceptual structures under consideration. *Possibility one* would result from strong opposition from the traditional sector of the village. This would be likely to occur immediately if the migrants attempt to implement the Agrarian Reform Law. If they attempt to alienate the comuneros from their privately held agricultural plots, then I predict strong opposition and a return to the traditional village structure, with intensification of the concept of the comuneros standing opposed to the outside world, which has become more threatening. *Possibility two* depends upon the availability of a common enemy against which both the migrants and the traditional comuneros might struggle. If this occurred, the migrants' chances of introducing urban ideas and concepts would be increased, due to their identification as members of the established, traditional "We." This situation might develop from the current court case concerning the formation of a village cooperative out of the Church's land and animals. *Possibility three* depends upon the success of the migrants in introducing new ideas and concepts. If the proposed cooperative is successful and benefits the village economically, the door will be open for integration into the national culture through participation in the national market.

The three possibilities outlined could occur serially, with one structure dominating for a period of time and then giving way to another. However, it is clear that the traditional structure of the village that has withstood previous onslaughts is currently under the strongest of pressures. It is very likely that the closed corporate organization that is maintained by the dichotomy of "We" versus the entire outside world will in time disappear. The basic Andean opposition of "We" versus "They," which has served as an interpretive device by which villagers have rendered their social world intelligible, will be transformed. The outcome of this transformation process will depend upon the dialectic between ideas and activity. Actually, in the case under consideration, there are two dialectical processes occurring simultaneously. One is between the ideologies of the villagers and the ideologies of the returned migrants; the other is the dialectic between ideology and the vicissitudes of history.

I have described the transformation of the key concept of "We" versus "They" effected by migrants in Lima, and I have proposed three logical possibilities for the transformation of the same concept in their village of origin. The basic assumption is that urban and rural ideologies are self-regulating, transformational structures which interact with one another as well as with events and the flow of activities. It is within these dimensions that a dialectical and structural point of view is profitable for the study of culture change. Many anthropological studies have created static pictures of the dynamic, dialectical struggles of social life (Murphy, 1971). I firmly believe that transformations and change are the reality, and stability and equilibrium are the fictions created by human societies—and anthropologists—to annul the entrophic effects of history.

NOTES

1. For the full text of the law, see Beltran (1971).
2. See Murra (1972) for a discussion of vertical control in the Andes.
3. The village is a classic example of the closed corporate community as defined by Wolf (1955, 1957, 1966).
4. In 1967 Carlos Delgado (1971: 125) conservatively estimated the squatter population of metropolitan Lima to be twenty-five percent of the city's total population of 2,100,000.

REFERENCES

BARTHES, R. (1972) "The structuralist activity," pp. 148-154 in R. T. DeGeorge and F. M. DeGeorge (eds.) The Structuralists from Marx to Lévi-Strauss. Garden City, N.Y.: Doubleday.
BELTRAN, A. (ed.) (1971) Estatuto de comunidades campesinas del Perú. Instituto Indigenista Interamericano, Anuario Indigenista, V. XXXI: 191-208. (México, D.F.)
BOLIVAR DE COLCHADO, F. (1967) "El Distrito de Chuschi," pp. 1-22 in V. H. Sarmiento Medina et al., Los Distritos de Vischongo, Chuschi, Concepción y Ocros. Lima: Instituto Indigenista Peruano.
DELGADO, C. (1971) "Tres planteamientos en torno a problemas de urbanización accelerada en areas metropolitanas: el caso de Lima," pp. 119-158 in C. Delgado (ed.) Problemas Sociales en el Perú Contemporáneo. Perú-Problema 6, Lima, Peru: Instituto de Estudios Peruanos.

DOUGHTY, P. L. (1968) Huaylas: An Andean District in Search of Progress. Ithaca: Cornell University Press.

——— (1970) "Behind the back of the city: 'provincial life in Lima, Peru," pp. 30-46 in W. Mangin (ed.) Peasants in Cities. Boston: Houghton Mifflin.

Instituto Nacional de Planificación Asesoría Geográfica (1969) Atlas histórico geográfico y de paisajes Peruanos. Lima, Perú: Instituto Nacional de Planificación.

ISBELL, B. J. (1972a) "Kuyaq: those who love me: an analysis of Andean kinship and reciprocity within a ritual context." Presented at the Seventy-First Annual Meeting of the American Anthropological Association, Toronto, Canada.

——— (1972b) "No servimos mas: un estudio de los efectos de disipar un sistema de la autoridad tradicional en un pueblo Ayacuchano." Revista del Museo Nacional 37: 285-298. (Also in: Actas y Memorias del Congreso Internacional de Americanistas V. 3: 285-298. Lima, Peru.)

——— (1973) "Andean structures and activities: towards a study of transformations of traditional concepts in a Central Highland peasant community." Ph.D. dissertation. University of Illinois.

La Prensa (1963) Diario, Lima, Peru, October 7: "Invaden tierras de cooperativa." October 8: "La caballería no pudo desalojar a invasores de Fundo Valdivieso." October 9: "Invadieron de nuevo el Fundo Valdivieso."

LEACH, E. R. (1965) Political Systems of Highland Burma. Boston: Beacon Press.

LEVI-STRAUSS, C. (1966) Savage Mind. Chicago: University of Chicago Press.

MANGIN, W. (1959) "The role of regional associations in the adaptation of rural population in Peru." Sociologus 9: 23-25.

——— (1960) "Mental health and migration to cities: a Peruvian case." Annals of New York Academy of Sciences 84: 911-917.

——— (1967) "Latin America squatter settlements: a problem and a solution." Latin American Research Review 2, 3: 65-98.

——— (1970) "Urbanization case history in Peru," pp. 47-54 in W. Mangin (ed.) Peasants in Cities. Boston: Houghton Mifflin.

MARANDA, P. (1972) "Structuralism in cultural anthropology," pp. 329-348 in J. B. Siegel (ed.) Annual Review of Anthropology. Palo Alto, Calif.: Annual Reviews Incorporated.

MARTINEZ, H. (1968) "Las migraciones internas en el Perú." Estudios de Población y Desarrollo 2, 1: 1-15. (Lima, Perú: Centro de Estudios de Población y Desarrollo.)

MATOS MAR, J. (1966) Estudio de las barriadas Limeñas. Lima: Departmento de Antropología, Universidad Nacional Mayor de San Marcos.

MURPHY, R. F. (1971) The Dialectics of Social Life. New York: Basic Books.

MURRA, J. V. (1972) "El 'control vertical' de un máximo de pisos ecológicos en la economía de las sociedades Andinas," pp. 427-476 in Vista de la Provincia de León de Huánuco. Huánuco, Perú: Universidad Hermilio Valdizán.

PALOMINO FLORES, S. (1970) "El sistema de oposiciones en la Comunidad Sarhua." Tésis para optar el grado de Bachiller. Universidad Nacional de San Cristóbal de Huamanga.

——— (1971) "Duality in the socio-cultural organization of several Andean populations." Folk 13 (Copenhagen): 65-88.

PIAGET, J. (1971) Structuralism. New York: Harper Torchbooks.

ROWE, J. H. (1963) "Inca culture at the time of the Spanish conquest," pp. 183-330 in Volume 3 of J. H. Steward (ed.) The Handbook of South American Indians. New York: Cooper Square.

TURNER, J. C. (1970) "Barriers and channels for housing development in modernizing countries," pp. 1-19 in W. Mangin (ed.) Peasants in Cities. Boston: Houghton Mifflin.

TURNER, V. (1969) The Ritual Process: Structure and Anti-Structure. Chicago: Aldine.

WILSON, M. (1954) "Myakyusa ritual and symbolism." American Anthropologist 56: 228-241.

WOLF, E. R. (1955) "Types of Latin American peasantry: a preliminary discussion." American Anthropologist 57: 452-471.

--- (1957) "Closed corporate peasant communities in Mesoamerica and Central Java." Southwestern Journal of Anthropology 13: 7-12.

--- (1966) Peasants. Englewood Cliffs, N.J.: Prentice-Hall.

SELECT

BIBLIOGRAPHY

1972-1974

SELECT BIBLIOGRAPHY, 1972-1974

CAPITAL OR MAJOR CITIES

Asunción, Paraguay

ESCOBAR, J. C. (1972) "Algunos indicadores del asentamiento en un sector del área metropolitana de Asunción." Revista Paraguaya de Sociología 9, 25 (September-December): 155-169.

MITCHELL, G. H. (1971) "Food marketing in Asunción, Paraguay, with emphasis on purchasing habits and consumption by household units in two working class barrios." Mimeographed report. International Education Office, New Mexico State University, University Park.

Bogotá, Colombia

BAILEY, S. M. (1971) "Political socialization among children in Bogotá, Colombia." Ph.D. dissertation. University of Michigan.

FLINN, W. L. (1971) "Rural and intra-urban migration in Colombia: Two case studies in Bogotá," pp. 83-93 in Latin American Urban Research, Vol. I. F. F. Rabinovitz and F. M. Trueblood (eds.) Beverly Hills, Calif.: Sage Publications, Inc.

HARKESS, S. (1973) "The pursuit of an ideal: Migration, social class, and women's roles in Bogotá, Colombia," pp. 231-254 in A. Pescatello (ed.) Female and Male in Latin America: Essays. Pittsburgh, Penna.: University of Pittsburgh Press.

HEY, S. M. (1970) "A study on municipal public finances in Bogotá, D.E., Medellín, and Cali, Colombia." Ph.D. dissertation. Johns Hopkins University.

Editors' Note: We would like to thank Elisa M.D.C.P. Reis, Leonidas F. Pozo-Ledezma, Charles J. Savio, Allyn Stearman, and Karen Yapita for their help in the preparation of this bibliography. Readers are cautioned that the bibliography is not exhaustive, with some foreign serial publications representing the most significant omissions. The bibliography covers primarily the period from 1972 to mid-1974. It also includes important items not available at the time our last bibliography was prepared (see *Latin American Urban Research*, Vol. II [1972], pp. 261-291). We invite readers to send to the Editors citations for inclusion in future bibliographies.

ORTEGA RICUARTE, C. (1972) "Aspectos históricos y lingüísticos del gamin bogotano."
   UN, Revista de la Dirección de Divulgación Cultural, Universidad Nacional de Colombia
   10 (April): 7-72.
SIMMONS, A. B. and R. CARDONA G. (1972) "Rural-urban migration: Who comes, who
   stays, who returns? –The case of Bogotá, Colombia." International Migration Review 6,
   2: 166-181.
VAN ES, J. C. and W. L. FLINN (1973) "A note on the determinants of satisfaction among
   urban migrants in Bogotá, Colombia." Interamerican Economic Affairs 27, 2 (Autumn):
   15-28.
VERNEZ, G. (1973) The Residential Movements of Low-Income Families: The Case of
   Bogotá, Colombia. Santa Monica, Calif.: Rand Corporation, Report No. P-5102,
   October.

Brasília, Brazil

EPSTEIN, D. (1973) Brasília, Plan and Reality: A Study of Planned and Spontaneous Urban
   Development. Berkeley and Los Angeles: University of California Press.
––– (1972) "The genesis and function of squatter settlements in Brasília." pp. 51-58 in T.
   Weaver and D. White (eds.) The Anthropology of Urban Environments. Boulder,
   Colorado: Society for Applied Anthropology (SAA Monograph Series No. 11).
SANDERS, T. G. (1973) "Urban growth and public policy in Brasília's satellite cities."
   American Universities Field Staff Reports, East Coast Latin America Series 17, 6 (June):
   1-9.

Buenos Aires, Argentina

CAMPOS, J. and R. PI HUGARTE (1973) "Migrantes de la clase baja en Buenos Aires."
   Revista Paraguaya de Sociología 10, 27 (May-August): 101-118.
CLEARY, E. L. et al. (1973) "Social selectivity in the secondary schools of Buenos Aires,
   La Paz, and Santiago de Chile." Sociology of Education.
MAKOBODZKI, R. (1972) "Urban planning in the Argentine: The Buenos Aires province
   experience." Journal of the Royal Town Planning Institute 58 (May): 201-208.
MOUCHET, C. (1972) "Buenos Aires," pp. 239-270 in W. A. Robson and D. E. Regan (eds.)
   Great Cities of the World, Vol. I. Beverly Hills, Calif.: Sage Publications.
RECCHINI DE LATTES, Z. L. (1971) La población de Buenos Aires: componentes
   demográficos del crecimiento entre 1855 y 1960. Buenos Aires: Instituto Torcuato Di
   Tella.
––– (1971) "The contributions of migration and natural increase to the growth of Buenos
   Aires, 1855-1960." Ph.D. dissertation. University of Pennsylvania.
ROCK, D. (1972) "Machine Politics in Buenos Aires and the Argentine Radical Party,
   1912-1930." Journal of Latin American Studies 4, 2 (November): 233-256.
SARGENT, C. S. (1973) The Spatial Evolution of Greater Buenos Aires, 1870-1930.
   Tempe, Arizona: Center for Latin American Studies, Arizona State University.
   Monograph Series No. 1.
SCHTEINGART, M. and H. TORRES (1973) "La estructura espacial interna de la región
   metropolitana de Buenos Aires en 1970." Revista Interamericana de Planificación 7, 26
   (June): 113-133.

Caracas, Venezuela

ACEDO MENDOZA, C. (1969) La vivienda en el área metropolitana de Caracas. Caracas:
   Fondo Editorial Común.

BLANK, S. B. (1971) "Social integration and social stability in a colonial Spanish American city, Caracas (1595-1627)." Ph.D. dissertation. University of Wisconsin.

GASPARINI, G. (1969) Caracas colonial. Buenos Aires: Centro Editor de América Latina.

––– and J. P. POSANI (1969) Caracas através de su arquitectura. Caracas: Fundación Fina Gómez.

KARST, K. L., M. L. SCHWARTZ and A. J. SCHWARTZ (1973) The Evolution of Law in the Barrios of Caracas. Los Angeles, Calif.: Latin American Center, University of California at Los Angeles, Latin American Studies Series, Vol. 20.

MARTZ, J. D. and P. B. HARKINS (1973) "Urban electoral behavior in Latin America: The case of metropolitan Caracas, 1958-1968." Comparative Politics 5, 4 (July): 523-549.

MORALES TUCKER, A. (1969) "Caracas 1990." El Farol 228 *(sic.)* should be No. 229 (April-May-June): 9-17.

SARMIENTO, P. (1969) "Tipología de los barrios de Caracas: intento de contrucción de tipos empíricos." Boletín, Centro Latinoamericano de Venezuela (CLAVE) 1 (December). Caracas: ETAPA.

SEHWERERT FERRER, A. (1969) Relaciones públicas e información en la administración municipal. Caracas: Fondo Editorial Común.

SOSA FRANCO, P. (1971) "Caracas," pp. 33-52 in A. A. Laquian (ed.) Rural-Urban Migrants and Metropolitan Development. Toronto, Canada: INTERMET, Metropolitan Studies Series.

Guadalajara, Mexico

RIVIÈRE D'ARC, H. (1970) Guadalajara et sa Région: Influences et Difficultes d'une Metropole Mexicaine. Paris: Centre d'Études Politiques, Économiques et Sociales.

SORIA-MURILLO, V. M. (1972) "Problems of urban transport in Guadalajara." Ph.D. dissertation. University of Colorado, Boulder.

WALTON, J. (1972) "Political development and economic development: A regional assessment of contemporary theories." Studies in Comparative International Development 7 (Spring): 39-63.

––– (1971) "An exploratory study of decision-making and development in a Mexican city," pp. 167-192 in F. M. Wirt (ed.) Future Directions in Community Power Research: A Colloquium. Berkeley, Calif.: Institute of Governmental Studies, University of California, Berkeley.

––– (1970) "Development decision making: A comparative study in Latin America." American Journal of Sociology 75, 5 (March): 828-851.

Guatemala City

GANDELL, M. and J. VAN DER TAK (1973) "The size and structure of residential families, Guatemala City, 1964." Population Studies 27, 2 (July): 305-322.

ROBERTS, B. R. (1973) Organizing Strangers: Poor Families in Guatemala City. Austin, Texas: University of Texas Press.

ROBERTS, B. and S. LOWDER (1970) Urban Population Growth and Migration in Latin America: Two Case Studies. Liverpool: Center for Latin American Studies, University of Liverpool, Monograph Series No. 2.

Mexico City

AGUIRRE, C. et al. (1972) Fuentes para la historia de la Ciudad de México, con una bibliografía sobre desarrollo urbano y regional de México. México, D.F.: Departamento de Investigaciones Históricas, Instituto Nacional de Antropología e Historia. Série: Catálogos y Bibliografías, No. 2.

BAKER, G. T. (1970) "Mexico City and the War with the U.S.: A Study in the Politics of Military Occupation." Ph.D. dissertation, Duke University.

BATAILLON, C. and H. RIVIÈRE D'ARC (1973) La Ciudad de México. México, D.F.: Sep/Setentas (Secretaría de Educación Pública).

BOYER, R. E. (1973) "Mexico City and the great flood: aspects of life and society, 1629-1635." Ph.D. dissertation. University of Connecticut.

BROWN, J. C. (1972) "Patterns of intra-urban settlement in Mexico City: An examination of the Turner theory." Latin American Studies Program Dissertation Series, No. 40 (August). Ithaca: Cornell University.

BUTTERWORTH, D. (1972) "Two small groups: A comparison of migrants and non-migrants in Mexico City." Urban Anthropology 1, 1 (Spring): 29-50.

CONTRERAS SUAREZ, E. (1972) "Migración interna y oportunidades de empleo en la Ciudad de México," pp. 359-418 in Jorge Martínez Ríos et al., El Perfil de México en 1980, Vol. 3. México, D.F.: Siglo Veintiuno.

CORNELIUS, W. A. (1974) "Urbanization and political demand-making: political participation among the migrant poor in Latin American cities." American Political Science Review 68, 3 (September).

——— (1974) "La urbanización y la participación política: el caso de los migrantes en la Ciudad de México." Demografía y Economía 8, 23.

——— (1973) "The impact of governmental performance on political attitudes and behavior: The case of the urban poor in Mexico City," pp. 213-251 in F. F. Rabinovitz and F. M. Trueblood (eds.), Latin American Urban Research, Vol. III. Beverly Hills, Calif.: Sage Publications.

——— (1972) "A structural analysis of urban caciquismo in Mexico." Urban Anthropology 1, 2 (Fall): 234-261. (Reprinted in revised form in R. Kern (ed.), The Caciques: Oligarchical Politics and the System of Caciquismo in the Luso-Hispanic World. Albuquerque: University of New Mexico Press, 1973.)

ECKSTEIN, S. (1972) "The poverty of revolution: A study of social, economic, and political inequality in a central city area, a squatter settlement, and a low cost housing project in Mexico City." Ph.D. dissertation. Columbia University.

FOX, D. J. (1972) "Patterns of mortality and morbidity in Mexico City." Geographical Review 62: 151-185.

FRIED, R. C. (1972) "Mexico City," pp. 645-688 in W. A. Robson and D. E. Regan (eds.), Great Cities of the World. 3rd ed. Beverly Hills, Calif.: Sage Publications.

GONZÁLEZ CASANOVA, P. and A. R. POZAS (1965) "Un estudio sobre la estratificación y movilidad social en la Ciudad de México." Revista Mexicana de Ciencia Política 11, 39: 115-185.

KAUFMAN, C. (1971) "Urbanization, material satisfaction, and mass political involvement: The poor in Mexico City." Comparative Political Studies 4, 3 (October): 295-319.

KEMPER, R. V. (1974) "Tzintzuntzeños in Mexico City: The anthropologist among peasant migrants," pp. 63-91 in G. M. Foster and R. V. Kemper (eds.), Anthropologists in Cities. Boston: Little, Brown.

——— (1973) "Factores sociales en la migración: el caso de los Tzintzuntzeños en la Ciudad de México." América Indígena 33, 4 (October-December): 1095-1118.

——— (1971) "Migration and adaptation of Tzintzuntzan peasants in Mexico City." Ph.D. dissertation. University of California, Berkeley.

LOMNITZ, L. (1973) "Supervivencia en una barriada de la Ciudad de México." Demografía y Economía 7, 1: 58-85.

——— (1973) "The survival of the unfittest." Paper presented at the Ninth International Congress of Anthropological and Ethnological Sciences, Chicago, Ill., August 28-September 8.

MOORE, B.E.A. (1970) "Some working women in Mexico City: Traditionalists and modernists." Ph.D. dissertation. Washington University.

MUÑOZ, C. and M. I. ULLOA (n.d.) Estudio sobre las escuelas particulares del Distrito Federal. México, D.F.: Publicaciones del Centro de Estudios Educativos.

MUÑOZ, H. and O. de OLIVEIRA (1973) "Migración interna y movilidad ocupacional en la Ciudad de México." Demografía y Economía 7, 2: 135-148.

——— and C. STERN (1972) "Migración y marginalidad ocupacional en la Ciudad de México," pp. 325-353 in J. Martínez Ríos et al., El Perfil de México en 1980, Vol. III. Mexico: Siglo Veintiuno.

——— (1971) "Categorías de migrantes y nativos y algunas de sus características socio-económicas: comparación entre las ciudades de Monterrey y México." Revista Paraguaya de Sociología 8, 21 (May-August): 40-59.

ORELLANA, C. L. (1973) "Mixtec migrants in Mexico City: A case study of urbanization." Human Organization 32, 3 (Fall): 273-283.

ORNELAS, C. (1973) "Land tenure, sanctions, and politization in México, D.F." Ph.D. dissertation. University of California at Riverside.

PIHO, V. (1973) "Life and labor of female textile workers in Mexico City." Paper presented at the Ninth International Congress of Anthropological and Ethnological Sciences, Chicago, Ill.: August 28-September 8.

UNIKEL, L. (1972) "La dinámica del crecimiento de la Ciudad de México." Revista de la Sociedad Interamericana de Planificación 6, 21 (March): 65-82.

Monterrey, Mexico

BALAN, J., H. L. BROWNING, and E. JELIN (1973) Men in a Developing Society: Geographic and Social Mobility in Monterrey, Mexico. Austin: University of Texas Press. Latin American Monographs,No. 30.

——— (eds.) (1973) Migración, estructura ocupacional, y movilidad social: el caso de Monterrey. México, D.F.: Instituto de Investigaciones Sociales, Universidad Nacional Autónoma de México.

BROWNING, H. L. and W. FEINDT (1971) "The social and economic context of migration to Monterrey, Mexico," pp. 45-70 in F. F. Rabinovitz and F. M. Trueblood (eds.), Latin American Urban Research, Vol. I. Beverly Hills, Calif.: Sage Publications.

FEINDT, W. and H. L. BROWNING (1972) "Return migration: Its significance in an industrial metropolis and an agricultural town in Mexico." International Migration Review 6, 2 (Summer): 158-165.

GAMBLE, S. H. (1971) The *Despensa* System of Food Distribution: A Case Study of Monterrey, Mexico. New York: Praeger.

——— (1970) "The efficiency and effectiveness of the *despensa* system of food distribution in Monterrey, Mexico." Ph.D. dissertation. University of Oregon.

MIR, D. (1968) "Movilidad social, educación y grupos de referencia en Monterrey, México: un estudio sociológico." Revista Mexicana de Ciencia Política 14, 52: 281-286.

WALTON, J. (1972) "Political development and economic development: A regional assessment of contemporary theories." Studies in Comparative International Development 7 (Spring): 39-63.

——— (1970) "Development decision making: A comparative study in Latin America." American Journal of Sociology 75, 5 (March): 828-851.

Montevideo, Uruguay

MEXIGES VITAL, R. and C. W. MAISSONAVE (1967) La programación presupuestaria en el Gobierno Departamental de Montevideo. Montevideo: Universidad de la República. Selección de Temas de Administración No. 50.

WILKIE, M. E. (1973) "The Lebanese in Montevideo, Uruguay: A study of an entrepreneurial ethnic minority." Ph.D. dissertation. University of Wisconsin.

La Paz, Bolivia

GUARDIA B., F. (n.d.) La evolución de la forma de la ciudad de La Paz, Bolivia. Buenos Aires: Centro de Investigaciones Socio-Económicas, Instituto Torcuato di Tella.

PACHECO JIMENEZ, V. (1969) Los intereses del Departamento de La Paz y los factores internacionales para su integración económica. La Paz.

SANJINES ROJAS, G. (1972) "The Acción Comunal program: La Paz, Bolivia," pp. 211-215 in G. Geisse and J. E. Hardoy (eds.) Latin American Urban Research, Vol. II. Beverly Hills, Calif.: Sage Publications.

Lima-Callao, Peru

ADURIZ, J. (1972) "Así viven y así nacen." Revista Latinoamericana de Estudios Urbano Regionales 2, 5 (July): 107-134.

BISHOP, M. E. (1973) "Media use and democratic political orientation in Lima, Peru." Journalism Quarterly 50, 1 (Spring): 60-67.

——— (1970) "Political information-seeking in the mass media, political knowledge, and democratic orientation in Lima, Peru." Ph.D. dissertation. University of Wisconsin.

COLLIER, D. (1971-72) "Política y creación de pueblos jóvenes en Lima." Estudios Andinos 2: 5-34.

——— (1971) "Squatter settlement formation and the politics of co-optation in Peru." Ph.D. dissertation. University of Chicago.

——— (1971) "Squatter settlement formation and the politics of co-optation in Peru." Paper presented at the Annual Meeting of the American Political Science Association, Chicago, Ill., September.

COTLER, J. and A. A. LAQUIAN (1971) "Lima," pp. 111-134 in A. A. Laquian (ed.), Rural-Urban Migrants and Metropolitan Development. Toronto, Canada: INTERMET, Metropolitan Studies Series.

DIETZ, H. A. (1974) "Becoming a *poblador:* Political adjustment to the Lima urban environment." Ph.D. dissertation. Stanford University.

——— (1973) "The office and the *poblador:* Perceptions and manipulations of housing authorities by the Lima urban poor." Paper presented at the Meeting of the American Society for Public Administration, Los Angeles, Calif., April 3.

DOUGHTY, P. L. (1974) "Social policy and urban growth in Lima," in D. Chaplin (ed.), Peruvian Nationalism. New York: E. P. Dutton-Transaction Books.

——— (1972) "Peruvian migrant identity in an urban milieu," pp. 39-50 in T. Weaver and D. White (eds.), The Anthropology of Urban Environments. Boulder, Colorado: Society for Applied Anthropology, Monograph Series No. 11.

ISBELL, B. J. (1973) "Andean structures and activities: Towards a study of transformations of traditional concepts in a Central Highland peasant community." Ph.D. dissertation. University of Illinois, Urbana.

——— (1972) "Migrants' adaptation of a traditional Andean kindred to the urban environment of Lima." Paper presented at the Annual Meeting of the American Anthropological Association, Toronto, Canada, November 29-December 3.

LEWIS, R. A. (1973) "Employment, income, and the growth of the barriadas in Lima, Peru." Ithaca, N.Y.: Cornell University, Latin American Studies Program Dissertation Series, No. 46 (May).

MANGIN, W. (1973) "Sociological, cultural, and political characteristics of some urban migrants in Peru," pp. 315-350 in A. Southall (ed.), Urban Anthropology. New York and London: Oxford University Press.

MARUSKA, D. (1972) "Government policy and neighborhood organizations in the squatter settlements of Lima." Honors Thesis, Department of Government. Harvard University.

MICHL, S. (1973) "Urban squatter organization as a national government tool: The case of Lima, Peru," pp. 155-178 in F. F. Rabinovitz and F. M. Trueblood (eds.), Latin American Urban Research, Vol. III. Beverly Hills, Calif.: Sage Publications.

PAREDES, M. K. de (1973) "Urban community organization in Peru." Ph.D. dissertation. Massachusetts Institute of Technology.

RODRIGUEZ, A. (1972) "Oferta de viviendas y terrenos en Lima metropolitana, 1940-1967: análisis de los avisos de periódicos." Revista Latinoamericana de Estudios Urbano Regionales 2, 6 (November): 83-100.

––– et al. (1973) Segregación residencial y desmovilización política: el caso de Lima. Buenos Aires: Sociedad Interamericana de Planificación.

––– G. RIOFRIO and E. WELSH (1972) "De invasores a invadidos." Revista Latinoamericana de Estudios Urbano Regionales 2, 4 (March): 101-142.

SMITH, M. L. (1973) "Domestic service as a channel of upward mobility for the lower-class woman: The Lima case," pp. 191-207 in A. Pescatello (ed.), Female and Male in Latin America: Essays. Pittsburgh, Penna: University of Pittsburgh Press.

––– (1971) "Institutionalized servitude: The female domestic servant in Lima, Peru." Ph.D. dissertation. University of Indiana.

UZZELL, D. (1973) "Bureaus and the urban poor in Lima." Paper presented at the Annual Meeting of the American Anthropological Association, New Orleans, La., November-December.

––– (1973) "Feedback models of the development of urban localities in Lima, Peru." Paper presented at the Ninth International Congress of Anthropological and Ethnological Sciences, Chicago, Ill., August 28-September 8.

––– (1972) "Bound for places I'm not known to: Adaptation of migrants and residence in four irregular settlements in Lima, Peru." Ph.D. dissertation. University of Texas, Austin.

Rio de Janeiro, Brazil

BRODY, E. B. (1973) The Lost Ones: Social Forces and Mental Illness in Rio de Janeiro. New York: International Universities Press.

EVENSON, N. (1973) Two Brazilian Capitals: Architecture and Urbanism in Rio de Janeiro and Brasília. New Haven, Conn.: Yale University Press.

LEEDS, A. (1973) "Locality power in relation to supra-local power institutions," pp. 15-41 in A. Southall (ed.), Urban Anthropology. New York and London: Oxford University Press.

––– (1973) "Political, economic, and social effects of producer and consumer orientations toward housing in Brazil and Peru: A systems analysis," pp. 181-211 in F. F. Rabinovitz and F. M. Trueblood (eds.), Latin American Urban Research, Vol. III. Beverly Hills, Calif.: Sage Publications.

LEITMAN, S. L. (1973) "A Brazilian urban system in the nineteenth century: Pelotas and Rio de Janeiro." Paper presented at the Ninth International Congress of Anthropological and Ethnological Sciences, Chicago, Ill., August 28-September 8.

MARTINE, G. (1972) "Migration, natural increase, and city growth: The case of Rio de Janeiro." International Migration Review 6, 2 (Summer): 200-215.

PARISSE, L. (1969) "As favelas na cidade: o caso do Rio de Janeiro." Revista Geográfica 70 (June): 109-130.

PERLMAN, J. E. (1971) "The fate of migrants in Rio's favelas." Ph.D. dissertation. Massachusetts Institute of Technology.

RICHARDSON, I. L. (1973) Urban Government for Rio de Janeiro. New York: Praeger.

RIOS, J. A. (1972) "Rio de Janeiro," pp. 821-852 in W. A. Robson and D. E. Regan (eds.), Great Cities of the World. 3rd ed. Beverly Hills, Calif.: Sage Publications.

––– (1971) "Social transformation and urbanization: The case of Rio de Janeiro." Paper presented at the Conference on Urbanization in Latin America, Latin American Center, University of Wisconsin, Milwaukee, December 9-11.

SALMEN, L. F. (1971) "The casa de cômodos of Rio de Janeiro: A study of the occupants and accommodations of inner city slums and a comparison of their characteristics with the favelas." Ph.D. dissertation. Columbia University.

––– (1970) "Housing alternatives for the Carioca working class: A comparison between favelas and casas de cômodos." América Latina 13, 4 (October-December): 51-70.

San Juan, Puerto Rico

SEDA BONILLA, E. (1971) "La condición urbana: San Juan, Puerto Rico." Caribbean Studies 11, 3 (October): 5-18.

Santiago, Chile

BARRA, T. de la and M. QUINTANA (1972) "Estudios sobre Santiago." Revista de la Sociedad Interamericana de Planificación 6, 23 (September): 96-117.

BEHRMAN, L. C. (1972) "Patterns of religious and political attitudes and activities during modernization: Santiago, Chile." Social Science Quarterly 53, 3 (December): 520-533.

––– (1972) "Political development and secularization in two Chilean urban communities." Comparative Politics 4 (January): 269-280.

CHELLEW, P. et al. (1973) "Planificación y gobierno para el área metropolitana de Santiago: Algunas alternativas." Revista Latinoamericana de Estudios Urbano Regionales 3, 8 (December): 99-120.

CLEAVES, P. S. (1972) "Bureaucratic politics and administration in Chile." Ph.D. dissertation. University of California, Berkeley.

CUELLAR, O. et al. (1971) "Experiencias de justicia popular en poblaciones." Cuadernos de la Realidad Nacional 8 (June): 153-172.

EQUIPO DE ESTUDIOS POBLACIONALES DEL CIDU (1972) "Reivindicación urbana y lucha política: los campamentos de pobladores en Santiago de Chile." Revista Latinoamericana de Estudios Urbano Regionales 2, 6 (November): 55-82.

FIORI, J. (1973) "Campamento Nueva Habana: Estudio de una experiencia de auto-administración de justicia." Revista Latinoamericana de Estudios Urbano Regionales 3, 7 (April): 83-102.

FRIEDMAN, J. and A. NECOCHEA (1970) "Algunos problemas de política de urban-ización en la región capital de Chile." Revista Latinoamericana de Estudios Urbano Regionales 1, 1 (October).

GAVAN, J. (1971) "Un enfoque económico de la pobreza urbana." Revista Latino-americana de Estudios Urbano Regionales 1, 3 (October): 69-94.

GIUSTI, J. (1971) "La formación de las 'poblaciones' en Santiago: Aproximación al problema de la organización y participación de los pobladores." Revista Latinoamericana de Ciencia Política 2, 2 (August).

––– (1971) "Social marginality in Chile: The process of squatter settlement formation in Santiago." Ph.D. dissertation. Washington University.

KAUFMAN, C., K. LINDENBERG, and B. JONES (1973) "Personal welfare and political performance: Testing a model in Chile and Peru." Paper presented at the Annual Meeting of the Southwestern Social Science Association, Dallas, Texas.

LINDENBERG, K.E.M. (1970) "The effect of negative sanction on politicization among lower class sectors in Santiago, Chile, and Lima, Peru." Ph.D. dissertation. University of Oregon.

PORTES, A. (1973) "A model for the prediction of lower-class radicalism." Paper presented at the Annual Meeting of the American Sociological Association, New York, August.
——— (1972) "Status inconsistency and lower-class leftist radicalism." The Sociological Quarterly 13 (Summer): 361-382.
——— (1971) "Political primitivism, differential socialization, and lower-class leftist radicalism." American Sociological Review 36, 5 (October): 820-835.
——— (1971) "The urban slum in Chile: Types and correlates." Land Economics 47, 3 (August): 235-248.
PRATT, R. B. (1971) "Community political organization and lower class politicization in two Latin American cities." Journal of Developing Areas 5 (July): 523-542.
——— (1971) "Parties, neighborhood associations, and the politicization of the urban poor in Latin America." Midwest Journal of Political Science 15, 3 (August): 495-524.
QUEVEDO, S. and E. SADER (1973) "Algunas consideraciones en relación a las nuevas formas de poder popular en poblaciones." Revista Latinoamericana de Estudios Urbano Regionales 3, 7 (April): 71-82.
RACZYNSKI, D. (1972) "Migration, mobility, and occupational achievement: The case of Santiago, Chile." International Migration Review 6, 2 (Summer): 182-199.
SANTA MARIA, I. (1973) "El desarrollo urbano mediante los 'asentamientos espontáneos': el caso de los 'campaments o' chilenos." Revista Latinoamericana de Estudios Urbano Regionales 7, 3 (April): 103-112.
VANDERSCHUEREN, F. (1973) "Political significance of neighborhood committees in the settlements of Santiago," pp. 256-283 in D. L. Johnson (ed.), The Chilean Road to Socialism. Garden City, N.Y.: Doubleday-Anchor Books.
——— (1971) "Pobladores y conciencia social." Revista Latinoamericana de Estudios Urbano Regionales 1, 3 (October): 95-124.
——— (1971) "Significado político de las juntas de vecinos en poblaciones de Santiago." Revista Latinoamericana de Estudios Urbano Regionales 1, 2 (June): 67-90.

São Paulo, Brazil

BLAY, E. A. (1972) "Trabalho, familia e clases sociais em São Paulo." Revista do Instituto de Estudos Brasileiros 13: 87-99.
BLOUNT, J. A. (1971) "The public health movement in São Paulo, Brazil. A history of the sanitary service, 1892-1918." Ph.D. dissertation. Tulane University.
CARDOSO, F. E. and O. IANNI (1959) "Condiciones y efectos de la industrialización en São Paulo." Revista Mexicana de Ciencia Política 5, 18: 577-585.
——— et al. (1971) "Consideraciones sobre el desarrollo de São Paulo: Cultura y participacion." Revista Latinoamericana de Estudios Urbano Regionales 1, 3 (October): 43-68.
DANGENBUCH, J. R. (1971) "O sistema viario da aglomerção paulistina apreciação geográfica da situação atual." Revista Brasileira de Geografía 33, 2 (April-June): 3-38.
DURHAN, R. and R. CARDOSO (1973) "The social mobility of Brazilian and Japanese rural migrants in São Paulo." Paper presented at the Ninth International Congress of Anthropological and Ethnological Sciences, Chicago, Ill., August 28-September 8.
HANSEN, E. C. and E. de G. R. HANSEN (1973) "Middle class-upper class relations in São Paulo, Brazil." Paper presented at the Annual Meeting of the American Anthropological Association, New Orleans, La., November-December.
HARBLIN, T. D. (1971) "Urbanization, industrialization, and low-income family organization in São Paulo, Brazil." Ph.D. dissertation. Cornell University.
MARCILIO, M. L. (1969) La Ville de São Paulo: Peuplement et Population. Rouen: Université de Rouen, Faculté de Lettres et Sciences Humaines.

MATTOON, R. H. (1971) "The Companhia Paulista de Estradas de Ferro, 1868-1900: A local railway enterprise in São Paulo, Brazil." Ph.D. dissertation. Yale University.

MORSE, R. M. (1971) "San Pablo: más alla de la metrópolis, 1955-1970." Revista de la Sociedad Interamericana de Planificación 5, 17 (March-June): 40-65.

––– (1971) "São Paulo: Case study of a Latin American metropolis," pp. 151-186 in F. F. Rabinovitz and F. M. Trueblood (eds.), Latin American Urban Research, Vol. I. Beverly Hills, Calif.: Sage Publications.

PRESSEL, E. J. (1971) "Umbamba in São Paulo: Religious innovation in a developing society." Ph.D. dissertation. Ohio State University.

ROSEN, B. C. (1973) "Social change, migration, and family interaction in Brazil." American Sociological Review 38, 2 (April): 198-212.

SHIRLEY, R. W. (1971) The End of a Tradition: Culture Change and Development in the Municipio of Cunha, São Paulo, Brazil. New York: Columbia University Press.

SINGER, P. (ed.) (1973) Urbanización y recursos humanos. Buenos Aires: Sociedad Interamericana de Planificación.

VIANNA, H. (1969) São Paulo no Arquivo de Mateus. Rio de Janeiro: Biblioteca Nacional. Coleção Rodolfo Garcia.

OTHER CITIES BY COUNTRY

Argentina

ACKERMAN, W. V. (1972) "A spatial strategy of development for Cuyo, Argentina." Ph.D. dissertation. Ohio State University, Columbus.

BASALDUA, R. O. and O. MORENO (1972) "The legal and institutional organization of metropolitan Rosario, Argentina," pp. 189-195 in G. Geisse and J. E. Hardoy (eds.), Latin American Urban Research, Vol. II. Beverly Hills, Calif.: Sage Publications.

REINA, R. (1973) Paraná: Social Boundaries in an Argentine City. Austin: University of Texas Press.

Bolivia

CISNEROS, A. J. (1973) Condiciones familiares relacionados a la vivienda en la ciudad de Copacabana. La Paz: Centro de Investigaciones Sociales, Academia Nacional de Ciencias. Série Estudios Urbanos, No. 1.

URQUIDI Z., J. (1967) La urbanización de la ciudad de Cochabamba. Cochabamba, Bolivia: Editorial Universitaria.

WHITEHEAD, L. (1973) "National power and local power: The case of Santa Cruz de la Sierra, Bolivia," pp. 23-46 in F. F. Rabinovitz and F. M. Trueblood (eds.), Latin American Urban Research, Vol. III. Beverly Hills, Calif.: Sage Publications.

Brazil

BYARS, R. (1973) "Culture, politics, and the urban factory worker in Brazil: The case of Zé Maria," pp. in R. E. Scott (ed.), Latin American Modernization Problems. Urbana: University of Illinois Press.

DAVIDOVICH, F. (1971) "Formas de projeção espacial das cidades na área de influência de Fortaleza." Revista Brasileira de Geografía 33, 2 (April-June): 3-38.

DIAS, F. C. and O. J. DOS SANTOS (1972) "Ipatinga: uma comunidade operaria." Revista Brasileira de Estudos Políticos 33 (January): 119-149.

DORIA, C. (1973) "Middle and upper class kinship networks in Belo Horizonte, Brazil: The functions of the urban parentela." Paper presented at the Annual Meeting of the American Anthropological Association, New Orleans, November-December.

GAUTHEROT, M. (1970) Aratu: The Heart of Industrial Bahia. Hamburg: Hamburger Verlags-Buchhandlung.

MAGNANINI, R. L. da C. (1971) "As cidades de Santa Catarina: base econômica, clasificação funcional." Revista Brasileira de Geografía 33, 2 (April-June): 85-122.

MIRANDA DE SIQUEIRA, M. (1972) "Mudança de capital de Minas: uma questão ideológica." Revista Brasileira de Estudos Políticos 33 (January): 89-101.

QUINN, M. (1972) "Technicians versus politicians: Administrative reform of local government in a developing country: A case study of Pôrto Alegre, Brazil." Ph.D. dissertation. University of Illinois, Urbana.

WOLFF, L. (1971) "The use of information for improvement of educational planning in Rio Grande do Sul, Brazil." Ph.D. dissertation. Harvard University.

Central America

BRUNN, S. and R. THOMAS (1972) "Socio-economic environments and internal migration: The case of Tegucigalpa, Honduras." Social and Economic Studies 21, 4 (December): 463-473.

DROUBAY, M. S. (1972) "Changes in urban morphology in developing countries: A case study of Escuintla, Guatemala." Ph.D. dissertation. University of Oregon, Eugene.

EBEL, R. (1971) "The decision-making process in San Salvador," pp. 189-213 in F. F. Rabinovitz and F. M. Trueblood (eds.), Latin American Urban Research, Vol. I. Beverly Hills, Calif.: Sage Publications.

HUGES, J. C. (1973) "Distributions of selected medical services in the San José, Costa Rica, and Topeka, Kansas metropolitan areas." Graduate Studies on Latin America (University of Kansas) 1: 7-16.

Colombia

ABELLO, G. E. (1968) Barranquilla debe promover su desarrollo. Barranquilla, Colombia: Cámara de Comercio de Barranquilla.

ASHTON, G. T. (1971) "Rehousing and increased working-class in Cali, Colombia." América Latina 14, 1-2 (January-June): 70-82.

――― (1972) "The differential adaptation of two slum groups and working-class segments to a housing project in Cali, Colombia." Ph.D. dissertation. University of Illinois at Urbana.

――― (1972) "The differential adaptation of two slum subcultures to a Colombian housing project." Urban Anthropology 1, 2 (Fall): 176-194.

COOMBS, D. W. (1971) "Value orientation and modernization in two Colombian cities." Ph.D. dissertation. University of Florida.

DELAVAUD, C. C. (n.d.) L'Armature Urbaine et la Régionalisation en Antioquia. Paris: Institute des Hautes Etudes. R.C.P. 147.

DENT, D. W. (1973) "Community cooperation in Colombia: A comparative study of public-private sector relationships in two urban centers (Medellín and Barranquilla)." Ph.D. dissertation. University of Minnesota.

――― (1973) "Cooperation and community development in Colombia: A comparative study of two urban communities." Paper presented at the Annual Meeting of the American Political Science Association, New Orleans, La., September 4-8.

DRAKE, G. F. (1973) "Elites and voluntary associations: A study of community power in Manizales, Colombia." Land Tenure Center, University of Wisconsin. Research Papers, No. 52 (June).

ELDRIDGE, R. L. (1972) "Urban development in Colombia: The four largest cities." Ph.D. dissertation. University of Denver.
HOLLINGSWORTH, J. S. (1970) "Value orientations of leaders and students in Popayán, Colombia." Ph.D. dissertation. University of Florida.
IBIZA DE RESTREPO, G. (n.d.) Essai sur la Décentralisation Industrielle de Medellín. Paris: Institute des Hautes Etudes de l'Amérique latine. R.C.P. 147.
LECUONA, R. A. (1970) "A comparative analysis of the perceptions of selected elementary school children from Tallahassee, Florida, USA, and Popayán, Colombia, South America, about politics, government, and citizenship." Ph.D. dissertation. Florida State University.
MARZAHL, P. G. (1970) "The Cabildo of Popayán in the 17th century: The emergence of a creole elite." Ph.D. dissertation. University of Wisconsin.
OCAMPO, J. F. (1971) "Democracy and class rule in a Colombian city." Ph.D. dissertation. Claremont Graduate School and University Center.
WALTON, J. (1972) "Political development and economic development: A regional assessment of contemporary theories." Studies in Comparative International Development 7 (Spring): 39-63.
——— (1970) "Development decision making: A comparative study in Latin America." American Journal of Sociology 75, 5 (March): 828-851.
WHITEFORD, M. B. (1974) "Barrio Tulcán: Fieldwork in a Colombian city," pp. 41-62 in G. M. Foster and R. V. Kemper (eds.), Anthropology in Cities. Boston: Little, Brown. (Popayán)
——— (1973) "Illness and curing in a Colombian barrio." Paper presented at the Annual Meeting of the American Anthropological Association, New Orleans, La., November-December.
——— (1972) "Barrio Tulcán: Colombian countrymen in an urban setting." Ph.D. dissertation. University of California, Berkeley. (Forthcoming, University of Florida Press, Gainesville, Fla., Latin American Monographs series.)

Ecuador

MIDDLETON, DeW. R. (1973) "Network and opportunity: Changing arenas of recruitment in an Ecuadorian city." Paper presented at the Annual Meeting of the American Anthropological Association, New Orleans, La., November-December.
——— (1972) "Form and process: A study of urban social relations in Manta, Ecuador." Ph.D. dissertation. Washington University, St. Louis.

Mexico

BUTTERWORTH, D. (1973) "Squatters or suburbanites? —The growth of shantytowns in Oaxaca, Mexico," pp. 208-232 in R. E. Scott (ed.), Latin American Modernization Problems. Urbana-Champaign: University of Illinois Press.
CHANCE, J. K. (1973) "Parentesco y residencia urbana: Grupo familiar y su organización en el suburbio de Oaxaca, Mexico." América Indígena 33, 1 (January-March): 187-212.
——— (1971) "Kinship and urban residence: Household and family organization in a suburb of Oaxaca, Mexico." Journal of the Steward Anthropological Society 2, 2: 122-147.
FAGEN, R. and W. S. TUOHY (1972) Politics and Privilege in a Mexican City. Stanford: Stanford University Press. (Jalapa)
FOSTER, D. (1971) "Tequío in urban Mexico: A case from Oaxaca City." Journal of the Steward Anthropological Society 2, 2: 148-179.
GARNER, R. L. (1970) "Zacatecas, 1750-1821: The study of a late colonial Mexican city." Ph.D. dissertation. University of Michigan.

MILLER, F. C. (1973) Old Villages and a New Town: Industrialization in Mexico. Menlo Park, Calif.: Cummings Publishing Co. (Ciudad Sahagún)

MILLON, R. (ed.) (1973) Urbanization at Teotihuacán, Mexico. (9 vols.) Austin: University of Texas Press.

PARSONS, J. B. (1971) "Teotihuacán, Mexico, and its impact on regional demography." Ekistics 182 (January): 51-56.

PELTO, P. J. (1972) "Research strategies in the study of complex societies: The 'Ciudad Industrial' project," pp. 5-20 in T. Weaver and D. White (eds.), The Anthropology of Urban Environments. Boulder, Colorado: Society for Applied Anthropology.

POGGIE, J. J., Jr. (1972) "Ciudad Industrial: A new city in rural Mexico," pp. 10-38 in H. R. Bernard and P. Pelto (eds.), Technology and Social Change. New York: Macmillan.

PRICE, J. A. (1973) "Tecate: An industrial city on the Mexican border." Urban Anthropology 2, 1 (Spring): 35-47.

––– (1973) Tijuana: Urbanization in a Border Culture. Notre Dame, Indiana: Notre Dame University Press.

ROLLWAGEN, J. R. (1973) "Tuxtepec, Oaxaca: An example of rapid urban growth in Mexico." Urban Anthropology 2, 1 (Spring): 80-92.

ROYCE, R. R. (1973) "Sociological correlates of bilingualism in Juchitan, Oaxaca." Paper presented at the Annual Meeting of the American Anthropological Association, New Orleans, La., November-December.

SIMON, B. (1972) "Power, privilege, and prestige in a Mexican town." Ph.D. dissertation. University of Minnesota.

UGALDE, A. et al. (1974) The Urbanization Process of a Poor Mexican Neighborhood: The Case of San Felipe del Real Adicional, Juárez. Austin, Texas: Institute of Latin American Studies, University of Texas, Austin.

Peru

BODE, B. (1973) "The role of religion in adjustment to disaster." Paper presented at the Annual Meeting of the American Anthropological Association, New Orleans, La., November-December.

BRADFIELD, S. (1973) "Selectivity in rural-urban migration: The case of Huaylas, Peru," pp. 351-372 in A. Southall (ed.), Urban Anthropology. New York and London: Oxford University Press.

Uruguay

DE WINTER, A.M.T. (1971) "Family interaction, family planning, and fertility in the city of Durazno, Uruguay." Ph.D. dissertation. University of Wisconsin.

Venezuela

CANNON, M. W., R. S. FOSLER, and R. WITHERSPOON (1973) Urban Government for Valencia. New York: Praeger.

CORRADA, R. (1972) "Una política de vivienda para Ciudad Guayana." Revista de la Sociedad Interamericana de Planificación 6, 21 (March): 5-23.

GARCIA, M. P. and R. LESSER BLUMBERG (1973) "The unplanned ecology of a planned industrial city: The case of Ciudad Guayana, Venezuela." Paper presented at the Ninth International Congress of Anthropological and Ethnological Sciences, Chicago, Ill., August 28-September 8.

GARRILLO, J. A. (1969) "El desarrollo urbano, Maracaibo y el Cuatricentenario." El Farol 228 (January-March): 1-9.

LOUVIERE, V. (1973) "Building a city in the wilderness: Puerto Ordaz." Nation's Business 61 (August): 62.

LYNCH, E. (1973) "Propositions for planning new towns in Venezuela." Journal of Developing Areas 7, 4 (July): 549-571.

McGINN, N. F. and R. G. DAVIS (1970) Build a Mill, Build a City, Build a School: Industrialization in Ciudad Guayana, Venezuela. Cambridge: M.I.T. Press.

MATHIASON, J. R. (1972) "Patterns of powerlessness among urban poor: Toward the use of mass communications for rapid social change." Studies in Comparative International Development 7, 1 (Spring): 64-84. (Ciudad Guayana)

PEATTIE, L. R. (1971) "The structural parameters of emerging life styles in Venezuela," pp. 285-298 in E. B. Leacock (ed.), The Culture of Poverty: A Critique. New York: Simon and Schuster. (Ciudad Guayana)

COUNTRIES IN GENERAL

Argentina

AGULLA, J. C. (1972) "Elites tradicionales, poder y desarrollo en Argentina: estudio de un estrato alto tradicional en el poder de una ciudad en desarrollo." Revista Española de Opinión Pública 29 (July-September): 183-225.

BAILY, S. L. (1969-70) "The Italians and the development of organized labor in Argentina, Brazil, and the United States: 1880-1914." Journal of Social History 3, 2 (Winter): 123-134.

CORTES CONDE, R. (1972) "The antecedent of the Argentine urban system." Paper delivered at the Fortieth International Congress of Americanists, Rome, Italy, September 3-9.

ELIZAGA, J. C. (1973) "La evolución de la población de la Argentina en los últimos cien años." Desarrollo Económico 12, 48 (January-March): 795-806.

HARDOY, J. E. and L. A. ROMERO (1971) "La ciudad Argentina en el período precensal (1516-1869)." Revista de la Sociedad Interamericana de Planificación 5, 17 (March-June): 16-39.

INSTITUTE IN THE CHURCH IN URBAN-INDUSTRIAL SOCIETY (ICUIS) (1971) "Argentina: The truth about the eradication of 'emergency villages'." ICUIS Occasional Paper No. 3 (June). (Reprinted from Cristianismo y Sociedad.)

KENWORTHY, E. (1973) "The function of the little-known case in theory formation, or what Peronism wasn't." Comparative Politics 6, 1 (October): 17-45.

KIRKPATRICK, J. (1971) Leader and Vanguard in Mass Society: A Study of Peronist Argentina. Cambridge, Mass.: M.I.T. Press.

LATTES, A. E. (1973) "Migration, population change, and ethnicity in Argentina." Paper presented at the Ninth International Congress of Anthropological and Ethnological Science, Chicago, Ill., August 28-September 8.

——— (1973) "Las migraciones en la Argentina entre mediados del siglo XIX y 1960." Desarrollo Económico 12, 48 (January-March): 849-866.

MARGULIS, M. (1972) Migración y marginalidad en la sociedad Argentina. Buenos Aires: Editorial Paidos.

RECCHINI DE LATTES, Z. (1973) "El proceso de urbanización en la Argentina: Distribución, crecimiento, y algunas características de la población urbana." Desarrollo Económico 12, 48 (January-March): 867-886.

——— and A. E. LATTES (n.d.) Migraciones en la Argentina: Estudio de las migraciones internas e internacionales, basado en datos censales, 1869-1960. Buenos Aires: Instituto Torcuato di Tella.

ROFMAN, A. (1972) "Aspectos del comportamiento del sistema socio-económico Argentino en el período 1943-1953 y sus efectos a escala espacial." Revista Latinoamericana de Estudios Urbano Regionales 2, 4 (March): 41-66.

RUBINSTEIN, J. C. (1972) "Urbanización, estructura de ingresos y movilidad social en Argentina (1960-1970)." Revista del Instituto de Ciencias Sociales 20: 379-419.

SMITH, P. H. (1972) "The social base of Peronism." Hispanic American Historical Review 52, 1 (February): 55-73.

TOBAR, C. (1972) "The Argentine national plan for eradicating Villas de Emergencia," pp. 221-228 in G. Geisse and J. E. Hardoy (eds.), Latin American Urban Research, Vol. II. Beverly Hills, Calif.: Sage Publications.

WHITEFORD, S. (1973) "Agricultural labor unions and the migrant worker." Paper presented at the Annual Meeting of the American Anthropological Association, New Orleans, November-December.

——— (1972) "Bolivian migrant labor in Argentina." Paper presented at the Seventy-First Annual Meeting of the American Anthropological Association, Toronto, Canada, November.

——— and R. N. ADAMS (1973) "Migration, ethnicity, and adaptation: Bolivian migrant workers in northwest Argentina." Paper presented at the Ninth International Congress of Anthropological and Ethnological Sciences, Chicago, Ill., August 28-September 8.

WILKIE, R. W. (1973) "Rural depopulation: A case study of an Argentine village," in E. S. Lee (ed.), Proceedings of the International Biological Programme, Fifth General Assembly. Washington, D.C.: National Academy of Sciences.

——— (1972) "Toward a behavioral model of rural out-migration: An Argentine case of peasant spatial behavior by social class level," pp. 83-114 in R. N. Thomas (ed.), Population Dynamics of Latin America: A Review and Bibliography. East Lansing, Mich.: Conference of Latin Americanist Geographers Publications, Inc.

——— (1972) "Urban-rural implications of migration from a rural village in Argentina." Paper presented at the International Biological Program Human Adaptability Workshop. Seattle, Washington, August 30-September 7.

——— (1968) "On the theory and process of human geography: A case study of migration in rural Argentina." Ph.D. dissertation. University of Washington, Seattle.

Bolivia

BUECHLER, H. (1972) "Fiesta cycles and urban-rural communications systems in Bolivia." Paper presented at the Fortieth International Congress of Americanists, Rome, Italy, September 3-9.

CALVIMONTES ROJAS, C. (1972) "Urban land reform in Bolivia during the Victor Paz Estenssoro administration," pp. 179-182 in G. Geisse and J. E. Hardoy (eds.), Latin American Urban Research, Vol. II. Beverly Hills, Calif.: Sage Publications.

GOOD, D. W. (1971) "A study of organizational climate in Bolivian urban elementary schools." Ph.D. dissertation. University of Illinois, Urbana-Champaign.

POL, G. P. (1973) "Competence required for the principalship: A methodology applied to the urban Bolivian setting." Ph.D. dissertation. University of Utah.

PRESTON, D. (1972) Post-Revolutionary Rural-Urban Interaction on the Bolivian Altiplano. Leeds, England: University of Leeds, Department of Geography. Working Paper No. 10.

——— (1972) "Rural-urban transformation in Bolivia." Paper presented at the Fortieth International Congress of Americanists, Rome, Italy, September 3-9.

Brazil

AMES, B. (1973) "Rhetoric and reality in a militarized regime: Brazil after 1964." Sage Professional Papers in Comparative Politics, No. 01-042. Beverly Hills, Calif.: Sage Publications. (Favela policy)

BARBAROVIC, I. (1972) "Development poles and rural marginality in Brazil: Toward a definition of regional policy," pp. 101-124 in G. Geisse and J. E. Hardoy (eds.), Latin American Urban Research, Vol. II. Beverly Hills, Calif.: Sage Publications.

BOISIER, S. (1973) "Localización, tamaño urbano y productividad industrial: un estudio de caso en Brasil." Revista Interamericana de Planificación 7, 26 (June): 87-112.

BROWN, D. (1973) "Folk catholicism and patronage: A critique of urban-rural dichotomies." Paper presented at the Annual Meeting of the American Anthropological Association, New Orleans, La., November-December.

CARMEN, J.E.R. (1973) "An urban family in Brazil: A case study of upward social mobility." Ph.D. dissertation. Rice University.

CARNOY, M. and L. L. KATZ (1971) "Explaining differentials in earnings among large Brazilian cities." Urban Studies 18, 1 (February): 21-37.

CORREIA DE ANDRADE, M. (1970) "Considerações sobre a metodología para a aplicação da teoría dos polos de desenvolvimento aos países do terceiro mundo: uma experiencia no nordeste do Brasil." Revista Mexicana de Sociología 32, 1 (January-February): 5-26.

DADD, C. M. (1973) "Estimating the influence of household size and composition on consumption patterns by adult equivalent scales for urban households in Brazil, 1960-1970." Ph.D. dissertation. University of Wisconsin.

DALAND, R. T. (1972) "Attitudes toward change among Brazilian bureaucrats." Journal of Comparative Administration 4, 2 (August): 167-204.

FAISSOL, S. (1972) "A estrutura urbana Brasileria: uma visão do processo Brasileiro de desenvolvimento econômico." Revista Brasileira de Geografía 34, 3 (July-September): 19-123.

––– (1970) "As grandes cidades Brasileiras: dimensões básicas de diferenciação e relações com o desenvolvimento econômico: um estudo de análise fatorial." Revista Brasileira de Geografía 32, 4 (October-December): 87-130.

GARDNER, J. A. (1973) Urbanization in Brazil. New York: The Ford Foundation, International Urbanization Survey Reports, No. 280.

GASPAR, L. M. (1970) "Migrações rurais e crescimento urbano." Revista de Ciencias Sociais 1, 1: 124-135.

GEIGER, P. P. (1970) "Cidades do nordeste: Aplicação de 'factor analysis' no estudo de cidades nordestinas." Revista Brasileira de Geografía 32, 4 (October-December): 131-172.

––– and S. OXNARD (1969) "Aspects of population growth in Brazil." Revista Geográfica 70 (June): 7-28.

HOLZNER, L. (1971) "The problem of rural-urban migration in Brazil and South Africa." Paper presented at the Conference on Urbanization in Latin America, Latin American Center, University of Wisconsin-Milwaukee, December 9-11.

INSTITUTO BRASILEIRO DE GEOGRAFIA, SETOR DE GEOGRAFIA URBANA (1970) "Cidade e região no sudoeste Paranaense." Revista Brasileira de Geografía 32, 2 (April-June): 3-156.

LEEDS, A. (1973) "Political, economic, and social effects of producer and consumer orientation toward housing in Brazil and Peru: A systems analysis," pp. 181-211 in F. F. Rabinovitz and F. M. Trueblood (eds.), Latin American Urban Research, Vol. III. Beverly Hills, Calif.: Sage Publications.

––– (1971) "The concept of the 'Culture of Poverty': Conceptual, logical, and empirical problems, with perspectives from Brazil and Peru," pp. 226-284 in E. B. Leacock (ed.), The Culture of Poverty: A Critique. New York: Simon and Schuster.

LEEDS, E. and A. LEEDS (1972) "Brazil in the 1960's: Favelas and polity, the continuity of the structure of social control." LADAC Occasional Papers (Institute of Latin American Studies, University of Texas, Austin), Series 2, No. 5.

LORDELLO DE MELLO, D. (1971) O municipio na organização nacional. Rio de Janeiro: Instituto Brasileiro de Administração Municipal.

MACHADO, L. A. (1973) "Assimilation of rural migrants in Brazil." Paper presented at the Ninth International Congress of Anthropological and Ethnological Sciences, Chicago, Ill., August 28-September 8.

MAYER, J. (1970) "The Brazilian household: Size and composition." Ph.D. dissertation. University of Florida.

MELVIN, H. W., Jr. (1970) "Religion in Brazil: A sociological approach to religion and its integrative function in rural-urban migrant adjustment." Ph.D. dissertation. Boston University School of Theology.

MORSE, R. M. (1972) "Brazil's urban development: Colony and empire." Paper presented at the International Symposium on Historical Dimensions of Modern Brazil, Johns Hopkins University, October 18-19.

MULLER, N. L. (1969) "Situação atual e renovação metodológica dos estudos de geografía urbana no Brasil, 1965-1969." Revista Geográfica 70: 163-180.

PEREIRA DE QUEIROZ, M. I. (1969) "Favelas urbanas, favelas rurais." Revista do Instituto de Estudos Brasileiros 7: 81-99.

REEVE, R. P. (1973) "Race relations and socioeconomic mobility in a Brazilian town." Paper presented at the Annual Meeting of the American Anthropological Association, New Orleans, La., November.

REIS, F. W. (1971) "Participación, movilización e influencia política: 'Neo-coronelismo' en Brazil." Revista Latinoamericana de Ciencia Política 2, 1 (April): 73-102.

ROBOCK, S. H. (1968) The Rural Push for Urbanization in Latin America: The Case of Northeast Brazil. East Lansing, Mich.: Michigan State University, Latin American Studies Center. Occasional Paper No. 1.

SALMEN, L. F. (1972) "Urbanization and development," pp. 415-438 in H. J. Rosenbaum and W. G. Tyler (eds.), Contemporary Brazil: Issues in Economic and Political Development. New York: Praeger.

SCHWARTZMAN, S. (1973) "Empresarios y política en el proceso de industrialización: Argentina, Brasil, Australia." Desarrollo Económico 49, 13 (April-June): 67-90.

VIOTTI, E. (1972) "The formation of the Brazilian urban system in the 19th century." Paper delivered at the Fortieth International Congress of Americanists, Rome, Italy, September 3-9.

Central America

CRONER, C. M. (1972) "Spatial characteristics of internal migration to San Pedro Sula, Honduras." Ph.D. dissertation. Michigan State University.

GIBSON, J. R. (1970) "A demographic analysis of urbanization: Evolution of a system of cities in Honduras, El Salvador, and Costa Rica." Ph.D. dissertation. Cornell University.

LOVELAND, C. (1973) "Rural-urban dynamics: The Miskito coast of Nicaragua." Urban Anthropology 2, 2 (Fall): 182-193.

TELLER, C. H. (1972) "Internal migration, socio-economic status, and health: Access to medical care in a Honduran city." Latin American Studies Program Dissertation Series (Cornell University, Ithaca, N.Y.), No. 41 (September).

TORRES-RIVAS, E. (1973) "Urbanización y diferenciación social en Centroamérica." Paper presented at the Ninth International Congress of Anthropological and Ethnological Sciences, Chicago, Ill., August 28-September 8.

――― (1972) "Restructuring urban-rural linkages in Central America." Paper presented at the Fortieth International Congress of Americanists, Rome, Italy, September 3-9.

Chile

ACHURRA L., M. (1972) "Los desequilibrios regionales en Chile y algunas reflexiones sobre el proceso de concentración." Revista de la Sociedad Interamericana de Planificación 6, 23 (September): 28-50.

――― (1972) "Chilean regional development policy," pp. 133-141 in G. Geisse and J. E. Hardoy (eds.), Latin American Urban Research, Vol. II. Beverly Hills, Calif.: Sage Publications.

ALVARADO, L. et al. (1973) "Movilización social en torno al problema de la vivienda." Revista Lationoamericana de Estudios Urbano Regionales 3, 7 (April): 37-70.

ANDRADE, F. J. (1971) "Some normative aspects of planning in the Maule region, Chile." Ph.D. dissertation. Iowa State University.

ARANDA B., S. (1972) "La planificación en el gobierno de la Unidad Popular." Revista de la Sociedad Interamericana de Planificación 6, 23 (September): 7-12.

BEDRACK, M. (1972) "Desarrollo urbano y vivienda en Chile." Revista de la Sociedad Interamericana de Planificación 6, 23 (September): 76-95.

BOISIER, S. (1971) "Algunas hipótesis sobre un modelo de desarrollo de la zona metropolitana." Revista Latinoamericana de Estudios Urbano Regionales 1, 2 (June): 19-32.

CASTELLS, M. (1973) "Movimientos de pobladores y lucha de clases." Revista Latinoamericana de Estudios Urbano Regionales 3, 7 (April): 9-36.

CONNING, A. M. (1972) "Rural-urban destinations of migrants and community differentiation in a rural region of Chile." International Migration Review 6, 2 (Summer): 148-157.

DUQUE, J. and E. PASTRANA (1972) "La movilización reivindicativa urbana de sectores populares en Chile: 1964-1972." Revista Latinoamericana de Ciencias Sociales 4 (December): 259-294.

EQUIPO MACROZONA CENTRAL, CIDU (1972) "Síntesis del estudio 'Región Central de Chile: perspectivas de desarrollo'." Revista Latinoamericana de Estudios Urbano Regionales 2, 6 (November): 9-30.

FRIEDMANN, J. (1972) "The spatial organization of power in the development of urban systems." Comparative Urban Research 1, 2 (December): 5-42.

――― (1971) "Urban-regional policies for national development in Chile," pp. 217-246 in F. F. Rabinovitz and F. M. Trueblood (eds.), Latin American Urban Research, Vol. I. Beverly Hills, Calif.: Sage Publications.

FRANKENHOFF, C. A. (1969) Hacia una política habitacional popular: el caso de Chile. Santiago: Universidad Católica, Centro Interdisciplinario de Desarrollo Urbano y Regional.

GIUSTI, J. (1972) "Participación y organización de los sectores populares en América Latina: los casos de Chile y Perú." Revista Mexicana de Sociología 34, 1 (January-March): 39-64.

GONGORA DEL CAMPO, M. (1971) "Social stratification of urban Chile during the 16th and 17th centuries." Paper presented at the Conference on Urbanization in Latin America, Latin American Center, University of Wisconsin-Milwaukee, December 9-11.

MAMALAKIS, M. (1973) "Urbanization and economic development: The case of Chile." Paper presented at the Ninth International Congress of Anthropological and Ethnological Sciences, Chicago, Ill., August 28-September 8.

MENANTEAU-HORTA, D. and R. E. CARTER (1972) "La comunicación colectiva en

Chile: Algunas características del campo y de la ciudad." Revista Española de la Opinión Pública 28 (April-June): 107-120.

MUJICA, R. A. (1970) "Satiation levels and consumer demand: analysis of a Chilean family expenditure survey." Ph.D. dissertation. University of California at Berkeley.

NECOCHEA, A. (1973) "Tendencias de movimiento demográfico chileno y exploración de algunas hipótesis sobre su futuro." Revista Latinoamericana de Estudios Urbano Regionales 3, 8 (December): 43-98.

PARISI, L. (ed.) (1973) Proceso de metropolización en Chile y en América Latina. Instituto Latinoamericano de Investigaciones Sociales (ILDIS), Serie "ILDIS-Estudios y Documentos," No. 23-24.

PETRAS, J. F. (1973) "Chile: Nationalization, socio-economic change, and popular participation," pp. 41-60 in J. F. Petras (ed.), Latin America: From Dependence to Revolution. New York: Wiley.

RABINOVITZ, F. F. (1974) "Municipal government performance: the cases of Venezuela and Chile." Working Paper No. 3, European Urban Research, University of California, Los Angeles, January.

SINDING, S. (1972) "The evolution of Chilean voting patterns: a reexamination of some old assumptions." Journal of Politics 34, 3 (August): 774-796.

VALENZUELA, A. (1973) "Local politics and political recruitment in Chile: The test of a hypothesis." Paper presented at the Annual Meeting of the American Political Science Association, New Orleans, La., September 4-8.

——— (1972) "The scope of the Chilean party system." Comparative Politics 4, 2 (January): 179-199.

VILLA, M. (1972) "La formación urbano-regional chilena en su perspectiva reciente." Revista de la Sociedad Interamericana de Planificación 6, 23 (September): 51-59.

Colombia

BROOKS, R. (1971) "Social planning in Colombia." Journal of the American Institute of Planners (November): 373.

CAMPOS, J. T. and J. F. McCAMANT (1972) Cleavage Shift in Colombia: Analysis of the 1970 Elections. Beverly Hills, Calif.: Sage Publications. (Sage Professional Papers in Comparative Politics, Vol. 3, No. 01-032.)

CARDONA GUTIERREZ, R. (1972) Las migraciones internas. Bogotá, Colombia: Asociación Colombiana de Facultades de Medicina, División de Estudios de Población.

——— (1969) Las invasiones de terrenos urbanos: elementos para un diagnóstico. Bogotá: Colección el Dedo en la Herida, No. 33.

——— and G. ECHEVERRIA A. (1971) "Estudio descriptivo-exploratorio sobre migración y familia." Revista Paraguaya de Sociología 8, 20 (January-April): 115-127.

CASTANO, H. (1971) "Las economías urbanas de Colombia." Revista de la Sociedad Interamericana de Planificación 5, 18-19 (September): 44-54.

FELSTEHAUSEN, H. (1971) "Planning problems in improving Colombian roads and highways." Ekistics 187 (June): 438-443.

FLINN, W. L. and J. W. CONVERSE (1970) "Eight assumptions concerning rural-urban migration in Colombia: A three shantytowns test." Land Economics 46, 4 (November): 456-466.

HARKESS, S. J. (1973) "The elite and the regional urban system of Valle, Colombia as a reflection of dependency." Ph.D. dissertation. Cornell University.

KOORMAN, T. E. (1970) "Urban emphasis in the contemporary Colombian novel." Ph.D. dissertation. University of Missouri.

McGREEVEY, W. P. (1971) "The structure of migration and policies of urban growth in

Colombia." Paper presented at the Conference on Urbanization in Latin America, Latin American Center, University of Wisconsin, Milwaukee. December 9-11.

MACHADO S., J. R. (1972) "La estructura regional del desarrollo de Colombia." *Revista de la Sociedad Interamericana de Planificación* 6, 24 (December): 126-130.

MORCILLO, P. P. (1972) "Urban reform laws in Colombia," pp. 183-187 in G. Geisse and J. E. Hardoy (eds.), *Latin American Urban Research*, Vol. II. Beverly Hills, Calif.: Sage Publications.

NEAL, J. H. (1971) The Pacific age comes to Colombia: The construction of the Cali-Buenaventura route, 1854-1882." Ph.D. dissertation. Vanderbilt University.

PINEDA, R. (1972) "The Colombian Instituto de Crédito Territorial: Housing for low-income families," pp. 197-201 in G. Geisse and J. E. Hardoy (eds.), *Latin American Urban Research*, Vol. II. Beverly Hills, Calif.: Sage Publications.

POLLOCK, J. (1973) "The political attitudes and social backgrounds of Colombia's urban housing bureaucrats," pp. 133-152 in F. F. Rabinovitz and F. M. Trueblood (eds.), *Latin American Urban Research*, Vol. III. Beverly Hills, Calif.: Sage Publications.

ROBIN, J. P. and F. C. TERZO (1973) Urbanization in Colombia. New York: The Ford Foundation, International Urbanization Survey Reports, No. 281.

ROTHER, H. (1971) "La participación ciudadana en la planificación urbana." *Revista de la Sociedad Interamericana de Planificación* 5, 18-19 (September): 71-78.

RUBINSTEIN, M. K. (1973) "The migration of Colombian women from the campo to the city." M.A. thesis. Stanford University.

SANDILANDS, R. J. (1971) "The modernization of the agricultural sector and rural-urban migration in Colombia." Glasgow, Scotland: Institute of Latin American Studies, University of Glasgow. Occasional Papers, No. 1.

SCHOULTZ, L. (1972) "Urbanization and changing voting patterns: Colombia, 1946-1970." *Political Science Quarterly* 87, 1 (March).

SOLAUN, M., F. CEPEDA and B. BAGLEY (1973) "Urban reform in Colombia: The impact of the 'politics of games' on public policy," pp. 97-130 in F. F. Rabinovitz and F. M. Trueblood (eds.), *Latin American Urban Research*, Vol. III. Beverly Hills, Calif.: Sage Publications.

VERNEZ, G. (1971) "El proceso de urbanización de Colombia." *Revista de la Sociedad Interamericana de Planificación* 5, 18-19 (September): 14-34.

WALTON, J. (1972) "Political development and economic development: A regional assessment of contemporary theories." *Studies in Comparative International Development* 7, 1 (Spring): 39-63.

——— (1970) "Development decision making: A comparative study in Latin America." *American Journal of Sociology* 75, 5 (March): 828-851.

Costa Rica

ALBERTS, J. (1971) La migración interna en Costa Rica. San José: Centro Latino Americano de Demografía.

ANTONINI, G. A. (ed.) (1972) Public Policy and Urbanization in the Dominican Republic and Costa Rica: Proceedings of the Twenty-Second Annual Latin American Conference, Gainesville, Fla.: Center for Latin American Studies, University of Florida, Gainesville.

BAKER, C., R. FERNANDEZ P., and S. Z. STONE (1972) El gobierno municipal en Costa Rica: sus características y funciones. San José: Escuela de Ciencias Políticas, Universidad de Costa Rica.

CARVAJAL, M. and D. L. GEITHMAN (1973) "An economic analysis of migration in Costa Rica." Paper presented at the Fourth National Meeting of the Latin American Studies Association, University of Wisconsin, Madison, May 3-5.

Cuba

ACOSTA LEON, M. and J. E. HARDOY (1972) "La urbanización en Cuba." Demografía y Economía 6, 1: 41-68.

——— (1972) "Urbanization policies in revolutionary Cuba," pp. 167-177 in G. Geisse and J. E. Hardoy (eds.), Latin American Urban Research, Vol. II. Beverly Hills, Calif.: Sage Publications.

LATINAMERICANIST (Center for Latin American Studies, University of Florida, Gainesville) (1971) "Latin urbanization: The case of Cuba." Latinamericanist 6, 3 (March): 3-7.

MESA-LAGO, C. (1972) The Labor Force, Employment, Unemployment, and Underemployment in Cuba: 1899-1970. Beverly Hills, Calif.: Sage Publications. (Sage Professional Papers in International Studies, No. 02-009.)

PEREZ, L. (1973) "The growth of population in Cuba, 1953-1970." M.A. thesis. University of Florida.

PETRAS, J. F. (1973) "Cuba: Fourteen years of revolutionary government," pp. 281-293 in C. Thurber and L. Graham (eds.), Development Administration in Latin America. Durham, North Carolina: Duke University Press.

Dominican Republic

ANTONINI, G. A. (ed.) (1972) Public Policy and Urbanization in the Dominican Republic and Costa Rica. Proceedings of the Twenty-Second Annual Latin American Conference. Gainesville, Florida: Center for Latin American Studies, University of Florida.

GONZALEZ, N. L. (1974) "The City of Gentlemen: Santiago de los Caballeros," pp. 19-40 in G. M. Foster and R. V. Kemper (eds.), Anthropologists in Cities. Boston: Little, Brown.

——— (1973) "Types of migratory patterns to a small Dominican city." Paper presented at the Ninth International Congress of Anthropological and Ethnological Sciences, Chicago, Ill., August 28-September 8.

PEREZ MONTAS, E. (1972) "Rural community development in the Dominican Republic," pp. 217-219 in G. Geisse and J. E. Hardoy (eds.), Latin American Urban Research, Vol. II. Beverly Hills, Calif.: Sage Publications.

Mexico

ALSCHULER, L. R. (1972) "Algunas consequencias políticas de la urbanización rápida en México." Revista Latinoamericana de Ciencia Política 3, 1 (April): 131-143.

APPENDINI, K. A. de., D. MURAYAMA and R. M. DOMINGUEZ (1972) "Desarrollo desigual en Mexico, 1900 y 1960." Demografía y Economía 6, 1: 1-40.

BAKER, M. W., Jr. (1970) "Land use transition in Mexican cities: A study in comparative urban geography." Ph.D. dissertation. Syracuse University.

BARKIN, D. (ed.) (1972) Los beneficios del desarrollo regional. México, D.F.: Sep/Setentas (Secretaría de Educación Pública).

BASURTO, J. et al. (eds.) (1972) Un análisis múltiple de la realidad nacional. México, D.F.: Siglo Veintiuno.

BATAILLON, C. (1972) La ciudad y el campo en el México Central. México, D.F.: Siglo Veintiuno.

BRAY, W. (1972) "The city state in central Mexico at the time of the Spanish conquest." Journal of Latin American Studies 4, 2 (November): 161-185.

BRITTON, J. A. (1973) "Urban education and social change in the Mexican Revolution, 1931-1940." Journal of Latin American Studies 5, 2 (November): 233-245.

BROWNING, H. L. and J. P. GIBBS (1971) "División intraindustrial del trabajo en las entidades federativas de México." Demografía y Economía 5, 3: 287-303.
BUSSEY, E. M. (1973) The Flight from Rural Poverty: How Nations Cope. Lexington, Mass.: Heath-Lexington Books.
CAMERON, D. R., J. S. HENDRICKS and R. I. HOFFERBERT (1972) "Urbanization, social structure, and mass politics: A comparison within five nations." Comparative Political Studies 5, 3 (October): 259-290.
CAMPBELL, H. L. (1972) "Bracero migration and the Mexican economy, 1951-1964." Ph.D. dissertation. American University.
CARDENAS, C. (1972) "Regional rural development: The Mexican Río Balsas Commission," pp. 143-150 in G. Geisse and J. E. Hardoy (eds.), Latin American Urban Research, Vol. II. Beverly Hills, Calif.: Sage Publications.
CARLOS, M. L. (1973) "Fictive kinship and modernization in Mexico: A comparative analysis." Anthropological Quarterly 46, 2 (April): 75-91.
CARRIER, J. M. (1972) "Urban Mexican male homosexual encounters: An analysis of participants and coping strategies." Ph.D. dissertation. University of California at Irvine.
CINTA, G., R. (1970) "Clases sociales y desarrollo en México." Revista Latinoamericana de Ciencia Política 1, 3 (December): 447-469.
CLIFFORD, R. A. (1970) "Sociological study of the growth and decline of Mexican population centers, 1940-1960." Ph.D. dissertation. University of Florida.
CONE, C. A. (1973) "Perceptions of occupations in a newly industrializing region of Mexico." Human Organization 32, 2 (Summer): 143-151.
——— (1973) "Regional migration patterns and residential histories: A Mexican case." Paper presented at the Annual Meeting of the American Anthropological Association, New Orleans, La., November-December.
CONTRERAS S., E. (1971) "Inestabilidad ocupacional y estratificacion urbana." Revista Mexicana de Sociología 33, 4 (October): 699-728.
CORNELIUS, W. A. (1973) "La urbanización como un agente en la inestabilidad política: el caso de México." Línea: Pensamiento de la Revolución (México, D.F.) 3 (May-June): 65-103.
CORWIN, A. E. (1973) "Mexican emigration history, 1900-1970: Literature and research." Latin American Research Review 8, 2 (Summer): 3-24.
CROSSON, P. R. (1973) "Economic consequences of urbanization in Mexico." Paper presented at the Conference on Urbanization in Latin America, Center for Latin American Studies, University of Wisconsin, Milwaukee.
DISKIN, M. (1971) "Persistence of tradition in the urbanization of the Oaxaca Valley." Urban Affairs Annual Reviews 5: 191-214.
——— (1969) "Estudio estructural del sistema de plaza en el valle de Oaxaca." América Indígena 29, 4: 1076-1099.
DOHERTY, P. and J. M. BALL (1971) "Central functions of small Mexican towns." Southeastern Geographer 11, 1: 20-28.
FURLONG, W. L. (1972) "Obstacles to political development: Case studies of center and periphery in northern Mexico." Paper presented at the Annual Meeting of the American Political Science Association, Washington, D.C., September.
HARMAN, R. C. (1973) "Innovations in a Maya Community of Mexico." Paper presented at the Annual Meeting of the American Anthropological Association, New Orleans, La., November-December.
HUBBELL, L. (1973) "The Mexican middle class as perceived by its members." Paper presented at the Annual Meeting of the American Anthropological Association, New Orleans, La., November-December.
KEESING, D. B. and A. S. MANNE (1971) "Proyecciones de la fuerza de trabajo de México." Demografía y Economía 5, 2: 169-192.

KEMPER, R. V. (1972) "Contemporary Mexican urbanization: A view from Tzintzuntzan, Michoacan." Paper presented at the International Congress of Americanists, Rome, Italy, September 3-9.

LOMNITZ, L. and M. PEREZ (1973) "Poor cousins and wealthy uncles: The evolution of an urban family group." Paper presented at the Annual Meeting of the American Anthropological Association, New Orleans, La., November-December.

MARKMAN, S. (1972) "The urban foundations of the Dominicans in Chiapas during the 16th century." Paper presented at the Fortieth International Congress of Americanists, Rome, Italy, September 3-9.

MORELOS, J. B. (1972) "Niveles de participación y componentes de cambio de la población activa de México, 1950-1970." Demografía y Economía 6, 3: 298-318.

MORENO TOSCANO, A. (1971) "Patterns of urbanization in 19th century Mexico." Paper presented at the Conference on Urbanization in Latin America, Latin American Center, University of Wisconsin-Milwaukee, December 9-11.

MUNDALE, C. I. (1971) "Local politics, integration, and national stability in Mexico." Ph.D. dissertation. University of Minnesota.

PEDERSEN, M. C. (1971) "Decentralizing in Mexico: The case of Nuevo León." Ph.D. dissertation. Yale University.

PURCELL, S. K. and J.F.H. PURCELL (1974) "Community power and benefits from the nation: The case of Mexico," pp. 49-76 in F. F. Rabinovitz and F. M. Trueblood (eds.), Latin American Urban Research, Vol. III. Beverly Hills, Calif.: Sage Publications.

RENGERT, G. F. and A. C. RENGERT (1973) "Who moves to cities: A multi-variate examination of migrants from rural Mexico." Paper presented at the Annual Meeting of the Population Association of America, New Orleans, La., April 26-28.

――― (1972) "Distance and human migration: A study in rural Mexico," pp. 488-490 in W. P. Adams and F. M. Helleiner (eds.), International Geography, 1972: Papers presented at the Twenty-Second International Geographical Congress, Montreal, Canada. Toronto: University of Toronto Press.

――― (1972) "Migration probabilities: A study of migration from the agricultural villages around Ojuelos, Mexico." Paper presented to the Sixty-Eighth Annual Meeting of the Association of American Geographers, Kansas City, April 25.

――― (1971) "Factors related to migration behavior: A univariate analysis of individuals from an area in rural Mexico," pp. 10-14 in J. W. Brownell and R. O. Riess (eds.), Proceedings of the Joint Divisional Meeting of the Association of American Geographers, Middle States Division, and the New England-St. Lawrence Valley Geographical Society, New York, October 29-30.

REYNA, J. L. (1971) "An empirical analysis of political mobilization: The case of Mexico." Latin American Studies Program Dissertation Series (Cornell University, Ithaca, N.Y.), No. 26 (September).

ROLLWAGEN, J. R. (1972) "A comparative framework for the investigation of the city-as-context: A discussion of the Mexican case." Urban Anthropology 1, 1 (Spring): 68-86.

SCHENSUL, J. J. (1973) " 'Mi hijo va a la escuela para adelantarse—verdad? ': The role of education in an industrializing area of Mexico." Paper presented at the Annual Meeting of the American Anthropological Association, New Orleans, La., November-December.

SCHERS, D. (1972) The Popular Sector of the Partido Revolucionario Institucional in Mexico. Tel Aviv: The David Horowitz Institute for the Research of Developing Countries, Tel Aviv University, Research Report No. 1. (Submitted as a Ph.D. dissertation in Political Science, University of New Mexico, Albuquerque, 1972.)

STOLTMAN, J. P. and J. M. BALL (1971) "Migration and the local economic factor in rural Mexico." Human Organization 30, 1 (Spring): 47-56.

TREJO, S. (1971) "Industrialization and employment growth: Mexico, 1950-1965." Ph.D. dissertation. Yale University.

UNIKEL, L. (1971) "The process of urbanization in Mexico: Distribution and growth of urban population," pp. 247-302 in F. F. Rabinovitz and F. M. Trueblood (eds.), Latin American Urban Research, Vol. I. Beverly Hills, Calif.: Sage Publications.

——— C. RUIZ CHIAPETTO, and O. LAZCANO (1973) "Factores de rechazo en la migración rural en México, 1950-1960." Demografía y Economía 7, 1: 24-57.

——— and G. GARZA (1971) "Una clasificación funcional de las principales ciudades de México." Demografía y Economía 5, 3: 329-359.

URQUIDI, V. L. and A. GARCIA ROCHA (1973) "La construcción de vivienda y el empleo en México." Demografía y Economía 7, 1: 1-23.

VERDUZCO, G., M. GONZALES R. and A. ROZADA (1973) Comunicación gubernamental y sectores populares urbanos. México, D.F.: Estudios Sociales, A.C.

WALTON, J. and J. A. SWEEN (1971) "Urbanization, industrialization, and voting in Mexico: A longitudinal analysis of official and opposition party support." Social Science Quarterly 52 (December): 721-745.

WILKIE, R. W. (1973) "Urban growth and the transformation of the settlement landscape of Mexico, 1910-1970." Paper presented at the Fourth International Congress of Mexican Studies, Santa Monica, Calif.: October 17-21.

WITTE, A. D. (1971) "Employment in the manufacturing sector of developing economies: A study of Mexico, Peru, and Venezuela." Ph.D. dissertation. North Carolina State University at Raleigh.

Peru

DOUGHTY, P. L. (1973) "Social networks and community as evoked in disaster." Paper presented at the Annual Meeting of the American Anthropological Association, New Orleans, La., November-December.

——— (1972) "What makes a city in Peru? —A question of public policy and public service," pp. 120-141 in G. A. Antonini (ed.), Public Policy and Urbanization in the Dominican Republic and Costa Rica: Proceedings of the Twenty-Second Annual Latin American Conference. Gainesville, Fla.: Center for Latin American Studies, University of Florida.

FURLONG, W. L. (1972) "Peruvian and northern Mexican municipalities: A comparative analysis of two political subsystems." Comparative Political Studies 5, 1 (April): 59-83.

LONG, N. (1973) "The role of regional associations in Peru," in M. Drake et al. (eds.), The Process of Urbanization. Bletchley: The Open University.

MARTINEZ, H. (1970) "Migración en las comunidades indígenas del Perú antes de la reforma agraria." Estudios de Población y Desarrollo 4, 5 (December): 1-15.

QUINTANILLA, A. (1973) "Effects of rural-urban migration on beliefs and attitudes toward disease and medicine in two areas of Peru." Paper presented at the Ninth International Congress of Anthropological and Ethnological Sciences, Chicago, Ill., August 28-September 8.

ROBIN, J. P. and F. C. TERZO (1973) Urbanization in Peru. New York: Ford Foundation, International Urbanization Survey Reports, No. 283.

ROBLES RIVAS, D. (1972) "Development alternatives for the Peruvian barriada," pp. 229-237 in G. Geisse and J. E. Hardoy (eds.), Latin American Urban Research, Vol. II. Beverly Hills, Calif.: Sage Publications.

VANDENDRIES, R. (1973) "Internal migration and economic development in Peru," pp. 193-208 in R. E. Scott (ed.), Latin American Modernization Problems. Urbana, Ill.: University of Illinois Press.

WESCHE, R. (1971) "Recent migration to the Peruvian montaña." Cahiers de Geographie de Quebec 15, 35 (September): 251-266.

WITTE, A. D. (1971) "Employment in the manufacturing sector of developing economies: A study of Mexico, Peru, and Venezuela." Ph.D. dissertation. North Carolina State University at Raleigh.

Puerto Rico

BOSWELL, T. D. (1973) "Municipio characteristics as factors affecting internal migration in Puerto Rico: 1935-1940 and 1955-1960." Ph.D. dissertation. Columbia University.
BRYCE-LAPORTE, R. S. (1973) "Relocalización urbana y adaptación familiar en Puerto Rico." Revista de Ciencias Sociales 17, 1 (May): 57-72.
HEALY, R. G. and J. SHORT (1970) Some Responses to Improved Housing in a Puerto Rican Town. Los Angeles, Calif.: University of California Graduate School of Business Administration (International Housing Productivity Study).
RAMIREZ, R. L. (1973) "Social structure and the political process: A study of squatter settlements and public housing in a Puerto Rican urban area." Ph.D. dissertation. Brandeis University.
SAFA, H. (1974) The Urban Poor of Puerto Rico: A Study in Development and Inequality. New York: Holt, Rinehart, and Winston.
STANTON, H. R. (1972) "Social detriments of housing policy in Puerto Rico: A case study of rapid urbanization." American Behavioral Scientist 15 (March): 563-580.

Uruguay

COLLIN DELAVAUD, A. (1972) Uruguay, Moyènnes et Petites Villes. Paris: Institute des Hautes Etudes de l'Amérique Latine.
GILIO, M. E. (1972) The Tupamaro Guerrillas: The Structure and Strategy of the Urban Guerrilla Movement. Trans. by Anne Edmondson. New York: Saturday Review Press.
PORZECANSKI, A. C. (1973) Uruguay's Tupamaros: The Urban Guerrilla. New York: Praeger.
TURIANSKY, W. (1973) El movimiento obrero uruguayo. Montevideo: Pueblos Unidos.

Venezuela

ACOSTA L., M. (1973) "Urbanización y clases sociales en Venezuela." Revista Interamericana de Planificación 7, 26 (June): 22-44.
BELANDRIA, F. (1971) "An empirical study of consumer expenditure patterns in Venezuelan cities." Ph.D. dissertation. Northwestern University.
RABINOVITZ, F. F. (1974) "Municipal government performance: The cases of Venezuela and Chile." Working Paper No. 3, European Urban Research, University of California, Los Angeles, January.
SAVIO, C. J. (1974) "Revenue sharing in practice: National-state-local subventions in Venezuela," pp. 79-93 in F. F. Rabinovitz and F. M. Trueblood (eds.), Latin American Urban Research, Vol. III. Beverly Hills, Calif: Sage Publications.
TORREALBA NARVAEZ, L. (1970) Aspectos jurídicos del urbanismo en Venezuela. Caracas: Fondo Editorial Común.
TRAVIESSO, F. (1973) "Desarrollo nacional, desarrollo regional, y urbanización en el caso de Venezuela." Revista de la Sociedad Interamericana de Planificación 7, 25 (March): 54-73.
WATSON, L. C. (1972) "Urbanization and identity dissonance: A Guajiro case." American Anthropologist 74, 5 (October): 1189-1207.
WITTE, A. D. (1971) "Employment in the manufacturing sector of developing economies: A study of Mexico, Peru, and Venezuela." Ph.D. dissertation. North Carolina State

GENERAL URBAN STUDIES ON LATIN AMERICA

ACEDO MENDOZA, C. (1973) América Latina: Marginalidad y subdesarrollo. Caracas: Fondo Editorial Común.

AGOR, W. A. (1972) "Local government and administration in Latin America: A summary of research findings in the 1960's and a recommended agenda for the 1970's." Paper presented at the American Society for Public Administration Conference, March 21-24, New York.

ANTONINI, G. A. (ed.) (1972) Public Policy and Urbanization in the Dominican Republic and Costa Rica: Proceedings of the Twenty-Second Annual Latin American Conference. Gainesville, Fla.: Center for Latin American Studies, University of Florida, Gainesville.

BALAN, J. (1973) "Urbanización, migraciones internas y desarrollo regional: notas para una discusión." Demografía y Economía 7, 2: 149-163.

BASIL, L. A. (1970) "Gobierno urbano: estudio tentativo para definir su estructura." Cuadernos de la Sociedad Venezolana de Planificación 80-81 (September-October): 3-32.

BEHRMAN, L. (1972) "The political role of African and Latin American Pentacostals: A suggestion for a comparative framework in urban studies in developing areas." Paper presented at the Annual Meeting of the African Studies Association.

BOISIER, S. (1972) "Industrialización, urbanización, polarización: hacia un enfoque unificado." Revista Latinoamericana de Estudios Urbano Regionales 2, 5 (July): 35-62.

BOYD, M. (1973) "Occupational mobility and fertility in metropolitan Latin America." Demography 10, 1 (February): 1-18.

――― (1971) "Occupational mobility and fertility in urban Latin America." Ph.D. dissertation. Duke University.

BOYER, R. E. and K. A. DAVIES (1973) Urbanization in 19th Century Latin America: A Supplement to the Statistical Abstract of Latin America. Los Angeles, Calif.: Latin American Center, University of California.

BROWNING, H. L. (1973) "Some consequences of migration on the class structure of communities of origin and of destination in Latin America," pp. 259-269 in Vol. I, International Union for the Scientific Study of Population, International Population Conference, Liège, 1973: Proceedings. Liège, Belgium: International Union for the Scientific Study of Population.

CEPAL, SERVICIOS INFORMATIVOS (1972) "Distribución comparada del ingreso en grandes ciudades y los países correspondientes." CEPAL Newsletter 96 (16 March).

CALDERON, J. F. and J. F. ENCINA M. (1972) "La contradicción campo-ciudad y la urbanización." Revista de Ciencias Sociales 3 (July): 107-122.

CARDONA, G., R. and A. B. SIMMONS (1973) "Hacia un modelo de la migración en América Latina." Paper presented at the Ninth International Congress of Anthropological and Ethnological Sciences, Chicago, Ill., August 28-September 8.

CARLOS, M. L. and L. SELLERS (1972) "Family, kinship structure, and modernization in Latin America." Latin American Research Review 7, 2 (Summer): 95-124.

CASIMIR, J. (1970) "Definición y funciones de la ciudad en América Latina." Revista Mexicana de Sociología 32, 6 (November-December): 1497-1511.

CASTELLS, M. (1972) Problemas de investigación en sociología urbana. Buenos Aires: Siglo XXI.

CENTRO LATINOAMERICANO DE DEMOGRAFIA (1972) "El crecimiento urbano como función del tamaño de las ciudades." Revista de la Sociedad Interamericana de Planificación 6, 24 (December): 118-125.

CHAPARRO, P. (1972) "Efectos sociales y políticos del proceso de urbanización." Revista Latinoamericana de Estudios Urbano Regionales 2, 6 (November): 101-116.

CORNELIUS, W. A. (1974) "Urbanization and political demand-making: Political participation among the migrant poor in Latin American cities." American Political Science Review 68, 3 (September).

――― (1974) "Out-migration from rural communities in Latin America: The impact of government policies and programs." Research proposal, Center for International Studies, Massachusetts Institute of Technology, Cambridge, Mass.

――― (1972) "The cityward movement: Some political implications," pp. 27-41 in D. A. Chalmers (ed.), Changing Latin America: New Interpretations of its Politics and Society. New York: Academy of Political Science, Columbia University. (Proceedings of the Academy of Political Science 30, 4.)

――― (1971) "The political sociology of cityward migration in Latin America: Toward empirical theory," pp. 95-147 in F. F. Rabinovitz and F. M. Trueblood (eds.), Latin American Urban Research, Vol. I. Beverly Hills, Calif.: Sage Publications.

――― and H. A. DIETZ (1973) "Urbanization, demand-making, and political system 'overload': Political participation among the migrant poor in Latin American cities." Paper presented at the Annual Meeting of the American Political Science Association, New Orleans, La., September 4-8.

COULARD, P. (1970) "Análisis rápido para problemas urbanos: Apuntes para un plan de trabajo." Cuadernos de la Sociedad Venezolana de Planificación 80-81 (September-October): 33-45.

CRAIG, A. (1971) "Urban guerrilla in Latin America." Survey 17, 3 (Summer): 112-128.

EBEL, R. H. (1972) "Governing the city-state: Notes on the politics of the small Latin American countries." Journal of Inter-American Studies and World Affairs 14, 3 (August): 325-346.

ECKSTEIN, S. (1972) "Ideological and intellectual biases in the study of Latin American urban poverty." Paper presented at the Annual Meeting of the American Sociological Association, Washington, D.C., September.

ELIZAGA, J. C. (1972) "Algunos problemas de estimación y proyección de la población urbana." Revista de la Sociedad Interamericana de Planificación 6, 24 (December): 110-117.

――― (1972) "Internal migration: An overview." International Migration Review 6, 2 (Summer): 121-126.

EQUIPO DE ESTUDIOS POBLACIONALES DEL CIDU (1972) "Pobladores y administración de justicia: informe preliminar de una encuesta." Revista Latinoamericana de Estudios Urbano Regionales 2, 5 (July): 135-150.

FAISSOL, S. (1972) "Análise fatorial: problemas e aplicações na geografía, especialmente nos estudos urbanos." Revista Brasileira de Geografía 34, 4 (October-December): 77-100.

FLISFISCH, A. (1970) "La estructura política local." Revista Latinoamericana de Ciencia Política 1, 3 (December): 415-446.

FOSTER, D. (1972) "Housing in low-income urban barrios in Latin America: Some cultural considerations." Paper presented at the Annual Meeting of the American Anthropological Association, Toronto, Canada, November 29-December 3.

FRENKEL, R. (1971) "Consideraciones económicas del proceso de urbanización." Revista Latinoamericana de Estudios Urbano Regionales 1, 2 (June): 9-18.

GERMANI, G. (1972) "Consideraciones metodológicas y teóricas sobre la marginalidad urbana en América Latina." Revista de la Sociedad Interamericana de Planificación 6, 24 (December): 17-37.

GUTIERREZ, R. C. and G. E. ALARCON (1971) "Estudio descriptivo-exploratorio sobre migración y familia." Revista Paraguaya de Sociología 8, 20 (January-April): 115-127.

HAMBURG, R. (1972) "Urbanization, industrialization, and modernization in Latin America: Soviet views." Studies in Comparative Communism 5, 1 (Spring): 1-20.

HARDOY, J. E. (ed.) (1974) Urban Problems in Latin America. Garden City, N.Y.: Doubleday-Anchor Books.

——— (1973) "Potentials for urban absorption: The Latin American experience," pp. 167-192 in T. T. Poleman and D. K. Freebairn (eds.), Food, Population, and Employment. New York: Praeger.

——— (1972) Las ciudades en América Latina. Seis ensayos sobre la urbanización contemporánea. Buenos Aires: Editorial Paidos.

——— (1972) "Contemporary Latin American urban hierarchies and sociopolitical systems." Paper delivered at the Fortieth International Congress of Americanists, Rome, Italy, September 3-9.

——— (1972) "Políticas de urbanización y políticas de la tierra urbana: la situación en Cuba, Haití, Jamaica, México, y la República Dominicana," pp. 142-175 in G. A. Antonini (ed.), Public Policy and Urbanization in the Dominican Republic and Costa Rica: Proceedings of the Twenty-Second Annual Latin American Conference. Gainesville, Fla.: Center for Latin American Studies, University of Florida, Gainesville.

——— (1972) Precolumbian Cities. New York: Walker & Co.

——— (1972) "Urbanization policies and urban reform in Latin America," pp. 19-44 in G. Geisse and J. E. Hardoy (eds.), Latin American Urban Research, Vol. II. Beverly Hills, Calif.: Sage Publications.

——— and O. A. MORENO (1973) "La reforma urbana en América Latina." Revista de la Sociedad Interamericana de Planificación 7, 25 (March): 7-35.

HASS, P. H. (1971) "Maternal employment and fertility in metropolitan Latin America." Ph.D. dissertation. Duke University.

HASSAN, M. F. (1973) "Unemployment in Latin America: Causes and remedies." American Journal of Economics and Sociology 32, 2 (April): 179-190.

HERRERA, F. (1971) "Nationalism and urbanization in Latin America." Ekistics 192 (November): 369-373.

HERRERA, L. (1972) "Ubicación de las ciudades en el espacio geográfico: México, Colombia, Perú, Chile, Venezuela, Argentina." Revista de la Sociedad Interamericana de Planificación 6, 24 (December): 101-109.

HERRICK, B. (1971) "Urbanization and urban migration in Latin America: An economist's view," pp. 71-81 in F. F. Rabinovitz and F. M. Trueblood (eds.), Latin American Urban Research, Vol. I. Beverly Hills, Calif.: Sage Publications.

JACOBSON, A. (1973) "Towards a theory of uncontrolled urban settlements in Latin America." Paper presented at the Annual Meeting of the American Sociological Association, New York, August 27-30.

KATZ, F. (1972) "The Inca and Aztec urban systems and their sociopolitical systems." Paper delivered at the Fortieth International Congress of Americanists, Rome, Italy, September 3-9.

KAUFMAN, C. (1972) "Urban structure and urban politics in Latin America." Journal of Comparative Administration 4, 3 (November): 343-364.

KEMPER, R. V. (1971) "Rural-urban migration in Latin America." International Migration Review 5 (Spring): 36-47.

KENSKI, H. C., Jr. (1971) "Urbanization and political change in Latin America, 1950-64." Ph.D. dissertation. Georgetown University.

LABADIA CAUFRIEZ, A. (1972) "Operación sitio: A housing solution for progressive growth," pp. 203-209 in G. Geisse and J. E. Hardoy (eds.), Latin American Urban Research, Vol. II. Beverly Hills, Calif.: Sage Publications.

LEEDS, A. (1971) "The metropole, the squatment, and the slum: Some thoughts on capitalism and secondary countries." Paper presented at the Conference on Dependency in Latin America, UCLA Conference Center, Lake Arrowhead, California, March 5-7.

LERNER, S. and R. DE LA PENA (eds.) (1973) Documentos de la Conferencia Regional Latinoamericana de Población, 2 vols. México, D.F.: El Colegio de México.

LOYKASEK, V. S. (1972) "Uma definição estadística da hierarquia urbana." Revista Brasileira de Geografía 34, 3 (July-September): 154-171.

MACISCO, J. J., Jr. (1972) "Some directions for further research on internal migration in Latin America." International Migration Review 6, 2 (Summer): 216-223.

MAMALAKIS, M. J. (1972) "Urbanization and sectoral transformation in Latin America, 1960-65," in Vol. II, Actas y Memorias del XXXIX Congreso Internacional de Americanistas, Lima, 1970. Lima, Peru: Congreso Internacional de Americanistas.

MARTINE, G. (1973) "Migrant fertility adjustment and urban growth in Latin America," pp. 293-313 in Vol. I, International Union for the Scientific Study of Population, International Population Conference, Liège, 1973: Proceedings. Liège, Belgium: International Union for the Scientific Study of Population.

MATEO, R. M. (1972) "La penetración pública en la propiedad urbana." Revista de la Sociedad Interamericana de Planificación 6, 22 (June): 79-91.

MATTOS, C. A. de (1972) "Algunas consideraciones sobre la movilidad espacial de recursos en los países latinoamericanos." Revista Latinoamericana de Estudios Urbano Regionales 2, 6 (November): 31-42.

MAURO, F. (1972) "El rol de las ciudades en el desarrollo regional en América Latina." Revista Mexicana de Sociología 34, 1 (January-March): 65-74.

MILLER, D. C. (1973) "The institutional approach as a strategy for comparative community power structure studies," in T. N. Clark (ed.), Comparative Community Politics. Beverly Hills, Calif.: Sage Publications.

MORSE, R. M. (1974) "The claims of tradition in urban Latin America," pp. 480-494 in D. B. Heath (ed.), Contemporary Cultures and Societies of Latin America. New York: Random House.

――― (1972) "A prolegomenon to Latin American urban history." Hispanic American Historical Review 52, 3 (August): 359-394.

――― (1972) "The development of Latin American urban systems in the 19th century." Paper delivered at the Fortieth International Congress of Americanists, Rome, Italy, September 3-9.

――― (1971) "Primaría, regionalización, dependencia: enfoques sobre las ciudades latino-americanas en el desarrollo nacional." Desarrollo Económico 11, 41 (April-June): 55-85.

――― (1970) "Internal migrants and the urban ethos in Latin America." Paper presented at the Seventh World Congress of Sociology, Varna, Bulgaria, September.

――― (1970) "The limits of metropolitan dominance in contemporary Latin America." Paper presented at the Thirty-Ninth International Congress of Americanists, Lima, Perú, August 2-9.

――― M. L. CONNIFF, and J. WIBEL (eds.) (1971) The Urban Development of Latin America, 1750-1920. Stanford: Stanford University, Center for Latin American Studies.

MOSS, R. (1970) "Urban guerrillas in Latin America." Conflict Studies (London) 8 (October): 1-15.

MUNOZ, H. y O. de OLIVEIRA (1972) "Migraciones internas y desarrollo: algunas consideraciones sociológicas." Demografía y Economía 6, 2: 248-260.

NELSON, J. (1972) "The search for useful hypotheses." Journal of Comparative Administration 4, 3 (November): 365-371.

NUTINI, H. G. (1972) "The Latin American city: A cultural-historical approach," pp. 89-96 in T. Weaver and D. White (eds.), The Anthropology of Urban Environments. Boulder, Colorado: Society for Applied Anthropology, Monograph Series No. 11.

OLIVEIRA, O. de and C. STERN (1972) "Aspectos sociológicos de las migraciones internas." Revista Economía Política (Mexico), 9, 34 (Cuarto Trimestre).

PASSOS, A. (1972) "Tendencias y dirección del crecimiento urbano en América Latina entre 1950 y 1970." Revista de la Sociedad Interamericana de Planificación 6, 24 (December): 5-16.

PEREIRA, L. (1970) "Urbanização 'sociopática' e tensões sociais na América Latina."
    Revista Mexicana de Sociología 32, 2 (March-April): 283-309.
PORTES, A. (1972) "Urbanización y política en América Latina." Revista Paraguaya de
    Sociología 9, 24 (May-August): 47-72.
——— (1972) "Rationality in the slum: An essay in interpretive sociology." Comparative
    Studies in Society and History 14, 3 (June): 268-286.
——— (1971) "Urbanization and Politics in Latin America." Social Science Quarterly 52
    (December): 697-720.
QUIJANO, A. (1972) "La constitución del 'mundo' de la marginalidad urbana." Revista
    Latinoamericana de Estudios Urbano Regionales 2, 5 (July): 89-106.
RABINOVITZ, F. F. and R. C. FRIED (1972) "Public policy determinants of urban growth
    in Latin America: An overview," pp. 6-22 in G. A. Antonini (ed.), Public Policy and
    Urbanization in the Dominican Republic and Costa Rica: Proceedings of the Twenty-
    Second Annual Latin American Conference. Gainesville, Fla.: Center for Latin American
    Studies, University of Florida, Gainesville.
ROFMAN, A. B. (1972) "The contemporary Latin American city." Paper delivered at the
    Fortieth International Congress of Americanists, Rome, Italy, September 3-9.
——— (1972) "El fenómeno de la concentración y centralización espacial en América Latina:
    elementos para una discusión." Revista Latinoamericana de Estudios Urbano Regionales
    2, 5 (July): 11-34.
SCHAEDEL, R. P. (1972) "Variations in the patterns of contemporary and recent
    urban-rural (macro-microsocietal) linkages in Latin America." Paper delivered at the
    Fortieth International Congress of Americanists, Rome, Italy, September 3-9.
SCHOULTZ, L. (1972) "Urbanization and political change in Latin America." Midwest
    Journal of Political Science 16, 3 (August): 367-387.
SCHTEINGART, M. (ed.) (1973) Urbanización y dependencia en América Latina. Buenos
    Aires: Sociedad Interamericana de Planificación.
——— and H. TORRES (1973) "Procesos sociales y estructuración metropolitana en América
    Latina: estudio de casos." Desarrollo Económico 12, 48 (January-March): 725-760.
SCHWARTZMAN, F. (1972) "Un enfoque teórico del regionalismo político." Revista de la
    Sociedad Interamericana de Planificación 6, 22 (June): 5-21.
SERAFINI, O. (1972) "La educación en los barrios populares urbanas de América Latina."
    Revista Paraguaya de Sociología 9, 25 (September-December): 170-187.
SINGER, P. (1972) "The transformational process in the 19th century Latin American
    city." Paper presented at the Fortieth International Congress of Americanists, Rome,
    Italy, September 3-9.
SOLA MORALES, M. de (1973) "Enseñanza del urbanismo: formación técnica vs.
    información pública." Revista Interamericana de Planificación 7, 26 (June): 140-148.
SOLOW, A. A. (1974) "National urbanization policies in Latin America." University Center
    for International Studies, University of Pittsburgh, Occasional Paper.
STEGER, H. A. (1973) "VIP-city and techno-science in Latin America." Paper presented at
    the Ninth International Congress of Anthropological and Ethnological Sciences, Chicago,
    Illinois, August 28-September 8.
STRAUSS, E. (1972) "El proceso de urbanización y las migraciones internas: un enfoque
    desde el ángulo de los recursos naturales." Revista de la Sociedad Interamericana de
    Planificación 6, 24 (December): 38-45.
TRINDADE, H. H. (1971) "Participação político-social ao nivel local." Dados 8: 129-151.
TURNER, J.F.C. and R. FICHTER (1972) Freedom to Build. New York: Free Press.
UNITED NATIONS, DEPARTMENT OF ECONOMIC AND SOCIAL AFFAIRS (1973)
    Urban Land Policies and Land-Use Control Measures, Vol. IV: Latin America. New
    York: United Nations.

URDANETA, A. (1973) "Costos del desarrollo urbano." Revista de la Sociedad Interamericana de Planificación 7, 25 (March): 80-100.

WALTER, J. P. (1973) "The city as a source of regional economic disparity in Latin America." Review of Social Economy 31 (April): 66-88.

WELLER, R. H. and J. J. MACISCO, Jr. (1971) "Fecundidad, migración y aspiraciones de mobilidad social en los países en desarrollo: sugerencias para investigación." Demografía y Economía 5, 1: 56-76.

––– and G. R. MARTINE (1971) "The relative importance of the components of urban growth in Latin America." Demography 8, 2 (May): 225-232.

WESTEBBE, R. M. (1971) "O desafío da urbanização." Revista de Administración Municipal 18, 105 (March-April): 49-62.

WILSON, S. (1972) "Occupational mobility and social stratification in Latin American cities." Latin American Studies Program Dissertation Series (Cornell University, Ithaca, N.Y.), No. 43 (May).

WITT, V. (1972) "La urbanización y su impacto sobre los niveles de salud y otros indicadores del bienestar." Revista de la Sociedad Interamericana de Planificación 6, 24 (December): 86-100.

URBAN AND REGIONAL PLANNING

COLOMBIA, DEPARTAMENTO NACIONAL DE PLANEACION (1970) "Políticas de desarrollo regional y urbano: modelo de regionalización." Revista de Planeación y Desarrollo 2, 3 (October): 303-352.

CORAGGIO, J. L. (1973) "Polarización, desarrollo e integración." Revista Latinoamericana de Estudios Urbano Regionales 3, 8 (December): 121-134.

DIAZ, A. (1972) "Organización del espacio y estudio de las actividades individuales." Revista de la Sociedad Interamericana de Planificación 6, 21 (March): 83-103.

GAKENHEIMER, R. (1971) "Análisis para la planificación metropolitana en América Latina: la adaptación de métodos." Revista Latinoamericana de Estudios Urban Regionales 1, 2 (June): 55-66.

GEISSE, G. and J. L. CORAGGIO (1972) "Metropolitan areas and national development," pp. 45-60 in G. Geisse and J. E. Hardoy (eds.), Latin American Urban Research, Vol. II. Beverly Hills, Calif.: Sage Publications.

GUILLEN, F. (1973) "Planificación y participación social en América Latina." Revista de la Sociedad Interamericana de Planificación 7, 25 (March): 101-111.

HANSEN, N. M. (1971) "Pobreza rural y la crisis urbana: una estrategia para el desarrollo regional." Revista de la Sociedad Interamericana de Planificación 5, 17 (March-June): 66-69.

HARDOY, J. E. and G. GEISSE (1973) Políticas de desarrollo urbano y regional en América Latina. Buenos Aires: Sociedad Interamericana de Planificación.

––– and O. A. MORENO (1972) "Primeros pasos de la reforma urban en América Latina." Revista Latinoamericana de Estudios Urbano Regionales 2, 4 (March): 83-100.

HERNANDEZ, O. (1973) La planificación urbana y el desarrollo urbano no controlado. Caracas: Fondo Editorial Común.

LANDER, L., F. TRAVIESO, and A. URDANETA (1971) "Desarrollo urbano y desarrollo nacional en Venezuela: conclusiones y recomendaciones." Cuadernos de la Sociedad Venezolana de Planificación 84-86 (January-March): 125-142.

LATORRE C., H. (1972) "La planificación regional en el gobierno popular." Revista de la Sociedad Interamericana de Planificación 6, 23 (September): 60-68.

MELCHIOR, E. R. (1972) "The integration of space in Latin America," pp. 85-100 in G. Geisse and J. E. Hardoy (eds.), Latin American Urban Research, Vol. II. Beverly Hills, Calif.: Sage Publications.

NEIRA ALVA, E. (1972) "Development strategy and the Recôncavo Baiano of Brazil," pp. 151-166 in G. Geisse and J. E. Hardoy (eds.), Latin American Urban Research, Vol. II. Beverly Hills, Calif.: Sage Publications.

ORGANIZACION DE LOS ESTADOS AMERICANOS (1972) "Consideraciones acerca de la formulación de un subsistema de planificación para el desarrollo local integrado." Revista de la Sociedad Interamericana de Planificación 6, 24 (December): 62-72.

——— (1972) "Criterios básicos para el establecimiento de sistemas de enseñanza e investigación en planificación urbano-regional en América Latina." Revista de la Sociedad Interamericana de Planificación 6, 24 (December): 73-85.

——— (1972) "Ideas generales para la reformulación de los instrumentos de planificación urbana en América Latina." Revista de la Sociedad Interamericana de Planificación 6, 24 (December): 54-61.

PONTUAL, R. (1973) "Racionalidad formal vs. racionalidad sustancial en el proceso de planificación del desarrollo urbano." Revista Interamericana de Planificación 7, 26 (June): 75-86.

PUMARINO, G. (1973) "Nuevo enfoque para la planificación en áreas metropolitanas: hacia un modelo alternativo." Revista Latinoamericana de Estudios Urbano Regionales 3, 8 (December): 11-42.

SLOAN, J. W. (1973) "Colombia's new development plan: An example of post-ECLA thinking." Inter-American Economic Affairs 27, 2 (Autumn): 49-66.

SOMS, G. E. (1972) "Los instrumentos de dirección económica regional." Revista de la Sociedad Interamericana de Planificación 6, 23 (September): 69-75.

STOHR, T. (1970) "Un esquema para la planificación del transporte." Cuadernos de la Sociedad Venezolana de Planificación 80-81 (September-October): 47-64.

STOHR, W. B. (1973) El desarrollo regional en América Latina: experiencias y perspectivas. Buenos Aires: Sociedad Interamericana de Planificación.

——— (1972) "The state of the art: Regional development programs in Latin America at the end of the 1960s," pp. 241-257 in G. Geisse and J. E. Hardoy (eds.), Latin American Urban Research, Vol. II. Beverly Hills, Calif.: Sage Publications.

TRAVIESO, F. (1972) Ciudad, región, y subdesarrollo. Caracas: Fondo Editorial Común.

——— (1970) "Estancamiento regional y marginalidad urbana en América Latina: hacia una crítica de las explicaciones existentes." Cuadernos de la Sociedad Venezolana de Planificación 76-77 (June): 3-17.

UTRIA, R. D. (1972) "The social variables of regional development in Latin America," pp. 61-84 in G. Geisse and J. E. Hardoy (eds.), Latin American Urban Research, Vol. II. Beverly Hills, Calif.: Sage Publications.

YUJNOVSKY, O. (1973) La estructura interna de la ciudad: el caso latinoamericano. Buenos Aires: Sociedad Interamericana de Planificación.

GENERAL URBAN STUDIES DEALING IN PART WITH LATIN AMERICA

BRIGG, P. (1973) "Some economic interpretations of case studies of urban migration in developing countries." International Bank for Reconstruction and Development, Bank Staff Working Paper No. 151. Washington, D.C., March.

BROWNING, H. L. (1971) "Migrant selectivity and the growth of large cities in developing societies," pp. 273-314 in National Academy of Sciences, Rapid Population Growth, Vol. 2. Baltimore, Md.: Johns Hopkins Press.

CLINARD, M. B. and D. J. ABBOTT (1973) Crime in Developing Countries: A Comparative Perspective. New York: Wiley-Interscience.

EAMES, E. and J. G. GOODE (1973) Urban Poverty in a Cross-Cultural Context. New York: Free Press.

FOSTER, G. M. and R. V. KEMPER (eds.) (1974) Anthropologists in Cities. Boston: Little, Brown.

FRIED, R. C. (1973) "Comparative urban performance." European Urban Research Program, University of California, Los Angeles, Working Paper No. 1, revised, September.

––– and F. F. RABINOVITZ (1974) Comparative Urban Performance. Englewood Cliffs, N.J.: Prentice-Hall.

FRIEDMANN, J. (1973) Urbanization, Planning, and National Development. Beverly Hills, Calif.: Sage Publications.

GERMANI, G. (ed.) (1973) Modernization, Urbanization, and the Urban Crisis. Boston: Little, Brown.

KOENIGSBERGER, O. H. et al. (1972) Infrastructure Problems of the Cities of Developing Countries. New York: Ford Foundation. International Urbanization Survey Reports, No. 287.

LESLIE, C. (1973) "Redfield's contribution to urban anthropology." Paper presented at the Annual Meeting of the American Anthropological Association, New Orleans, La., November-December.

McGEE, T. G. (1971) The Urbanization Process in the Third World. London: G. Bell.

PRADILLA, E. and C. JIMENEZ (1973) Arquitectura, urbanismo y dependencia neocolonial. Buenos Aires: Sociedad Interamericana de Planificación.

ROBIROSA, M. C. (n.d.) "Internal migration, human resources, and employment within the context of urbanization." International Review of Community Development 18, 25-26: 49-65.

ROBSON, W. A. and D. E. REGAN (eds.) (1972) Great Cities of the World: Their Government, Politics, and Planning. Beverly Hills, Calif.: Sage Publications.

RODWIN, L. (1973) Países y ciudades: comparación de estrategias para el crecimiento urbano. Buenos Aires: Sociedad Interamericana de Planificación.

SADOVE, R. (1973) "Urban needs of developing countries." Finance and Development 10 (June): 26-31.

WEAVER, T. and D. WHITE (eds.) (1972) The Anthropology of Urban Environments. Boulder, Col.: Society for Applied Anthropology, Monograph Series No. 11.

WEITZ, R. (ed.) (1973) Urbanization and the Developing Countries: Report on the Sixth Rehovot Conference. New York: Praeger.

WORLD BANK (1972) Urbanization Sector Working Paper. Washington, D.C.: World Bank.

BIBLIOGRAPHIES

AMMON, A. et al. (1973) Planificación y estudios urbano-regionales en Chile y America Latina: Bibliografía. Instituto Latinoamericano de Investigaciones Sociales (ILDIS), Série "ILDIS-Estudios y Documentos," No. 25.

BRUNN, S. D. (1971) Urbanization in Developing Countries: An International Bibliography. East Lansing, Mich.: Latin American Center, Michigan State University.

CORNELIUS, W. A. (1974) Bibliography on Comparative Urban Politics and Development. Department of Political Science, Massachusetts Institute of Technology, Cambridge, Mass., February.

––– (1972) "Urbanization and political development: a course syllabus." Comparative Urban Research 1, 2 (December): 43-55.

FRIEDMANN, J. (1972) "Urbanization and national development: a course syllabus." Comparative Urban Research 1, 1 (Spring): 32-41.

FRIBERG, J. C. (1971) Migraciones hacia la ciudad y las consecuencias de la urbanización en Latinoamérica: una bibliografía preliminar. Bucaramonga, Colombia: Universidad Industrial de Sontonder, División de Investigaciones.

GUTKIND, P.C.W. (1973) "Bibliography on urban anthropology," pp. 425-489 in A. Southall (ed.), Urban Anthropology: Cross-Cultural Studies of Urbanization. New York and London: Oxford University Press.

KEMPER, R. V. (1971) "Bibliografía comentada sobre la antropología urbana en América Latina." Boletín Bibliográfico de Antropología Americana 33-34: 83-140. (Reprinted in Institute of International Studies, University of California, Berkeley, Latin American Reprint Series, No. 393.)

SABLE, M. H. (1971) Latin American Urbanization: A Guide to the Literature, Organizations, and Personnel. Metuchen, N.J.: Scarecrow Press.

VAUGHAN, D. R. (1970) Urbanization in Twentieth Century Latin America: A Working Bibliography. Austin, Texas: University of Texas Press, for the Institute of Latin American Studies and Population Research Center.

ADDENDA: Papers Presented at the Seminar on New Directions of Urban Research, Institute of Latin American Studies, University of Texas, Austin, Texas, May 16-18, 1974

AMARO, N. "Exports, growth poles and urbanization: the Central American case."

LOMNITZ, L. "Migration and network in Latin America."

ROBERTS, B. R. "The provincial urban system and the process of dependency."

SALMEN, L. F. "Perspectives for long-term co-sponsored (U.S.-Latin American) research in urbanization."

SILVERS, A. L. and M. de MELLO MOREIRA "The absorption of urban and rural poor in the Brazilian state of Minas Gerais."

WALTON, J. "Urban hierarchies and patterns of dependence in Latin America: theoretical bases for a new research agenda."